Philosophical Issues in Tourism

PEFC
PEFC/16-33-111
CATG-PEFC-052
www.pefc.org

ASPECTS OF TOURISM
Series Editors: Chris Cooper *(Nottingham University Business School, UK)*, **C. Michael Hall** *(University of Canterbury, New Zealand)* and **Dallen J. Timothy** *(Arizona State University, USA)*

Aspects of Tourism is an innovative, multifaceted series, which comprises authoritative reference handbooks on global tourism regions, research volumes, texts and monographs. It is designed to provide readers with the latest thinking on tourism worldwide and push back the frontiers of tourism knowledge. The volumes are authoritative, readable and user-friendly, providing accessible sources for further research. Books in the series are commissioned to probe the relationship between tourism and cognate subject areas such as strategy, development, retailing, sport and environmental studies.

Full details of all the books in this series and of all our other publications can be found on http://www.channelviewpublications.com, or by writing to Channel View Publications, St Nicholas House, 31-34 High Street, Bristol BS1 2AW, UK.

ASPECTS OF TOURISM
Series Editors: Chris Cooper *(Nottingham University Business School, UK)*, C. Michael Hall *(University of Canterbury, New Zealand)* and Dallen J. Timothy *(Arizona State University, USA)*

Philosophical Issues in Tourism

Edited by
John Tribe

CHANNEL VIEW PUBLICATIONS
Bristol • Buffalo • Toronto

Library of Congress Cataloging in Publication Data
A catalog record for this book is available from the Library of Congress.
Philosophical Issues in Tourism/Edited by John Tribe.
Aspects of tourism: 37
Includes bibliographical references and index.
1. Tourism–Philosophy. I. Tribe, John. II. Title. III. Series.
G155.A1P49 2009
910.01–dc22e2009001600

British Library Cataloguing in Publication Data
A catalogue entry for this book is available from the British Library.

ISBN-13: 978-1-84541-097-1 (hbk)
ISBN-13: 978-1-84541-096-4 (pbk)

Channel View Publications
UK: St Nicholas House, 31-34 High Street, Bristol BS1 2AW, UK.
USA: UTP, 2250 Military Road, Tonawanda, NY 14150, USA.
Canada: UTP, 5201 Dufferin Street, North York, Ontario M3H 5T8, Canada.

The policy of Multilingual Matters/Channel View Publications is to use papers that are natural, renewable and recyclable products, made from wood grown in sustainable forests. In the manufacturing process of our books, and to further support our policy, preference is given to printers that have FSC and PEFC Chain of Custody certification. The FSC and/or PEFC logos will appear on those books where full certification has been granted to the printer concerned.

Typeset by Datapage International Ltd.
Printed and bound in Great Britain by MPG Books Ltd.

Contents

Contributors

Irena Ateljevic received her doctoral degree in human geography in 1998 at the University of Auckland, New Zealand. She is currently positioned within the Socio-Spatial Analysis Group at Wageningen University, Netherlands. Interested in human development potential, she explores tourism as a powerful agent of socioeconomic change with the particular focus on issues of women empowerment and leadership. She is a co-founder of the Critical Tourism Studies network (CTS) through which she has been promoting the epistemological issues of reflexivity in the production of tourism knowledge.

Maureen Ayikoru completed her PhD in Tourism at the University of Surrey, UK and currently is a lecturer in Tourism at Middlesex University London. Her research concentrates on methodological issues in tourism inquiry, higher education policies, globalisation, environmental education and sustainability issues in the Ugandan tourism sector. She has authored a book chapter on interpretive and critical methodology in tourism education inquiry and a journal article (recently accepted) on tourism education and neoliberalism.

Jim Butcher lectures at Canterbury Christ Church University, UK in the Faculty of Applied and Social Sciences. His two main contributions to discussions on ethical tourism are the books *The Moralisation of Tourism: Sun, Sand ... and Saving the World?* (Routledge, 2003) and *Ecotourism, NGOs and Development* (Routledge, 2007). He is a Fellow of the RSA, and regularly contributes to debates in the media on tourism.

Tim Coles is Associate Professor in Management at the University of Exeter where he is also Co-Director of the Centre for Tourism Studies. Tim's research examines the interface between studies of tourism and of business and management. His current research, which is funded by the British Academy and the Economic and Social Research Council, concentrates on how environmental behaviours among consumers

interact with business innovation, regulation and governance to produce
new patterns of travel and tourism.

David Timothy Duval is Associate Professor in the School of Business,
University of Otago. David's research interests, for the most part, centre
upon aviation management. He has published on issues of aeropolitics,
alliances, international air service agreements and aviation emissions
management.

David Fennell is Professor in the Department of Tourism and Environment at Brock University, Canada, where he teaches and researches
mainly in the areas of ecotourism and tourism ethics. He has published
widely in these areas, including sole authored books on ecotourism
programme planning, a general text on ecotourism, tourism ethics, and a
title focusing on codes of ethics in tourism (he has edited two other
books). He is the founding Editor-in-Chief of the *Journal of Ecotourism*,
and is an active member on the editorial boards of many academic
journals.

C. Michael Hall is Professor of Marketing at the University of Canterbury, Christchurch, New Zealand and Docent, Department of Geography, University of Oulu, Finland. Co-editor of *Current Issues in Tourism*,
he has published widely on tourism and human mobility, regional
development and environmental history.

Kevin Hannam is Professor of Tourism Development and Head of
Tourism at the University of Sunderland. He has a PhD in geography
from the University of Portsmouth, UK and specialises in the area of
tourism development with a particular regional interest in India. He has
published many journal articles and book chapters on various aspects of
heritage tourism and has recently edited a book with Irena Ateljevic on
backpacker tourism. He is also founding co-editor of the journal
Mobilities (with John Urry and Mimi Sheller). He has been a Fellow of
the Royal Geographical Society since 1998.

Tazim Jamal is an Associate Professor in the Department of Recreation,
Park and Tourism Sciences, Texas A&M University, College Station,
Texas. Her research areas are community-based tourism planning,
heritage tourism management, collaborative processes for sustainable
development, as well as theoretical/methodological issues related to
tourism and sustainability. Her study areas include mountain resorts

communities in Western Canada, rural communities in Texas and coastal tourism in Quintana Roo, Mexico.

Balvinder Kaur Kler is a Lecturer in Tourism at Universiti Malaysia Sabah. Her research concerns the phenomenology of tourist experience, with specific focus on Sense of Place and Restorative Environments. Her doctoral thesis (University of Surrey) used Interpretative Phenomenological Analysis (IPA) to investigate the place experience of scuba divers and the restorative potential of the subaquatic environment. Her work continues to explore restoration as an explanatory and motivational component of tourist experience.

Scott McCabe is Lecturer in Tourism Management and Marketing at the Christel DeHaan Tourism and Travel Research Institute of Nottingham University Business School. His research interests include tourist experience and behaviour, nonparticipation and social equity issues in tourism, sociolinguistics and communication in tourism and ethnographic and qualitative research methodologies. He is the author of a number of journal articles and book chapters on these subjects and the forthcoming book: *Marketing Communications in Tourism and Hospitality: Concepts, Strategies and Cases.*

Robert Maitland is Reader in Tourism and Director, the Centre for Tourism Research, at the University of Westminster, London, UK. His research focuses on tourism in cities, particularly world cities and national capitals, and on tourism policy. He has authored articles and books and advised government on these themes. Current research examines tourism and the everyday, visitors' role in the creation of new tourist areas in London, and tourism in national capitals. *World Tourism Cities – developing tourism off the beaten track* was published in 2008.

Christopher Menzel is an Associate Professor in the Department of Philosophy, Texas A&M University, College Station, Texas. His central research areas are metaphysics and the philosophy of logic, though he dabbles in ethics when he feels the need to work on something relevant to the real world.

Alexandre Panosso Netto graduated in Philosophy and Tourism and has a Masters in History and PhD in Communication Sciences. He is a lecturer in Leisure and Tourism at the School of Arts, Sciences and

Humanities of the University of São Paulo (Brazil). He has published more than a dozen books on tourism. He is the author of *Filosofia do turismo: teoria e epistemologia* – published too in Spanish (São Paulo: Aleph, 2005); *Teoria do turismo: conceitos, modelos e sistemas,* with Guilherme Lohmann (Aleph, 2008); and *Epistemología del turismo: estúdios críticos,* with Marcelino Castillo Nechar (Trillas, 2008).

Shalini Singh is Associate Professor in the Department of Recreation and Leisure Studies at Brock University, Ontario, Canada. Her research interests span themes of sustainability, communities, spirituality, tourism curricula and tourism in developing countries (especially India). She has recently completed an edited volume on Asian domestic tourism. Dr Singh is the Executive Editor of the international journal *Tourism Recreation Research.* She also serves as India National Representative of the Asia Pacific Tourism Association (APTA).

Tej Vir Singh is Professor and founding Director of the Centre for Tourism Research & Development, Lucknow, India. He is also the Editor-in-Chief of the International Journal *Tourism Recreation Research.* A specialist in Himalayan Tourism, Dr Singh has produced more than a dozen international books on Himalayan resource use and conservation, impact studies and tourism on the margin. Dr Singh is a Fellow of the International Academy for the Study of Tourism (since 1989). He has consulted for the UNEP, the Ford Foundation and ICIMOD.

Andrew Smith is a Senior Lecturer in Tourism at the University of Westminster, UK. He previously lectured at the University of Kent and at Sheffield Hallam University and completed a doctoral thesis (on sport initiatives in city marketing) in 2002. Andrew has published research on city images, urban regeneration and urban monuments in various journals including *Urban Studies* and *Annals of Tourism Research.* His recent research focuses on the use of events within tourism and urban regeneration strategies.

Mick Smith is Associate Professor in Environmental Studies and Philosophy at Queen's University, Ontario, Canada. Originally trained as an ecologist, his main focus of interest is environmental ethics and politics. He is the author of *An Ethics of Place: Radical Ecology, Postmodernity and Social Theory* (SUNY, 2001) and with Rosaleen Duffy of *The Ethics of Tourism Development* (Routledge, 2003) together with two edited volumes. He is on the editorial board of Environmental Ethics and Environmental Values and an editor of Emotion, Space, and Society.

Cain Samuel Todd is Lecturer in Philosophy at the University of Lancaster, UK. His research interests lie primarily in aesthetics and ethics, focusing on the nature and objectivity of aesthetic judgement, fiction and imagination, environmental aesthetics, and the connections between aesthetic and ethical value. He is the author of various articles on these topics and also has a philosophical interest in areas of practical aesthetics, such as the appreciation of sport and wine tasting.

John Tribe is Professor of Tourism and subject group leader at the University of Surrey, UK. His research concentrates on sustainability, epistemology and education and he has authored books on strategy, economics, education and environmental management in tourism. He is co-chair of the UN World Tourism Organisation Education and Science Council and editor of *Annals of Tourism Research* and the *Journal of Hospitality, Leisure Sport and Tourism Education (JoHLSTE)*.

Brian Wheeller is Professor of Tourism at the University of Tasmania, Australia and Visiting Professor at NHTV, Breda, Netherlands. He holds degrees in Economics, Applied Economics, in the Economic Impacts of Tourism and in American Studies. His Doctorate is in Critiquing Sustainability. His research revolves around the links between travel, tourism and popular culture … in particular literature, art, film and music, and their relevance to contemporary tourism thinking. Brian's interests also embrace humour, the visual and the use of image in tourism and tourism education.

Part 1

Introduction

Chapter 1

Philosophical Issues in Tourism

JOHN TRIBE

Introduction

The more I have studied tourism, the more I have been drawn to three questions that are perennial ones in philosophy. These are questions about truth, beauty and virtue. Indeed, I have made some preliminary forays into these areas in previous writings such as 'The truth about tourism' (Tribe, 2006), 'The art of tourism' (Tribe, 2008) and 'Education for ethical action' (Tribe, 2002). Yet despite the geometric expansion of tourism knowledge, it seems that some areas have remained stubbornly underdeveloped and a full or comprehensive consideration of the philosophical issues of tourism represents one such significant knowledge gap. A key aim of this book therefore, is to provide an initial mapping of, and insights into this territory.

In fact, two of these areas – truth and virtue – have attracted pockets of interest, with methodology being the main driver of interest in truth and sustainability sometimes interpellating wider issues of virtue. On the other hand, with the exception of de Botton's popular writing on *The Art of Travel* (2003), beauty has attracted scant attention indeed. This is curious. For tourism has become a significant creator of forms in the contemporary world. At a micro level, tourism creates souvenirs and representations. It affects dress. It generates signage and interpretative clutter. It causes buildings (restaurants, terminals, accommodation, galleries) to rise into being with their exterior architecture and interior design. At a macro level it scapes parts of the world into seasides, ski resorts and whole tourism cities such as Las Vegas. It causes some land and city scapes to be revered and preserved, others to be overturned by development.

Indeed the word development (Pearce, 1995) and that of planning (Gunn, 1994) each suggests an interest in and an ability to affect the way in which tourism will be delivered in the future. These words further suggest that there are particular ends that have been thought out to which development is directed. Against this notion of a tourism world created through rational planning, the sociologist Anthony Giddens (2002) employed the term *Runaway World* as the title for a series of lectures and a book. He used the term to describe a world that was developing quickly and out of our control. In his book, Giddens (2002: 2) notes that post-Enlightenment philosophers shared a belief that 'with the further development of science and technology the world should become more stable and ordered'. But instead Giddens (2002: 2) finds that:

> The world in which we find ourselves today, however, doesn't look or feel much like they predicted it would. Rather than being more and more under our control, it seems out of our control – a runaway world.

In many cases tourism proceeds in an essentially unplanned and barely controllable way. Hence, it is possible to appropriate Giddens' idea to talk about Runaway Tourism. This is because, like most things, tourism is delivered in a largely uncontrolled neoliberal market environment, which often precedes and overpowers attempts at planning and management. But more importantly, neoliberalism is a deeply ideological project. That Adam Smith (1904) talked about the *invisible hand* is significant here as neoliberalism creates and forms our (tourism) world in a seemingly unconscious, routine, common sense way almost as if it were the natural way and that there was no alternative. Tourism development seems to happen without much conscious effort. Moreover, the study of economics often lays claim to the importance of value-freedom. But there are implicit values at work in neoliberalism. These include individualism, competition, technology, the reification of markets and (after Adam Smith) the belief that the pursuit of self-interest leads to socially beneficial results. Indeed against the themes of this book – truth, beauty and virtue – it might be said that neoliberalism promotes a particular set of values – performativity, consumerism and profitability. The idea of performativity is particularly potent for, as Lyotard explained, it is a key force driving the progress of technological knowledge. Technology is dominated by performativity (the maximum output for the minimum input) and the importance of this is that 'an equation between wealth, efficiency and truth is thus established' (Lyotard, 1984: 45). Here, useful knowledge is favoured so that

> The production of proof ... thus falls under control of another language game, in which the goal is no longer truth, but performativity – that is the best possible input/output equation. (Lyotard, 1984: 46)

This analysis gives a special significance to a considered enquiry into what truths are in tourism.

The ability to locate ourselves in a tourism world that has runaway qualities and identify and question its powerful neoliberal driving forces is in itself a philosophical act. For at its very simplest, philosophising is the ability to extract ourselves from the busy, engaged world of making and doing things, to disengage and to pause for refection and thought especially about meaning and purpose. The word philosophy is derived from the Greek term meaning love of wisdom and the *Concise Oxford Dictionary* defines philosophy as:

> Seeking after wisdom or knowledge, esp. that which deals with ultimate reality, or with the most general causes and principles of things and ideas and human perception and knowledge of them, physical phenomena (*natural philosophy*), and ethics (*moral philosophy*); advanced learning in general (*doctor of philosophy*); philosophical system; system of principles for the conduct of life; serenity, calmness.

The unpacking of this definition provides a further indication of the interests of this book since it merely raises more questions. What is wisdom? What is it to know something? What is the nature of reality? Why are some things considered beautiful and desirable? What are ethics and what is good and bad? What are desirable ends? It is these questions that are now addressed more fully in the three main sections of this book under the headings of truth, beauty and virtue.

Truth: Reality, Knowledge and Disciplines

Tourism is often portrayed as a new subject of research and activity in universities, but despite its relative youth it has already generated substantial amounts of knowledge. For example *Annals of Tourism Research* has been producing articles since 1973, the number of specialist research journals stands at over 50 and a recent search of the CABI abstract service revealed the existence of around 50,000 items (mainly articles but also including books and chapters) recorded under the subject head of tourism. The field also generates a substantial programme of conferences. Amazon lists over 7500 book titles that include the word tourism. But most of the knowledge produced in these ways is what might be termed additive knowledge, that is knowledge that seeks to add or adapt theories, insights or understandings about the phenomenon of tourism. In contrast, the task of this section is to place the process of tourism knowledge production under scrutiny and to consider more carefully what it means to know.

Such an enquiry is perhaps particularly necessary in the present era, which is witnessing an explosion of information largely enabled by rapid developments in digital communications and media. For example, a Google search for the term tourism generates 166 million hits. These include all sorts of representations of tourism, including websites, images, blogs, postings, videos, discussion groups etc. The question of web-based information immediately raises a number of questions requiring clarification.

The first of these is about scope and framing and this relates to what is meant by the concepts of the tourist and tourism, how we frame these concepts and hence what are the boundaries of the concepts, what are the consequences of such framings and what lies inside and outside of our fields of enquiry. The second question for clarification is about the meaning of knowledge itself. This concerns questions such as what is knowledge, what is it to know something and how do we distinguish between truth, assertion, lies and propaganda? Here, Plato set the scene, stating that in order to count as knowledge, statement must be justified, true and believed.

The conceptualisations and problematiques of the terms tourists and tourism are covered in Chapters 2 and 3, respectively. In Chapter 4, consideration is given to issues in the production of knowledge about tourism, specifically those of how we know things (epistemology) and the nature of the tourism world we wish to know (ontology). Chapter 5 presses at our conventional discipline-based way of understanding tourism and develops the idea of post-disciplinarity epistemology. The section ends with Chapter 6, which considers recent challenges to the concept of tourism and possible replacement concepts such as mobilities which allow a much wider framing (Bernstein, 1971) than that offered by tourism. The discussion of one aspect of this section invariably involves consideration of another and so some key ideas weave their way across the chapters of this section.

It seems that much of the population prefers to see itself as traveller rather than tourist, but as Scott McCabe argues this has considerable implications for tourism research and its findings. In Chapter 2, he poses a fundamental philosophical question and implied approach to answering it: Who is a Tourist? Conceptual and Theoretical Developments. His purpose is to illuminate the problematic relationships between the use of the term tourist by the industry, the academy and with its use as a lay construct by ordinary people in everyday conversation. Part of McCabe's interest arises from observing an established discourse that connotes 'tourist' as a pejorative term and his aim is to discover how tourists construct the activities of themselves and others as social practices, as well as to warn of the dangers of working with a category that is so saturated with particular meaning.

The chapter commences by outlining the main definitions of tourists, including industry and social science perspectives. McCabe uses dictionary and literature sources to arrive at a common definition of a tourist, roughly 'the act of travelling, or making a journey which starts and finishes in the same place ... for pleasure, interest, culture, holiday, recreation etc'. But, this is not his destination – merely a stop over – for he warns that definitions are not able to encompass the multiplicity of experiences often desired by travellers in the same trip. To address this, the chapter then moves on to discuss and evaluate critical and poststructuralist conceptualisations of tourist activities and behaviour in the tourism literature. It discusses postmodernist empirical research which emphasises the subjective and negotiated characteristics of an individual's experiences. Such research tends to focus more deeply on the nature of tourist roles, experiences and meanings, and attitudes avoiding more reductionist and rigid conceptualisations.

The discussion then moves on to assess the epistemological basis through which knowledge claims about tourists and their identifying characteristics are made. McCabe argues that social sciences of tourism, and particularly postmodern and poststructuralist interpretations of tourists (as well as sociological and psychological research coming from an ethnographic and qualitative perspective) often fails in its attempts to understand tourists' behaviour. This critique stems from Jacobsen's (2000) idea of an 'anti-tourist'. It is re-enforced from noting a comprehensively pejorative use of the concept 'tourist' by tourists when they contrast their own activities with those of others. Here, ethnomethodological techniques, membership categorisation analysis and conversation analysis offer useful tools in getting to the heart of the term. The term 'tourist', McCabe concludes, turns out to be little more than a rhetorical device, an ideological and political construct. We should therefore be very wary of using the term. For as the lay concept 'tourist' is used as an ideological construct, this has important consequences on the ways in which it is operationalised in social science research in tourism. Consequently, a great deal of care needs to be taken in using empirical data that is premised on the use of this term. In simple terms, using the expression 'tourist' in research instruments may influence the results we get in unexpected and hidden ways. It is loaded and freighted with much hidden ideological baggage.

The word tourism describes an activity and this activity has given rise to academic interest and study. In Chapter 3, Alexandre Panosso Netto considers the question: What is Tourism? Definitions, Theoretical Phases and Principles. In the first part of the chapter, he presents and analyses different explanations of what tourism is according to different organisations and researchers. These might be termed issues of framing tourism. In the second part of the chapter, he turns to the study of tourism. His discussion uses Kuhn (1962) to classify some of the key theoretical models and approaches. Panosso Netto proposes that general systems theory became established as the basic paradigm of tourism studies. This realisation enables Panosso Netto to suggest a division of tourism studies into three distinct phases: the preparadigmatic, the paradigm and new approaches. Included in the latter is Nechar's (2005) 'critical epistemology'. This foregrounds certain habits that have taken root in tourism academic life (i.e. the operation of a paradigm) and advocates critical, reflexive and hermeneutic moves to advance the understanding of new knowledge and meanings. Along with each of these three phases, Netto identifies a transition area, constituted of researchers that are migrating from one phase to another.

In the final part of his chapter, Panosso Netto returns to the concept of tourism and offers a normative schedule of tourism principles. These are divided into fundamental principles and desirable ones. These principles are condensed into a new proposal for the definition of tourism.

In Chapter 4 – Epistemology, Ontology and Tourism – Maureen Ayikoru engages with two of the key concepts that are central to understanding truth, knowledge and representation. These are epistemology and ontology and these concepts recur throughout the chapters in this section. Ayikoru defines ontology as that branch of philosophy that studies the nature of reality. Ontology asks what is the nature of that which is to be known. Epistemology is referred to as that branch of philosophy that studies knowledge. Epistemological questions ask about how we know things. Knowledge has a knowing subject and epistemology focuses on the relationship between the knower (researcher) and that which is to be known. Like Panosso Netto in the previous chapter, Ayikoru invokes Kuhn (1962) to organise her argument, in her case according to scientific (post)positivism and interpretive paradigms.

Positivism adopts a realist ontological perspective whereby it is assumed that there exists a reality out there, driven by immutable natural laws. This reality is therefore objective and independent from the knowing subject. (Postpositivism adopts a critical realist ontological viewpoint which assumes reality to be imperfectly apprehendable but nevertheless apprehendable.) Positivist epistemology operates on the principle that the knower and the object of inquiry are independent entities. Its emphasis is therefore on objective rigorous scientific method by corroboration or falsification of factual evidence.

However, Ayikoru points out that knowledge of the social (as opposed to the physical) world of tourism is imbued with meaning-making mechanisms of the social, mental and linguistic worlds of the knowing subjects. In this case, what is to be known cannot be separate from the knower. Hence the importance of the interpretive paradigm that subscribes to a relativist ontology. Here, Ayikoru explains, knowledge does not exist independently and is not waiting to be discovered, but rather enquirers contribute to its construction, imbuing meaning according to different historical and sociocultural influences. She adds that the constructivist epistemology is usually described as being transactional and subjectivist as the inquirer and the inquired-into closely interact with each other.

Post-disciplinary Tourism is the title of Chapter 5. Here, Tim Coles, Michael Hall and David Duval tackle the question of disciplinarity, thus extending the epistemological enquiry initiated by Ayikoru in Chapter 4. In epistemological terms disciplines are the bedrock of knowledge quality control. It is the disciplines that provide well-established, well-tested ways of knowing and an organised academic community for peer review of new knowledge claims. So why should Coles, Hall and Duval wish to lead us beyond disciplines? Their rationale is threefold. First, disciplines can restrict what their adherents see. Second, disciplines may not provide sufficient breadth to address many complex contemporary problems, and third many disciplines have not adapted sufficiently quickly so that they reflect the conditions evident when they were initially developed. Thus, according to Coles *et al.* 'there is the danger that we may be attempting to address contemporary subjects (such as tourism) through outdated and ageing frameworks for scholarly activity and academic administration'.

The authors draw on a literature that is developing in the broader social sciences which has emphasised the limitations of established and orthodox disciplinary boundaries and dogmas. In particular, they adapt and extend the arguments of Sayer (1999) and propose and unpack the concept of post-disciplinarity in the study of tourism. Sayer's explanation of a 'post-disciplinary' approach is offered where 'scholars forget about disciplines and whether ideas can be identified with any particular one; they identify with learning rather than with disciplines'.

For tourism, Coles *et al.* argue that a post-disciplinary approach is especially well-suited to the emergent study of mobilities (which is discussed at length in Chapter 6). Thus, their argument extends not only to new ways of knowing, but also to the reframing of what is to be studied and known. They also see post-disciplinarity as central to progress in understanding and responding to climate change, noting that human behaviour and its impact on the environment is complex, messy and uncertain and that post-disciplinarity is needed to capture the complexity that may be overlooked by disciplinary-focussed studies.

Where Chapter 5 makes an interesting challenge to the study of tourism, in Chapter 6 Kevin Hannam submits a broad ontological challenge to the concept of tourism itself. In The End of Tourism? Nomadology and the Mobilities Paradigm, his argument is that the concept of tourism is a somewhat dated one and one that frames itself too narrowly. Rather, according to Hannam, tourism needs to be understood as an activity within a wider ontological context, namely that of mobility or mobilities. This move situates the study of tourism within a wider social theory context.

Mobility is defined in contrast to fixity, involving a kind of displacement and being the act of moving between locations. Hannam, citing Sheller and Urry two other protagonists of the concept of mobilities (Hannam *et al.*, 2006), notes that everything seems to be in perpetual movement throughout the world. They find that most people travel – academics, terrorists, tourists, military people, business people, homeless people, celebrities, migrants, refugees, backpackers, commuters, students and friends. They note that mobility barriers have been significantly lowered in contemporary society by political, technological, financial and transportation changes. This has led to a blurring of tourism, leisure, transport, business, travel, migration and communication and it is this 'fluid interdependence' that causes Hannam to assert that tourism should not be analysed discretely, but rather in the wider context of mobilities.

Hannam also develops the wider epistemological point that fixities of older forms of philosophy have also come into question through developments in mobility and points to Foucault's critique denying objective truth and emphasising the fluidity of knowledge and its relationship to power. A more specific epistemological observation is also made that mobile methodologies, such as mobile ethnographies, offer the best way of understanding contemporary mobilities.

Beauty: Wellbeing, Aesthetics and Art

Understanding the meaning and nature of beauty is a central concern of the branch of philosophy that deals with aesthetics. In this section, three aspects of beauty are considered. First, beauty is considered as a subjective experience. This can manifest itself in feelings of warmth, attraction, emotional wellbeing and even euphoria. Here, tourists might find feelings of flow, human connection or harmony with nature. Second, beauty can involve the evaluation and appreciation of an external object such as an attractive person, a sublime landscape or a moving cultural performance. Third, art attempts in different ways to capture the spirit of things freeing us from the conventional limitations of words and language and offering poetic, visual and musical representations that can engender deeper and different engagements with their subjects. Indeed, art also interrogates the other themes of this book – truth (it can help us to see things differently and confront our lazy perceptions) and virtue.

This section initially considers the contribution of tourism to individual wellbeing and spirituality. The restorative and transcendental aspects of tourism are analysed in Chapters 7 and 8. It then investigates the aesthetics that result from the way in which tourism and spaces co-create places. Tourism is contingent upon the beauty of place and can both contribute to and detract from this as it (re)constructs place. Chapters 9 and 10 discuss these issues as they apply to the natural and built environments, respectively. Chapter 11 concludes this section with an examination of how tourism is depicted through the arts.

In Chapter 7, Balvinder Kaur Kler considers the relationship between Tourism and Restoration with specific reference to the natural environment. She notes that relaxation, the refreshment of body and mind, as well as restoration, continue to be listed as key physical motivations to travel. In further investigating the concept of restoration, she is drawn to understandings offered by environmental psychology and specifically to Kaplan's (1995) attention restoration theory. This describes how the need for psychological restoration (particularly for directed attention which can lead to fatigue) can motivate individuals to seek contact with the natural environment and postulates the importance of both the individual and the environment in this process. Kaplan and Kaplan (1989) further explain that people's preference for nature is driven both by their need for restoration and particular properties of the natural environment that allow it to provide restoration. Additionally, they identify four properties that an environment must possess in order to provide restoration: fascination, being away, extent and compatibility and that an environment possessing these properties would be a restorative environment. 'Fascination' refers to an environment's potential for eliciting involuntary attention (as opposed to the directed attention of say reading a book or writing). 'Being away' offers a freedom from any mental activity requiring directed attention and therefore facilitates fascination to occur. 'Extent' occurs where the immediate setting is part of some larger place or whole. 'Compatibility' represents a positive fit between an individual and the environment.

Kler discusses attention restoration theory in relation to relevant tourism writings and notes that this theory currently concentrates on the physical aspects of restoration environments and does not consider what role the presence of other people in such environments might have. Here she notes the possible roles of others in providing safety and in guiding attention. Finally, Kler distinguishes between passive and active restoration through tourism. She notes that wellbeing tourism (typically focused on the use of spa facilities such as massages, exercises and pampering) appears to be oriented towards a passive approach to relaxation. In contrast, restoration is not about passively escaping perception. Instead, it offers escape from fatiguing modes of interaction with the world and activates a more primal and natural mode of perception based on effortless fascination, with relaxation as its consequence.

Shalini Singh and Tej Vir Singh continue the theme of this section in Chapter 8 titled Aesthetic Pleasures: Contemplating Spiritual Tourism. Their discussions are organised around the concepts of spirituality, travel and tourism, wandering journeys and pilgrimages and they begin by articulating a conundrum. If, the authors postulate, tourism is concerned with the pleasures of the material world and spirituality embodies renunciation of the same – can these two aspects be reconciled?

Singh and Singh consider the various meanings of the term spiritual and within the broad term of tourism distinguish questing journeys from regular tourism as special odysseys for personal fulfilment and enlightenment. They allude to the limens of the sacred and secular that afford transformative learning experiences and suggest that a quest that sets off a need to go forth is at the heart of spirituality. Their chapter encompasses sacred and secular quests, and considers both the role of sacred centres as well as nature as sources of spiritual quest and quench. The authors note the transformative outcomes of spiritual quests that can generate virtuous conduct in people (see Chapter 13). In concluding, Singh and Singh point to spiritually meaningful experiences being accessible through varieties of alternative tourism such as solidarity trips, educational travel, dark tourism, volunteering vacations, New Age and/or postmodern travel, as well as religious pilgrimages and note these as pointers for optimism for the future (see Chapter 16).

Chapters 9 and 10 each investigate different aspects of the aesthetics of tourism. Nature often provides an important pull for tourists. But in doing so it brings pressures for development and change. This raises questions of what it is to value nature. In Chapter 9, Cain Todd considers the relationship between Nature, Beauty and Tourism, addressing questions such as whether 'beauty' is a useful concept, what is aesthetic appreciation of 'nature' and what are the implications of the contemporary debates about aesthetics for thinking about tourism?

Todd sets out the main contending philosophical theories of the aesthetic appreciation of nature, dividing the theories into two broad types, cognitive and noncognitive. Starting with the cognitive natural-environment model, he then considers various noncognitivist alternatives to it, including the arousal model, the engagement model as well as a more sceptical position that there can be no one model for the aesthetic appreciation of nature. Todd applies these ideas to tourism in a section titled 'Beauty and the Tourist Gaze', where he makes a number of observations. First, he invokes Carlson (2000) who critiques a certain tourism gaze (that which artificially frames nature through brochure apertures, through photo stops and viewpoints) as one that falsifies nature. Todd proceeds to consider thin encounters in tourism (characterised by speed of engagement, over-easy access, simplification, depth of engagement) which may be contrasted with thick encounters (characterised by slow appreciation, hard won labour of access, deeper intellectual and physical engagement), hinting that the former may lead to a loss of important experiences of qualities of nature such as wonder, awe and the sublime.

But Todd is wary of judging one form of tourism as being necessarily aesthetically richer than another and here he notes three important caveats. First, he asks who is to discount the judgment of any appreciator how ever their experience is obtained. Second, he notes that it is often consequential ethical concerns that lead to critique of the aesthetics of certain experiences (e.g. a critique of mass tourism that in fact concentrates on environmental damage) (see Chapter 14). Finally, Todd notes that overly serious tourism engagement can lead to an over-concentration on technique or difficulty or an overwhelming experience of exhilaration or danger or fatigue. These factors may distance the participant from the aesthetics of the natural context in which their travails take place.

In Chapter 10, Robert Maitland and Andrew Smith consider the relationship between Tourism and the Aesthetics of the Built Environment. The authors point out that aesthetics often refers narrowly to artistic merit and that although the built environment may induce profound and inspirational responses, they note the difficulties in applying a narrow view of aesthetics to architecture. The aesthetics of experience are offered a way of reconciling these difficulties. The authors embark on their analysis with a section that uncovers the philosophies embedded in urban design, pointing out various traditions such as functionalism, formalism and even façadism (the latter apparently derided by purists but appreciated by tourists).

The next section includes discussion of how tourism's influence on cities has become stronger. The authors note the move from the elite Grand Tour and its concern with decorum aesthetics and orderliness, to mass tourism that prompted architectural experimentation, from the ostentatious Blackpool Tower to the modernist De La Warr Pavilion in Bexhill. They also note that tourists return with altered aesthetic tastes and that divisions between home and away are becoming more blurred. Witness, they say, London bar styles borrowed from Manhattan and Barcelona and the new ubiquity of pavement cafes. The authors also map the changing eras of city architecture. They note that the city beautiful movement rarely consciously considered tourists. Modern cities started to incorporate spectacles (such as the Golden Gate Bridge and the viewing tower at the Empire State Building). Modernist cities with an emphasis on functionalism often failed as tourism cities and here UK New Towns are noted for their particular lack of tourist potential. Postmodern cities, where power has shifted from governments to developers and users are seen to promote eclectic design and appeal to the playfulness of tourists.

Next, this chapter considers the ways in which tourism has contributed to the aesthetics of places from the 1970s. First, tourism can be seen as contributing to an aesthetic that is more consumer-focused. Here the city of Baltimore is cited as an example of tourism as an antidote to industrial decline (especially with regard to regenerating industrial buildings and docks) and thus cities transform from places of production to places of consumption. Second, cities can be seen promoting heritage and amenity with a need for a balanced environment that meets the needs of residents and tourists (but with some criticisms of sameness and uniformity arising). Third, the introduction of 'iconic' buildings in the urban landscape is noted, for example the Guggenheim in Bilbao. Here, tourism has been a key driver in this form of city marketing and the promotion of spectacular environments and 'brandscapes' for an experience economy.

The authors conclude that the various words used to describe a tourist's aesthetic experience of built environments (reading, consuming, perceiving, conceiving) are testament to the wide range of related positions on this matter. They point to the quandary as to an ideal epistemology that will allow us to gain a comprehensive understanding of urban aesthetics. They also assert the tentative proposition that the tourism imperative is more influential now than it has ever been in understanding the aesthetics of the built environment. However, they caution that this does not necessarily mean that city developers are giving tourists what they want. For they point to the paradox that cities are often designed for tourism, rather than for tourists. A worrying gap is thereby noted between what city developers think tourists want and what tourists actually want when they are in their own city and when they visit others.

Concluding this section, in Chapter 11, Brian Wheeller considers Tourism and the Arts, a title that he has approached in a characteristically iconoclastic, innovative, broad-ranging way and with considerable artistic licence. Indeed it is a highly philosophical chapter, but one where the reader is left to do much of the interpretation and provide the analytical structure. In this way it acts somewhat as a piece of art itself – in its rhetoric, structure and overall form. Wheeller introduces it as 'my take on things: a personal, value-laden, anecdotal perspective based on experience'. He almost immediately sounds a warning about any naïve view (possibly mindful of the themes of this book) of art's relationship with aesthetics or truth by pointing out the relentless pressures of business and money on the arts. The arts, he notes in the context of tourism supply, are ever increasingly being seen as a business opportunity and cultural/heritage tourism often erodes the arts. Both the arts and tourism he concludes are primarily industries.

What, asks Wheeller constitutes 'the arts'? His answer includes not only theatre, opera, ballet, museums, exhibitions, literature, the cinema (art house), architecture, art, photography and classical music, but also blockbuster films, pop music and best-seller books. But the arts, he notes, like tourism, are riven by class. A schism between high and low culture appears to mimic the divide between the traveller and the (mass) tourist.

Wheeller's artistic tour begins with art as a tourist attraction, including Gorman's *Angel of the North* and his *Another Place* at Crosby. City artscapes (see Chapter 10) include St Pancras Station, London, Madrid airport and the Guggenheim Bilbao. Then there are art exhibitions, for example *If*

Everyone Had an Ocean, at Tate St Ives, Cornwall (dedicated to artwork inspired by Beach Boy Wilson's early music) and Hopper, Monet and Tutankhamen exhibitions in capital cities. There are even tourism art exhibitions *Censored at the Seaside* – the Art of Donald McGill (Brunswick Centre, 2004), *Universal Experience. Art, Life and the Tourist Eye* (Hayworth Gallery, 2005), *The Impressionists by the Sea* (Royal Academy, 2007) and *All-Inclusive: A Tourist World* (Schirn–Kunsthalle, Frankfurt, 2008). He points to art consciously or unconsciously selling places through for example *Paradise Found, California Dreaming, Bohemian Rhapsody* and Liverpool's *Hard Day's Night* Hotel. Books such as Saint-Expuery's *Little Prince* provide escapism and songs like the Mammas and Pappas *California Dreaming* can be nostalgic for place. His tour includes the politics of art – exemplified by the deliberate deception of tourists surfaced in Mann's *Death in Venice* and Benchley's *Jaws*.

Wheeller shows how art can be used in tourism teaching: 'Give them [he says]... Carey's ... *American Dreams* to analyse ... [or] *The Beach*: or ask them to think about a few paintings ... Casper David Friedrich's *The Traveller* or Fischeli's interpretations of beach life: or ... some of McGill's exquisite, risqué postcards ... and ... throw in a few of Parr's iconoclastic images depicting England's decaying coastal resorts'. Finally, Wheeller considers 'the truth' (see Chapter 4) in art by considering travel writing. Here he sets out a contrast. On the one hand he invites us to witness the romantic, glossy, highly selective views of Britain, such as BBC books' *The Coast* and *A Picture of Britain*. Against these he places Harland Miller's art works based on the reworking of book covers depicting the darker side of Northern towns in England: *Bridlington: 93 Million Miles from the Sun* and *Blackpool: Its All Fun and Games until Someone Loses an Eye*.

Virtue: Ethics, Values and the Good Life

The final part of the book engages with the concept of virtue in tourism. Virtue signifies moral excellence and goodness and belongs with ethics in the branch of philosophy that analyses values, right conduct and considers the meaning of the good life. A distinction may be made between ethics which encompasses the theory of what is right and wrong and good and bad as opposed to morals which denotes ethically governed action and behaviour. In this section, Chapter 12 offers a general overview of ethics and tourism, whilst Chapter 13 considers what it is to be good and how we can encourage good actions in tourism. Chapter 14 discusses the view that tourism has been the subject of over-moralisation and Chapter 15 reaffirms the place for ethical tourism. Finally, Chapter 16 sets its sights on the ends of tourism. It asks what those ends might be, analyses means and power and invokes a new paradigm of transmodernity for remaking the tourism world.

We are, according to David Fennell, ethical beings by nature and in Chapter 12 he considers the relationship between Ethics and Tourism. This offers a basis from which to understand the more formal side of ethics along with discussion of key philosophical traditions. It helps us locate our bearings in thinking about and applying ethics, beginning with a distinction between ethics (principles that dictate right conduct) and morality (the rational and natural inclinations of humanity to do good and avoid evil). We are next offered a practical guide to the steps needed to implement an ethical dimension in decision making, from problem recognition and analysis to values analysis and prioritisation. Values, then, are at the heart of ethical analysis and Fennell offers a powerful definition of values that incorporates an action imperative. A paradigm of values is next presented, distinguishing between four different grounds of value: preference, consensus, consequence and principle. Each of these is seen to have a psychological and a philosophical dimension.

Fennell then guides us through the major philosophical traditions of ethics. The first of these concentrates on ends – what is our ultimate goal? Here Fennell offers two approaches. On the one hand Aristotle's concept of *eudaimonia* (flourishing) tempered by moderation is offered as the desirable end for humans. On the other hand the pursuit of happiness is sometimes invoked as a moral end. Here a distinction is made between hedonism (the pursuit of individual pleasure) and utilitarianism (the greatest good for the greatest number). The second major tradition considered is deontology or means – that is action based on duty. This may include the following of religious principles, social contract ethics (Locke, Rousseau) or categorical imperatives (Kant). Additionally, Fennell considers authenticity and existentialism (Kierkegaard) as well as justice and rights (Rawls). Fennell concludes by noting the somewhat marginal interest taken in ethics in tourism research and urges a stronger understanding of values, their link to ethics and ethical traditions to better prepare us in considering what we ought to do in order to be good in tourism. Understanding ethical theory, he underlines, is a crucial prerequisite for achieving sustainable and responsible tourism.

Where Chapter 12 offers us a broad perspective of ethical traditions, Chapter 13 offers us some guidance on selecting and combining key ideas and a tentative recipe for action. Here Tazim Jamal and Chris

Menzel further examine the notion of the good in tourism, specifically, what constitutes Good Actions in Tourism. To do this they combine the ideas of three of the philosophers – Bentham (utilitarianism), Kant (respect for others) and Aristotle (virtue ethics) alluded to in the previous chapter. They argue that the starting point for ethical deliberation in regard to good actions in tourism is utilitarian. That is that other things being equal, significant actions ought to maximise utility, where utility is understood broadly to include such 'goods' as pleasure, wealth, security and general happiness.

The authors argue that the qualification 'other things being equal' is a critical one. As they note, it takes little reflection to see that maximising utility can be overridden by clear Kantian desiderata regarding the respect of persons. This is the second ethical consideration presented by Jamal and Menzil as a necessary constraint on utilitarian action. In illustration of this point, they consider a tourist development that would bring substantial wealth to a region – and hence very high overall utility – but which might do so at the expense of the cultural survival of a small indigenous group. In such a scenario, the members of the indigenous community would be treated as means to an end (maximisation of utility for a large number of people) and not as ends in themselves. Under-standing this, developers would design attractions and destinations so as to facilitate respect for local people (who in turn would treat visitors with respect – a mutual relationship between visitors and residents). The authors also argue that an Aristotelian 'virtue' ethic ties together the utilitarian and Kantian perspectives vis-à-vis good actions in tourism. Here it is the development of character that enables an agent to temper judgments motivated with maximisation of utility with concern and respect for persons. The chapter offers examples of actions in tourism that are discussed in relation to these three ethical perspectives.

Jim Butcher argues in Chapter 14 against 'Ethical Tourism'. Butcher finds the concept of ethical tourism a thoroughly bad idea. He contends that it amounts to a slight on the holidaymaker in search of fun and relaxation and is premised upon assumptions that are profoundly reactionary when viewed from a humanist standpoint. First of all, Butcher rounds up his targets and/or specific works that include among others Krippendorf (1984), Croall (1995), Smith and Duffy (2003), Fennell (2006), NGOs, Industry Groups, the media (especially the *Guardian*), journalists (Monbiot, 1999) and tour operators. Next, he summarises typical ethical tourism critiques. For example, there is the view that package tourists are thoughtless with regard to their environmental footprint and unaware of their damaging impact on host cultures.

Because of this, Butcher argues, the ethical tourism lobby seeks to rein in the pleasure-seeking of mass tourists for the sake of the planet and the cultures that inhabit it and to control their activities through codes of conduct. This same ethical lobby is seen by Butcher as demonstrating a one-sided sympathy for hosts as victims of cultural imposition, rather than an empathy with the aspirations of hosts (for development or indeed travel). Against what he sees as the prevailing ethical tide, Butcher puts up the case of Torremolinos in Spain as a counter-argument. Hardly, he points out, a site of ethical tourism and yet symbolising Spain's development and a move which transformed its hosts from a poor fishing community to wealthy cosmopolitanism.

Ecotourism (offered as a paradigm example of ethical tourism) is treated with particular contempt by Butcher as a development model. He pinpoints ecotourism's claims to be 'sustainable' and 'ethical' in its ability to offer development within limits set by conservation. But this is problematic for Butcher because in his view it means a limited development that denies hosts the opportunity to participate fully in the possibilities of wealth and material improvement generated by unfettered economic growth. This explains Butcher's preference for mass tourism and large projects with their promise of poverty reduction through economic growth. In concluding, Butcher states his enthusiasm for more rather than less mobility as part of a humanist philosophy. Here the opportunity to travel is seen as a significant part of a common human progress so that its benefits – pleasurable, educational and commercial – are made available for all. That, according to Butcher, would be a truly ethical vision. It is unlikely, he says, to be one that finds favour with those who have lost sight of equality and development, caught up in moralising about our holidays. He may be referring here to some of his fellow authors in this section!

In Development and its Discontents: Ego-tripping Without Ethics or Idea(l)s? Mick Smith begins Chapter 15 by revisiting Freud's essay on 'Civilisation and its Discontents' and uses it to open up an understanding of one of Jim Butcher's previous works *The Moralisation of Tourism* (2003), especially in relation to three points. These are the antagonism between instinctive human behaviour and civilised society, the futility of the struggle between ethics and human instinct, and 'on ethics as a repressive conjuring trick played on the gullible' and as a means of guilt-tripping people into fulfilling their social responsibilities. Beyond this, Smith points up Butcher's other key theses which are the belief that tourism development is always in the best interest of everyone and the notion of tourism as innocent fun which moralising undermines. To rebut

Butcher's arguments (and hence, as the title of this chapter suggests, critique ego-tripping without ethics or idea(l)s) Smith invokes the work of Bauman and Arendt. Following their lead, Smith dismisses any simplistic and negative view of ethics as a form of social repression, but rather suggests that ethics are important in composing who we are. Smith also rejects the idea that ethics is necessarily opposed to pleasure. According to Smith, individual responsibility is the starting point for ethics and ethics is not about mindlessly following rules. Rather, the question as to what is good is always an open question that is never quite settled. Finally, we are reminded that each of us is potentially one of civilisations discontents and that is why we should struggle within both for and against social and economic restrictions.

It is fitting that a book on philosophical issues in tourism should conclude with a chapter that thinks about the ends of tourism. What would be 'good' tourism and in what ways can tourism contribute to a 'good' world? This task falls to Irena Ateljevic who is perhaps best known for convening a recent series of conferences in Croatia – the last of which (2007) was titled 'Towards an Academy of Hope' – a theme that she relentlessly pursues in this chapter. In Transmodernity: Remaking our (Tourism) World? Ateljevic offers a detailed analysis of transmodernity and consideration of what the term means for tourism. In this unashamedly upbeat chapter (devoted largely to discovering 'what is positive and possible in our human development potential') Ateljevic locates us (after Rifkin, 2005) at a crossroads between a dying old order and the rise of a new age. She argues that transmodernity represents a profound paradigm shift that is being played out through changes in sociocultural, economic, political and philosophical thought and practice.

Ateljevic's analysis points to a major global consciousness change (albeit one that is sometimes rather hidden). The move represents a rejection of the dominant European/Euro-American capitalist/patriarchal/modern/materialist/colonial world-system. Transmodernity represents a vision for the whole planet and all its inhabitants (including plants and animals), recognising that we are all connected in one system and stressing our interdependence, vulnerability and responsibility for the Earth as an indivisible living community. Equally, transmodernity opposes mindless economic progress and the pursuit of material wealth as an end in itself and instead promotes the concept of quality of life as the measure of progress. Ateljevic relates the concept of transmodernity to other contemporary critiques/visions that emanate from critical economics, social anthropology, cultural studies, political science, social psychology, popular culture and social activism literature.

Ateljevic concludes that tourism is in fact one of the main indicators that a major shift in global consciousness and human activity is underway and that this has been staring us in the face for quite some time. Witness, she says, the early claims of MacCannell's (1999) theory of international tourism as a quest, as well as the whole array of postmodern forms of travel, such as the boom in backpacking and new age and spiritual tourism. These she claims are indicators of possibilities of hope for tourism to be remade and to remake the world.

References

Bernstein, B. (1971) On the classification and framing of educational knowledge. In M. Young (ed.) *Knowledge and Control: New Directions for the Sociology of Education* (pp. 47–69). London: Collier-Macmillan.

Butcher, J. (2003) *The Moralisation of Tourism*. London: Routledge.

Carlson, A. (2000) *Aesthetics and the Environment: The Appreciation of Nature, Art and Architecture*. London: Routledge.

Croall, J. (1995) *Preserve or Destroy? Tourism and the Environment*. London: Calouste Gulbenkian Foundation.

de Botton, A. (2003) *The Art of Travel*. London: Penguin Books.

Fennell, D. (2006) *Tourism Ethics*. Clevedon: Channel View Publications.

Giddens, A. (2002) *Runaway World*. London: Profile Books.

Gunn, C. (1994) *Tourism Planning*. New York: Taylor and Francis.

Hannam, K., Sheller, M. and Urry, J. (2006) Editorial: Mobilities, immobilities and moorings. *Mobilities* 1, 1–22.

Jacobsen, J. (2000) Anti-tourist attitudes: Mediterranean charter tourism. *Annals of Tourism Research* 27, 284–300.

Kaplan, S. (1995) The restorative benefits of nature: Toward an integrative framework. *Journal of Environmental Psychology* 15, 169–182.

Kaplan, R. and Kaplan, S. (1989) *The Experience of Nature. A Psychological Perspective*. Cambridge: Cambridge University Press.

Krippendorf, J. (1984) *The Holiday Makers*. Oxford: Butterworth Heinemann.

Kuhn, T. (1962) *The Structure of Scientific Revolutions*. Chicago, IL: University of Chicago Press.

Lyotard, J. (1984) *The Postmodern Condition: A Report on Knowledge*. Manchester: Manchester University Press.

MacCannell, D. (1999) *The Tourist: A New Theory of the Leisure Class*. Berkeley, CA: University of California Press.

Monbiot, G. (1999) An Unfair Exchange. *The Guardian*.

Nechar, M. (2005) *La modernización de la política turística. Retos y perspectivas*. México: Centro de Investigación y Docencia en Humanidades del Estado de Morelos.

Pearce, D. (1995) *Tourist Development*. Harlow: Longman.

Rifkin, J. (2005) *The European Dream: How Europe's Vision of the Future is Quietly Eclipsing the American Dream*. New York: Penguin Group.

Sayer, A. (1999) *Long Live Postdisciplinary Studies! Sociology and the Curse of Disciplinary Parochialism/imperialism*. On WWW at http://www.comp.lancs.ac. uk/sociology/papers/Sayer-Long-Live-Postdisciplinary-Studies.pdf.

Smith, A. (1904) *An Inquiry into the Nature and Causes of the Wealth of Nations* (5th edn). London: Methuen and Co.

Smith, M. and Duffy, R. (2003) *The Ethics of Tourism Development*. London: Routledge.

Tribe, J. (2002) Education for ethical tourism action. *Journal of Sustainable Tourism* 10, 309–324.

Tribe, J. (2006) The truth about tourism. *Annals of Tourism Research* 33, 360–381.

Tribe, J. (2008) The art of tourism. *Annals of Tourism Research* 35, 924–944.

Part 2

Truth: Reality, Knowledge, and Disciplines

Chapter 2

Who is a Tourist? Conceptual and Theoretical Developments

SCOTT MCCABE

Introduction

This chapter aims to assess the relevance of the term tourist to contemporary debates in tourism. It aims to illuminate the problematic relationships between the use of the term tourist by the academy of tourism studies and sciences with its use as a lay construct (its use by ordinary people in everyday conversation). Hence, a differentiation is sought between functional definitions of the term tourist used to define and measure activities of people for the purposes of sorting and collecting data about those activities, and that of the concept of a *tourist*, which has a much less well-understood value. I argue that this latter could and should become the object of analysis to help develop understandings of the former which will contribute to both the study of tourism and the wider social sciences whose interest is in mobile cultures (Urry & Sheller, 2004) and has relevance to the wider interest in globalisation of cultures (Appardurai, 1990). This is proposed through an analysis of the *tourist* as a membership categorization device.

The chapter argues that despite the many problems of definitions and lack of concreteness surrounding the term *tourist*, a distinction needs to be made between its use at a practical level, in enumerating various types of activity within and across international borders and its use as a discursive construct. The chapter contends that there is little point in trying to ascribe meaning or experiential values to the definition of a tourist as this will add no practical value to the methods used to determine types of tourist activities. Indeed, the chapter will debate that the tourism industry has little overall interest in the category tourist because of increasingly sophisticated consumer segmentation and marketing techniques, which seek to imbue a deeper sense of meaning to the development, promotion and communication of tourism services, based on multivariate constructs and experiential attributes. In segmenting markets into discrete and categorical niche groups, the term tourist is rendered a vestige that makes no contribution to overall product-market strategy decisions.

However, the chapter indicates that there is scope to develop and increase our understanding of tourist-as-consumer attitudes and orientations towards products and services offered by the industry through the analysis of the *tourist* (as a concept). This would be fruitful because the overwhelmingly pejorative use of the word tourist within lay sociological reasoning and such analysis can be useful in contributing to our understanding of how tourists construct their activities and those of others as social practices, which, in turn, would uncover layers of social mores that make up this vast and dynamic aspect of consumer society, which is tourism. Analysis of the concept *tourist* can yield deeper meanings attributable to contemporary travel given that a *tourist* can be conceived as an identity marker used pervasively in ordinary interaction as people narrate their experiences (cf. McCabe, 2005; Stokoe & McCabe, 2004). This type of analysis does have relevance to industry, as knowing and understanding how tourists position themselves and their activities as tourists in relation to others can help the industry position, promote and communicate its services more effectively.

The chapter elaborates these issues firstly by outlining the main definitions of tourists from a range of perspectives. It moves on to discuss and evaluate research on tourist experience. Through the analysis, knowledge claims about tourists and their identifying characteristics are made. The discussion concludes that social sciences of tourism often fails in its attempts to understand tourists' behaviour and experiences through a lack of attention to the perspective of interview respondents and the categories they use to describe themselves and others. Ethnographic research on tourist experience has often paid undue regard to reflexivity, researchers often neglecting their own role as an influencing factor in determining responses about attitudes towards other tourists. As social scientists, we all need to engage much more positively with the methods people use to topicalise talk about *tourists* either in terms of their own behaviour, motives or experiences or those of others. The chapter outlines one method that is useful to apply to interaction (conversation, interview and textual data).

Defining tourists: The changing context

A great deal of effort has been put into defining tourists, which is good social science. The importance of being able to define and differentiate between different types of travel is critical not only in allowing information to be gathered concerning the numbers of tourists entering and leaving a region, but also so that we can classify and add deeper levels of understanding to the activities and experiences that go into making tourism a distinctive set of activities as opposed to other forms of travel. In terms of the official recording of data, the UN World Tourism Organisation (UNWTO) has spent a great deal of time working with the international community to develop and implement the Tourism Satellite Accounts (TSA) based on the categories of international travellers and activities outlined in Figure 2.1. The classificatory system is needed to try to establish the significance of international tourism and to understand broad-based descriptive statistics on the types and reasons for travel. The classification has some recognition of temporal qualities of tourists – same-day visitors, tourist but not permanent or temporary migrants for example. Types of activities as well as purposes of travel are also identified: leisure, recreation and holidays; visiting friends and relatives (VFR); business and professional travel; health treatments; religious and pilgrimage trips; as well as others. A range of travel activities is also encompassed in the official definition of tourists: crews; returning non-nationals; day visitors etc.

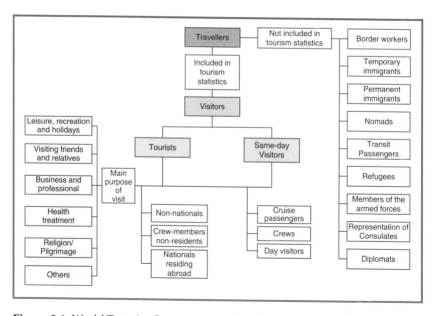

Figure 2.1 World Torusim Organisation classification of international travelers

The main problem with the UNWTO classification of tourists centres on the problem of stasis. The categories are necessarily broad and fixed and yet it is this fixity that hampers any progress in utility of the measures. Therefore, the relevance of debates about the definition of tourists remains critical because what has become very clear over the last decade – particularly in the developed world where tourism has become an increasingly important aspect of contemporary consumer societies – is that tourist's consumption of travel is being radically changed.

The nature of these changes can be characterised by the following factors: uptake and diffusion of broadband internet connections; change in the structure of the industry through fragmentation and depackaging of products; increasing importance of individual principal component sectors – such as airlines and hotels; the move to increasing independence for self-arranged travel components, the so-called DIY packaging by consumers; the increase in numbers of shorter breaks taken and the correlate decrease in longer holidays; the openness of borders and the subsequent increase in security and border controls to combat terrorism activities, which have reduced the capacity to monitor tourist activities. Yeoman *et al.* (2007) argue that increasingly, there is a desire for authentic tourist experiences. Although the nature, context and possibility of 'authentic experiences' remains contested, what is interesting is that regardless of the 'type' of travel experience, short city break, package holiday or long-haul independent trips, tourists appear to be placing a greater emphasis on the nature and quality of the experience, and increasingly seek to match up a range of interests and activities within each trip. One example is the rise in ethical or responsible travel, whereby people make active choices to visit a destination in order to undertake some voluntary work (see Wearing, 2001 for example) as well as to see the country and gain a better understanding or connection with the local culture.

Although these examples might be classified as niche aspects of the tourism industry, even in the context of mass travel more and more people are making choices that reflect or tap into their networks of family and/or friends through independent travel and accommodation booking, the rise in second home ownership and the diversity of travel motivations suggesting that combinations of purposes can easily be achieved in one trip: business AND pleasure; holiday AND visiting friends and relatives; and increasing 'work' and holiday, especially in deregulated labour markets such as the EU. Young people from various parts of the EU find that cities such as London are too expensive to visit purely as 'tourists', and so when jobs are easy to find, they can stay longer and have a deeper experience of the city. Therefore, consumers are changing in their attitudes to travel and their consumption of places, the tourism industry is changing in structure and shape, orienting its services to an increasingly fragmented and segmented market.

All of these factors make it just as important that we know how to categorise what people are doing when they travel and understand what travel means to individuals and for wider society. For example, it is important not only for industry, but also for government. Funding is allocated by central government in proportion to the contribution to the wider economy and social good of certain activities. Tourism balance of payments and statistics on traveller numbers feeds into budget allocation to national and regional tourism authorities. The extent to which tourism statistics are valid and reliable will surely impact upon government's spending revues. At the wider level, if being a tourist is deemed to be good for you, in that tourism yields personal and social benefits, then tourism might become an issue for social and health policy. Thus, the enterprise of defining *tourists* has both a practical and theoretical value. But, I argue that although there will always be contested ground between competing definitions based on different factors, and variability concerning the validity of broad statistical measures of tourist activities, especially given these changing circumstances and structure of the industry, debate must be addressed at the philosophical level in order to inform and contribute towards clearer understanding of who is a tourist. Some of the key issues underpinning these debates concerning conventional measures will now be outlined.

Defining tourists: The practical way

In beginning a discussion on definitions of terms, their use and meaning, it is usual to draw on the major dictionary definitions to understand the broad cultural sense in which they are understood. In this section, my aim is also to delve a little into the etymological basis for the use of the term *tourist* in order to get a nuanced picture of the underlying meanings of its contemporary use. A number of different dictionary definitions throw up some immediate and interesting contrasts:

> Tour- ist-*noun*. One who travels for pleasure. (The *American Heritage Dictionary*)

The *American Heritage Dictionary* makes the immediate causal leap between travel and pleasure as the connecting principles underpinning the definition of a tourist. A tourist is therefore defined in terms of the act of travel and the purpose of the trip. The *Merriam-Webster Dictionary* includes a broader set of purposes to encompass cultural motives

> one who travels for pleasure or culture. (www.merriam-webster.com)

A tourist in this sense infers the possibility of an engagement with the peoples of a destination as well as places. The Cambridge online dictionary (www.dictionary.cambridge.org) expands this to encompass a broader category of 'interest', which is useful as a means to include a wider range of possible motivations, and also clearly links the possibility of pleasure *and* interest. The Cambridge definition makes explicit the link between tourist activities and holidays. This dictionary also includes the popular sporting use of the term 'tourist' to refer to the visiting team, particularly in the context of international games of Rugby and Cricket.

1. someone who visits a place for pleasure and interest, usually while they are on holiday:
2. UK a member of a sports team who is travelling from place to place in a foreign country, playing games

It is interesting that there are differences in emphasis in all these definitions, but at the same time, there are two constant elements, the act of travel and the purpose, motive or experiential quality that characterises the action, as being pleasurable, driven by interest or at least a sense of a lack of obligation. It is possible, therefore, to define being a tourist in terms of what it is not: travel which is 'forced' in that there is a lack of choice, either by cause of weather (recent flooding in England meant that people had to be 'evacuated' from their homes) or driven by economic necessity.

The etymological basis for the contemporary use of the word tourist is usually traced back to Stendhal's *Memoires d'un Touriste,* a short recount of his journey around Brittany and Normandy first published in 1838. There is evidence that the word *tourist(e)* was used in the French to refer to people visiting England – or to refer to the practices of the English, but the word moved into more common parlance in relation to travelling for pleasure after Stendhal's book and coincided with the beginnings of the 'modern tourist industry'. This is generally attributed to Thomas Cook's organised excursions in the Midlands of England after the initial wave of growth of railway infrastructure, which greatly reduced the times of journeys.

In these definitions, it is noted that the root word is *tour* – in that a *tour- ist* is one who undertakes a 'tour'. In order to develop a deeper understanding of the possible definitional qualities of the term 'tourist', it may be useful to probe the etymological basis for the word 'tour'. The Etymological online dictionary defines a tour thus:

> c. 1320, "a turn, a shift on duty", from O.Fr. *tour, tourn* "a turn, trick, round, circuit, circumference", from *torner, tourner* "to turn", from L. *tornare* "to polish, round off, fashion, turn on a lathe". Sense of "a traveling around, journey" is first recorded 1643. The verb is attested from 1746. (http://www.etymonline.com/)

The historical context of the word tour provides more detail on the meanings of the activities that are encompassed by tourism. The word 'tour' is derived from the Latin word *Tornus* meaning a lathe, in the sense that *tornare* is to 'round off' or 'to turn on a lathe'. The tour implies roundedness, a circular movement. It is also connected to the old French *tourner* meaning to 'turn about' and in Middle English *a turn*, originating from the old English *tyrnan* and *turnian* (cf: http://www.merriam-webster.com/dictionary/turn) meaning to go or pass around by turning, which could be used in relation to 'taking a turn of the park' a short walk out and back, but could imply a tour of duty, a shift on the watch. Of course, a link is also made in connection with the word *return*, which is the act of coming or going back, inferring a reply, recurrence, a reflection or being sent back. In this sense, a tour infers that the starting and ending points are the same.

The dictionaries are able to provide a much more detailed and richer description of the word tour than tourist as this example from the *American Heritage Dictionary* shows:

tour – *noun*

1. a traveling around from place to place.
2. a long journey including the visiting of a number of places in sequence, esp. with an organized group led by a guide.
3. a brief trip through a place, as a building or a site, in order to view or inspect it: The visiting prime minister was given a tour of the chemical plant.
4. a journey from town to town to fulfill engagements, as by a theatrical company or an entertainer: to go on tour; a European concert tour.
5. a period of duty at one place or in one job.
   –verb (used without object)
6. to travel from place to place.
7. to travel from town to town fulfilling engagements.
   –verb (used with object)

8. to travel through (a place).
9. to send or take (a theatrical company, its production, etc.) from town to town.
10. to guide (someone) on a tour: He toured us through the chateaus of the Loire Valley.

In this set of definitions, the temporal factor is broad, encompassing shorter as well as long journeys, a sense of moving about from place to place, incorporating a number of different places on an itinerary, or an inspection. But, in this we have lost the sense of pleasurable purpose that underlies the act of being a *tourist*. Other words whose dictionary definition may hold importance for understanding what it means to be a tourist would include *holiday*.

A holiday is an official, authorised day(s) when a person does not have to go to school or work, and is free to either relax or travel. Accordingly, the etymological basis of holiday was clearly in reference to a 'holy' 'day', a day of religious observance, but also in connection with a period of time for recreation. The etymological dictionary notes that St George's feast day has been a holiday in England since 1222. The Latin word *Vacare* which was transferred into early French *Vacation* referred to being free or released from obligation or duty from the 14th century, but in reference to schools and courts, and did not take on its current sense of equivalency to the English word *holiday* until the late 19th century.

In summary, a 'tourist' can be characterised by the following factors: through the act of travelling, or making a journey that starts and finishes in the same place. I refrain from stating that the journey must start and end at 'home' because people can be 'tourists' within or as part of a different type of travel experience. Take, for example, an international student visiting a country to undertake a period of further or higher education, who takes a tourist trip during that stay, either internationally or regionally. These travellers would be included within the TSA as tourists (see Figure 2.1) in any case, and this highlights the inherent problems with definitions that are used to develop meaningful statistical data on this type of activity. Secondly, a tourist can be defined by the purpose or experiential qualities of the trip; for pleasure, interest, culture, holiday, recreation etc. However, the problem with all the definitions is that they are not able to account for or encompass the multiplicity of experiences often desired by travellers in their trips. Perhaps a more detailed analysis of the literature on tourist experience would add more fruitfully to the understanding of what it means to be a tourist.

The Tourist Experience

In a previous paper (McCabe, 2005) I have argued that the relative focus on the experiential aspects of tourist behaviour often fails to acknowledge and accept that the concept *tourist* is not ideologically neutral and is often used at the level of practical reasoning (everyday discourse) and in a wider cultural context (culturally embedded discourses), in a pejorative sense. This lack of attention to the ideological and philosophical positions taken by both the researchers and the researched on the concept of *tourists* in these studies represents a missed opportunity to understand how people position their own activities in relation to those of others and to make claims about their understandings of the cultural discourses underpinning the activities. In this section, I want to briefly review those arguments and explain how tourist experience research can be linked to matters of social identity.

Theoretical interest in tourist experiences can be traced back to the work of Erik Cohen who identified and defined the nature of experiences. Cohen's 'sociology of international tourism' was based on a fourfold typology of tourist experiences: the organised mass tourist, the individual mass tourist, the explorer and the drifter (Cohen, 1972). Up until that point, tourists had been conceived as a largely homogenous group. Cohen argued that the main differentiating factor consisted of a continuum of familiarity/strangeness sought by tourists that could be used to delineate between varying qualities of experience (Cohen, 1972: 177). Cohen then developed this analysis of the variability of touristic experience and asked, 'Who is a tourist?' (Cohen, 1974: 527). He observed that the study of tourism accepted the unreflective, commonsensical stereotype of a tourist, which led him directly to link together types of experiences to types of tourist roles, drawing largely on the work of Goffman, proposing a range of tourist roles with common characteristics such as: permanency, voluntary-ness, direction, distance, recurrence and purpose of trip (Cohen, 1974). Cohen's (1979: 180) later work drew on Turner's ideas about tourist experiences being related to an individual's orientation to a 'centre'. Tourism was conceived as a reversal of everyday activities, a temporary break from the 'centre', which was conceived along a spectrum of types.

This range of types of experience was further conceptualised in relation to notions of authenticity seeking (Wang [1999] provides an excellent summary of these debates). Wang proposes that rather than the nature of the activities and the type of experience being the defining characteristics of tourist-ness, it is the act of being a tourist that defines the experience as such in a self-referential and indivisible way. Hom Cary (2004) shares this view and develops the notion of the interpellation between the 'tourist' as 'subject' and the wider representations of the tourist experience. In framing her analysis in the context of touristic narrative, Hom Cary draws together the fundamental link between conceptualising 'the tourist' as a defined subject and a cultural discourse of the *tourist* as a product of cultural construction.

Tourist experiences have often been characterised in relation to the expectations and behaviours of different groups as identified by Cohen above in relation to the types and/or forms of tourist experience. Pearce (2005) described the differences in behaviours between tourists and backpackers. Uriely *et al.* (2002) argue that despite the fact that the study of backpacking behaviour has developed as a distinct – but largely homogenous – category separate from and distinguished in contrast to mass tourism, this differentiation is false as there are different *forms* of backpacker tourism and there are consequently many different ways in which tourists doing essentially the same form of activity, cannot be categorised as being the same *type* of tourist.

This approach accords with a more general shift towards postmodernism thinking, which has tended to emphasise the subjective, multiple and negotiated characteristics of individual's experiences over more reductionist and rigid conceptualisations. This has been translated into empirical research focusing more deeply on the plethora of tourist roles, experiences and meanings, and attitudes. Jacobsen (2000) draws on Goffman's role theory as his basis for an empirical study of Mediterranean charter vacationers, asking them how they see themselves in relation to their stated attitudes towards other vacationers. This study's focus on the expressed attitudes and descriptions of tourist's experiences produces a critical departure from theoretical explanations of the *tourist* to ones that are founded on tourists' own expressions. This raises a philosophical question about the extent to which it is possible to theorise about the nature of tourist experiences based on tourists' own judgements about the behaviours of others.

For example, Jacobsen proposes the idea of an 'anti-tourist' attitude, which is described as an expected or perceived shallowness of experience of place within traditional tourism, a tendency to condemn the superficiality of tourist experience – typified by brief stops in each place. This is what Jacobsen defines as the 'touristic role'. The concept of anti-tourist roles, or role distance, is used to describe individuals who are attached and committed to a role, but who wish to distance themselves from the identity that accompanies it (Goffman, 1961: 110). In this conception, roles seem to challenge a sense of identity and individuality for people, so role distance becomes a means of maintaining a feeling that individuals' experiences are distinct from all the other occupants and players of a role. Role distance therefore, 'constitutes a wedge between the individual and the role, between doing and being' (Jacobsen, 2000: 286). Jacobsen argues that the notion of setting one's own activities apart from those of others might be something connected to status, akin to Bourdieu's concept of 'distinction'; 'it is often assumed that many anti-tourists believe that the possibilities of experiencing something authentic and typical are inversely proportional to the number of tourists present in an area' (Jacobsen, 2000: 287). However, Jacobsen's analysis is very useful but limited in its ability to account for such attitudes or to go beyond a simple definition to cut through to a theoretical position about the nature of being a *tourist*. Jacobsen could have drawn deeper from Goffman's (1959) ideas about self-presentation and the demands this places on individuals to create and sustain social roles, or 'identities' through all social interaction – including responses to research questions about tourism – in what Goffman calls the dramaturgical production of everyday life. The theatre of everyday life was understood to be created for, and directed towards, others in society, that made the direct link between the 'self' and society:

> When we allow that the individual projects a definition of the situation when he appears before others, we must also see that the others, however passive their role may seem to be, will themselves effectively project a definition of the situation by virtue of their response to the individual and by virtue of any lines of action they initiate to him. (Goffman, 1959: 20)

Goffman argued that participants contribute altogether to a single definition, not based on real agreement but on whose claims will be honoured (temporarily), which Goffman (1959: 21) calls 'working consensus'. In varying social circumstances, social actors present themselves according to competency, power relations and type of interactional setting. Goffman uses the concept of a performance to argue that individuals orient to presenting themselves through expressive equipment – fronts, including sex, age, race, clothes, facial expressions and gestures to ensure that the performance meets with what is expected of them in each interaction situation. As such, notions of identities become fluid, as individuals slip between negotiated selves according to the demands of the interactional setting. Goffman later developed the idea of an interactional order for 'self'-production in social encounters (1979). These interactional relationships Goffman called 'footings', which were equivalent to identity roles.

Tourists own classifications of their/others activities as 'touristic', or their classifications of themselves or others as *tourists* is then better positioned as a natural process of language practice rather than in terms of being conceived as an ascription of meaning about the nature of tourist experiences. McCabe and Stokoe (2004) argued that one feature of tourists' accounts is a tendency to construct one's own experiences in relation to, contrasting with or in distinction to those of others. Such 'contrasting work' is a natural and intrinsic feature of accounts for behaviour. If we do not ask people to account for their behaviour then there is every reason to assume that people do not naturally need to account for the experiences of others.

A good example is provided by Uriely *et al.* (2002). In their study on backpackers, the respondents described the activities and experiences of others in a largely positive light. However, their study also revealed how backpackers experiences were contrasted with those of mass tourists and also how backpacking as an ascribed activity was only deemed to be positive provided the experience conformed to certain characteristics:

> Specifically, the backpackers develop attitudes that approve of and respect those who fully comply with the form-related attributes, which signify their identity ... On the contrary, those who deviate from these norms are considered "fake" or "not serious". An interesting indication of this approach is that many tend to downplay the parts of their trip during which they did not follow these form-related codes of the backpacking ideology. This pattern of behavior was clearly illustrated in the interviewees' accounts regarding visits to popular attractions. In this context, almost all emphasized their attempts to avoid destinations that are "too touristy". (Uriely *et al.*, 2002: 534)

In the studies by Jacobsen (2000), Uriely *et al.* (2002) and McCabe and Stokoe (2004) similar 'anti-tourist' constructions were noted. Respondents tend to play down their own activities and experiences that might be deemed inappropriate or that might not accord with the way they want to project themselves to the interviewers as 'good' and moral people/tourists. This is a most important and fascinating aspect of these accounts, yet this inherent reflexivity in interview data between respondent and interviewer often remains unacknowledged (McCabe, 2005).

Thus, the experiential dimensions of tourist's activities provide additional details on the types and forms of experience, but which are inconclusive in terms of being able to develop theoretical understandings of what it means to be a *tourist*. The pejorative use of the concept *tourist* in tourist accounts to contrast their own activities with those of others provides us with more substantial evidence that the *tourist* could be little more than a rhetorical device, an ideological and political construct as opposed to a concept able to encompass experiential dimensions. This is a philosophical point as all that we can possibly know about *tourists* is from what other people say about themselves in their interviews with researchers or in natural conversation. This stance towards the term *tourist* used as a language device to achieve some aspect of local social order in the context of its use is essentially derived from Wittgenstein's analysis of language games (Wittgenstein, 1965). This approach to theorising the *tourist* avoids the problems of conventional sociological essentialising experiences and postmodernism's irreconcilable relativity. The final section of this chapter goes on to discuss how such an approach might be operationalised by conceptualising the *tourist* as a membership categorization device.

The 'tourist' as a member's category

Membership categorization analysis (MCA) is the study of ordinary terms and knowledge used in everyday interaction. As Francis and Hester (2004: 21) argue: MCA is 'concerned with the organisation of common-sense knowledge in terms of the categories members employ in accomplishing their activities in and through talk'. Although it is most often associated in connection with the strand of qualitative sociology called conversation analysis (CA), there are differences in emphasis and yet, the two approaches share an orientation to an ethnomethodological position. Ethnomethodology is a branch of sociology that takes as its focus the practical activities and reasoning of ordinary people as the basis from which to draw theorising about social facts (see McCabe, 2007). It takes a radical stance, which is in opposition to traditional Durkheimian sociology because it is interested in how social order is 'built up' through actions by ordinary members of society as they seek to 'create and maintain a sense of order and intelligibility in social life' (ten Have, 2004: 14). Studies in CA and MCA have, therefore, often focused on, respectively, the sequential organisation of topics and the categories developed within ordinary conversations as their empirical source of data from which to theorise about how social order is created and maintained. However, Stokoe (2006) points out that MCA has also been used to study a variety of different types of discourse, including newspaper texts, television and radio debates and interview data (see Stoke, 2006: 3 and also Baker, 1997).

Stokoe (2006) provides a detailed and useful summary to the origins of MCA, outlined in Sack's Lectures on Conversation (1992) in which he was interested in how speakers categorised themselves and others. Sacks theorised that within a culture, speakers use categories (membership categorization devices; MCD) which do not need a full explanation or account because their use allowed hearers to link categories to concepts in a way that made sense to the production of local social order. In other words, in natural conversation, speakers deploy categories and their meaning appears to be understood and/or taken for granted, using commonsense knowledge. MCDs are then collections of categories that are linked together by rules of application. Stokoe (and also see McCabe & Stokoe, 2004) recounts Sack's example of the MCD 'family', which allows hearable links between the categories of 'mommy' and 'baby' in the line from a children's story: 'The baby cried. The mommy picked it up', whereby the categories are linked together by actions – category-bound activities – and characteristics – natural predicates – so that expectations are made about the normative behaviour associated with the category members, which accounts for the absence of detailed explanation.

Of course, categories can have different interpretations in different occasions of their use and so the context of their use becomes important, as Stokoe argues: 'The practical reasoning by which categories and their inferences "go together" is not, however, a strictly linguistic or logical kind of entailment. Rather, it is a common sense, normative practice in which inferences and implications are generated and managed in actual stretches of talk, with regard to particular states of affairs or narrative accounts' (Stokoe, 2006: 5). And further, Stokoe goes on to argue that because anyone can be categorised in any number of different ways, the choice of category used in any given situation or interaction allows for quite rich inferential analysis.

Using this approach, the category *tourist* can be understood to belong to the categorization device 'leisure travel' alongside other possible categories such as 'traveller', 'holidaymaker', 'vacationer', 'pilgrim' and so on, with potentially endless numbers of possible categorizations. These may also have nothing whatsoever to do with the actual travel trip such as 'scuba-diver', 'mountain-biker', 'climber', which are obvious examples whereby the activity presupposes the appropriate terrain/sous-terrain that may necessitate travel in order to qualify. Stokoe argues that such categories are *inference rich* in that a great deal of cultural knowledge is stored in them.

I have argued that the category *tourist* comes with a set of features or 'natural predicates' and in an earlier paper (McCabe & Stoke, 2004) it was shown how *tourists* appear to be identified with a set of normative behaviours: they 'swarm' in that they move about in a destination in large groups together; they visit places in such a way that they cannot know it deeply, by 'ticking' places off a list for example; and they do not appreciate the space of the destination, and thus the concept of the *tourist* is inferentially loaded with '... implicit moral evaluations about the activities that comprise the category, the incumbents of it and the place that is characterised by it [*their activity*]' (McCabe & Stokoe, 2004: 617). Of course, this analysis was developed out of a reflection on the context of the interview data in which these categorisations were used, by tourist day-visitors to the Peak District National in an interview with a tourism researcher. In that context at that time, it was perhaps natural that respondents chose these categories together with their incumbent characteristics and features to describe the behaviour of others in contrast to their own behaviour. However, in McCabe (2005), I drew on data from a web-blog to show how similar categorisation work was deployed and in the studies cited earlier by Uriely *et al.* (2002) and Jacobsen (2002), in different cultural contexts and with different categories of research respondents (backpackers and package tourists), similarly pejorative constructions were used to elaborate on the characterisations of 'tourists'. This demonstrates that as Edwards (1997) points out, categorisations like *tourist* are prone to being invoked implicationally, to manage accounts for and of behaviour. These are thus functional semantic properties, they are not fixed and innate, they are rhetorical constructs serving a purpose in their use. Often, this choice of category is linked to identity constructs as people's choices of leisure travel and destination are often linked to status and identity needs.

Concluding Remarks

The purpose of this chapter was to critically review the concept of a *tourist* and its philosophical value to knowledge development in tourism studies. It did this through an examination of dictionary definitions and the etymological basis of the term tourist, and a discussion of industry and academic definitions. Philosophical questions were raised about the usefulness of research on tourist experience to illuminate theorisations of *tourists.* An alternative approach was discussed that focused on how the concept *tourist* is deployed as a rhetorical device. I argued that the idea of a *tourist* has taken on a cross-cultural and cross-contextual ideological significance as a pejorative term with implicit political and moral implications in its use. As such, problems are created for social science researchers in tourism, but also opportunities. *Tourist* as a categorisation device can be subjected to analysis using social science techniques. I have argued that there is a range of potential research strategies and studies to develop research into 'tourist' as a categorisation device.

There is also a need to recognise that at the macro-level of the TSAs, the classification of tourist is unlikely to change, however it is interesting to note that the original definitions of tourists as leisure and pleasure travellers have been expanded and extended to capture a wider range of purposes and types of travel experiences, I would suggest specifically in order to acknowledge the larger scale and value of travel to national economies and to improve the profile of the sector. Industry certainly seems to be moving towards ever more fragmented and 'niched' categorisations of people and experiences, and has little use for the concept of an overarching category of tourist. However, industry could benefit from a greater analysis of the use of the term as a lay construct, as it may benefit in terms of product development, delivery and communications to customers. Tourists are discretionary leisure travellers whose trips begin and end at the same place, but the ways in which the concept of a *tourist* is deployed as a lay philosophical construct, a person category which is rich in identity associations, incumbent with characteristics and meanings, provides opportunities to explore in much more nuanced ways how travel experiences relate to contemporary society and individuals lives, and in turn influence industry and policy.

References

Appadurai, A. (1996) *Modernity at Large: Cultural Dimensions of Globalization.* Minneapolis, MN: University of Minnesota Press.

Baker, C. (1997) Membership categorisation and interview accounts. In D. Silverman (ed.) *Qualitative Research: Theory, Method and Practice* (pp. 162–176). London: Sage.

Berger, P.L. and Luckmann, T. (1966) *The Social Construction of Reality.* New York: Doubleday.

Bruner, E.M. (1994) Abraham Lincoln as authentic reproduction: A critique of postmodernism. *American Anthropologist* 96, 397–415.

Cohen, E. (1972) Toward a sociology of international tourism. *Social Research* 39, 164–189.

Cohen, E. (1974) Who is a tourist? A conceptual review. *Sociological Review* 22, 27–53.

Cohen, E. (1979) A phenomenology of tourist experiences. *Sociology* 13, 179–201.

Cohen, E. (1984) The sociology of tourism: Approaches, issues, and findings. *Annual Review of Sociology* 10, 373–392.

Dann, G. (1999) Writing out the tourist in space and time. *Annals of Tourism Research* 26 (1), 159–187.

Desforges, L. (2000) Travelling the world: Identity and travel biography. *Annals of Tourism Research* 27 (4), 929–945.

Elsrud, T. (2001) Risk creation in traveling: Backpacker adventure narration. *Annals of Tourism Research* 28 (3), 597–617.

Erb, M. (2000) Understanding tourists: Interpretations from Indonesia. *Annals of Tourism Research* 27 (3), 709–736.

Goffman, E. (1959) *The Presentation of Self in Everyday Life.* London: Penguin.

Goffman, E. (1961) *Encounters: Two Studies in the Sociology of Interaction.* Harmondsworth: Penguin.

Goffman, E. (1979) Footing. *Semiotica* 25, 1–29.

Graburn, N. (2002) The ethnographic tourist. In G.M.S. Dann (ed.) *The Tourist as a Metaphor of the Social World* (pp. 19–40). Wallingford: CAB International.

Hom Cary, S. (2004) The tourist moment. *Annals of Tourism Research* 31 (1), 61–77.

Jack, G. and Phipps, A. (2005) *Tourism and Intercultural Exchange: Why Tourism Matters.* Clevedon: Channel View Publications.

Jacobsen, J.K.S. (2000) Anti-tourist attitudes: Mediterranean charter tourism. *Annals of Tourism Research* 27 (2), 284–300.

Jaworski, A. and Pritchard, A. (eds) (2005) *Discourse, Communication and Tourism.* Clevedon: Channel View Publications.

MacCannell, D. (1976) *The Tourist: A New Theory of the Leisure Class.* London: Macmillan.

Mathieson, A. and Wall, G. (1982) *Tourism: Economic, Physical and Social Impacts.* Harlow: Longman.

McCabe, S. (2007) The beauty in the form: Ethnomethodology and tourism studies. In I. Ateljevic, A. Pritchard and N. Morgan (eds) *The Critical Turn in Tourism Studies: Innovative Research Methodologies* (pp. 227–244). Oxford: Elsevier (Advances in Tourism Research Series).

McCabe, S. (2005) Who is a tourist? A critical review. *Tourism Studies* 5 (1), 85–106.

McCabe, S. and Stokoe, E.H. (2004). Place and identity in tourist accounts. *Annals of Tourism Research* 31 (3), 601–622.

Moore, K. (2002) The discursive tourist. In G.M.S. Dann (ed.) *The Tourist as a Metaphor of the Social World* (pp. 41–60). Wallingford: CAB International.

Morgan, N. and Pritchard, A. (1998) *Tourism Promotion and Power: Creating Images, Creating Identities.* Chichester: John Wiley.

Pearce, P.L. (2005) *Tourist Behaviour: Themes and Conceptual Schemes.* Clevedon: Channel View Publications.

Pickett, J.P. (2000) *The American Heritage Dictionary of the English Language* (4th edn). Boston, MA: Houghton Mifflin Co.

Potter, J. (2005) Making psychology relevant. *Discourse and Society* 16 (5), 739–747.

Potter, J. and Wetherell, M. (1987) *Discourse and Social Psychology. Beyond Attitudes and Behaviour.* London: Sage.

Random House (2006) *Random House Webster's Unabridged Dictionary*. London: Random House Reference Publishing.

Rojek, C. (1995) *Decentring Leisure: Rethinking Leisure Theory*. London: Routledge.

Rojek, C. and Urry, J. (eds) (1997) *Touring Cultures*. London: Routledge.

Sacks, H. (1992) *Lectures on Conversation*. G. Jefferson (ed.). Oxford: Blackwell.

Schegloff, E.A. (1997) Whose text? Whose context? *Discourse and Society* 8 (2), 165–187.

Schegloff, E.A. (1998) Reply to Wetherell. *Discourse and Society* 9 (3), 413–416.

Schutz, A. (1972) *The Phenomenology of the Social World*. London: Heinemann (first published 1938).

Schutz, A. and Luckmann, T. (1974) *The Structures of the Life-World*. London: Heinemann.

Selwyn, T. (1996) Introduction. In T. Selwyn (ed.) *The Tourist Image: Myths and Myth Making in Tourism* (pp. 1–31). New York: John Wiley.

Silverman, D. (1993) *Interpreting Qualitative Data: Methods for Analysing Talk, Text and Interaction*. London: Sage.

Silverman, D. (ed.) (1997) *Qualitative Research: Theory, Method and Practice*. London: Sage.

Stokoe, E. (2006) On ethnomethodology, feminism, and the analysis of categorial reference to gender in talk-in-interaction. *Sociological Review* 54 (3), 467–494. (Special issue 'New Horizons in Ethnomethodology').

Turner, V. (1973) The center out there: Pilgrim's goal. *History of Religion* 12, 191–230.

UNWTO (2004) *World Tourism Statistics*. Madrid: WTO.

Uriely, N. (2005) The tourist experience: Conceptual developments. *Annals of Tourism Research* 32 (1), 199–216.

Uriely, N., Yonay, Y. and Simchai, D. (2002) Backpacking experiences: A type and form analysis. *Annals of Tourism Research* 29 (2), 520–538.

Urry, J. (1994) Cultural change and contemporary tourism. *Leisure Studies* 13, 233–238.

Urry, J. (2002) *The Tourist Gaze* (2nd edn). London: Sage.

Urry, J. and Sheller, M. (eds) (2004) *Tourism Mobilities: Places to Stay, Places in Play*. London: Routledge.

Wang, N. (1999) Rethinking authenticity in tourism experience. *Annals of Tourism Research* 26 (2), 349–370.

Wearing, S. (2001) *Volunteer Tourism: Experiences that Make a Difference*. Oxford: CABI Publishing.

Wearing, S. and Wearing, B. (2001) Conceptualising the selves of tourism. *Leisure Studies* 20 (2), 143–159.

Wetherell, M. (1998) Positioning and interpretive repertoires: Conversation analysis and post-structuralism in dialogue. *Discourse and Society* 9 (3), 387–412.

Wickens, E. (2002) The sacred and the profane: A tourist typology. *Annals of Tourism Research* 29 (3), 834–851.

Wittgenstein, L. (1965) *Philosophical Investigations*. New York: Macmillan.

Yeoman, I., Brass, D. and McMahon-Beattie, U. (2007) Current issue in tourism: The authentic tourist. *Tourism Management* 28 (4), 1128–1138.

Chapter 3

What is Tourism? Definitions,
Theoretical Phases and Principles

ALEXANDRE PANOSSO NETTO

Introduction

Some of the main concepts related to tourism are leisure, entertainment, hospitality and recreation. However, tourism is the most difficult to define and researchers have not yet come to a consensus about it. Authors like Fuster (1971), Leiper (1979), Sessa (1985), Molina (1991), Palomo (1991), Ascânio (1992), Jafari (1995), Beni (1988) and Boullón (2002), didn't graduate in tourism, but in other fields like administration, architecture, biology, communication among others. This creates problems as researchers have a tendency to 'reduce' the explanation to one of these fields. Each researcher will start from the paradigms and presuppositions of the science that they are graduated in, and so won't agree with each other. In other words: there will be different approaches for similar issues.

This chapter approaches the difficulty in coming to a definition for tourism. It will present and analyze some explanations of what is tourism given by organizations and researchers. It discusses some of the theoretical models, based in Kuhn (2001), and also proposes an academic division of the tourism theories developed so far. At the end of the paper, I will emphasize some of the fundamental and desirable principles in tourism. I will also present a new proposal for the definition of tourism.

Tourism's Definitions

At the outset, it is necessary to ask what is the importance in establishing a definition for tourism.

Burkart and Medlik (1974: 39) answer this question stating that:

> [...] a more precise definition of tourism is required for various purposes. First, for purposes of study: in order to examine a phenomenon systematically, it is necessary to define what it covers.

43

Secondly, for statistical purposes: when a phenomenon is measured, it must be defined; in practice available techniques of measurement frequently define what is measured. Thirdly, for legislative and administrative purposes: legislation may apply to some activities and not to others. Fourthly, for industrial purposes: particular economic activities may give rise to market studies and provide the vases for the formation of industrial organizations.

Despite the need, there is still no unanimous definition among researchers and professionals (not even the definition created by the World Tourism Organization – UNWTO: www.unwto.org) of tourism. Definitions proposed are criticized and can often be improved upon and this underlines the problem that tourism is a complex phenomenon. Fuster (1971) states that in 1800, *The Shorter Oxford English Dictionary* published for the first time the word 'tourist': 'One who makes a tour or tours, sp. One who does this for recreation; one who travels for pleasure or culture, visiting a number of places for their objects of interest, scenery or the like'. In 1811, the word 'tourism' was defined as: 'The theory and practice of touring; travelling for pleasure. According to Haulot (in Fuster, 1971), the word tour comes from the Hebrew and has its origin in the Bible, in the book of Numbers (13:17) and it corresponds to the concept of discovering, trip, recognition and exploration.

Wahab (1977) signals that the first academic definition was created in 1911 by Herman von Schullern in his work *Fremdenverkehr und Volkswirkschaft* as: 'the sum of the operations, mainly the economic ones which are directly connected to the entrance, permanence and displacement of foreigners in an out of a country, city or region' (Wahab, 1977: 3).

The UNWTO has mainly been concerned with political, commercial and normative principles and doesn't approach the conceptual aspects. Its definition is adopted by several countries and organizations and has been the 'official' definition of tourism. It is a technical definition according to the following text:

> It comprises the activities of persons traveling to and staying in places outside their usual environment for not more than one consecutive year for leisure, business and other purposes not related to the exercise of an activity remunerated from within the place visited. (www.unwto.org)

Some definitions exclude the concept of tourism as the displacement motivated by work or remunerated activity. If this happens, I cannot talk about the segment 'Business Tourism'. But people who travel for work are also surely part of tourism as they are making use of the infrastructure and tourist services. Additionally, on a business trip there is the possibility of including some activities of leisure or entertainment. However, nowadays the word tourism is mainly associated with leisure trips and in many cases people do not like to admit that they are tourists.

Wahab (1977: 26) defined tourism as:

> A human intentional activity that serves as a mean of communication and as a link of interaction between the peoples, inside a country or even beyond its geographical demarcations. It involves the temporary displacement of people from one region to another, country or even continent, with the objective of satisfying necessities and not the realization of remunerated activity. For the visited country, tourism is an industry whose products are consumed in loco, producing invisible exports.

This is the most complete definition, but it also excludes remunerated displacement. Jafari (1995: 5) also received some criticism of his definition:

> Tourism is the study of man [the tourist] away from his usual habitat, of the touristic apparatus and networks, and of the ordinary [non-tourism] and non-ordinary [tourism] worlds and their dialectic relationship.

Jafari's definition is related to a key element: the study. In this definition, tourism became the study (1) of the displacement, (2) of companies of the sector and (3) of the impacts caused by the displacement of people. About this I agree with Tribe (1997) who called attention to the fact that it is important to know how to define the *tourism phenomenon* and the *study of tourism*. Jafari mixes the phenomenon with the study. Tribe (1997: 640) also proposes his definition:

> tourism is essentially an activity engaged in by human beings and the minimum necessary features that need to exist for it to be said to have occurred include the act of travel from one place to another, a particular set of motives for engaging in that travel (excluding commuting for work), and the engagement in activity at the destination.

Cooper *et al.* (1993: 4), starting from the conception of tourism in the form of a system proposed by Leiper (1979), state that:

Tourism can be thought of as a whole range of individuals, businesses, organizations and places which combine in some way to deliver a travel experience. Tourism is a multidimensional, multifaceted activity, which touches many lives and many different economic activities.

In spite of the confusions and difficulties in the definitions, there are a number of researchers who are interested in this theme, some making use of the theoretical basis of investigation offered by epistemology and invoking philosophers of science such as Thomas Kuhn, Karl Popper, Edmund Husserl, Mario Bunge and Imre Lakatos.

With the objective of overcoming the impasses of the definitions, in 1991 the UNWTO organized the International Conference on Travel and Tourism Statistics, which created specific definitions for the sector. However, not even these are free from critics and the issue of definition still exists. However, in recent years the concept has been refined and the sector is coming to an agreement on its meaning and definition.

Models and Conceptualizations of Tourism

Theoretical phases in tourism

Having discussed various issues relating to definition it is clear that *defining* is different to *explaining*. In this sense, the importance of a deeper study on the theories elaborated on the theme is important. Three basic groups of authors use the theory of scientific paradigms by Kuhn (2001) to understand tourism. But before these are discussed, a brief explanation of the theory of scientific paradigms is necessary.

Each science has its own patterns (paradigms, models, foundations and principles) that serve as an orientation for researchers. Kuhn realized that the advance of sciences occurs in the form of leaps or ruptures. For him, the scientist who is not satisfied with the present paradigm can search for another theory that better explains the studied object. Paradigms are the theoretical and value concepts accepted by a scientific community that uses these concepts and values in its researches. Paradigms define the rules that are universally recognized in a subject and that validate the advance of the science.

According to Kuhn (2001), there is a stage before the formation of a paradigm in a science, which is the preparadigmatic stage. This is considered as the moment in which a theory is being created and faces the challenges and obstacles of a science in formation, for example, the lack of credibility and difficulty in answering new problems, due to the creation of new approaches for these problems. In this stage, the advances are perceived only for the people who are working actively in this new theory.

If I use Kuhn's theory, the systems view can be viewed as a paradigm in tourism studies that is most accepted by this academic community (according to Leiper, 1979; Cardenas, 1981; Bernardi, 1985; Krippendorf, 1985; Lainé, 1985; Sessa, 1985; Beni, 1988; Boullón, 1995; Cooper *et al.*, 1993; Acerenza, 2002, among other authors). However, in the field of tourism there is no unique theory able to join researchers in the same study methodology. To prove this statement, I consider the different approaches to the subject.

This consideration of approaches divided into theoretical phases is useful for the following reasons: first, it permits the researcher to have a large and global idea of the studies in the sector. Second, it permits that any theory or author can be classified according to his or her approach. Third, it is a useful instrument for the student who wishes to comprehend the theories and lastly it classifies and characterizes the various theories in tourism.

The first group is identified as the 'preparadigmatic'. It is formed by the first authors who suggested a theoretical analysis of tourism. Some of the authors represented in this phase are Hunziker and Krapf (1942), Fuster (1971), Burkart and Medlik (1974) and Jafari and Ritchie (1981). The second phase is the 'system of tourism' formed by authors that disseminated the general systems theory. The authors in this group are Cuervo (1967), Wahab (1977), Leiper (1979), Sessa (1985), Beni (1988), Boullón (1995) and Martinez (2005) among others. The 'system of tourism' is a paradigm in tourist studies because the systemic vision has a great diffusion, reach and utilization in the studies of this field and, up to the moment, is the theory that best explains the dynamic of the phenomenon, although it still presents elements that make it difficult to comprehend.

From the theory of systems there is a transition area composed of authors who are situated between the second and the third phase. This area is formed by Krippendorf (1985, 1989), Molina (2003), Ascânio (1992) and Garcia (2005) among others – who still base their studies on the general theory of systems, but who demonstrate advances that are almost new approaches.

The third theoretical phase is called 'new approaches'. It differentiates itself from the first by proposing diversified and innovative analysis. Some authors of this phase propose schemes and interpretation with the objective of overcoming the paradigm 'system of tourism'. This group is

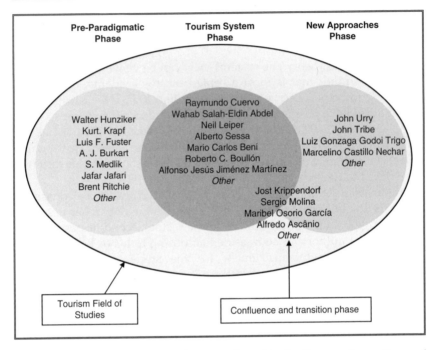

Figure 3.1 Theoretical phases of tourism based in the theory of paradigms of Thomas S. Kuhn. (*Source*: Based in Panosso Netto [2005].)

formed by authors like Urry (1996), Tribe (1997), Trigo (1998, 2003) and Nechar (2005) among others. Figure 3.1 illustrates this explanation. Dozens of others authors could have been classified in each of these phases, but this is not the objective of this chapter. I chose to mention only some representatives and analyze two theories of each phase.

Preparadigmatic phase

  Luis Fernandez Fuster.   Fuster (1971) divides his approach into theory and practice. For him the existence of a technical theory does not mean that the concept of tourism should be seen as a science; this will only happen by establishing a systematized, logical and valid doctrine. His position in relation to academic studies is that the subject should be treated as a specialization of a scientific area: 'It is clear that our phenomenon nowadays is a set of knowledge with its own entity that is sufficient to be able to request the category of scientific specialization' (Fuster, 1971: 21).

The author makes it clear that the theme must be approached as a science, but not as a science apart from the others, 'since the studies of the tourist phenomenon are accomplished, logically, with the aid of other sciences: economy, statistics, social sciences, etc.' (Fuster, 1971: 21). For this author, the systematization of the general study of tourism (or the tourist science) depends on its method of study, but he also considers that:

> In tourism no method has been applied, for the only reason that tourism has been only an object of study in its integrity in spite of the existence of a great bibliography on its particular aspects. (Fuster, 1971: 21)

The establishment of a method in tourism would depend on the content to be researched, because if the tourist is approached in an individual way, psychology would be necessary to study the object. Consequently, I suppose that the method to be utilized for the research will be the method of theories in psychology. Thus, this author does not propose the creation of a specific method, but the use of methods belonging to other disciplines. For him, the tourist phenomenon cannot be reduced to the study of the *homo turisticus, homo politicus* or *homo economicus*, its study must establish relations among these several approaches. His attitude was to condemn the partial approach of tourism and propose a holistic analysis.

Jafar Jafari and Brent Ritchie.   Jafari and Ritchie (1981) have as an objective to offer a basis for the analysis and discussion of education in the field, and they consider the trandisciplinary way, the best to study the tourism. But, due to the several limitations that this approach presents, the best thing to do is to accept the multidisciplinary or interdisciplinary way (Jafari & Ritchie, 1981: 26). Their proposal of interdisciplinary study is presented in Figure 3.2.

According to this model, the field of study, 'tourism', would be the center of the discussion that would be situated in a tourism department. The disciplines that study it are around this circle, originating from other contributing departments. As an example, the geography of tourism would be located in the geography department and from there, I would have the basis for the study of the geographical aspects of the phenomenon.

This approach was innovative for the time when it was published and it was the basis for the configuration of several pedagogical projects of graduation courses in Argentina, Brazil, Mexico and Venezuela among

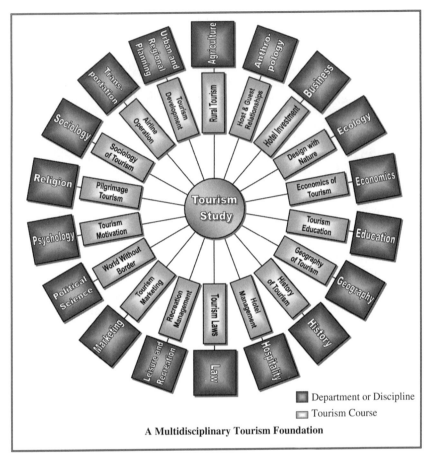

A Multidisciplinary Tourism Foundation

Figure 3.2 Model of knowledge production in tourism of Jafar Jafari. (*Source*: Originally proposed by Jafari in 1981 and updated in 2005.)

other countries. Despite its positive aspects, it was analyzed in a critical way by Tribe (1997) and Panosso Netto (2003).

Phase system of tourism

   Raymundo Cuervo.   Cuervo (1967) was the first researcher to make use of and to propose a referential model of the general system theory applied to tourism. This statement is also confirmed by Acerenza (2002) and Martinez (2005). According to Cuervo (1967: 29), tourism would be a great set composed of the following subsets:

C_1) the means of aerial, automobilist, rail, maritime and fluvial communication etc;

C_2) the hospitality accommodations as hotels, motels, hostels and lodging houses;

C_3) the travel agencies;

C_4) the tour guides;

C_5) the restaurants, cafes and other establishments where a fluctuating population receives services of alimentation;

C_6) the commercial establishments dedicated to the sale of souvenirs, articles for the travel and other consume articles common to the travelers;

C_7) the manufacturers of souvenirs, articles for travel and other consume articles common to travelers;

C_8) the workmanship dedicated the production of typical objects;

C_9) the centers of leisure whose clients are integrated in an important proportion for the fluctuating population

Each of these subsets would be divided into other subsets as for example (Cuervo, 1967: 29–30):

$C_1 = \{A_1, A_2, A_3, \ldots, A_n\}$
Being $C_1 =$ transportation
$A_1 =$ national air transportation
$A_2 =$ international air transportation
$A_3 =$ national bus transportation
$\vdots$
$A_n =$ other kinds of transportation

The analysis is also based on the presupposition of this being a set whose function is communication as explained in the text below:

If I accept that during a trip a communication occurs I can accept as a valid hypothesis that the set tourism is a "system" and that I can also pre determinate a function for this system which in this case, is the communication. (Cuervo, 1967: 33)

Finally, the author proposes that tourism is a system of communication, able to transmit positive and useful information for world peace, but that can also be negative and affects the harmony of the human relations. This raises the challenge for the system to work or maintain itself as an operator of positive communication.

Salah-Eldin Abdel Wahab.   Wahab (1977: 3–4) states that the human being is one of the main elements of tourism:

The anatomy of the tourist phenomenon would be basically composed of three elements: the *human being* (human element as the author of the tourist act), *the space* (physical element necessarily covered by the act) and *the time* (temporal element that is used by the travel and by the stay in the destination).

His point of view is that tourism is a *phenomenon* (a new word for the analysis at the time) that refers to the movement of people. For him, 'a behavior approach of the tourist phenomenon study would be the appropriate method to emphasize the human side of the phenomenon and its role in the formation of a communication link among the peoples of several nations' (Wahab, 1977: 3).

Tourism in its current form represents a system basis on the social sphere. This happens principally due to the interdependency and the interaction of its many components, which with the objective of a "healthier" tourism industry should function coherently.

Later he mentions: 'all the system consists of two parts, the description of its "state" in a certain moment and its "dynamic" which is the description of the successive states in the dimensions of time and space',

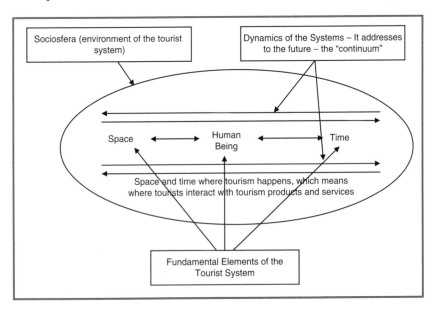

Figure 3.3 Possible model of the system proposed by Wahab.
(*Source*: Panosso Netto [2005], according to the propositions of Wahab [1977].)

and he continues explaining that the analysis through dynamic systems and 'the perception of pattern in the "continuum" time-space, [makes possible] the formation of future images, which permits, having the basis in the current behaviors, that I take decisions for the future' (Wahab, 1977: 16).

This author has not presented a model of how his system would be but, from his proposal, I infer that his model would be similar to the one presented in Figure 3.3.

Transition between the system of tourism phase and the new approaches phase

Sérgio Molina.   The proposal of Molina (2003) is that of post-tourism, which rests on the understanding of the phenomenon divided into three basic stages of evolution since its appearance: pretourism, tourism and post-tourism. It is in this last stage that there is the greatest academic contribution.

Pretourism would be the tourism practiced during the Grand Tour era, in the 17th and 18th centuries, when the 'eldest sons of the wealthy and nobles businessmen families' would travel around. In this period, the level of technology was relatively low and it also lacked administrative and accounting systems, with rudimentary installations. Currently, there are companies that offer attractions with pretourism characteristics, but 'the existence of the Pre – Tourism doesn't involve any pejorative sense' (Molina, 2003: 23).

The second stage is tourism, subdivided in three categories:

(1)   The primitive industrial that originated in the 19th century and continued up to the period of the Second World War.
(2)   The mature industrial from the decade of 1950s up to the decade of 1990s.
(3)   The postindustrial that originated in the mid-1980s.

Finally, there is the phase of post-tourism originated in 1990 and that:

Contributes to a new paradigm, a historical category which changes some fundamental considerations of the tourism previously originated. The high efficiency technologies and the social and cultural phenomena of 1990s explain the development of the post tourism in contrast with the principle that alternate the continuity of the industrial types of tourism (Molina, 2003: 27).

His analysis is made by categories and uses other definitions to explain his own approach. When the author states that post-tourism is characterized by the technology used in amusement parks, he is making use of the technology category to explain his approach. Post-tourism is an analysis category that has a strong relation with postmodernity in historical analysis.

Alfredo Ascânio.   This author proposes the creation of a new scientific discipline with the focus on tourist studies, the Social Science of Travels. According to Ascânio, this new science should refer to all kinds of trips and their various contexts. 'It represents the conscious continuation of studying the tendencies of the travelers and hosts behavior in an interdisciplinary way, as well as the relations among them, the geographical space and the context' (Ascânio, 1992: 188). The task of the Social Science of Travels would be to 'find out and explain the internal and external relations of the distinct aspects of the ways of traveling, the use of the trip and the effects of it, as well as a way of analyzing the distinct disciplines' (Ascânio, 1992: 189).

Ascânio also proposes that inside each science like geography, psychology and economy there could be a field of performance of the Social Science of Travels. He believes that tourism is a science and states:

> Tourism is a science concerned about the phenomenon that can increase or not the quality and the way of life of a determined community whose role is to receive tourists; and the basic issue is to be able to know the benefits or not of a tourist activity, with the objective that the receptive community receives more benefits than costs. (Ascânio, 2007)

For Ascânio, the study of tourism would be the relations between the visitor, the host and the impacts produced or in other words the interdependent connections of a receptive community and the temporal visitors. His proposal is innovative; however, it is probable that the relations between the visitors and the host are better studied by hospitality, sociology and anthropology. The author also does not scientifically justify the proposal of a science of tourism.

New approaches phase
Marcelino Castillo Nechar.   The proposal of Nechar (2005) is called 'critical epistemology'. Its objective is to practice the reflexive and interpretative critique of tourism in face of the constructions of *critical contents* and not the *critique of contents*. It is an activity that examines the reason, the measurement and the interpretation of all the contents which one can expect in the construction of the knowledge. Associated with the critical concept is the concept of interpretation. To interpret is more than

a simple description, referred to the basic world of essentialities, as a mere mental construction. To interpret is about constructing, it is about putting into practice what reason is constructing in an abstract way. To interpret implies detecting firmness in the senses that is communicated; the search of senses is something abstract.

Nechar (2005) states that not only are I in a crisis of scientific knowledge, but also in a philosophic one and therefore in a crisis of the basis of thinking. He proposes a recovering of the deductive-inductive process of thinking, which implies the construction of rigorous knowledge of tourism. This is not about the rigor of 'traditional scientific logos' nor even of the criteria which rule the 'science' of a logical process and the supports its rationality which delimitates the inclusive and exclusive of the scientific knowledge. It is about the way in which the reality is deceived by language, where language configures thought, articulates reality and correlates discourses. New proposals of apprehension and signification of the 'tourist reality', using hermeneutics, phenomenology and dialects, among other postpositivist schemes, permit a critical proposal of tourist reality.

This critical proposal foregrounds certain logical moves that have turned into habits in sectors of academic life. It also shows the lack of rationality in evaluating the level of certainty, rigor and the measurement of tourist knowledge in researches that rely on the 'correct use' of the pre-established methodological rules, without examining the logic, the meaning and the implications of constructed knowledge. This critical, reflexive and hermeneutic proposal in tourism epistemology could postulate a distinct epistemic matrix, along with a system of establishing different meanings and operational processes.

Luiz Gonzaga Godoi Trigo.   Tourism in the context of postmodernity is the center of the analysis of Trigo (1998). His study considers the services sector at the end of the 20th century. His proposal is to comprehend the problems that permeate present societies in face of the new technologies, the world of work, changes in education and the conceptions of time and space related to the mass tourism.

He also discusses what would be a suitable education philosophy to structure the professionals' work in the tertiary sector in post-industrial societies. Having in mind the principle that the market needs 'thinking people', he states that the philosophy contributes to improve the formation of the services professionals.

He analyses the new international order molded by the changes in world conditions and proposes tourism and leisure as fundamental elements in the establishment of new social models, according to the text below:

> The post modern condition induces to a new style of life based on comfort and well being. The high technology and economic power of the developed countries made possible investments in important projects in the fields of the tourism and leisure. (Trigo, 1998: 65)

Trigo analyses tourism as one of the transforming powers of the contemporary world and demonstrates how this power acts and develops itself. His proposal for study is by means of philosophy as this science can make people more reflexive in their actions and their role in the social world. Philosophy is one of the tools that can reveal the contradictions, paradoxes and miscomprehended facets of this field. Such criticism can cause distress as it uncovers the sector, showing its negative aspects (impacts, economic and sexual exploitation, existential relativism etc.). However, the same critique can encourage reflexive study, the promotion of information and scientific knowledge, a fuller comprehension of society and the return of philosophy as fundamental aspects to redirect cultures to a more social and self-sustainable practice.

Principles of Tourism

The term 'principle' is considered to be a basic and elementary proposition that serves as the basis for the development of a knowledge, a law, a theory or a concept. When I talk about a principle, I also refer to the origin of something. What is the essence of tourism? What is invariable? Which are the attributes that must exist for us to say that something is tourism? The lack of answers brings imperfection to the concept and this is sometimes viewed with some incredulity and distrust in the productive and intellectual sectors. It also hints at a scientific deficiency in the epistemological basis of tourism.

Hence, the importance of establishing principles is fundamental and this will allow the boundaries to be drawn showing what is and what is not tourism. According to the previous definitions and approaches analyzed, two principles are identified: the *fundamental* and the *desirable*.

Fundamental principles

Subject

In order for tourism to exist, the tourist must be present. However, this tourist interacts with the host. In the host category, there are the service suppliers (in the origin and at the destination) as well as the host, the person that receives somebody.

Displacement

Displacement is classified in two categories: internal – inside the tourist origin country and the external – outside the origin country. The displacement of refugees, migrations motivated by natural and human catastrophes as well as trips of embassy staff must not be included in this category.

Principle of return

The action of leaving home, the residence or living place implies a return to these places. This concept is already in the root of the word tourism (tour) – the trip in a circle, I go and return.

Principle of motivation

There will always be a reason for the tourist to travel, be it explicit or not.

Principle of hospitality

Hospitality represents a social-cultural phenomenon that includes the food, drink and accommodation offered to the guest. It is also the basis for an act that has been happening for thousands of years and it is rooted in the matter of survival of the human species. It is a fundamental element for the development of tourism, as it is related to the act of receiving and being received by somebody in the domestic, public or commercial contexts.

Domestic hospitality originated the other kinds of hospitality and it is related to the act of receiving, providing accommodation, feeding and entertaining somebody in a domestic context.

Commercial hospitality occurs in the commerce context of hotels, hostels, restaurants, tourism agencies and establishments that offer services and receive a monetary value for that. Finally, public hospitality is the act of receiving people in the public context. It should be applied in urban parks, squares, public places of concentration of people like bus stops, bus stations, railways, airports, tourist information booths as well as public offices.

Principle of experience

Tourism is composed of a range of immaterial and intangible services, as a consequence of sensorial and psychological experience (no matter if it is good or bad), making experience the main marker of a tourist trip. Besides, people also travel in search of new experiences.

Principle of communication
   Tourism is the act of communicating. Tourists relate with other people as well as with other cultures. It is impossible to travel without communicating with others.

Technology
   Any kind of tourism will make use of technology, even the kind of tourism that happens in natural or inhabited areas. Communication and transportation technologies are the most important in this principle.

Desirable principles

Sustainability
   Sustainable tourism, i.e. the use of tourist resources in a way that permits the continuity of use should be guaranteed. It is divided into social, cultural, economic and environmental sustainability. Additionally, political and psychological sustainability should be included although these are implicit in the first four.

Principle of equality
   Human beings, no matter their social or financial level, religion, color and race are all the same according to the laws of tourism and must be treated as so in human and professional relations as well as in space and place.

Principle of public and private supremacy
   The will of public power should be above private and personal interests. This being so, if the desire of a tourist would negatively affect the order and the desire of a social group, it should not be permitted.

Principle of alterity
   Alterity means respect for the difference. It should exist in tourist relations with regard to the host, among tourists and among the hosts.

Principle of ethics
   Ethics is understood as the science of morals and customs. It also refers to a correct way of acting. This principle is related to four subjects: (a) the profession of tourism, (b) the tourist, (c) the host community and (d) public authorities.
   The above principles may cause some controversy, as there are other principles that were not mentioned, such as: the principle of the free market, the principle of the immaterial product, the principle of inviolability and the principle of the secondary activity. However, the objective is to explain the thematic basics so that a better comprehension

of tourism may be possible. To talk about definitions of tourism, as pointed out previously, is complex. It would be much easier to talk about contextualization, characterization and comprehension, because from the moment the term is defined, some frontiers are established and I have the risk of creating limited approaches. Even if I consider this fact, being based in the theories and principles mentioned, I propose the following definition of tourism:

> Tourism is the phenomenon caused by the departure and return of human beings from their place of habitual residence, for reasons that can be revealed or concealed. It presupposes hospitality, encounters and communication with other people, companies which offer services and technology so that the act of coming and going is possible. It generates sensorial and psychological experiences as well as positive and negative effects on the economical, political, environmental and socio cultural environments.

Final Considerations

As the above discussion shows, there is concern by researchers in defining and establishing a solid theoretical basis for tourism. However, for any theory to be considered useful it must be validated and pass peer review. I believe that a single researcher **cannot** construct a theoretical complete model that is able to explain the innumerous facets of tourism. Besides that, there is the problem of concept commercialization, which avoids the search for a clear characterization of tourism in favor of one that concentrates on impacts, mainly economic ones. Society faces the commercialization of values, behavior and human beings themselves. Tourism for large companies is simply understood as economic and commercial practices. The sector offers comfort, security and sanitized experiences as if this was the phenomenon itself. However, tourism is much more than that. In a trip, there are elements involved that at the first moment do not show up, like the wishes and longings of the tourist, the search for the new, the necessity of new experiences. The study of tourism should help to comprehend the role of human beings in the context of their trips and the search for new solutions to old problems, such as the relationship between guests and hosts, which is often discussed, but has achieved little advances in practical terms. New paradigms must continue to be proposed, because when I push ourselves away from the normal and the taken for granted, I have the possibility of looking at ourselves and our habitat in a different way.

References

Acerenza, M. (2002) *Administração do turismo.* Bauru-SP: Edusc.

Ascânio, A. (1992) Turismo: La ciencia social de los viajes. *Estudios y Perspectivas en Turismo* 1 (3), 185–197.

Ascânio, A. (2007) *El objeto del turismo: ¿Una posible ciencia social de los viajes?* On WWW at http://servicios.universia.edu.ve/webprofesor/prf_rsc.php. Accessed 20.5.08.

Beni, M.C. (1988) Sistema de turismo: Construção de um modelo teórico referencial para aplicação na pesquisa em turismo. PhD thesis, Universidade de São Paulo.

Beni, M.C. (1998) *Análise estrutural do turismo.* São Paulo: Senac.

Bernardi, R. (1985) Le dicisioni di investimento nel quadro di un approccio sitemico del fenômeno turístico. In A. Sessa (ed.) *La scienza dei sistemi per lo sviluppo del turismo* (pp. 195–211). Roma: Agnesotti.

Boullón, R.C. (1995) *Las actividades turísticas y recreacionales.* México: Trillas.

Boullón, R.C. (2002) *Planejamento do espaço turístico.* Bauru-SP: EDUSC.

Burkart, A.J. and Medlik, S. (1974) *Tourism: Past, Present and Future.* London: Heinemann.

Cardenas, F. (1981) *Comercialización del turismo.* México: Trillas.

Cooper, C. *et. al.* (1993) *Tourism, Principles and Practice.* London: Pitman Publishing.

Cuervo, R. (1967) El turismo como medio de comunicación. In R. Cuervo (ed.) *El turismo como medio de comunicación humana* (pp. 27–40). México: Departamento de Turismo del Gobierno de México.

Fuster, L.F. (1971) *Teoría y técnica del turismo.* Madrid: Nacional, Tomo I.

García, M.O. (2005) El análisis del turismo desde la perspectiva de los sistemas funcionales. PhD thesis, Universidad Iberoamericana.

Hunziker, W. and Krapf, K. (1942) *Algemeine frendenverkehrslehre.* Berna University: Zurique.

Jafari, J. (1995) Structure of tourism: Three integrated models. In S.F. Witt and L. Moutinho (eds) *Tourism Marketing and Management Handbook* (pp. 5–17). London: Prentice Hall International.

Jafari, J. (2005) Tourism research: Revamping old challenges for *integrative* paradigms. *Anais:* VII Congreso Nacional y I Internacional de Investigación Turística. Guadalajara, México.

Jafari, J. and Ritchie, J.R.B. (1981) Toward a framework for tourism education – problems and prospects. *Annals of Tourism Research* 8 (1), 13–34.

Krippendorf, J. (1985) Le tourime dans le systeme de la societe industrielle. In A. Sessa (ed.) *La scienza dei sistemi per lo sviluppo del turismo* (pp. 167–184). Roma: Agnesotti.

Krippendorf, J. (1989) *Sociologia do turismo: Para uma nova compreensão do lazer e das viagens.* Rio de Janeiro: Civilização Brasileira.

Kuhn, T.S. (2001) *A estrutura das revoluções científicas.* São Paulo: Perspectiva.

Lainé, P. (1985) Utilisation de la théorie des systèmes pour l'amenegement touristique. In A. Sessa (ed.) *La scienza dei sistemi per lo sviluppo del turismo* (pp. 185–194). Roma: Agnesotti.

Leiper, N. (1979) The framework of tourism: Towards a definition of tourism, tourist, and the tourist industry. *Annals of Tourism Research* 6, 390–407.

Martínez, A.J.J. (2005) *Una aproximación a la conceptualización del turismo desde la Teoria General de Sistemas.* México: Universidad del Caribe.

Molina, S. (1991) *Conceptualización del turismo.* México: Limusa.

Molina, S. (2003) *O pós-turismo.* São Paulo: Aleph.

Nechar, M.C. (2005) *La modernización de la política turística. Retos y perspectivas.* México: Centro de Investigación y Docencia en Humanidades del Estado de Morelos.

Nechar, M.C. and Cortés, M.L. (2006) *Notas a la investigación turística.* México: Universidad de Quintana Roo.

Palomo, M.F. (1991) *Elementos para el estudio de la economía de la empresa turística.* Madrid: Síntesis.

Panosso Netto, A. (2003) Jafar Jafari x John Tribe: Um diálogo de teorias. *Boletim de Estudos em Hotelaria e Turismo* 1 (1), 1–9.

Panosso Netto, A. (2005) *Filosofia do turismo: Teoria e epistemologia.* São Paulo: Aleph.

Sessa, A. (1985) La scienza dei sistemi per i piani regionali di sviluppo turistico. In A. Sessa (ed.) *La scienza dei sistemi per lo sviluppo del turismo* (pp. 53–107). Roma: Agnesotti.

Tribe, J. (1997) The indiscipline of tourism. *Annals of Tourism Research* 24 (3), 638–657.

Trigo, L.G.G. (1998) *A Sociedade pós-industrial e o profissional em turismo.* Campinas: Papirus.

Trigo, L.G.G. (2003) *Entretenimento: Uma crítica aberta.* São Paulo: Senac São Paulo.

Urry, J. (1996) *O olhar do turista. Lazer e viagens nas sociedades contemporâneas.* São Paulo: Studio Nobel/Sesc.

Wahab, S-E.A. (1977) *Introdução à administração do turismo.* São Paulo: Pioneira.

Chapter 4

Epistemology, Ontology and Tourism

MAUREEN AYIKORU

Introduction

This chapter focuses on theoretical explication of ontological and epistemological issues in the production of tourism knowledge. Ontology refers to that branch of philosophy that studies the nature of reality (Jennings, 2001). Meanwhile, epistemology, the theory of knowledge encapsulates such issues as 'the nature of perception, the relationship between knowledge and belief, and alternative theories of truth' (Cahn, 1971: 10). The chapter explores some tensions in the production of knowledge and how an understanding of ontological and epistemological issues can potentially broaden the horizon within which tourism knowledge is produced.

The chapter is divided into three main parts. This first part, the introduction, presents the general overview and sets the context of the chapter. The second part (the main body) is covered under the following subheadings: 'tourism and knowledge production' (briefly reviewing some existing literature that closely highlights the rationale behind the chapter and thus tensions in the production of knowledge about tourism); and 'ontological' and 'epistemological' issues in the production of knowledge about tourism. This subheading encapsulates the review of common philosophical paradigms in social sciences and how an understanding of their central assumptions can be used to select the most appropriate perspective to underpin knowledge production in a given tourism inquiry. The final part constitutes the concluding remarks.

Tourism and Knowledge Production

Knowledge production about tourism, until recently, struggled with (sometimes compulsive) debates about its (post) disciplinary status and hence identity within the academe (see, e.g. Coles *et al.*, 2006; Echtner & Jamal, 1997; Leiper, 1981; Tribe, 1997). However, there is now a considerable body of work that touches upon the problematic of tourism and knowledge production in a way that portrays it as a field exhibiting signs of maturation (Ryan *et al.*, 2007). Rather than belabour a rehearsal of all that has been done in this area, three examples suffice in providing plausible insights into these fundamental shifts in the debate. The first focuses on methods level (qualitative and quantitative divide) and the second (an extension of the first example) entails paradigmatic under-pinnings of tourism inquiry. These are clearly captured by Riley and Love's (2000) article on the state of qualitative tourism research and Phillimore and Goodson's (2004) edited collection on *Qualitative Research in Tourism: Ontologies, Epistemologies and Methodologies*. The third example entails a deconstructive reading of the power political discourses in which knowledge production about tourism are entangled (Hall, 2004; Page, 2005; Pritchard & Morgan, 2007; Tribe, 2004).

The first two examples draw upon Denzin and Lincoln's (1998) explication of the history of qualitative social research categorised into five evolutionary moments (the 2005 edition has eight moments, with three more additions to the 1998 version, namely the traditional, modernist, blurred genres, crisis in representation, the fifth moment/ postmodern period, postexperimental inquiry, the methodologically contested present and the fractured future) as a basis for analysing the pre and post-1996 state of tourism research. Two fundamental issues raised by these studies deserve mention in this chapter. First is the realisation that much of tourism knowledge production is dominated by quantitative and thus positivistic methodologies (Riley & Love, 2000; cf. Zahra & Ryan, 2005). Secondly, the observation by Phillimore and Goodson (2004: 4; cf. Jamal & Hollinshead, 2001) that 'tourism scholars have generally been more hesitant in ... developing their understanding of the philosophical and theoretical process that underpins knowledge production and practices'.

A general response to the last observation is contained in the first part of Phillimore and Goodson's edited collection. Here, Hollinshead (2004) explicates the ontological assumptions that ought to be considered prior to the conduct of social (tourism) research (cf. Zahra & Ryan, 2005). Grounding his arguments in the complex issues of being, meaning and identity as well as raising some crucial ontological issues for the entire tourism studies, Hollinshead (2004: 84) argues that 'matters of ontology should always precede the choice of particular research method'. Meanwhile, Tribe (2004) in the same edition offers a cogent analysis of epistemological issues in tourism research by highlighting the discipli-nary position or lack thereof of tourism prior to problematising tourism knowledge under the lenses of sociology of knowledge. A noteworthy observation by Tribe (2004: 59) is that tourism knowledge 'is a social and political construct' that is not necessarily 'interest free' and that 'the social and political forces at work in the production of tourism knowledge' function in such a way as to legitimise some understandings of tourism while marginalising others.

The third example focuses on the concerted efforts to deconstruct the seemingly stable power political structures through which tourism knowledge is produced and how the researcher's position on matters of reflexivity play out in tourism. Writing from a feminist perspective, Aitchison (1996) exposed some ways and means through which patriarchal power and control unfold in leisure and tourism (see also Swain, 2004; Yule, 1997), citing research and consultancy, publications and educational management and teaching among other things as exemplars. Aitchison further suggests that such issues are closely associated with knowledge construction and dissemination and how such knowledge is legitimated and reproduced. In a similar vein, Pritchard and Morgan (2007) in their chapter on 'De-centring Tourism's Intellectual Universe' proffer a critique of the discourse of knowledge production (in and about tourism) by highlighting the crucial role played by the tourism's academic gatekeepers (cf. Tribe, 2004). They reiterate the observations made previously (Aitchison, 1996) that 'at the beginning of the 21st century, the tourism academe remains highly patriarchal and continues to privilege the knowledge systems of its first generation scholars, many of whom have failed to problematise their middle class white identities' (Pritchard & Morgan, 2007: 16). They crucially suggest that 'time has come to scrutinise just how this masculine, Anglo-Saxon, business-focused domination of the field of tourism has shaped its architecture of knowledge' (Pritchard & Morgan, 2007: 17).

In close tandem with the third example are the voices that increasingly urge the tourism academe to engage with issues of reflexivity. The notion of reflexivity originally deployed in ethnographic research is increasingly finding usage in other social inquiries, particularly in nonpositivistic studies (Seale, 1999). Perceived in terms of reflexive accounting (Seale, 1999) it encompasses the deliberate efforts by an inquirer to reflect on their position within the inquiry, in terms of: the methodology chosen; the type of research question; the inquirer's background (race, gender, class, ethnicity, citizenship, ideology and so forth); the various biases they bring to the research; what they have omitted and what they have chosen to represent in the course of their studies (Lincoln & Guba, 2003; Phillimore & Goodson, 2004).

Within the tourism literature, Michael Hall (2004: 143) in a chapter dedicated to discussing 'reflexivity and tourism research' notes that

> in tourism there is very little discussion of the role that ... gate-keepers (of which I would be counted as one) have in determining the scope and direction of tourism knowledge ... The field of tourism studies is partly influenced by the relationships that exist within the research community rather than depending solely on so-called objective academic merit.

In a detailed exploration of the notion of reflexivity and tourism research, William Feighery (2006: 269) criticises tourism scholars for 'sidestep[ing] the issue of subjectivity in their research practice and in its reporting'. Feighery (2006: 279) concludes by posing the question 'As tourism studies and tourism research continues its maturation, is it now time for us to tell an (other) story – the story of our self?'. Having highlighted some existing works that closely reflect the rationale behind this chapter, it is now possible to turn to ontological and epistemological issues in tourism inquiry.

Ontological and Epistemological Issues in the Production of Knowledge about Tourism

Before engaging directly with the ontological and epistemological issues in this chapter, it is imperative to elucidate the notion of a paradigm. The term 'paradigm' is normally associated with Thomas Kuhn who challenged the claim that there is some rational basis for comparing and choosing between (scientific) theories (Lazar, 1998). A paradigm for Kuhn (1970: 175) stood for 'the entire constellation of beliefs, values, techniques shared by members of a given community' of inquirers. Kuhn in his *magnum opus The Structure of Scientific Revolution* (1970) claimed that conventional (normal) science is not always critical of its paradigm. Kuhn argued that if there was no fit between theory and facts (implicitly referring to Popper's falsification thesis to be discussed later), then there would be need to reinterpret the facts.

Guba (1990: 18) maps out the fundamental characteristics of para-digms, which he frames into three main questions, namely ontological, epistemological and methodological questions as follows: ontological question: what is the nature of the 'knowable'? or what is the nature of 'reality'? Epistemological question: what is the nature of the relationship between the knower (inquirer) and the known (or knowable)? And finally, methodological question: how should the inquirer go about finding out knowledge? (cf. Lazar, 1998; Lincoln & Guba, 1998, 2003). Guba adds that the responses offered to these fundamental questions are tantamount to a paradigm or the basic belief systems that, in turn, act as the starting point that shapes what inquiry is and how it is to be practised (cf. Hollinshead, 2004; Zahra & Ryan, 2005). This section discusses the key ontological and epistemological issues in social (tourism) inquiry by evaluating the central assumptions of scientific (post) positivism followed by the interpretive philosophies.

The scientific (post) positivist philosophy

Carr and Kemmis (1986) have noted that positivism is a doctrine that is not systematically elaborated and that it is commonly linked to the general philosophical thinking that surfaced as the most powerful intellectual current in Western thought during the second half of the 19th century. And that although the genealogy of positivist thought can be traced to the work of Francis Bacon as well as the British empiricists of the 18th and 19th century, the French writer Auguste Comte coined the term 'positive' (Turner, 2001; Halfpenny, 2001). The latter, they argue was aimed at relaying 'an opposition to any metaphysical or theological claims that some kind of non-sensorily apprehended experience could form the basis of valid knowledge' (Carr & Kemmis, 1986: 61). The following discussion explains the (post) positivist philosophy in terms of its ontological and epistemological beliefs.

The positivist tradition is premised on the principle that what can be upheld as reliable knowledge of any field of phenomena is that which can be experienced using the senses (Carr & Kemmis, 1986; Habermas, 1987; Harré, 1981). It upholds a worldview in which rules do explain the behaviour of observable phenomenon through establishment of causal relationships (Jennings, 2001). So that for Guba (1990: 19), positivism is governed by a realist ontological perspective whereby it is presumed that

> There exists a reality out there, driven by immutable natural laws ...
> the business of science is to discover the "true" nature of reality and
> how it "truly" works ... the ultimate aim of science is to predict and
> control natural phenomenon.

Harré (1981: 3) further adds that within this tradition, laws are regarded as the 'probabilistic generalisation of patterns of sensation ... their only role is to enhance the prediction of future sensory experience'. Making a cogent description of how positivism works, Habermas (1987: 74) observes that

Positivism adopts the basic rule of the empiricist schools that all knowledge has to prove itself through the sense certainty of systematic observation that secures inter-subjectivity. Only perception can claim evidence with regard to reality ... sense experience defines access to the domain of facts. Science that makes statements about reality is always empirical science.

Although founded in the natural sciences, the positivist paradigm views the social world – of which tourism is part – as organized by universal laws and truths (Phillimore & Goodson, 2004). This is largely regarded as the legacy of Comte's 'positive philosophy' that sought to appropriate the scientific progress made during the enlightenment period (particularly Isaac Newton's discovery of the law of gravity), to understand social phenomenon (Turner, 2001). With such a perception it can be said that the positivists believe it is possible to predict (social) behaviour and even find ways through which it can be controlled as long as cause–effect relationships are ascertained (cf. Halfpenny, 2001; Turner, 2001). However, it should be noted that social behaviour as opposed to natural behaviour is enmeshed in a complexity of differing value systems, beliefs and attitudes all of which render the whole notion of predictability very problematic.

This observation not only highlights the inappropriateness of subsuming human (social) behaviour in terms of laws that govern explanations of natural phenomena, but also points to how knowing in the human (social) context might be different from that in a natural context. Put differently, the positivist ontological perspective that necessitates the adoption of an objectivist epistemology may not be transposed neatly onto an understanding of social phenomena. This positivist epistemology operates on the principle that

If there is a real world operating according to natural laws, then the inquirer must behave in ways that put questions directly to nature and allow nature to answer back directly. Objectivity in the "Archimedean point"... permits the inquirer to wrest nature's secrets without altering them in any way. (Guba, 1990: 19)

This emphasis on objectivity stems from the enlightenment prescription for knowledge of the physical world that it perceived as being separate and distinct from the inquirer (Polkinghorne, 1989; Turner, 2001). According to Polkinghorne (1989), at the core of the notion of objectivity was the attempt to overcome the 'ordinary way of knowing' in favour of pure objective knowledge. The ordinary human knowing was regarded error-prone, hence not well placed in providing accurate comprehension of reality (Polkinghorne, 1989). It was also believed that ordinary knowledge is grounded in perspective and a point of view that is relative to individual knowledge (Polkinghorne, 1989). To this end, the proponents of objectivity assert that

> Knowledge of the truth must represent reality ... independent of the perspective from which it is viewed. The strategy for overcoming the limits of personal and cultural points of view is to establish a method of inquiry that will assure that all who follow it will come to the same true view. (Polkinghorne, 1989: 22)

However, if knowledge of the social (as opposed to the physical) world is imbued with meaning-making mechanisms of the social, mental and linguistic worlds of the knowing subjects then knowledge cannot be separate from the knower. Instead it is to be found in the latter's mental and linguistic understandings of that world (Polkinghorne, 1989). Habermas (1987) however contends that communities of inquiry create knowledge, underpinned in turn by procedures (which may be sets of rules or conventions or norms) that justify propositions and theories (Kuhn, 1970). These procedures embody three deep-seated anthropological interests of mankind in control, in understanding and in freedom from dogma. He then suggests the possibility of differentiating three forms of knowledge, one of which (the empirical analytic sciences) entails what the positivists perceive as definitive of all genuine knowledge (Geuss, 1981; Keat, 1981). Habermas argues that empirical analytic science comprises and thus presupposes the technical interest so that the theories put forward by this group of sciences can be used in a specific form of practices (Habermas, 1987). That is, the instrumental control of natural or social processes (Habermas, 1987).

To Habermas, the discourse of knowledge constructed through deployment of criteria of control over the physical environment was given the status of all possible knowledge under the positivist doctrine. This state of affairs is famously described as scientism, the idea that it is science alone that encompasses a genuine form of human knowledge (Carr & Kemmis, 1986; Geuss, 1981; Halfpenny, 2001; Keat, 1981). 'Scientism means science's belief in itself; that is, the conviction that we can no longer understand science as one form of possible knowledge, but rather must identify knowledge with science' (Habermas, 1987: 4; cf. Foucault, 1980: 27). It should be noted that scientism entails a little more than just a distinction between science and nonscience (Keat, 1981). Rather, all that is presumed to be nonscientific, such as the discourses of religion, metaphysics, ideology, politics and ethics or tourism for that matter are bracketed as inferior, cognitively meaningless or even nonsensical (Keat, 1981), trenchantly described by Halfpenny (2001: 373) in the following manner,

> Propositions that are properly scientific are factual or logical, and all other expressions are without sense, that is, nonsensical. … Since they are meaningless, arguments for and against them are undecidable and therefore pointless. They must be purged from positive science. In this way, moral discourse was expunged, since statements about what ought to be cannot be logically derived from empirically grounded statements about what is.

However, Keat (1981) observes that scientism and the positivist views of science do not necessarily go hand in hand. Rather, continues Keat (1981), that one can uphold a positivist idea of what counts as scientific knowledge without having to believe that science entails the only form of genuine knowledge.

What has been said up to this point entails a caricature of the positivist philosophy, particularly in terms of the two main characteristics of a paradigm explained in the introduction. A caricature because positivist philosophy is not only complex, but also Keat (1981) shows that there are many variants of this positivist philosophy thus making it inappropriate to talk about positivism in the singular form. However, the caricature draws on Habermas' (1987) categorisation of the empirical analytic sciences as entailing what the positivists perceive as definitive of all genuine knowledge. So, the foregone discussions entailed an evaluation of the application of this positivist paradigm founded in the natural/physical sciences to social or human inquiry in general.

Positivistically conceived studies have been common in areas such as market segmentation and demand forecasting (Crouch, 1994; Song & Li, 2008) among others. For instance, the Jang *et al.* (2002) study in which they deployed a factor cluster analysis to define three segments of the Japanese outbound travel market to the USA and Canada. Meanwhile, Mazanec (1992) applied artificial neural networks as a methodological tool to conduct market segmentation analysis of Austrian tourists. Another example entails the application of spectral analysis to establish cycles within and between the time-series of tourism flows by air and sea from the UK to France, Belgium and the Netherlands (Coshall, 2000).

The positivist philosophy has been criticised from within its own tradition in what was later labelled as postpositivism (Guba & Lincoln,

1994; Lincoln & Guba, 1998). Postpositivism is normally linked to the work of Karl Popper, particularly his publication in 1957 on the logic of scientific discovery, in which he argued that the truth-value of a theory could not be conclusively discerned from the number of true deductive inferences arrived at (Hetherington, 2003; Lazar, 1998). In terms of Guba's characterisation of paradigms described earlier, Lincoln and Guba (1998, 2003) describe postpositivism as upholding a critical realist ontological viewpoint. The latter believes in the existence of a 'real' reality just like the positivists, but deviates from the latter in that instead of a 'real' apprehendable reality, postpositivism presumes reality to be 'imperfectly and probabilistically apprehendable' (Guba & Lincoln, 2005: 258). This deviation from the positivist ontology, however, did not translate into a similar trend in postpositivist epistemology for the latter is described as being modified dualist/objectivist with a crucial role played by the critical community in the form of critique (Guba & Lincoln, 2005).

The interpretive philosophies

Schwandt (1998) has noted that the terms interpretive, interpretivism, constructivist and constructivism are commonly encountered in the lexicon of social science methodologists and philosophers, and that their particular meanings depend on the user's intentions. He then explains the commonalities between these two sets of terms, one of which is that these approaches share the goal of understanding the complex world of the lived experience from the vantage point of those who inhabit that world. And that this common goal is variously described in terms of the pressing concern for the life world, for the *emic* perspective, for understanding meaning, for grasping the actors' definition of a situation, for *verstehen* (Schwandt, 1998, 2003; cf. Walle, 1997; Wang, 1999). The main emphasis here is that the reality experienced by individuals and the specific meanings ascribed to a situation that in turn forms the object of social inquiry depicts the socially constructed view of reality by those individuals (Hetherington, 2003). The other shared feature of these terms is the belief that the only way of comprehending meanings inherent in the world is through interpretation.

To this end, Denzin and Lincoln (1998: 26) while describing the interpretive paradigm note, 'all research is interpretive, guided by a set of beliefs and feelings about the world and how it should be understood and studied'. This should, however, not be construed as interpretive approaches being homogenous in any way, contrarily, Guba and Lincoln

(1994, 2005) clearly explain the heterogeneity amongst them in terms of the three paradigm questions. What follows is a brief discussion of the central features of two main interpretive philosophies, namely constructivism and critical theory, respectively (Zahra & Ryan [2005] offer a similar undertaking but in a different research context).

The constructivist approach to social inquiry

There are various ways in which this approach is described and moreover no particular explanations offered as to why adherents would refer to either constructivist paradigm or just constructivism (professed to by Lincoln and Guba throughout their articulation of research paradigms) or constructionist/constructionism (as seen in the works of Burr, 1995; Gergen, 1985; Schwandt, 1998, 2003). There are suggestions that constructivism evolved as a reaction against (post) positivism and that it is not only similar to, but also derived from postmodernism (Hemmingway, 1999; Hetherington, 2003). Lincoln and Guba (1998: 206) intimate that constructivism is underpinned by a relativist ontological worldview that perceives reality as existing in the form of

> Multiple, intangible mental constructions [is] socially and experientially based, local and specific in nature (although elements are often shared among many individuals and even across cultures), and dependent on their content on the individual persons or groups holding the constructions.

In essence, constructivists reject what they perceive as a naïve realist view of the world to the extent of denying any form of interest in the positivists' preoccupations with ontological issues (Laclau & Mouffe, 1985). The constructivists further differentiate their ontological beliefs from other approaches by claiming that the constructions that result from the multiple realities apprehended by individuals do not conform to absolute truth (Hetherington, 2003; Lincoln & Guba, 1998; Wang, 1999). Rather such constructions may be more or less informed or sophisticated (Hetherington, 2003; Lincoln & Guba, 1998; Wang, 1999). Those constructions are fluid in nature, changing in as much as the associated realities change (Hetherington, 2003; Lincoln & Guba, 1998; Wang, 1999). Contrary to the positivists' belief in apprehending objective knowledge and truth, constructivists subsume these aspects to be perspectival, and thus created but not discovered by the mind (Schwandt, 1998). Perspectivism encompasses the belief that all truth claims and the subsequent criteria used to evaluate them occur within a conceptual framework that acts as a lens through which the phenomenon in question is explained and described (Schwandt, 2000).

Constructivists argue that reality is pluralistic as it can be expressed in many different symbolic and language systems and that it is plastic in as far as it is stretched and shaped to encompass purposeful acts of intentional social agents (Schwandt, 2000). In a way, all these ontological viewpoints espoused by constructivist philosophies tend to point at an all-encompassing idea that

> Human beings do not find or discover knowledge so much as we construct it. [Rather] we invent concepts, models, and schemes to make sense of experience, and we continually test and modify these constructions in the light of new experience. ... [These constructions are intricately linked to] historical and socio-cultural influences [all of which occur] against the back drop of shared understandings, practices, language and so forth. (Schwandt, 2000: 197)

All that has been said up to this point distinguishes the constructivist ontological worldview from that upheld by positivists. The constructivist epistemology is usually described as being transactional and subjectivist (Lincoln & Guba, 1998, 2000) in that the inquirer and the inquired-into are viewed as closely interacting with each other (Lincoln & Guba, 1998). The findings of inquiry are regarded as having been created in the process of investigation (Lincoln & Guba, 1998). This somehow dissolves the conventional boundaries between ontology and epistemology and also sets apart the constructivist epistemology from the objectivist positivist epistemology (discussed previously).

Closely associated with this constructivist epistemology is the rejection of any form of essentialism or the predisposition that presumes certain aspects of the world to be self-evident (for instance categories such as man, woman, self, truth and so forth) (see, e.g. Benhabib, 1992; hooks, 1993). This implies that constructivists believe the social world is constructed socially and discursively, but not in any naturally predetermined way. In the final analysis, the constructivist philosophies do not support the notion of separating the knower and the known, which is a common feature of positivism. In other words, this approach challenges the notion of objectivity of inquiry process commonly advocated by the positivist methodology as a means to attaining value-free knowledge claims. To this end, Guba and Lincoln (1989) assert that the inquirer cannot be separated unproblematically from the object of inquiry in the process of knowledge construction. The findings of an inquiry not only reflect the literal creation or construction of the inquiry process, but also that the constructions themselves reside in the minds of the constructors.

An example of a constructivist undertaking in tourism knowledge production can be traced to Ning Wang who sought to provide a conceptual clarification of the meaning of authenticity in tourism experience. Wang (1999) explored the concept of authenticity as perceived through the lenses of objectivism, constructivism and post-modernism, demonstrating the way these various perspectives argue about whether and how toured objects are experienced as real, prior to suggesting existential authenticity as an alternative approach.

The critical (theory) paradigm

Critical theory is often associated with the 'Frankfurt School', a term which refers to the work of members of the Institute for Social Research, established in Frankfurt, Germany during 1923 as the first formally unaffiliated Marxist-oriented research centre in Europe (Best & Kellner, 1991; Bronner & Kellner, 1989; Keat, 1981). Jürgen Habermas, seen by some people as the most prominent second generation theorist of the Frankfurt school (Bronner & Kellner, 1989), worked to espouse 'the distinctive epistemological character of social theory supposedly represented in much of Marx's work: social theory as critique' (Keat, 1981: 1). So that a critical social theory's conception of social science stands apart from both the positivist tradition and the main historical alternative to the latter, that is, the hermeneutic or interpretive tradition (Keat, 1981). However, Kincheloe and McLaren (2005: 303) intimate that

> There are many critical theories, not just one. [That] the critical tradition is always changing and evolving and critical theory attempts to avoid too much specificity, as there is room for disagreement among critical theorists.

Crucial though is the idea that critical theorists disavow any attempts 'to lay a set of fixed characteristics of the position' which if happens would imply the 'production of blue prints of sociopolitical and epistemological beliefs' (Kincheloe & McLaren, 2005). Nevertheless, critical theory as a paradigm subscribes to historical realism, an ontological conception in which reality is regarded as apprehendable but shaped by and enmeshed in a combination of factors such as social, political, cultural, economic, gender, ethnic and so forth (Guba & Lincoln, 2005; Lincoln & Guba, 1998, 2000, 2003). These various factors eventually crystallise over time into a series of structures and institutions espousing the values inherent but for some reason they assume the status of the 'real', that is, natural and immutable. For all practical purposes 'the structures are "real", a virtual or historical reality' (Lincoln & Guba, 1998: 205). Historical realism differs from both naïve realism and critical realism by recognising that the reality that is regarded natural and immutable at the present is in fact manifest to a combination of historical factors that have constituted and shaped it. So that critical theory's perception of historical realism permits a critique of attempts to establish universal laws that govern social phenomena, arguing that such laws result in 'misrepresentation as eternal or natural of what should instead be seen as historically specific and alterable' (Keat, 1981: 2; cf. Burr, 1995; Gergen, 1985).

Consequently, one of the main concerns of critical theory is to be explicit about its partisan role with the intent to challenge the status quo and make moral/political judgements that have the potential to expose the representations of the world as natural/immutable. Kincheloe and McLaren (2005: 308) describe this scenario as critical emancipation under their so-called reconceptualised critical theory, noting,

> Those who seek emancipation attempt to gain the power to control their own lives in solidarity with justice-oriented community. [In this case] critical research attempts to expose the forces that prevent individuals and groups from shaping the decisions that crucially affect their lives.

Such would be the task of a critical social science (Bronner & Kellner, 1989; Geuss, 1981; Keat, 1981). Within tourism studies, explicit interest in some form of emancipation can be seen in Tribe's (2000, 2002) attempts to extend the predominantly vocational tourism higher education curriculum into the realm of the liberal ideology. Likewise, an explication by Aitchison (1996), Pritchard and Morgan (2007), Hollinshead (1999) and Hall (2004) *inter alia*, the dominant and power-laden discourses inherent in the tourism academe that tend to not only be gender insensitive, but also set the limits and direction of knowledge construction and scholarship in the field of tourism.

As in the constructivist paradigm, critical theory is rooted in an epistemology that is transactional and subjectivist in nature (Guba & Lincoln, 2005; Lincoln & Guba, 1998, 2000). In this case, the inquirer and inquired-into participate interactively in the study environment and the values of the inquirer as a 'transformative intellectual' inevitably influences the inquiry (Guba & Lincoln, 2005; Lincoln & Guba, 1998, 2000). This is the main reason that the findings resulting from critical inquiry are labelled value-mediated and also lead to dissolving the conventional distinction between ontology and epistemology as practised in the positivist sciences (Guba & Lincoln, 2005; Lincoln & Guba, 1998, 2000). It is also by adopting such a position that critical theory places emphasis on the role of values, judgements and human interests and their integration into social inquiry (Carr & Kemmis, 1986).

Concluding Remarks

In this chapter, three research philosophies were explored, that is, scientific (post) positivist philosophy, the constructivist and the critical theory philosophies. The discussions centred on the main features of a paradigm outlined by Guba (1990) in which it was shown that a paradigm is a set of beliefs that guides disciplined inquiry and can be understood in terms of three sets of questions. These questions have to do with the nature of reality (ontological issues), the nature of the relationship between the knower and the known (epistemological issues) and finally the way in which the inquirer goes about gaining knowledge of the world (methodological issues). The importance of underpinning (social) inquiry with a broad understanding of philosophical issues prior to, and as opposed to the conventional focus on selecting and defending methods and techniques was reiterated (cf. Hollinshead, 2004; Phillimore & Goodson, 2004; Zahra & Ryan, 2005).

The fundamental point in this chapter was to demonstrate how a thorough reflection on various ontological and epistemological perspectives can serve to situate the inquiry into a proper philosophical context in the process of knowledge construction. This is important because it is not uncommon for those in the tourism academe to be challenged to defend their subject matter in different environments. Although existing studies have shown a tremendous familiarity with the intellectual resources at our disposal, the chapter serves to remind us of the need to have an inquiring mind that remains cognisant of the various ontological and epistemological contentions in the process of knowledge production. This is envisaged to be a better way of defending ourselves compared to a correct application of widely accepted standards of knowledge production when the very foundation of our beliefs are shaken by critiques within and without the academe.

References

Aitchison, C. (1996) Patriarchal paradigms and the politics of pedagogy: A framework for a feminist analysis of leisure and tourism studies. *World Leisure and Recreation* 38 (4), 38–40.

Benhabib, S. (1992) *Situating the Self: Gender, Community and Post Modernism in Contemporary Ethics*. New York: Routledge.

Best, S. and Kellner, D. (1991) *Postmodern Theory: Critical Interrogations*. London: The Macmillan Press.

Bronner, S. and Kellner, D. (1989) *Critical Theory and Society: A Reader*. London: Routledge.

Burr, V. (1995) *An Introduction to Social Constructivism*. London: Routledge.

Cahn, S.M. (1971) *A New Introduction to Philosophy*. New York, Evanston, San Francisco, London: Harper & Row.

Carr, W. and Kemmis, S. (1986) *Becoming Critical: Education, Knowledge and Action Research*. London: RoutledgeFalmer.

Coles, T., Hall, C.M. and Duval, D.T. (2006) Tourism and post-disciplinary enquiry. *Current Issues in Tourism* 9 (4&5), 293–319.

Coshall, J.T. (2000) Spectral analysis of international tourism flows. *Annals of Tourism Research* 39 (1), 85–89.

Crouch, G.I. (1994) The study of international tourism demand: A review of practice. *Journal of Travel Research* 33, 41–54.

Denzin, N.K. and Lincoln, Y.S. (eds) (1998) *The Landscape of Qualitative Research: Theories and Issues* (1st edn). Thousand Oaks, CA: Sage.

Echtner, C.M. and Jamal, T.B. (1997) The disciplinary dilemma of tourism studies. *Annals of Tourism Research* 24 (4), 868–883.

Feighery, W. (2006) Reflexivity and tourism research: Telling an (other) story. *Current Issues in Tourism* 9 (3), 269–282.

Foucault, M. (1972) *The Archaeology of Knowledge*. London: Tavistock.

Foucault, M. (1980) Power/knowledge. Selected interviews and other writings 1972–1979. In C. Gordon (ed.) *Michel Foucault. Power/Knowledge. Selected Interviews and Other Writings 1972–1979*. London: Harvester Press.

Gergen, K. (1985) The social constructionist movement in modern social psychology. *American Psychologist* 40 (3), 266–275.

Gergen, K.J. and Gergen, M.M. (1991) Toward reflexive methodologies. In F. Steier (ed.) *Research and Reflexivity* (pp. 76–95). London: Sage.

Geuss, R. (1981) *Idea of a Critical Theory: Habermas and the Frankfurt School*. Cambridge: Cambridge University Press.

Guba, E.G. (1990) *The Alternative Paradigm Dialog*. Thousand Oaks, CA: Sage.

Guba, E.G. and Lincoln, Y.S. (1989) *Fourth Generation Evaluation*. London: Sage.

Guba, E.G. and Lincoln, Y.S. (1994) Competing paradigms in qualitative research. In N.K. Denzin and Y.S. Lincoln (eds) *Handbook of Qualitative Research* (1st edn, pp. 105–117). Thousand Oaks, CA: Sage.

Guba, E.G. and Lincoln, Y.S. (2005) Paradigmatic controversies, contradictions, and emerging confluences. In N.K. Denzin and Y.S. Lincoln (eds) *The Sage Handbook of Qualitative Research* (3rd edn, pp. 191–215). Thousand Oaks, CA: Sage.

Habermas, J. (1987) *Knowledge and Human Interests* (J. Shapiro, trans.). Cambridge: Polity Press.

Halfpenny, P. (2001) Positivism in the twentieth century. In G. Ritzer and B. Smart (eds) *Handbook of Social Theory* (pp. 371–385). London: Sage.

Hall, M. (2004) Reflexivity and tourism research: Situating myself and/with others. In J. Phillimore and L. Goodson (eds) *Qualitative Research in Tourism: Ontologies, Epistemologies and Methodologies* (pp. 137–155). London: Routledge.

Harré, R. (1981) The positivist-empiricist approach and its alternative. In P. Reason and R. Rowan (eds) *Human Inquiry* (pp. 3–17). Milton, Sydney, Melbourne: John Wiley & Sons.

Hemmingway, J.L. (1999) Critique and emancipation: Toward a critical theory of leisure. In E.L. Jackson and T.L. Burton (eds) *Leisure Studies. Prospects for the Twenty-first Century* (pp. 487–506). State College, PA: Venture Publishing, Inc.

Hetherington, S. (2003) *Reality? Knowledge? Philosophy! An Introduction to Metaphysics and Epistemology.* Edinburgh: Edinburgh University Press.

Hollinshead, K. (1999) Surveillance of the worlds of tourism: Foucault and the eye-of power. *Tourism Management* 17 (2), 133–139.

Hollinshead, K. (2004) A primer in ontological craft: The creative capture of people and places through qualitative research. In J. Phillimore and L. Goodson (eds) *Qualitative Research in Tourism: Ontologies, Epistemologies and Methodologies* (pp. 63–82). London: Routledge.

hooks, b. (1993) *Sisters of the Yam: Black Women in Self-Recovery.* Boston, MA: South-End Press.

Jamal, T. and Hollinshead, K. (2001) Tourism and the forbidden zone: The underserved power of qualitative inquiry. *Tourism Management* 22, 63–82.

Jang, S.C., Morrison, A.M. and O'Leary, J.T. (2002) Benefit segmentation of Japanese pleasure travellers to the USA and Canada: Selecting target markets based on the profitability and risk of individual market segments. *Tourism Management* 23 (4), 367–378.

Jennings, G. (2001) *Tourism Research.* Milton, QLD: John Wiley & Sons.

Keat, R. (1981) *The Politics of Social Theory: Habermas, Freud and the Critique of Positivism.* Oxford: Basil Blackwell.

Kincheloe, J.L. and McLaren, P.L. (2005) Rethinking critical theory and qualitative research. In N.K. Denzin and Y.S. Lincoln (eds) *The Sage Handbook of Qualitative Research* (3rd edn, pp. 303–342). Thousand Oaks, CA: Sage.

Kuhn, T. (1970) *The Structure of Scientific Revolutions* (2nd edn, enlarged). Chicago, IL: University of Chicago Press.

Laclau, E. and Mouffe, C. (1985) *Hegemony and Socialist Strategy.* London: Verso.

Lazar, D. (1998) Selected issues in the philosophy of social science. In C. Seale (ed.) *Researching Society and Culture* (pp. 7–22). London: Sage.

Leiper, N. (1981) Towards a cohesive curriculum in tourism: The case for a distinct discipline. *Annals of Tourism Research* 8 (1), 69–84.

Lincoln, Y.S. and Guba, E.G. (1998) Competing paradigms in qualitative research. In N.K. Denzin and Y.S. Lincoln (eds) *The Landscape of Qualitative Research: Theories and Issues* (pp. 195–220). Thousand Oaks, CA: Sage.

Lincoln, Y.S. and Guba, E.G. (2000) *The Sage Handbook for Research in Education: Engaging Ideas and Enriching Enquiry.* Thousand Oaks, CA: Sage.

Lincoln, Y.S. and Guba, E.G. (2003) Paradigmatic controversies, contradictions and emerging confluences. In N.K. Denzin and Y.S. Lincoln (eds) *The Landscape of Qualitative Research: Theories and Issues* (2nd edn, pp. 253–291). Thousand Oaks, CA: Sage.

Mazanec, J.A. (1992) Classifying tourists into market segments: A neural network approach. *Journal of Travel and Tourism Marketing* 1 (1), 39–59.

Page, S.J. (2005) Academic ranking exercises: Do they achieve anything meaningful? – a personal view. *Tourism Management* 26, 663–666.

Phillimore, J. and Goodson, L. (eds) (2004) *Qualitative Research in Tourism: Ontologies, Epistemologies and Methodologies.* London: Routledge.

Polkinghorne, D. (1989) Changing conversations about human science. In S. Kvale (ed.) *Issues of Validity in Qualitative Research* (pp. 13–45). Lund: Studentlitteratur.

Pritchard, A. and Morgan, N. (2007) De-centring tourism's intellectual universe, or traversing the dialogue between change and tradition. In I. Ateljevic, A. Pritchard and N. Morgan (eds) *The Critical Turn in Tourism Studies: Innovative Research Methodologies* (pp. 11–28). Oxford: Elsevier.

Riley, R. and Love, R.R. (2000) The state of qualitative tourism research. *Annals of Tourism Research* 27 (1), 164–187.

Ryan, C., Page, S. and Roche, T. (2007) New development for the journal. *Tourism Management* 28 (5), 1167.

Schwandt, T.A. (1998) Constructivist and interpretivist approaches to human inquiry. In N.K. Denzin and Y.S. Lincoln (eds) *The Landscape of Qualitative Research: Theories and Issues* (pp. 221–259). Thousand Oaks, CA: Sage.

Schwandt, T.A. (2000) Three epistemological stances for qualitative inquiry: Interpretivism, hermeneutics, and social constructionism. In N.K. Denzin and Y.S. Lincoln (eds) *Handbook of Qualitative Research* (2nd edn, pp. 189–213). Thousand Oaks, CA: Sage.

Schwandt, T.A. (2003) Three epistemological stances for qualitative inquiry: Interpretivism, hermeneutics, and social constructionism. In N.K. Denzin and Y.S. Lincoln (eds) *The Landscape of Qualitative Research: Theories and Issues* (2nd edn, pp. 222–331). Thousand Oaks, CA: Sage.

Seale, C. (1999) *The Quality of Qualitative Research.* London: Sage.

Song, H. and Li, G. (2008) Tourism demand modelling and forecasting – A review of recent research. *Tourism Management* 29 (2), 203–220.

Swain, M. (2004) (Dis)embodied experience and power dynamics in tourism research. In J. Phillimore and L. Goodson (eds) *Qualitative Research in Tourism: Ontologies, Epistemologies and Methodologies* (pp. 102–118). London: Routledge.

Tribe, J. (1997) The indiscipline of tourism. *Annals of Tourism Research* 24 (3), 638–657.

Tribe, J. (2000) Balancing the vocational: Theory and practice of liberal education in tourism. *Tourism and Hospitality Research* 2 (2), 9–25.

Tribe, J. (2002) The philosophic practitioner. *Annals of Tourism Research* 29 (2), 338–357.

Tribe, J. (2004) Knowing about tourism: Epistemological issues. In J. Phillimore and L. Goodson (eds) *Qualitative Research in Tourism: Ontologies, Epistemologies and Methodologies* (pp. 46–62). London: Routledge.

Turner, J.H. (2001) The origins of positivism: The contributions of Auguste Comte and Herbert Spencer. In G. Ritzer and B. Smart (eds) *Handbook of Social Theory* (pp. 30–42). London, Thousand Oaks, New Delhi: Sage.

Walle, A.H. (1997) Quantitative versus qualitative tourism research. *Annals of Tourism Research* 24 (3), 524–536.

Wang, N. (1999) Rethinking authenticity in tourism experience. *Annals of Tourism Research* 26 (2), 349–370.

Yule, J. (1997) Engendered ideologies and gender policy in the UK Part 1: Gender ideologies. *Leisure Studies* 16 (2), 61–84.

Zahra, A. and Ryan, C. (2005) Reflections on the research process: The researcher as actor and audience in the world of regional tourist organisations. *Current Issues in Tourism* 8 (1), 1–21.

Chapter 5

Post-disciplinary Tourism

TIM COLES, C. MICHAEL HALL and DAVID TIMOTHY DUVAL

Introduction: Knowledge Production and Disciplines

Scholars interested in tourism have been criticised for a lack of interest in the ontological and epistemological (and hence methodological) foundations of their work, including the notion that some tourism knowledges are created for tourism knowledges' sake in a fragmented, incoherent and unsystematic manner (Tribe, 2006; Weed, 2006). But the indictment reads further: as a consequence, research on tourism has been limited in its ability to contribute substantively to the development of social theory, concept and hence deeper understanding (Franklin & Crang, 2001; Ioannides, 2007).

Such allegations form part of a debate about how knowledges of tourism can and indeed should be produced (cf. Coles *et al.*, 2006). A more prominent feature of this discussion is whether there is a coherent and clearly identifiable academic discipline centred on, and defined by its interest in, tourism; or, alternatively, is knowledge about tourism as a field of study generated by scholars within and across (other established) academic disciplines? An impasse has been reached and the conflicting positions are characterised by their contrasting approaches towards defining academic disciplines (e.g. Tribe, 1997, 2000; Leiper, 2000; Hall *et al.*, 2004). Fundamentally, though, the need for and existence of disciplines is taken as read when they should not be (Klein, 1996). In this chapter, we explore the opportunities and possibilities for the study of tourism 'beyond disciplines'; that is, post-disciplinary studies of tourism (see also Coles *et al.*, 2005, 2006). We consider the relevance of recent discussions, particularly in the social sciences, on knowledge production characterised by more reasonableness, flexibility and freedom from the constraints of established and orthodox disciplinary boundaries and dogmas (Sayer, 1999; Massey, 1999; Toulmin, 2001; Hellström *et al.*, 2003). Several academic disciplines as we know them today originate in the late 19th and early 20th century. Hence, they do not necessarily reflect current issues, themes and imperatives, so much as academic divisions of labour relevant to former times. Thus, there is the danger that we may be attempting to address contemporary subjects (such as tourism) through outdated and ageing frameworks for scholarly activity and academic administration.

Set against this background, two interconnected sets of implications for tourism scholars are raised here: first, discussions of the disciplinarity (or not) of tourism need to be recast and reappraised; and second, many present-day research foci require knowledge production that is not intellectually straightjacketed by disciplinary antecedents. For instance, we have argued that a post-disciplinary approach is especially well-suited to the emergent study of tourism mobilities as a more appropriate central construct for studies of contemporary tourism (Coles *et al.*, 2005, 2006; Hall, 2005a, 2005b), although from a more spatially oriented approach than discussed in the present volume (Chapter 6). Mobilities is not the only potential beneficiary, though. Several new analytical possibilities are considered, with special reference to the relationship between tourism and 'climate change' (as it is more routinely labelled in popular discourse). For years there have been calls for greater dialogue among physical and social scientists in view of the central role of the environment in tourism (Butler, 1999). Less parochialism and greater communication between scholars is the only viable strategy towards building an effective body of knowledge on global environmental change – currently the most urgent global agenda (Stern, 2007) – and its connections to tourism.

The Trouble with Tourism: Locating Tourism on the Disciplinary Map

Tourism has become a popular subject for study and research. In the UK alone, a recent estimate placed the number of undergraduate students on tourism programmes at around 10,500, with 700 registered for postgraduate study and around 90 for research degrees (Tribe, 2004a: 69). The last (2001) census of research activity (Research Assessment Exercise – RAE) demonstrated that tourism has become a relatively common focus (cf. Tribe, 2003, 2004a; Coles, 2008). Although tourism appeared to be most frequently addressed by scholars in business and management and sports-related studies, it also featured on the academic radars of those in geography, economics, sociology and town and country planning (Tribe, 2003: 228).

These data hint at the difficulty in placing tourism on the established disciplinary map and the diverse intellectual influences that are (we would argue) helpfully brought to bear in the study of tourism. They are emblematic of just how willing academic governors and administrators are to silo knowledge of particular subjects for administrative tidiness rather than for reasons of intellectual cogence. In New Zealand, for instance, the Performance Based Research Fund (PBRF) considers research on tourism together with marketing. In Australia, the Research Quality Framework (RQF) has tourism primarily located in the 'economics, commerce, management and information management' assessment panel. In both cases, clearly not all tourism research (i.e. on tourism and global environmental change – see below) would appear appropriate to their codesignations.

Several scholars have attempted to chart the development of tourism scholarship within particular disciplinary arenas (cf. Coles *et al.*, 2006). This is a difficult task, especially when carried out across the social sciences (Holden, 2005), and it requires an almost encyclopaedic knowledge of historiography in a number of disciplines. What emerges from such a reading is the quite different extent to which there has been engagement with tourism among disciplines in the social sciences and humanities. Geographers, for instance, are more acutely aware of how the study of tourism has developed within their discipline, comparative international differences in geographical approaches to studying tourism, and the wider contribution of geographical perspectives to tourism studies (Butler, 2004; Coles, 2004; Kreisel, 2004; Hall & Page, 2006; Ioannides, 2007). In contrast, Semmens (2005: 2–3) notes with no little accuracy of her discipline that 'unlike economists, ecologists, anthropologists, sociologists, semioticians and geographers, historians have only recently turned to tourism', and a 'lack of carefully researched, genuinely academic syntheses is keenly felt'. Be this as it may, it presupposes that academics are willing to synthesise, especially with those beyond their usual disciplinary purview (cf. Weed, 2006). Some academics appear reluctant to synthesise precisely in order to establish the credentials of their discipline and/or work as the most authoritative (and hence to obtain research institutional and financial support) (Holden, 2005: 2; Coles *et al.*, 2006: 296). Insular attitudes of this type result in fragmented knowledge production and artificially constructed 'truths' subsequently emerge (Botterill, 2001; Tribe, 2006; Weed, 2006).

Some commentators have questioned whether tourism knowledge production is best advanced through exclusivist disciplinary approaches (cf. Holden, 2005: 1). According to Graburn and Jafari (1991: 7–8), 'no single discipline alone can accommodate, treat or understand tourism; it can be studied only if disciplinary boundaries are crossed and if multi-disciplinary perspectives are sought and formed'. Echtner and Jamal (1997: 878) differentiate between the potentials and possibilities associated with multi and interdisciplinary approaches (see also Jamal & Kim, 2005). A multi-disciplinary approach recognises and incorporates information derived in other disciplinary arenas without scholars stepping beyond their own boundaries. This approach is, though, somewhat instrumental because it simply concedes that knowledge derived from other disciplines has a certain value or purpose, without necessarily engaging with knowledge production processes and practices elsewhere. By contrast, interdisciplinary approaches require (temporary) forays outside 'home' disciplinary boundaries in order to advance knowledge production. Echtner and Jamal (1997), following Leiper's (1981: 72) earlier work, view interdisciplinarity as 'working *between* disciplines, *blending* various philosophies and techniques so that particular disciplines do not stand apart but are brought together intentionally and explicitly to seek a synthesis' (in Echtner & Jamal, 1997: 878–879, emphasis original).

The Trouble with Disciplines: Appropriate Frameworks for Knowledge Production?

The positions presented above exclude the possibility that there may be an academic discipline in its own right centred on tourism. Nevertheless, audiences of potential students, sponsors and clients, funding councils, colleagues and higher education administrators have been presented with the position that 'tourism studies' or 'tourism management' is an institutionally coherent and textually defined area of knowledge production (Hall *et al.*, 2004; Hall & Page, 2006; Leiper, 1981, 2000; Tribe, 2003, 2004b). For Leiper (2000: 5), this pragmatic stance is eminently sensible and necessary because 'tourism-related phenomena are too complicated, with too many implications, for knowledge to be adequately developed by specialists favouring one [established social sciences] discipline'. In this view, disciplines emerge to reflect the themes and imperatives of the times, as is the case with the disciplines of 'geography' and 'policy science' (Skole, 2004; Pielke, 2004). The importance of tourism as a major contemporary economic, social, cultural, political and environmental phenomenon justifies the apparent *de facto* emergence of a distinctive discipline centred on the subject.

Indeed, if one were sympathetic to Toulmin's (2001) view that disciplines are contrived intellectual and institutional divisions of labour, a case may be made, as Hall *et al.* (2004) argue, under three practical criteria to legitimate the existence of tourism studies. Johnston (1991) validates the existence of geography as a discipline in the Anglo-American world through a well-established presence of the subject, including professorial positions; formal institutional structures, including associations and university departments; and avenues for academic publications. For instance, the ATLAS Body of Tourism Knowledge (Hall, 2005a) or the (United Nations) World Tourism Organisation's (UNWTO) TedQual programme (UNWTO, 2006) are schemes that effectively act as blueprints for the content and concerns of tourism studies programmes around the world.

An alternative viewpoint is championed by Tribe (1997, 2000), who argues that disciplinary status should be assessed through the dual lenses of the philosophy and sociology of scholarly enquiry. In this case, tourism studies do not conform to the desiderata necessary of a discipline (Tribe, 1997, 2004b: 47–48). For him, to describe tourism as a discipline fails on logical grounds, nor should it necessarily be a desirable ambition. As he points out in a view with which we have sympathy, 'disciplines are not the *sine qua non* of knowledge production' (Tribe, 1997: 646). While Tribe's assessment does not preclude future reconsideration (Hall, 2005a), at the present time he suggests that tourism is better understood as two related fields of study: one which in a later contribution he terms [tourism] 'business inter-disciplinarity', and the other, 'non-business related tourism' which is more difficult to label because of its diverse concerns and origins (Tribe, 2004b: 50).

Tribe (2004a: 51) elucidates a framework developed by Gibbons *et al.* (1994), which is widely discussed in the social sciences, in order to identify two modes of knowledge production in tourism. Briefly put, in Mode 1 'knowledge is generated within a disciplinary, primarily cognitive context' (Gibbons *et al.*, 1994: 1) and by its nature, may extend to include multi and interdisciplinary tactics. This is complemented by Mode 2, which he describes as 'extra-disciplinary' (cf. Tribe, 2004b: 51) where knowledge emerges from the 'context of application with its own distinct theoretical structures, research methods and modes of practice which may not be locatable on the prevailing disciplinary map' (Gibbons *et al.*, 1994: 168). Mode 1 appears to be the dominant type in higher education these days (cf. Coles, 2008) as 'the traditional centre for knowledge production' (Tribe, 2004b: 51), whereas Mode 2 was originally anticipated as taking place outside university structures (Gibbons *et al.*, 1994: vii). Mode 2 is routinely conducted in the public and private sectors for an applied purpose, such as consultancy work in the service industries. Within tourism research, there have been criticisms of the preponderance of business-focused perspectives, which, it is alleged, have frustrated greater theory-building and conceptualisation (Franklin & Crang, 2001). By and large these perspectives have their origins in Mode 2 knowledge production, but Mode 2 knowledge production does not, though, necessarily have to defy advanced or higher level knowledge production (Grabher, 2004; Coles, 2007a).

For some, this type of discussion may seem arid, even irrelevant. However, it is vital to how we come to construct and engineer knowledge about tourism and how tourism scholars relate to the world ontologically. Moreover, as scholars in higher education institutions in countries like the UK (and increasingly Australia and New Zealand and elsewhere in the world) are increasingly forced to seek out alternative sources of research funding beyond the state, Mode 2 findings produced in the context of application may play an increasingly important role in future academic knowledge production and theory-building (Coles, 2008). Crucially, this dispute exposes and embodies many of the dilemmas, predicaments and tensions faced by those active in tourism scholarship. To identify 'tourism studies' as a discipline is clearly awkward when certain criteria from the philosophy and sociology of scholarship are applied and when research assessment frameworks like the RAE, PBRF and RQF fail to offer administrative legitimacy to the case (Tribe, 2004a; Coles, 2008). Notwithstanding, the simple fact is that many departments, institutes, centres and schools as divisions of academic labour function around tourism as a subject and attract notable volumes of students and funding based on their thematic interest. In parallel to this standoff, interdisciplinary approaches to tourism studies are far from unproblematic because of the contested nature of disciplines *per se* and of interdisciplinarity.

Mode 1 knowledge production, and hence contemporary interdisciplinarity, takes as read the existence of a number of disciplines that are relevant in their form and function to contemporary, i.e. early 21st century conditions. In agreeing to make temporary transgressions into other disciplinary terrains, we assume that these other disciplines are appropriate, meaningful and capable of delivering coherent bodies of knowledge (as is our own disciplinary 'home') (Klein, 1996). Several disciplines in the form we largely know and understand them today are manifestations of 19th and 20th century rationalisations of intellectual enquiry (cf. Coles *et al.*, 2006: 300). Where once it may have made sense to package theory, concept and method under particular disciplinary monikers, the same (degree of) justification may persist nowadays perhaps more for administrative rather than purely intellectual reasons.

Witness, for instance, the current tensions between physical and human geographers with their widely different ways of understanding and producing knowledge about their common rallying point, the environment (Harrison *et al.*, 2004). Several historical accounts demonstrate how disciplines (and subdisciplines – Butler, 2004) as we understand them today have mutated in their form, paradigms and approaches over time, not least because of generational turnover among the most influential thinkers and/or advocates (Sayer, 1999; Toulmin, 2001; Jessop & Sum, 2001; Bainbridge, 2003; Pielke, 2004; Pelletier, 2004).

Massey (1999) has discussed the limits of interdisciplinarity to further knowledge production, while Sayer (1999) has highlighted how operational issues mediate against excursions beyond usual disciplinary boundaries. Disciplines have to be policed, regulated and promoted in order to survive and there are a number of devices to achieve this, such as research assessment (Tribe, 2003; Coles *et al.*, 2006; Coles, 2008). Policing defines not only which particular subjects, modes of inquiry and critical research questions may be studied by those in a discipline, but also, more importantly, those that are excluded (see also Markham, 2005). Scholars concede that there are areas beyond the remit of their disciplines, sometimes for pragmatic reasons of securing (greater) resources for themselves or denying others (Coles, 2008). While the general intellectual merits of interdisciplinary enquiry appear to bridge the gap between disciplines in principle, in practice scholars may act to defend their resource access and 'intellectual turf'. As a result, contrasting perspectives from different disciplines may not after all be so readily reconciled (Keyfitz, 1995; Turner, 2002).

Practice prevails over principle in other respects. The tendency for scholars to limit themselves to what lies within their intellectual 'comfort zones' is indicative of an ignorance of what lies across the disciplinary divide and risk aversion to explore otherwise unknown territories. As Sayer (1999: 5) argues, many interdisciplinary collaborations are actually little more than a pretence. Members of different disciplines come together to work on an interdisciplinary project, but retreat back into their sanctuaries once it is completed. Outside the lifetime of the collaboration, there is little commitment to knowledge production beyond their disciplinary 'homes'. If scholars are committed to genuinely interdisciplinary exchanges, they should be conversant with the traditions in those disciplines where they wish dialogue; moreover, they should be aware of, and have the skills to overcome, any differences in ontology, epistemology and methodology compared to their discipline. In this respect, it has been noted that tourism scholars would appear to lack the necessary skills and sensitivity to work across disciplines (see Coles *et al.*, 2006: 299–300; Coles & Church, 2007).

Post-disciplinary Knowledge Production

Scholarly interest in tourism may be flourishing through a rich blend of insights emerging from an array of disciplinary and (apparently) interdisciplinary knowledge production processes. Nevertheless, it is useful to reiterate that the nature of inter or multi-disciplinary enquiry is contested and cannot be taken for granted, nor can the existence of disciplines. Hellström *et al.* (2003: 251–252) argue that disciplinarity and paradigmatic policing within disciplines have traditionally guided researchers towards particular problems, especially within the sciences. They advocate the need for greater flexibility and tolerance in the manner anticipated by Gibbons *et al.*'s Mode 2 knowledge production (see also Toulmin, 2001). Contemporary, relevance-driven agendas are widening the sphere for legitimate academic activity. Many current themes are much wider in scope than previously and as such are inherently 'transdisciplinary' in nature. They call for more knowledge production that is elaborated in the 'context of application' through extended peer communities of practice, and that challenges and destabilises 'received understandings' of disciplinarity (see also Beier & Arnold, 2005). This has been described as a 'post-disciplinary' approach, the basic merits of which are, as Sayer (1999: 5) describes, that 'scholars forget about disciplines and whether ideas can be identified with any particular one; they identify with learning rather than with disciplines'.

One advantage of post-disciplinarity is that it allows scholars to free themselves from the intellectual shackles applied by disciplinary policing. Freedom encourages the valorisation of knowledge produced elsewhere. It allows ideas and connections to be followed to their logical conclusions, not to some contrived or preordained end point determined by artificial disciplinary strictures (Exhibit 1) (Coles *et al.*, 2006). According to Massey (1999: 6), in this context academic identities should be defined in a relational sense that highlights particularity within a complex network of scholarly inter-relations. As Hellström *et al.* (2003) argue, post-disciplinary knowledge production encourages greater specialisation among academics in their chosen area of expertise. A strictly disciplinary approach would suggest that academics need to build competence in each of the areas of techniques, methods and instrumentation; theory development; and subject matter knowledge. In contrast, post-disciplinary modes of enquiry encourage academics to devote

Exhibit 1 – Don't just save the whales: On the need for more flexible thinking about tourism research problems

In 2007 there was a discussion on trinet about the Global Ecotourism Conference that was to be held later that year in Norway. Some of this explored whether it was ethical for academics to support or attend this event. Norway was alleged to have a shoddy reputation because of its support of whaling, in contrast to the dominant global discourse against this practice. One of the more interesting contributions to this strand was posted by Stefan Gössling, a German citizen who is currently an Associate Professor in the Department of Service Management at Lund University in Sweden and the Research Co-ordinator of the Centre for Sustainable and Geotourism at the Western Norway Research Institute. Stefan studied geography and biology at Münster in Germany and he holds a PhD in Human Ecology from Lund. His response highlights the need to be finely attuned to the nuances and multiply connected scholarly dimensions of the issue, and to pursue it as far as possible to several logical conclusions rather than simply limit discussion to a simplified and truncated exchange on whether it is 'right' or 'wrong' to whale.

Stefan wrote that '[i]f you follow Norwegian or Icelandic debates on whaling (which, in many whale-watching areas, such as Husavik in Iceland, are also local debates between the whale watching versus whaling industry), you will soon realise that whaling is not just about economic values. Whaling is far more about cultural values, not least cultural independency, which has to be understood against the background of Norwegian and Icelandic history. Both countries gained independenc[e] rather late (Norway in 1905, separation from Sweden) or very late (Iceland in 1944, separation from Denmark), and both countries have been invaded (Norway by Germany in 1940 during WWII) or been involved in conflicts brought upon them by more powerful nations (the Icelandic cod wars with the UK). From my point of view, any debate about whaling has to be seen against this background: whatever you "advocate" in Oslo, be careful it is not understood as superimposing your values, as this may have an effect contrary to what you wish to achieve.

At this point, I'd like to say that I am against whaling; however, I do not see the major difference between whales and a larger number of other species we are driving to extinction. You may think this is a little far-fetched, but you mention long-distance journeys you want to make in the future to visit Iceland or Japan (as soon as they have stopped whaling). I see a link here to climate change, which is one of the major factors driving species extinction. Thomas *et al.* (2004), for instance, wrote that between 15 and 37% of species belonging to different taxa such as birds and butterflies are likely to become extinct because of climate change by 2050. If that's not enough, it also seems clear that particularly the livelihoods of the poorest people in the world will be affected by climate change.

To all of you thus one provocative question: any trip by air over 10,000 km (return distance) will exceed emissions of 3.5 t of CO_2-equivalent, or what can be assumed to be the globally sustainable amount of emissions per capita and year in the 2000s. Note that this amount will decline substantially in the future, both because of reduction needs (Kyoto) as well as a growing world population. As many of you will argue that technological change is going to solve this problem, the fact is that in aviation we face a situation where absolute (net) growth in fuel use is in the order of $> 3\%$ per year (i.e. despite of efficiency gains). Biofuels, a potential solution, need huge hinterlands for production, potentially another threat to biodiversity.

Against this background: what are the ethics of long-distance travel?'

Source: Adapted from Stefan Gössling posting to trinet on International Year of Ecotourism 08/5/07.

themselves to a single aspect, in the process developing their specialisation further and becoming able to contribute in a wider variety of contexts (Hellstöm *et al.*, 2003: 254). Similarly, the unwarranted and artificial parochialism of paradigms as regulatory measures is rejected, and this is a vital difference between inter and post-disciplinary studies (Smith, 1998: 311; Jessop & Sum, 2001; Rosamond, 2005). Kuhn's (1969) established and dominant view of the paradigm is dismissed because 'either it is so unspecific to function as an analytical tool in its right, or it is too suffocating in its specificity and discrimination that it leaves nothing to analyse in the first place' (Hellström *et al.*, 2003: 254).

Post-disciplinarity encourages new hybrid, more flexible forms of knowledge production, but they are not intended to be intellectual 'free-for-alls'. Post-disciplinary approaches are shaped by two sets of guiding principles, namely: they are framed by reference to what preceded them; and by the four components of (shared) interests, competencies, worldview (i.e. general assumptions about reality) and outlook (i.e. assumptions that of what should be involved in the field) (see Hellström *et al.*, 2003: 255). In the case of the former, the need for a post-disciplinary approach is only revealed after there has been a critical consideration of the merits of predisciplinary and disciplinary-based (i.e. also interdisciplinary) approaches (Jessop & Sum, 2001). With respect to the latter, the four components are intended to be more flexible terms of reference to shape academic collaborations and dialogues. Post-disciplinary knowledge production may reject the need for disciplines, but it demands a degree of autoregulation.

In some subject areas there have been attempts to set out how more flexible approaches may contribute to scholarly enquiry in the coming years. The need for alternatives has been discussed in political economy (Goodwin, 2004; Hay & March, 1999; Jessop & Sum, 2001; Painter, 2003; Rosamond, 2005). For instance, Hay and Marsh (1999) identify three among several possible new orientations to the study of international political economy (cf. Coles *et al.*, 2006: 306–308):

- 'Old problems, new approaches' – there has not been a qualitative shift in the nature of the political and the economic. Nevertheless, a fresh perspective is required to improve analysis of the past, present and processes of transformation.
- 'New problems, old approaches' – contemporary conditions of capitalism are qualitatively different. Nevertheless, old models of inquiry remain analytically and methodologically valid, with the challenge to ensure they are redeployed appropriately to ensure they explain contemporary conditions.
- 'New times, new political economy' –contemporary conditions of capitalism are qualitatively different and they cannot be explained alone by existing modes of analysis and bodies of theory.

Post-disciplinarity and Tourism

Hay and Marsh's (1999) work set out to be provocative, but it presents some interesting possibilities for the social sciences more generally and to studies of tourism more specifically in two respects. First, as Goodwin (2004: 72) highlights, where the limitations of old political economy are identified, research workers are required to go beyond current, established disciplinary boundaries to exploit new modes of knowledge production. In effect, the first and third approaches concede that understanding in political economy cannot (and should not) be exclusively advanced solely by those who have been formally trained in political economy in its orthodox, contemporary form. Following this line of thinking, elsewhere we have argued for a reorientation of studies of tourism with the concept of mobility (more widely conceived) as a central unifying construct (Coles *et al.*, 2004, 2005, 2006; Hall, 2005a, 2005b). Standard UNWTO definitions of tourism that have their origins in the 1970s are somewhat blunt taxonomical instruments (albeit still widely used in practice) that fail to reflect the changes, nuances and innovations in tourism mobilities particularly in the past decade. Increased human and nonhuman movements under conditions of globalisation, of which tourism mobilities are just one distinctive component, cannot be captured and understood by those residing in single disciplines, like geography or sociology (see also Sheller & Urry, 2006; Hannam *et al.*, 2006). Existing analytical frameworks are unable to cope with the widespread and complex, interconnected arrays of flows of people, goods, capital, data, ideas and biological organisms. The presence and prevalence of blogs, listservs and meetings dedicated to mobilities demonstrates how far more flexible and distinctive communities of practice among academics are forming to advance knowledge on a primarily thematic rather than disciplinary basis.

The second point is that none of these three approaches is privileged at the expense of the others in a misguided search for the next single 'meta-approach' as past precedents with paradigms may have otherwise suggested. Rather, there are important analytical opportunities associated with all three approaches. This is perhaps fortunate because it can sometimes be difficult to ascribe a particular theme to a specific category: in the case of contemporary medical tourism, is this an established research theme – that is, a long-term academic project still in progress – in need of new analytical approaches to reinvigorate the research effort? (i.e. Hay & Marsh's first approach); or alternatively, is contemporary medical tourism qualitatively different to previous times (i.e. there are significant disjunctures between past and present forms) and hence in need of altogether new analytical approaches (i.e. Hay & Marsh's third approach)?

Within studies of tourism, it is possible to identify instances whereby each of the three approaches has significant analytical potential (Coles *et al.*, 2006: 309–312). For example, with respect to medical tourism, we would contend that new approaches are required to an established and enduringly relevant research problem (i.e. Hay & Marsh's first approach), albeit the key point is the need to inject new analytical impetus. Health and medical reasons have long been identified as motives for travel, with early visitors to spas and resorts travelling to enjoy their recuperative properties. The current multibillion dollar global medical tourism sector has emerged over time on the basis of much wider demand for medical treatment (TRAM, 2006). Where once this might have been for spa treatments or climatic conditions for respiratory complaints, now this ranges from standard procedures for routine complaints such as hip replacements, cataract removals, dentistry and cosmetic enhancements to more intricate and involved courses of treatment on cancers, HIV-AIDS, fertilisation and xeno-transplantation – the transplantation of nonhuman cells and tissue into humans (Coles, 2007b). Standard approaches to tourism (through 'business interdisciplinarity' as Tribe may term it) enable us to identify the considerable volume and value in medical tourism flows and their importance to host destinations and state economies. Without embracing insights from medical sciences, bioethics and political science, we would not be able to develop as full an understanding of these visitor flows in terms of issues such as citizenship, health provision and bioregulation as key push-pull factors (Hall, 2007; Coles, 2007b).

In the area of the growth of airline traffic through the deregulation of the skies in the past decade, old approaches are still relevant to solving new research problems (i.e. Hay & Marsh's second approach). Connectedness and flows may be hallmarks of contemporary times (Urry, 2000), but more and greater transgressions into fields with longer and richer heritages of exploring networks, or for that matter international relations (e.g. through aeropolitics and the complex regulation of international transport and accessibility), widens and deepens our knowledges of bilateral tourism flows and tourism production (Goodman, 2006; Michael *et al.*, 2007; Duval, 2007). For several decades, networks have been the subject of extensive academic attention in sociology, anthropology, human geography, migration studies and political science, culminating in the development of distinctive bodies of theory and concept, methods and techniques that have as yet only partially made their way into studies of tourism.

Nevertheless, it is perhaps in the third approach ('new times, new tourism studies') that we may begin to identify the greatest need for flexibility in knowledge production. Scholars in the social sciences, along with their counterparts in the physical sciences, have started to shift their attention to the next and arguably far bigger, more urgent post-disciplinary theme: 'climate change', and the wider array of global environmental changes that are connected with climate (Gössling & Hall, 2006). As several commentators have noted, it has not always been straightforward to reap the intellectual rewards by harnessing scholars from the physical and social sciences to a specific knowledge production task (Kinzig, 1996; Redman *et al.*, 2004; Roux *et al.*, 2006). Released in 2006 and published in 2007, *The Stern Review* explores the economic implications of climate change, and has become a widely read and quoted work in a range of industry, practitioner and academic circles. As the large mass of evidence compiled for, and integrated within, the report makes clear, there is little room for disciplinary parochialism on this matter. Indeed, the opening paragraph offers,

The economics of climate change is shaped by the science. That is what dictates the structure of the economic analysis and policies; therefore we start with the science. (Stern, 2007: xiii)

By science, the report is referring here to physical science primarily in the form of climatology, meteorology and palaeo-environmental studies. Indeed, palaeo-environmental research – which focuses on the nature of past environments – is certainly interdisciplinary, arguably post-disciplinary in nature comprising as it does work among physical geographers, geophysicists, geochemists, geologists and biologists among others.

Repeatedly the text refers to the ability of *economics*, in collaboration with science 'to inform policies aimed at slowing and eventually bringing a stop to human-induced climate change' (cf. Stern, 2007: 319). As the principal author is an eminent practising economist, this may be understandable. An orientation towards the economic may provide the sort of factual substance and benchmarks to which business people, politicians and the general public may be able to relate. However, such confidence is misplaced because, as the substance of the report makes clear, issues like the ethics of climate change, the identification of winners and losers in global environmental transition, and behavioural change in terms of adaptation and mitigation, are not always convincingly understood or fully revealed by economic analysis. Human behaviour and its impact on the environment is far more complex, messy and uncertain (Law, 2004), and hence it is beyond the intellectual purview of many of the positivist, rationalist interpretations presented in the *Stern Report*.

In this respect, those with other backgrounds beyond economics have important contributions to make. For instance, there is still some lingering uncertainty over the 'science' of climate change and in particular the trajectories and impacts of further changes in global temperatures (Stern, 2007). Discourse analysis is a well-established technique used in the humanities and in the social sciences outside economics. As (Mode 2) research for the Institute for Public Policy Research (IPPR) in the UK makes clear, what scientists regard as healthy debate translates into the public domain quite differently, sometimes as vagueness and ambiguity. Ereaut and Segnit's (2006: 7–8) inspection of media coverage of climate change in the UK in 2006 reveals a range of positions from claims of outright pessimistic 'alarmism' to more positive 'nihilism and settlerdom' (it'll be alright) and 'small measures' (it'll be alright as long as we do something'). As they note, the public is required to make a vital contribution to reduce the dangerous effects of climate change, but not everyone subscribes to the same message. Their analysis demonstrates that the contested nature of the science hardly delivers a compelling or coherent single message to convince the public of the need to change behaviour to adapt to climate change.

Indeed, for all the alleged explanatory power of science and economics, one of the dismal features of the *Stern Report* is just how little reference is made to tourism. The term 'tourism' is not indexed nor is 'travel' in this 692-page volume, although 'tourism' is mentioned on 19 occasions in the main body of the text (Stern, 2007). Brief reference is made to changing snowfall patterns in the Alps and the bleaching of the Great Barrier Reef in Australia (Stern, 2007: 144). By and large, although some commentators may like to describe it as the 'world's largest industry', popular cliché or not, tourism is nevertheless largely invisible to the text authors. This is despite the contribution tourism – and in particular international tourism – would appear to make to global environmental change. Recent data compiled for the United Nations World Tourism Organisation (UNWTO/UNEP/WMO, 2007) would suggest that, at a best estimate, the tourism industry is responsible for around 5% of global CO_2 emissions. Arguably, this is a conservative estimate because it appears to exclude other Kyoto Greenhouse Gases (GHGs) and their role in radiative forcing (Stern, 2007: 389).

A number of policy solutions are presented in the *Stern Report* from adapting current behaviours in space and time to reflect new environmental conditions, to mitigating the environmental damage by current and future behaviours through such devices as carbon offset schemes and emissions quotas (and trading schemes). The so-called 'Stabilisation Wedge' strategy to which these initiatives are intended to contribute, suggests that a number of smaller, more modest behavioural changes should contribute to reductions in emissions, the sum of which is required to retard global warming (Stern, 2007: 235). Research on tourism influenced by ideas and methods from several diverse intellectual arenas (such as geography, biology, psychology, [environmental] economics and even engineering), suggests that there are inherent difficulties in applying this 'bigger picture' to the tourism industry. For example, Gössling *et al.* (2008) show there are differences in the scope, cost and efficiency of voluntary carbon offsetting schemes that challenge their perceived credibility among consumers. Becken (2004) notes that many tourists recognise the importance of planting trees in carbon offsetting as a form of mitigation, yet there is an important gap to close because they participate in carbon intensive long-haul travel. To overcome the intention-behaviour gap among tourists is one matter, but as Gössling and Peeters (2007) argue, it is an altogether more difficult and pressing task to alter the behaviours of the air travel industry. They identify what they term a strong 'psychology of denial' as well as gaps between the performance of airlines and their communicated discourses, both of which may contribute to public ignorance about the environmental consequences of air travel and a lack of willingness to respond in terms of behavioural changes (see also Hall & Higham, 2005; Gössling & Hall, 2006; Becken & Hay, 2007).

Conclusion

Disciplines are long-standing and well-established organisational features in knowledge production in higher education (Klein, 1996). Disciplinarity continues to be relevant, but more in the sense that it is how the majority of academic managers, governors and regulators understand the intellectual division of labour and allocate resources (Tribe, 2003; Hall *et al.*, 2004; Coles, 2008). In many instances, scholars working on new subjects have aspired to elevate their field of study to disciplinary status as a means of demonstrating the academic legitimacy and standing of their scholarship as well as to potentially gain better access to resources. The debate as to whether tourism has attained such a position remains unresolved and we would advocate that discussion of knowledge production on tourism should move forwards. By this, we do not mean that interdisciplinary studies of tourism or other discipline-based insights represent the only adequate or acceptable alternatives. Interdisciplinarity is not an uncontentious construct and it should not be regarded as an unproblematic, almost default solution to the issue of disciplinarity. Instead, it is time to consider tourism knowledge production beyond the restrictive dogma and parochialism of disciplines, although consideration of the administrative and regulatory confines of tourism may be another matter. Contemporary conditions have created several themes that transgress traditional disciplinary boundaries and interests, and which are only adequately addressed by more reasonable, flexible and inclusive approaches to knowledge production. Post-disciplinary research involving tourism does not mean an intellectual free-for-all; rather it stresses the need to research issues and questions to their logical conclusion rather than some preordained or contrived end point as dictated by disciplinary policing or the *de facto* limits to inter-disciplinary collaboration.

From a managerial perspective, the next five to ten years in higher education worldwide will prove intriguing in terms of situating disciplines and their natural (or otherwise) permeability. The Australian tertiary system is set to join New Zealand, South Africa and the UK by introducing a system of performance measures within institutions that considers the impact of the research generated. What remains to be seen, however, is whether the Australian example will be any more or less sympathetic to endeavours beyond traditional disciplinary boundaries. Both the Australian and UK counterparts have employed disciplinary experts in order to assess submissions by either individuals (New Zealand) or units (UK). As a result, they have solidified the perception that those tasked with oversight in tertiary-based research do not see much beyond the disciplinary boundaries many of us try to transgress and even dismantle. Therefore, as noted several times in the text, while the intellectual boundaries of tourism are capable of being stretched, the administrative boundaries may prove to be far less elastic.

Acknowledgements

We would like to thank Channel View Publications for permission to reproduce, refine and adapt ideas we first presented in *Current Issues in Tourism* (Coles *et al.*, 2006). We would like to thank Stefan Gössling for permission to reproduce the comments that appear in Exhibit 1.

References

Bainbridge, W.S. (2003) The future of the social sciences. *Futures* 35, 633–650.
Becken, S. (2004) How tourists and tourism experts perceive climate change and carbon-offsetting schemes. *Journal of Sustainable Tourism* 12 (4), 332–345.
Becken, S. and Hay, J.E. (2007) *Tourism and Climate Change. Risks and Opportunities.* Clevedon: Channel View Publications.
Beier, J.M. and Arnold, S.L. (2005) Becoming undisciplined: Towards the supradisciplinary study of security. *International Studies Review* 7 (1), 41–62.
Botterill, D. (2001) The epistemology of a set of tourism studies. *Leisure Studies* 20, 199–214.
Butler, R. (1999) Sustainable tourism: A state-of-the-art review. *Tourism Geographies* 1 (1), 7–25.
Butler, R.W. (2004) Geographical research on tourism, recreation and leisure: Origins, eras and directions. *Tourism Geographies* 6 (2), 143–162.
Coles, T.E. (2007a) The implementation of sustainable tourism: A project-based approach. Unpublished conference paper. Presented at Achieving Sustainable Tourism, Helsingborg, September.
Coles, T.E. (2007b) Citizenship and the state: Hidden features in the internationalisation of tourism. In T.E. Coles and C.M. Hall (eds) *International Business*

and Tourism. Global Issues, Contemporary Interactions (pp. 55–69). London: Routledge.

Coles, T.E. (2008) Tourism studies and the governance of higher education in the United Kingdom. *Tourism Geographies* (in press).

Coles, T.E., Duval, D.T. and Hall, C.M. (2004) Tourism, mobility and global communities: New approaches to theorising tourism and tourist spaces. In W. Theobold (ed.) *Global Tourism* (pp. 463–481). Oxford: Butterworth Heinemann.

Coles, T.E., Hall, C.M. and Duval, D.T. (2005) Mobilising tourism: A post-disciplinary critique. *Tourism Recreation Research* 30 (2), 53–63.

Coles, T.E., Hall, C.M. and Duval, D.T. (2006) Tourism and post-disciplinary enquiry. *Current Issues in Tourism* 9 (4&5), 293–319.

Duval, D.T. (2007) Aeropolitics, global aviation networks and the regulation of international visitor flows. In T.E. Coles and C.M. Hall (eds) *International Business and Tourism. Global Issues, Contemporary Interactions* (pp. 91–105). London: Routledge.

Echtner, C. and Jamal, T. (1997) The disciplinary dilemma of tourism studies. *Annals of Tourism Research* 24 (4), 868–883.

Ereaut, G. and Segnit, N. (2006) *Warm Words. How are We Telling the Climate Story and Can We Tell it Better?* London: Institute for Public Policy Research.

Franklin, A. and Crang, M. (2001) The trouble with tourism and travel theory? *Tourist Studies* 1 (1), 5–22.

Gibbons, M., Limoges, C., Nowotny, H., Schwartzmann, C., Scott, P. and Trow, M. (1994) *The New Production of Knowledge: The Dynamics of Science and Research in Contemporary Society.* London: Sage.

Gössling, S., Broderick, J., Upham, P., Ceron, J-P., Dubois, G., Peeters, P. and Strasdas, W. (2007) Voluntary carbon offsetting schemes for aviation: Efficiency, credibility and sustainable tourism. *Journal of Sustainable Tourism* 15 (3), 223–248.

Gössling, S. and Hall, C.M. (eds) (2006) *Tourism and Global Environmental Change.* London: Routledge.

Gössling, S. and Peeters, P. (2007) 'It does not harm the environment!' An analysis of industry discourses on tourism, air travel and the environment. *Journal of Sustainable Tourism* 15 (4), 402–417.

Goodman (2006) Tourism development on the Island of Koh Chang, Thailand: The applications and limitations of a social network theory perspective. Unpublished PhD thesis, University of Exeter.

Goodwin, M. (2004) Recovering the future: A post-disciplinary perspective on geography and political economy. In P. Cloke, M. Goodwin and P. Crang (eds) *Envisioning Human Geography* (pp. 65–80). London: Arnold.

Grabher, G. (2004) Learning in projects, remembering in networks? Communality, sociality, and connectivity in project ecologies. *European Urban and Regional Studies* 11 (2), 103–123.

Graburn, N. and Jafari, J. (1991) Introduction. Tourism social science. *Annals of Tourism Research* 18, 1–11.

Hall, C.M. (2005a) *Tourism: Rethinking the Social Science of Mobility.* Harlow: Pearson Education.

Hall, C.M. (2005b) Time, space, tourism and social physics. *Tourism Recreation Research* 30 (1), 93–98.

Hall, C.M. (2007) Regulating the international trade in tourism services. In T.E. Coles and C.M. Hall (eds) *International Business and Tourism. Global Issues, Contemporary Interactions* (pp. 33–54). London: Routledge.

Hall, C.M. and Higham, J. (eds) (2005) *Tourism, Recreation and Climate Change.* Clevedon: Channel View Publications.

Hall, C.M. and Page, S.J. (2006) *The Geography of Tourism and Recreation* (3rd edn). London: Routledge.

Hall, C.M., Williams, A.M. and Lew, A. (2004) Tourism: Conceptualisations, institutions and issues. In A. Lew, C.M. Hall and A.M. Williams (eds) *Companion to Tourism* (pp. 3–21). Oxford: Blackwell.

Hannam, K., Sheller, M. and Urry, J. (2006) Editorial: Mobilities, immobilities and moorings. *Mobilities* 1 (1), 1–22.

Harrison, S., Massey, D., Richards, K., Magilligan, F.J., Thrift, N. and Bender, B. (2004) Thinking across the divide: Perspectives on the conversations between physical and human geography. *Area* 36 (4), 435–442.

Hay, C. and Marsh, D. (1999) Introduction: Towards a new (international) political economy. *New Political Economy* 4 (1), 5–22.

Hellström, T., Jacob, M. and Wenneberg, S. (2003) The 'discipline' of post-academic science: Reconstructing paradigmatic foundations of a virtual research institute. *Science and Public Policy* 30 (4), 251–260.

Holden, A. (2005) *Tourism Studies and the Social Sciences.* London: Routledge.

Ioannides, D. (2006) Commentary: The economic geography of the tourist industry: Ten years of progress in research and an agenda for the future. *Tourism Geographies* 8 (1), 76–86.

Jamal, T. and Kim, H. (2005) Bridging the interdisciplinary divide: Towards an integrated framework for heritage tourism research. *Tourist Studies* 5 (1), 55–83.

Jessop, B. and Sum, N-L. (2001) Pre-disciplinary and post-disciplinary perspectives. *New Political Economy* 6 (1), 89–101.

Johnston, R.J. (1991) *Geography and Geographers: Anglo-American Human Geography Since 1945* (4th edn). London: Edward Arnold.

Keyfitz, N. (1995) Inter-disciplinary contradictions and the influence of science on policy. *Policy Sciences* 28, 21–38.

Kinzig, A.P. (2001) Bridging disciplinary divides to address environmental and intellectual challenges. *Ecosystems* 4 (8), 709–715.

Klein, J.T. (1996) *Crossing Boundaries: Knowledge, Disciplinarities and Interdisciplinarities.* Charlottesville, VA: University Press of Virginia.

Kreisel, W. (2004) Geography of leisure and tourism in the German-speaking world: Three pillars to progress. *Tourism Geographies* 6 (2), 163–185.

Kuhn, T. (1969) *The Structure of Scientific Revolutions* (2nd edn). Chicago, IL: University of Chicago Press.

Law, J. (2004) *After Method. Mess in Social Science Research.* London: Routledge.

Leiper, N. (1981) Towards a cohesive curriculum in tourism: The case for a distinct discipline. *Annals of Tourism Research* 8, 69–83.

Leiper, N. (2000) An emerging discipline. *Annals of Tourism Research* 27 (3), 805–809.

Markham, A.N. (2005) Disciplining the future: A critical organization of analysis of internet studies. *The Information Society* 21, 257–267.

Massey, D. (1999) Negotiating disciplinary boundaries. *Current Sociology* 47 (4), 5–12.

Michael, E., Gibson, L., Hall, C.M., Lynch, P., Mitchell, R., Morrison, A. and Schreiber, C. (2007) *Micro-clusters and Networks: The Growth of Tourism*. London. Elsevier.

Painter, J. (2003) Towards a post-disciplinary political geography. *Political Geography* 22, 637–639.

Pielke, R.A. (2004) What future for the policy sciences? *Policy Sciences* 37, 209–225.

Pelletier, D. (2004) Sustainability of the policy sciences: Alternatives and strategies. *Policy Sciences* 34, 237–245.

Redman, C.L., Grove, J.M. and Kuby, L.H. (2004) Integrating social science into the long-term ecological research (LTER) network: Social dimensions of ecological change and ecological dimensions of social change. *Ecosystems* 7 (2), 161–171.

Rosamond, B. (2005) Globalization, the ambivalence of European integration and the possibilities for a post-disciplinary EU studies. *Innovation* 18 (1), 23–43.

Roux, D.J., Rogers, K.H., Biggs, H.C., Ashton, P.J. and Sergeant, A. (2006) Bridging the science-management divide: Moving from unidirectional knowledge transfer to knowledge interfacing and sharing. *Ecology and Society* 11 (1), 4. On WWW at www.ecologyandsociety.org/vol11/iss1/art4. Accessed 22.5.06.

Sayer, A. (1999) *Long Live Postdisciplinary Studies! Sociology and the Curse of Disciplinary Parochialism/imperialism*. Lancaster: Department of Sociology, Lancaster University. On WWW at http://www.comp.lancs.ac.uk/sociology/papers/Sayer-Long-Live-Postdisciplinary-Studies.pdf. Accessed 15.4.04.

Semmens, K. (2005) *Seeing Hitler's Germany. Tourism in the Third Reich*. Basingstoke: Palgrave Macmillan.

Sheller, M. and Urry, J. (2006) The new mobilities paradigm. *Environment and Planning A* 38, 207–226.

Skole, D.L. (2004) Geography as a great intellectual melting pot and the preeminent interdisciplinary environmental discipline. *Annals of the Association of American Geographers* 94 (4), 739–743.

Smith, M.J. (1998) *Social Science in Question. Towards a Post-Disciplinary Framework*. London. Sage.

Stern, N. (2007) *The Economics of Climate Change. The Stern Review*. Cambridge: Cambridge University Press (Originally published in PDF form in 2006).

Thomas, C.D., Cameron, A., Green, R.E., Bakkenes, M., Beaumont, L.J., Collingham, Y.C., Erasmus, B.F.N., de Siqueira, M.F., Grainger, A., Hannah, L., Hughes, L., Huntley, B., Van Jaarsveld, A.S., Midgley, G.F., Miles, L., Ortega-Huerta, M.A., Townsend Peterson, A., Phillips, O.L. and Williams, S.E. (2004) Extinction risk from climate change. *Nature* 427, 145–148.

Tourism Research and Marketing (TRAM) (2006) *Medical Tourism: A Global Analysis*. London: ATLAS for Tourism Research and Marketing.

Tribe, J. (1997) The indiscipline of tourism. *Annals of Tourism Research* 24 (3), 638–657.

Tribe, J. (2000) Indisciplined and unsubstantiated. *Annals of Tourism Research* 27 (3), 809–813.

Tribe, J. (2003) The RAE-ification of tourism research in the UK. *International Journal of Tourism Research* 5, 225–234.

Tribe, J. (2004a) Extracts from the ATHE Response to the Consultation Document 'RAE 02/2004: Panel Configuration and Recruitment' for the UK Research Assessment Exercise 2008. *Journal of Hospitality, Leisure, Sport & Tourism Education* 3 (1), 71–74.

Tribe, J. (2004b) Knowing about tourism: Epistemological issues. In J. Phillimore and L. Goodson (eds) *Qualitative Research in Tourism. Ontologies, Epistemologies and Methodologies* (pp. 46–62). London: Routledge.

Tribe, J. (2006) The truth about tourism. *Annals of Tourism Research* 33 (2), 360–381.

Turner, B. II (2002) Response to thrift's 'the future of geography'. *Geoforum* 33 (4), 427–429.

Toulmin, S. (2001) *Return to Reason.* Cambridge, MA: Harvard University Press.

United Nations World Tourism Organization (UNWTO) (2006) TedQual Certified Institutions. On WWW at http://www.world-tourism.org/education/tedqual.htm. Accessed 22.5.06.

United Nations World Tourism Organization, United Nations Environment Programme, World Meteorological Organization (UNWTO/UNEP/WMO) (2007) *Climate Change and Tourism. Responding to Global Challenges. Advanced Summary.* Madrid: UNWTO.

Urry, J. (2000) *Sociology Beyond Societies: Mobilities for the Twenty-First Century.* London: Routledge.

Chapter 6

The End of Tourism? Nomadology and the Mobilities Paradigm

KEVIN HANNAM

Introduction

This chapter situates the study of tourism within a wider social theory context. It takes as its premise not that tourism no longer exists *per se*, but that tourism needs to be understood as a specific process within a wider ontological context, namely that of mobility or mobilities. The chapter begins by outlining the concept of mobility before discussing the strengths and weaknesses of some of the recent Deleuzian-inspired poststructuralist philosophical accounts of mobility (so called nomadology or nomad philosophy). Such theory is not seen as 'an orderly system of tested propositions' as in positivism, but rather as a way of socially constructing reality and asking new questions (Calhoun, 1995: 4–5).

The chapter then goes on to highlight various theoretical aspects of the new mobilities paradigm that have recently been asserted. In particular, it notes how conceptualisations of power have been used in order to develop ontological understandings of the relative mobilities and immobilities in everyday life. It is argued that contemporary mobilities encompass both the large-scale movements of people, objects, capital and information across the world, as well as more local processes of daily transportation, movement through public space and the travel of material things within everyday life (Urry, 2007). The chapter goes on to examine how recent developments in transportation and communications infrastructures, along with new social and cultural practices of mobility (including forms of tourism) have led to a number of new research initiatives. Finally, mobile methodologies are discussed.

Understanding Mobility

In his seminal book, *On the Move*, Tim Cresswell (2006) discusses the concept of mobility. He notes that it is ubiquitous in the pages of academia – as critics find it an exciting but elusive object of study.

Mobility is a fundamental geographical aspect of existence and '... provides a rich terrain from which narratives – and, indeed, ideologies – can be, and have been constructed' (Cresswell, 2006: 1). Activities like walking, moving home, going on holiday, immigrating, travelling and exploring are, in one way or the other, different forms of mobility. Yet, despite a number of meanings circulating widely in the modern Western world – mobility as progress, as freedom, as opportunity – 'mobility' itself, what it means, has been relatively unspecified.

Mobility has been expressed in contrast to any kind of fixity: 'It is a kind of blank space that stands as an alternative to place, boundedness, foundation and stability' (Cresswell, 2006: 2). The simplest understanding of mobility is that it involves a kind of displacement – the act of moving between locations. 'Movement is the general fact of displacement before the type, strategies, and social implications of that movement are considered' (Cresswell, 2006: 3). The displacement of an object between locations consumes time and traverses space. So, movement is made up of time and space; more clearly it is the 'spatialization of time and temporalization of space'. Time and space both provide the context for movement and are an outcome of movement. But crucially, the movements (of people and of other things) are always meaningful – both products and producers of power. Mobility, rather than movement, then, is considered by Cresswell (2006) as a dynamic equivalent of 'place'. Indeed, a 'place' is not as neutral as that of a 'location'. Place – imbued with various meanings and power – is always experienced and so is mobility: 'Mobility is just as spatial – as geographical – and just as central to the human experience of the world, as place' (Cresswell, 2006: 3).

In this regard, mobility could be captured in three relational moments (Cresswell, 2006). Firstly, it is about mobility as a potentially observable, measurable fact – an empirical reality that is evident in transport planning or in migration theory. Here, mobility signifies pure motion and is at its most abstract state. This abstract concept of mobility often jumped scale spatially. For example, with William Harvey's discovery of the body's circulation system: health came to be connected with 'circulation'. This notion of circulation then appeared in the new context of urban planning. Words such as 'artery' and 'vein' became familiar in the discourses of the new urbanists.

Secondly, mobility is also conveyed through various modes of representation – film, photography, literature, philosophy and law, etc. These representations of mobility produce meanings that are predominantly ideological. Here, mobility 'becomes synonymous with freedom, with transgression, with creativity, with life itself' (Cresswell, 2006: 3).

The third moment of mobility is that mobility which is practiced, is experienced, and is embodied. Human mobility is, as such, a deeply embodied experience. And, direct experience of human mobility is connected to the representational meanings of mobility. Similarly, representations of mobility are based on the ways mobility is embodied and practiced. It is thus argued that we need to read the moments of mobility as an integral process. As Cresswell (2006: 4) notes: 'To understand mobility without recourse to representation on the one hand or the material corporeality on the other is ... to miss the point'.

As Cresswell (2006) goes on to discuss, the transformation of the senses of mobility in the modern Western society can also be traced out historically. In European feudal society, mobility was a luxury item. There was a persistent mobility involved in working on the land, but the scale of mobility was restricted with the exception of pilgrimages, warfare, etc. The rise of mercantile capitalism in early modern Europe facilitated mobility in relation to trade and, this, eventually, loosened the groundedness of feudal society. The new types of mobility that developed required, in turn, new forms of social surveillance and control. The establishment of European nationstates brought larger markets for goods and waged labour. Labour became mobile on a national scale, and thus, feudal power to control mobility became diminished. With the transformation of mobility at both an ideological and a more mundane level, people began to inhabit more of the landscapes of Europe. Mobility became a right: a right to move at will within the bounds of the nationstate, along with the advent of another modern mobile figure, namely *the tourist.*

Mobility, then, as a concept, has circulated metaphorically. Various metaphors of mobility include the nomad, the vagabond, the tourist, the *au pair*, the ship and the hotel. And these fill contemporary discourses of social and spatial mobility (Morris, 1988; Gilroy, 1993; Clifford, 1997; Jokinen & Veijola, 1997; Bauman, 2000). The anthropologist James Clifford (1997), for example, has argued that the contemporary world is characterised by a new mobile world of nomads and travellers travelling hopefully, making connections and experiencing speed. He utilises the metaphor of the hotel lobby, contra the metaphor of home and stasis, with the former constructing a stage that is open to movement and unexpected encounters (see, of course, MacCannell, 1999). Thus, the apparent fixities of older forms of philosophy have come under question through the various metaphors of mobility (Cresswell, 2001).

Nomadology

At an epistemological level, theorisations of mobility appear to have a transgressive character where sedentarist metaphysics have been arguably replaced by a nomadic metaphysics. In their philosophical writings, Deleuze and Guattari (1988: 52) for example, use the figure of the nomad as a motif of smooth and mobile space, of the deterritorialisation of societies: 'The nomad has no point, paths or land ... If the nomad can be called the Deterritorialized *par excellence*, it is precisely because there is no reterritorialization *afterwards* as with the migrant'. Cresswell (2006: 49) explains that 'While the migrant goes from place to place, moving with a resting place in mind, the nomad uses points and locations to define paths. ... The nomad is never reterritorialized, unlike the migrant who slips back into the ordered space of arrival'. Urry (2000: 240) explains further that: 'Nomadism is associated with the notion that academic and political writing can itself be conceived of as a journey. In order to theorise one leaves home and travels. There is no "home" or fixed point from which the theorist departs and then returns. The theorist is seen as travelling hopefully, neither being at home or away'. It is towards this mobile thought and philosophy that we now turn.

Much of Western philosophy has been concerned with a search for order in the world, whether this is with social order or spatial order: patterns and processes, models and theories of how things work are propounded. However, rather against the grain, there has always been another movement within Western philosophy that sought not to understand the ordering of life, but its fundamental disorder and complexity. This latter movement develops a Nietzschean critique of both modern Western society and scientific reason. This reaches its climax in the work of the French poststructuralist philosophers Gilles Deleuze and Michel Foucault, who developed a critique of the production of knowledge, arguing that there is no objective truth or order to be found, rather all knowledge is bound up with relations of power: 'There is no power-relation without the correlative constitution of a field of knowledge, nor any knowledge that does not presuppose and constitute at the same time power-relations' (Foucault, 1977: 27). Foucault's critique of modernity argued that the emergence of modern society is not a process of liberation, but merely the installation of new disciplinary power-knowledge regimes (see Cheong & Miller [2000] in a tourism context).

Deleuze's nomadological critique meanwhile developed a similar strategy. As D'Andrea (2006: 107) writes:

Nomadology refers to a style of critical thinking that seeks to expose and overcome the sedentary logic of the state, science and civilization. ... It denounces a categorical binary of civilization whereby the dweller is positively assessed over the wanderer, seen as menace, distortion and problem. ... The privilege of fixity over mobility – of roots over routes – hinges on the issue of conventional modes of subjectivity: a dialectic of identification/alterity sustains a model of identity that constrains the self within rigid and exclusionary boundaries.

In *A Thousand Plateaus*, Deleuze and his co-author Felix Guattari (1988) thus 'counterpose the metaphor of the tree and its roots – hierarchical, structured, and authoritarian, implying a social world that is necessarily stratified – to that of the rhizome – whose roots ramify laterally, escaping confinement in any specific territory, an anarchic and uncontainable multiplicity' (Callinicos, 2007: 333). Deleuze and Guattari (1988: 7) argue that 'a rhizome ceaselessly establishes connections between semiotic chains, organizations of power, and circumstances relevant to the arts, sciences and social struggles'. Rhizomic thinking, then, can be likened to wandering around Amsterdam's canals and contrasts with the structured, dualistic thinking of much Western philosophy (Shurmer-Smith & Hannam, 1994). Such nomadological thinking thus asks us to rethink social identities, for example, as 'always mobile and processual, partly self-construction, partly categorization by others, partly a condition, a status, a label, a weapon, a shield, a fund of memories, etc. It is a creolized aggregate composed through bricolage' (Malkki, 1992: 37).

Furthermore, Deleuze and Guattari argue that we live in basically two types of space-time. Striated space is over-ordered and segmented, like a map it gives us our exact bearings and orientation. Nomad or smooth space holds nonsegmentary and directionless variation. However, 'the simple opposition "smooth-striated" gives rise to far more difficult complications, alternations and superpositions ... because the differences are not objective: it is possible to live striated on the deserts, steppes, or seas; it is possible to live smooth even in the cities, to be an urban nomad' (Deleuze & Guattari, 1988: 481–482).

Such flows of capital, people and materials characterise the global hypermobility of the contemporary world and D'Andrea (2006: 98) puts forward 'a dialogue between the anthropology of nomadism and [the] philosophy of nomadology as conceptual grounds for addressing the impact of hypermobility on identity and subjectivity forms'. The problem with this dialogue, however, is the underlying romanticisation of the figure of the nomad. As Cresswell (2006: 54) argues: '... the use of the nomad is often nothing more than a form of imaginative neo-colonialism'. The epistemological premise of nomadology may be a very worthy critique of Western society and its rational abstract science, yet it is only in the ontological understandings of mobilities that we can move forward.

Hence, rather than viewing society as being *wholly* organised according to 'globally integrated networks' (GINs), that is, enduring structures (such as transnational corporations) with predictable connections that nullify time-space constraints, Urry (2003: 101) posits the ontological notion of 'global fluids' – highly mobile and viscous formations whose shapes are uneven, contingent and unpredictable and which 'create over time their own context of action'. However, Hannam *et al.* (2006) acknowledge that it is only in the analysis of the combination of mobilities, immobilities and moorings (the smooth and the striated) that produces contemporary global complexity (of which tourism is a part) that we can develop an adequate ontological account of human behaviour.

The Mobilities Paradigm

Tourism is increasingly viewed not as an ephemeral aspect of social life that is practised outside normal, everyday life. Rather it is seen as integral to wider processes of economic and political development and even constitutive of everyday life (Franklin, 2003; Edensor, 2007). Indeed, Franklin and Crang (2001: 3) point out that, 'tourism has broken away from its beginnings as a relatively minor and ephemeral ritual of modern national life to become a significant modality through which transnational modern life is organised'. Hence, perhaps it is not so much the end of tourism as much as the beginning of our understanding of contemporary mobilities that is the point being made.

Sheller and Urry (2006: 1) go as far as to argue that: 'It seems that a new paradigm is being formed within the social sciences, the "new mobilities" paradigm'. Broadly, they argue that the concept of mobilities is concerned with mapping both the large-scale movements of people, objects, capital and information across the world, as well as the more local processes of daily transportation, movement through public space and the travel of material things within everyday life. Indeed, Urry (2007: 18) goes on to argue that:

> thinking through a mobilities 'lens' provides a distinctive social science ... a mobilities paradigm is not just substantively different,

in that it remedies the neglect and omissions of various movements of people, ideas and so on. But it is transformative of social science, authorizing an alternative theoretical and methodological land-scape ... this paradigm brings to the fore theories, methods and exemplars of research that have been mostly subterranean, out of sight.

Thus, from a post-disciplinary mobilities perspective the notion of just tourism *per se* is now perhaps arguably rather obsolete:

Mobilities of people and objects, airplanes and suitcases, plants and animals, images and brands, data systems and satellites, all go into "doing" tourism. Tourism is also concerned with the relational mobilizations of memories and performances, gendered and racia-lized bodies, emotions and atmospheres. (Sheller & Urry, 2004: 1)

Again, tourism and more importantly travel is increasingly seen as a process that has become integral to social life. It is not just about the purchase of second homes and the interconnections between tourism and migration. Rather, every thing seems to be in perpetual movement throughout the world. *Most* people *travel* – academics, terrorists, tourists, military people, business people, homeless people, celebrities, migrants, refugees, backpackers, commuters, students, friends – filling the world's planes, trains, ships, buses, cars and streets. In the contemporary world, all sorts of political, technological, financial and transportational changes have been critical in significantly lowering the mobility barriers for many. Tourism, leisure, transport, business, travel, migration and communication are thus all blurred and need to be analysed together in their fluid interdependence rather than discretely (Sheller & Urry, 2006; Hannam *et al.*, 2006).

On the one hand, moving between places physically or virtually can be a source of status and power for some tourists such as backpackers (see Richards & Wilson, 2004; Hannam & Ateljevic, 2007). On the other hand, where mobilities are coerced it can generate deprivation as with many migrants and refugees around the world (see Indra, 1998; Kofman, 2002) or forced resettlement schemes for tribal populations in the face of tourism mobilities (see Hannam, 2005). Such mobilities and immobilities become particularly apparent in the so-called tourism 'contact zones' at the interstices of different countries where notions of citizenship can become highly contested and where multiple identities become increa-singly fluid (see Bianchi, 2000; Sparke, 2006). Analysing contemporary mobilities thus involves examining many consequences for different peoples and different places located in the fast and slow lanes of societies (Sheller & Urry, 2006; Hannam *et al.*, 2006).

A Mobilities Agenda for Tourism

We can sketch out a rough agenda for mobilities research as we attempt to continue to view tourism as part of a wider mobility system. For example, we need to ask questions of how and *when* tourists become migrants (O'Reilly, 2003). The relations between migration, return migration, transnationalism and tourism need to be further researched. And, of course, the ways in which physical movement pertains to upward and downward social mobility are also central here. In such a context we need to examine how tourists negotiate their identities and their notions of citizenship in the so-called contact zones mentioned above. Moreover, it is perhaps too obvious to perceive tourists as being continually on the move, as being hypermobile when in fact being a tourist sometimes has more to do with being in places, of being relatively immobile and in the relative slow lane, through choice or finance. Places, technologies and 'gates' enhance the mobilities of some, while reinforcing the immobilities (or demobilisation) of others. And such (im)mobilities are also, of course, heavily gendered and age-specific.

At an ontological level, such studies of tourism within the broader context of global human mobilities also need to be brought together with more 'local' concerns about everyday transportation, material cultures and spatial relations, as well as with more 'technological' concerns about mobile information and communication technologies and emerging infrastructures of security and surveillance. Social life seems full of multiple and extended connections often across long distances, but these are organised through certain nodes. Mobilities entail distinct social spaces that orchestrate new forms of social life around such nodes, for example, stations, hotels, motorways, resorts, airports, leisure complexes, cosmopolitan cities, beaches, galleries, roadside parks and so on. Or connections might be enacted through less privileged spaces, on the street-corners, subway stations, buses, public plazas and back alleys. Also, *contra* much transport research, the time spent traveling is not dead time that people always seek to minimise. While the transport literature tends to distinguish travel from activities, the emerging mobilities paradigm posits that activities occur while on the move, that being on the move can involve sets of 'occasioned' activities (Lyons & Urry, 2005). Tourism research within the emerging mobilities paradigm would thus examine the embodied nature and experience of the different modes of travel that tourists undertake, seeing these modes in part as forms of material and sociable dwelling-in-motion, places of and for various activities (see Jokinen & Veijola, 1994; Crouch, 2000; Johnston, 2001; Featherstone *et al.*, 2004). These 'activities' can include specific forms of talk, work or information-gathering, but may involve simply being connected, maintaining a moving presence with others that holds the potential for many different convergences or divergences of physical presence. Not only does a mobilities perspective lead us to discard our usual notions of spatiality and scale, but it also undermines existing linear assumptions about temporality and timing, which often assume that actors are able to do only one thing at a time, and that events follow each other in a linear order (Hannam *et al.*, 2006).

Furthermore, a clear distinction is often drawn between places and those travelling to such places. Places have frequently been seen as pushing or pulling people to visit. Places are often presumed to be relatively fixed, given and separate from those visiting. Instead, we recognise that the notion of place, although deceptively simple, needs to be problematised (Shurmer-Smith & Hannam, 1994; Cresswell, 2004). The emerging mobilities paradigm thus argues against the ontology of distinct 'places' and 'people'. Rather, there is a complex relationality of places and persons connected through both performances (see Edensor, 1998; Sheller & Urry, 2004) and performativities (Knox, 2001). Crucial to the recognition of the materialities of mobilities is the recentring of the corporeal body as an affective vehicle through which we sense place and movement, and construct emotional geographies (Crouch, 2000; Bondi *et al.*, 2005). Imaginative travel, for example, involves experiencing or anticipating in one's imagination the 'atmosphere of place'. Atmosphere is neither reducible to the material infrastructures nor to the discourses of representation. There is a complex sensuous relationality between the means of travel and the traveller (Rodaway, 1994). Hence, we arguably need better maps of the sensuous, emotional geographies of tourism in a mobile context (Hannam *et al.*, 2006).

Mobile Methodologies

Moving on from our philosophical and conceptual discussion of mobilities, we now turn briefly to a discussion of mobile methodologies. If we are to adequately understand the ontology of contemporary mobilities and if a mobilities *paradigm* has truly emerged, then we also need to have mobile methodologies in order to 'capture' the fluid (dis)order and (dis)embeddedness of contemporary (de)territorialised social life. We argue that mobile ethnographies offer the best way of doing this research, but mobile ethnographies need to be distinguished from the conventional highly localised ethnographies (Appadurai, 1996; Marcus, 1998). Methods of data collection need to become much more 'flexible, informal and context dependent, partly mimicking mobile subjects being studied in their own suppleness' (D'Andrea, 2006: 113). By expanding his or her own viewpoints, the ethnographer 'will then perceive and experience the trembling of slowly moving entities running at high-speed through blurred surroundings' (D'Andrea, 2006: 114). Such research is thus 'designed around chains, paths, threads, conjunctions or juxtapositions of location in which the ethnographer establishes some form of literal, physical presence with an explicit logic of association or connection among sites that in fact defines the argument of ethnography' (Marcus, 1998: 90).

D'Andrea (2006: 114) asserts that such research:

> ... must consider political economies and socio-cultural processes that envelop hypermobile phenomena. At an economic level, it is necessary to ask, what is the role of material contexts ... At a cultural level, it must be asked: what is the nature of motivations and meanings implied in subjects engaged with hypermobile formations, in given locales and circuits; how specific sites of experience and meaning sustain their everyday life; and, how these sites host ritual practices that express and constitute forms of subjectivity, intimacy and sociability imbricated with hypermobility.

Appadurai (1996) thus proposes a 'macro-ethnography of translocal sites'. D'Andrea (2006: 115) develops this further and argues that mobile ethnographies can be developed at three levels. Firstly, there can be ethnographies of mobile subjectivities, lifestyles and identities, where at each specific geographical site the researcher 'must identify and translate subscenes, practices and imaginaries that constitute hypermobile formations locally'. Secondly, research needs to analyse the socioeconomic context of mobile scenes, subjects and communities: 'It is necessary to understand how economies (e.g. tourism, leisure, advertising), mainstream/sedentary moralities and state surveillance affect trajectories and strategies of mobile subjects and deterritorialized communities' (D'Andrea, 2006). And, thirdly, translocal ethnographies at multiple sites allow us to identify the fluid and connective nature of hypermobile formations across different spaces. Here, the researcher can 'identify which and how translocal flows, circuits or webs sustain hypermobile subjects and communities' (D'Andrea, 2006). Such research methods 'on the move' will provide a new critical window on the mobilities, immobilities and moorings of contemporary social life (Urry, 2007).

Conclusions

This chapter has situated the study of tourism within a wider social theory context. It took as its premise not that tourism no longer exists per se, but that tourism needs to be understood as a specific process within a wider ontological context, namely that of mobility or mobilities. As discussed, the strengths of nomadology is its critique of Western science at an epistemological level. However, its weakness is its ontological romanticisation of the figure of the nomad. The ontology of mobilities seeks to avoid this through its analysis of the complexity of contemporary global society. Finally, this chapter has also sought to demonstrate how mobile methodologies may help break the methodological stasis in contemporary research.

References

Appadurai, A. (1996) *Modernity at Large: Cultural Dimensions of Globalization*. Minneapolis, MN: University of Minnesota Press.

Bauman, Z. (2000) *Liquid Modernity*. Cambridge: Polity.

Bianchi, R. (2000) Migrant tourist workers: Exploring the contact zones of post-industrial tourism. *Current Issues in Tourism* 3 (2), 107–137.

Bondi, L., Smith, M. and Davidson, J. (eds) (2005) *Emotional Geographies*. London: Ashgate.

Calhoun, C. (1995) *Critical Social Theory*. Oxford: Blackwell.

Callinicos, A. (2007) *Social Theory: A Historical Introduction*. Cambridge: Polity.

Cheong, S-M. and Miller, P. (2000) Power and tourism: A Foucauldian observation. *Annals of Tourism Research* 27 (2), 371–390.

Clifford, J. (1997) *Routes: Travel and Translation in the Late Twentieth Century*. London: Harvard University Press.

Cresswell, T. (ed.) (2001) *Mobilities*. Special Issue of *New Formations* 43 (Spring).

Cresswell, T. (2004) *Place: A Short Introduction*. Oxford: Blackwell.

Cresswell, T. (2006) *On the Move: Mobility in the Modern Western World*. London: Routledge.

Crouch, D. (2000) Places around us: Embodied lay geographies in leisure and tourism. *Leisure Studies* 19, 63–76.

D'Andrea, A. (2006) Neo-nomadism: A theory of post-identitarian mobility in the global age. *Mobilities* 1 (1), 95–120.

Deleuze, G. and Guattari, F. (1988) *A Thousand Plateaus*. London: The Athlone Press.

Edensor, T. (1998) *Tourists at the Taj: Performance and Meaning at a Symbolic Site*. London: Routledge.

Edensor, T. (2007) Mundane mobilities, performances and spaces of tourism. *Social & Cultural Geography* 8 (2), 199–215.

Featherstone, M., Thrift, N. and Urry, J. (eds) (2004) Cultures of automobility (Special issue). *Theory, Culture and Society* 21, 1–284.

Foucault, M. (1977) *Discipline and Punish*. London: Allen Lane.

Franklin, A. (2003) *Tourism: An Introduction*. London: Sage.

Franklin, A. and Crang, M. (2001) The trouble with tourism and travel theory? *Tourist Studies* 1 (1), 5–22.

Gilroy, P. (1993) *The Black Atlantic: Modernity and Double Consciousness*. London: Verso.

Hannam, K. (2005) Tourism management issues in India's National Parks. *Current Issues in Tourism* 8 (2/3), 165–180.

Hannam, K. and Ateljevic, I. (eds) (2007) *Backpacker Tourism*. Clevedon: Channel View.

Hannam, K., Sheller, M. and Urry, J. (2006) Editorial: Mobilities, immobilities and moorings. *Mobilities* 1 (1), 1–22.

Indra, D. (ed.) (1998) *Engendering Forced Migration*. Oxford: Berghahn.

Johnston, L. (2001) (Other) bodies and tourism studies. *Annals of Tourism Research* 28 (1), 180–201.

Jokinen, E. and Veijola, S. (1994) The body in tourism. *Theory, Culture & Society* 11 (3), 125–151.

Jokinen, E. and Veijola, S. (1997) The disoriented tourist: The figuration of the tourist in contemporary cultural critique. In C. Rojek and J. Urry (eds) *Touring Cultures* (pp. 23–51). London: Routledge.

Knox, D. (2001) Doing the Doric: The institutionalization of regional language and culture in north-east Scotland. *Social & Cultural Geography* 2 (3), 315–331.

Kofman, E. (2002) Contemporary European migrations, civic stratification and citizenship. *Political Geography* 21, 1035–1054.

Lyons, G. and Urry, J. (2005) Travel time use in the information age. *Transport Research A: Policy and Practice* 39 (2–3), 257–276.

MacCannell, D. (1999) *The Tourist: A New Theory of the Leisure Class*. Berkeley, CA: University of California Press.

Malkki, L. (1992) National Geographic: The rooting of peoples and the territorialization of national identity among scholars and refugees. *Cultural Anthropology* 7 (1), 24–44.

Marcus, G. (1998) *Anthropology Through Thick and Thin*. Princeton, NJ: Princeton University Press.

Morris, M. (1988) At Henry Parkes motel. *Cultural Studies* 2, 1–47.

O'Reilly, K. (2003) When is a tourist? *Tourist Studies* 3 (3), 301–317.

Richards, G. and Wilson, J. (eds) (2004) *The Global Nomad: Backpacker Travel in Theory and Practice*. Clevedon: Channel View Publications.

Rodaway, P. (1994) *Sensuous Geographies: Body, Sense and Place*. London: Routledge.

Sheller, M. and Urry, J. (eds) (2004) *Tourism Mobilities: Places to Play, Places in Play*. London: Routledge.

Sheller, M. and Urry, J. (2006) The new mobilities paradigm. *Environment and Planning A* 38 (2), 207–226.

Shurmer-Smith, P. and Hannam, K. (1994) *World's of Desire, Realm's of Power: A Cultural Geography*. London: Edward Arnold.

Sparke, M. (2006) A neoliberal nexus: Economy, security and the biopolitics of citizenship on the border. *Political Geography* 25, 151–180.

Urry, J. (2000) *Sociology Beyond Societies: Mobilities for the Twenty-first Century.* London: Routledge.

Urry, J. (2003) *Global Complexity.* Cambridge: Polity.

Urry, J. (2007) *Mobilities.* Cambridge: Polity.

Part 3

Beauty: Well-being, Aesthetics and Art

Chapter 7

Tourism and Restoration

BALVINDER KAUR KLER

Introduction

The theoretical underpinnings of tourism research are cross-disciplinary and ever evolving. A convincing theoretical account of tourists' preferences for destination types and motivations for travel is of central importance, both to explain existing trends in tourist behaviour and to predict those of the future. Two such trends, evident from statistics and requiring explanation, are a significant preference for the natural environment as travel destination and a desire for relaxation as the motivation for that travel. It is the contention here that the environmental psychology concept of *restoration*, 'the process of renewing or recovering physical, psychological and social capabilities that have become depleted in meeting ordinary adaptational demands' (Hartig & Staats, 2005) may be useful to explain some of tourists' preference for natural environments and relaxation in a way that existing motivational theories do not. This chapter will discuss Kaplan's (1995) attention restoration theory (ART) and the theory of restorative environments to consider how they can explain known tourist behaviour. These theories are compared to existing accounts of tourist motivation and the chapter ends with a discussion of the implications of restoration for tourism practice.

Tourism to natural areas or nature-based tourism is an important part of the world tourism industry (Lindberg *et al.*, 1998) and it is travel that primarily involves direct enjoyment of undisturbed natural environments (Weiler & Davis, 1993). Natural environments are those areas that on the whole tend to retain their natural characteristics and are not modified to any large extent by human interference with the natural landscape or processes (Newsome *et al.*, 2002: 3). Whilst destinations for nature-based tourism vary considerably, national parks and conservation reserves constitute the largest components (Eagles, 1999). The World Tourism Organisation (WTO) suggests that nature-based tourism is worth US$20 billion a year (WTO, 1998). Nature-based tourism has increased from approximately 2% in the late 1980s to about 20% of all leisure travel in the late 1990s (Newsome *et al.*, 2002). Tourism to natural areas includes coastal and marine tourism (beaches, islands, estuarine areas, coral reefs and oceans, including boating and diving); alpine tourism (visits to mountains and mountain resorts, including hiking and snow skiing); inland, natural area tourism or noncoastal, and nonalpine dispersed tourism directed toward enjoying wildlife or other natural features (Newsome *et al.*, 2002). Relaxation has also been identified as the primary motivation for travel in past tourism research (Gray, 1970; Dann, 1977; Crompton, 1979; Iso-Ahola, 1982; Pearce, 1988). Recreational travel has been theorised as an escape from routine responsibilities and stress (Mannell & Iso-Ahola, 1987) and the motivational dimensions of escape/ relax have been confirmed as important travel motivation factors within the travel career pattern approach (Pearce, 2005).

Can existing theories of tourist motivation convincingly explain this preference for nature and relaxation? Pearce (1993) claims that an ideal theory of tourist motivation would do the following: it would function as a true theory, be easy to communicate, account for both intrinsic and extrinsic motivations, be methodologically accessible, adopt a multi-motive approach, appeal to different users and adopt a dynamic approach. The latter three criteria imply that an ideal theory of tourist motivation would be general, that is its explanations and predictions should apply to all tourists and all tourism researchers, now and in the future. Though a daunting task, a number of such general theories have been developed though none have achieved universal acceptance. These theories include Gray's (1970) sunlust and wanderlust; Plog's (1973) model on allocentrics and psychocentrics; Dann's (1977) anomie and ego-enhancement; Crompton's (1979) push and pull factors; Iso-Ahola's (1982) optimal arousal; and Pearce's (1988) travel career ladder. Aside from debate about their relative correctness, there is another problem: these theories achieve generality at the expense of describing practical specifics for particular tourist behaviours (Schiffman & Kanuk, 1997); none have deeply considered the role of nature. For example, the push-pull theory's (Dann, 1981) presumed claim that the decision to travel to nature comes from needs within an individual (push) and perceived properties of the natural environment (pull) may well be true, but what are those specific push and pull factors? Some particular push and pull factors for tourists are known: escape from the mundane, exploration and evaluation of self, relaxation, prestige, regression to childhood, bonding with family and friends, social interaction (Crompton, 1979), but these are acknowledged as limited (Pearce, 1993) and none are specifically oriented towards nature. 'Research into why individuals travel has been hampered by the lack of a universally agreed upon conceptualisation of the tourist motivation construct' (Pearce, 1993: 114). Knowing the mechanisms at work within an individual and those properties of natural environments that motivate a preference for nature would be of considerable importance to tour operators and marketing executives. These theories also do not meet Pearce's (1993) requirement of methodological accessibility – that is, they do not provide practical methods for measuring motivation and any mediating motivational constructs. As a consequence, their empirical validation is unclear.

The motivational construct considered here is that of *restoration* because it may be capable of addressing some of the shortcomings of existing tourist motivation theories in explaining the preference for nature and relaxation. The term restoration is occasionally used within tourism theory (e.g. Leiper, 1995), but is never clearly defined, never related to nature and never fully theorised or tested. In contrast, Kaplan's (1995) ART describes how the need for psychological restoration motivates individuals to seek contact with the natural environment and does so in terms of specific and clearly measurable properties of both the individual and the environment itself. Although it is claimed here that ART can help explain tourism statistics and provide a worthwhile cross-disciplinary addition to the expanding canon of tourist motivation theory, this discussion does not claim that all of nature tourism is motivated by restoration. The explanatory limits of restoration will have to be determined and any shortcomings addressed with other theories, but what should make us think that restoration is an aspect of tourist motivation at all? The essential argument is as follows: environmental psychologists have found the same preference for nature as that found in tourism and have explained it with theories that predict the kind of relaxation also known to motivate tourists. These theories are specific, methodologically accessible and have been empirically verified. Is it possible that there is a shared explanatory mechanism at work in both cases and that tourism theory could benefit from it?

The Preference for Natural Environments and Relaxation

Environmental psychology is 'the study of transactions between individuals and their physical settings ... (whereby) individuals change the environment and their behaviour and experiences are changed by the environment' (Gifford, 2002: 1). Although tourism hinges on the environment and much tourist experience could be seen as a transaction with it, tourism scholars (with the exception of Holden [2005]) have largely neglected findings and theory from this field. However, a preference for nature and relaxation evident in tourism statistics has also displayed itself strongly in studies conducted by environmental psychologists.

In the seminal book by Kaplan and Kaplan (1989) *The Experience of Nature*, results of a series of experiments found that people preferred natural over urban environments and that nature was restorative. This book offered the first research-based analysis of the vital psychological role that nature plays in fostering tranquillity and wellbeing for humans.

This trend continued within the field of environmental psychology where evidence indicates that viewing natural scenes improves mental wellbeing including mental alertness, attention and better cognitive performance (Hartig *et al.*, 1991, 1996; Cimprich, 1993, 2003; Tennessen & Cimprich, 1995). In their article, Mace *et al.* (1999) present over 100 studies that have found convincing evidence that natural environments contribute to relaxation. For example, Tennessen and Cimprich (1995) found that compared to university dormitory residents with less natural views from their windows, those with more natural views scored better on tests of directed attention and rated their attentional functioning as more effective. Notably, preference is not limited to the visual aspect of a given environment, it includes preference 'for a given environment as a place in which to carry out particular behaviours and fulfil particular roles' (Hartig & Staats, 2005: 282).

In subsequent experiments on environmental preference, Hartig *et al.* (2003) compared walking in a nature reserve versus walking in an urban surrounding and found that walking in the nature reserve fostered blood pressure change indicating stress reduction. Moreover, positive affect increased and anger decreased in the nature reserve by the end of the walk whereas the opposite pattern emerged in the urban environment. Other experiments also found participants preferred a one-hour walk through a forest as opposed to a walk through the city centre with a similar duration (Staats & Hartig, 2004; Hartig & Staats, 2005). In studies on gardening satisfactions and wilderness experience benefits, self-reports of sustained attention, feelings of peacefulness and opportunities for reflection appear to be the salient aspects of contact with nature (Kaplan & Talbot, 1983; Talbot & Kaplan, 1986; Kaplan & Kaplan, 1989). In itself, this preference for nature and relaxation is interesting, but only reinforces the preference found in tourism statistics. However, Kaplan (1995) goes beyond bare facts to explain the preference with ART.

Attention Restoration Theory

ART is situated within the *adaptive* paradigm in environmental psychology where human behaviour, perceptions and preferences are seen as having evolved to facilitate functioning and survival in an uncertain information environment (Saegert & Winkel, 1990). 'Some might dismiss people's desire for contact with nature as the result of an anti-urban bias in conjunction with a romantic view of nature. However, research in environmental psychology suggests that people's desire for contact with nature serves an important adaptive function, namely psychological restoration' (Van den Berg *et al.*, 2007: 79).

Indeed, Kaplan and Kaplan's (1989: 10) basic assumption for explaining a preference for nature was that environmental preferences are intimately tied to basic human concerns – they are an expression of underlying human needs and how the natural environment is capable of fulfilling them:

> Preference can be expected to be greater for settings in which an organism is likely to thrive and diminished for those in which it may be harmed or rendered ineffective. Thus humans, like other animals are far more likely to prefer a setting in which they can function effectively. Aesthetic reactions thus reflect neither a casual nor a trivial aspect of the human makeup. Rather, they appear to constitute a guide to human behaviour that is both ancient and far-reaching. Underlying such reactions is an assessment of the environment in terms of its compatibility with human needs and purposes. Thus aesthetic reaction is an indication of an environment where effective human function is more likely to occur.

This affinity for nature has been studied through the concept of environmental preference. The specific aspect of human information processing that the Kaplans associate with a preference for natural settings is that of selective *attention*, the crucial psychological mechanism that directs mental resources toward certain objects and properties of our environment to the exclusion of others. It is, in other words, our ability to focus and to concentrate. Following the philosopher William James (1892), a crucial distinction is made between two modes of processing: involuntary and voluntary (or directed) attention. When attention is in involuntary mode it is effortlessly drawn to inherently interesting stimuli, a state James called *fascination*. However, attention directed towards stimuli one cannot easily understand or has no real interest in requires effort and the continual use of directed attention can lead to the fatigue of vital mental faculties that manifests itself in a number of ways. In discussing the importance of directed attention, Kaplan (1995) highlights that mental fatigue can affect the capacity to solve problems and to make plans; impair perception leading to errors in performance; lead to irritability and avoidance of social interaction. 'Directed attention is, thus, a key ingredient in human effectiveness. The fatigue of directed attention is similarly a key ingredient in ineffectiveness and human error' (Kaplan, 1995: 172). Therefore, when attention becomes fatigued, it requires a period of *restoration* where the demand for directed attention is eliminated and effortless involuntary attention is allowed to operate. The outcome of restoration is an increased ability to concentrate, improved mood and sense of wellbeing and a feeling of relaxation (Kaplan, 1995).

The need for restoration arises from meeting everyday adaptational demands, and the preference for the natural environment arises due to its ability to meet the need for restoration. Using the concept of directed attention fatigue, Kaplan and Kaplan explain people's preference for nature as driven by the need for restoration, and discussed next, those properties of the natural environment that allow it to provide restoration. For this explanation of preference to be true, it is necessary that the natural environment actually does restore people and several studies have been conducted that strongly support this (Hartig *et al.*, 1991, 1996, 2003; Herzog *et al.*, 1997, 2003; Kaplan, 1995; Kaplan & Talbot, 1983; Laumann *et al.*, 2001; Talbot & Kaplan, 1986). These studies directly measured the regeneration of attentional capacity or the recovery of mental fatigue in natural environments.

For example, Hartig *et al.* (1991) presented an attentionally demanding proofreading task to three sets of subjects: wilderness vacationers, nonwilderness vacationers and a nonvacationing control group. The proofreading test was presented before and after the subjects' trip and the wilderness vacationers displayed significant improvement in post-trip performance. In contrast, the other two groups actually displayed a decline in post-trip performance. In a second study, Hartig *et al.* (1991) compared the restorative potential of three types of settings: the natural environment, the urban environment and a setting of passive relaxation that consisted of listening to soft music and reading magazines. All subjects completed the same attentionally demanding proofreading task before walking or relaxing in their respective settings for 40 minutes. Then, the task was repeated again and the result was also that those in the natural environment displayed an improvement in proofreading performance, but those in urban settings or passively relaxing did not. In addition to these objective measures, a self-report measure based upon a 'perceived restorativeness scale' also revealed a high correlation between proofreading performance and subjective feelings of restoration.

ART is also supported by research where perceived restorative quality in environments was measured (Berto, 2005; Hartig *et al.*, 1997; Herzog *et al.*, 2002; Korpela & Hartig, 1996). In a comparison of natural and urban environments, these studies found in general, participants perceived natural environments as more restorative than urban environments. In a recent study, Berto (2005) tested the hypothesis that exposure to restorative environments facilitates recovery from mental fatigue. 'Parti- cipants were asked to view a set of slides based on colour photographs depicting lakes, rives, seas, hills, woods, orchards, forests, city riversides, city streets, industrial zones, housing, porches, urban areas and sky- scrapers' (Berto, 2005: 251). Each participant was then asked to rate the restorative value of each scene using a version of Korpela and Hartig's (1996) perceived restorativeness scale (PRS). Results showed that nature- based scenes were given the highest ratings of restorativeness and that attentional capacity was regenerated in such environment. Findings provide support for ART's premise that natural environments are more restorative than urban environments.

As presented so far, ART accounts for those properties of the individual that require restoration, and studies show that restoration of an individual's attention is known to take place in the natural environ- ment, but not usually in manmade settings. In terms of motivation theory, we have explained the 'push' factors in a preference for nature, but have not yet fully specified the 'pull' factors that explain why nature and not manmade settings provides restoration. In other words, what is it about the natural environment that allows it to restore us and makes us seek it out thus? If tourists really are motivated to seek nature by the need for restoration, such a description of environmental properties would be invaluable for tourism research because it would provide clear properties of travel destinations to preserve, enhance and to market.

Theory of Restorative Environments

Based on an analysis of unique properties of the natural environment and extrapolating from James' concept of *fascination*, Kaplan and Kaplan (1989) identify four properties that an environment must possess in order to provide restoration: 'fascination', 'being away', 'extent' and 'compat- ibility'. An environment possessing these properties is considered to be a *restorative environment*.

'Fascination' refers to an environment's potential for eliciting *involuntary attention*. Involuntary attention requires little or no effort, is likely to be resistant to fatigue, and kicks into motion when out of interest, or curiosity, the contents and processes in the surroundings capture and hold one's attention. 'Fascination' is important for two reasons. First, 'it attracts people and keeps them from getting bored, and secondly it allows them to function without having to use directed attention' (Kaplan & Kaplan, 1989: 184). When involuntary attention is engaged, the demands on directed attention diminish and restoration becomes possible. Experiencing this form of 'fascination' is a pause in time, a moment to rejoice, to be truly alive. There are a range of sources and types of fascination, some derived from content or 'soft fascination' and others from process or 'hard fascination'. 'Fascination' is derived along a continuum of a 'soft-hard' dimension based on the elements of the stimuli, or content. 'Soft fascination', characteristic of certain natural settings, has a special advantage in terms of providing an opportunity for reflection, which can further enhance the benefits of recovering from directed attention fatigue (Kaplan, 1995). 'Soft fascination' would include elements of nature such as sunsets and waterfalls, caves and fires (Kaplan & Kaplan, 1989), leaves moving in a breeze and cloud formations (Kaplan, 1995). 'Hard fascination' involves dramatic attention-grabbing stimuli such as staring at giant trees and vast waterfalls (Herzog *et al.*, 1997). 'Fascination', however, is not always enough to allow restoration to take place; an environment must also allow an individual the opportunity of 'being away' with 'extent' and 'compatibility'.

'Being away' frees a person from any mental activity requiring directed attention, allowing fascination to take over. Two different types of 'being away' are identified: being away physically in a different geographical location, and being away psychologically or a conceptual shift (Kaplan, 1995). A restorative environment should offer the opportunity and qualities to be in a different location, away from the everyday routines and tasks of one's life. This is usually what is meant by a holiday. Secondly, Kaplan explains, 'a different environment is not as essential as much as a change in the direction of one's gaze' (Kaplan, 1995: 173). Indeed, where one is 'being away' *to* is every bit as important as to where one is being away *from*. For example, Kaplan (1995) stresses that travelling to a different environment alone is not restorative, if daily routines and tasks are accessible while being away. An example of this is expressed by De Botton (2002) on the first morning of his much-anticipated holiday to Barbados; he walks out to the beach and takes in the beauty of the resort with its beach, coconut trees and turquoise sea. He acknowledges,

I may have noticed a few birds careering through the air in matinal excitement, but my awareness of them was weakened by a number of other, incongruous and unrelated elements, among these, a sore throat that I had developed during the flight, a worry at not having informed a colleague that I would be away, a pressure across both temples and a rising need to visit the bathroom. A momentous but until then overlooked fact was making its first appearance: that I had inadvertently brought *myself with me* to the island. (De Botton, 2002: 20)

The everyday environment in which we function can become quite familiar and limited in scope of new information to process, or, quite demanding in terms of uninteresting information to process. Kaplan and Talbot (1983) explain that a restorative environment must have extent, offering elements of 'being away' to new worlds of mental exploration; it should be rich enough, and coherent enough to constitute 'a whole other world' that is, of sufficient scope to sustain exploration and interpretation. 'Extent' refers to the sense that the immediate setting is part of some larger place or whole. 'Extent' can be defined by the presence of two subcomponents: *connectedness* and *scope*, which again refer either to the physical environment or to psychological processes (Kaplan & Kaplan, 1989). *Connectedness* is expressed by a series of relationships between environmental features. *Scope* refers to breadth and indicates there is more than the immediate environment available, either physically just out of sight or even within the imagination that suggest that further information is available upon exploration (Hartig *et al.*, 1991).

'Compatibility' is the agreement between how one wants to function, both mentally and physically, within an environment and how that environment affords the opportunity to function as desired (Hartig *et al.*, 1991). For an environment to be restorative, it must not only support the specific activities, but also any inclinations of the individual. Therefore, 'compatibility' is a function of environmental dictates and personal intentions (Hartig *et al.*, 1991). If the environment or elements of the environment are not, or are perceived to be not supportive of specific activities proposed, then the environment is not compatible (Kaplan, 1995).

Are Tourists Motivated by Restoration?

It is clear from the preceding that many people are motivated to experience nature by the need for psychological restoration, but are tourists among them? Kaplan and Kaplan believe that restoration is a need shared by all humanity faced with adaptational demands, but it does not follow that *all* behaviour is driven by that need. The position taken here is that restoration can explain some of tourists' motivation for nature: Environmental psychologists have found the same preference for nature as that found in tourism and have explained it with ART that predicts the kind of relaxation also known to motivate tourists. This explanation is at least consistent with what is known about tourist behaviour, and the specifics of the theory of restorative environments also resonate with other known tourist motivations. The potential for 'being away' is inherent in any travel experience and is akin to Pearce's (2005) suggested core motivations of 'escape and relaxation', whereas 'fascination' and 'extent' are consistent with 'novelty' and 'compatibility' similar to 'relationships and personal development'.

Settling the question definitively will require dedicated studies and these can be performed using the existing ART methods discussed earlier. To establish the occurrence of restoration, tourists can be subjected to the proofreading, Necker cube tasks or other prescribed tasks to gauge mental fatigue before and after their holiday. However, even if restoration is found to occur, it must also be established that this is what motivates tourists to choose the natural environment for a destination. This might be achieved using interviews where tourists are asked questions related to the four components of the theory of restorative environments to understand the importance of each component as a 'pull' factor. One possible difficulty with restoration as a tourist motivation is that restoration is an ongoing issue of maintenance that arises, more or less, everyday and must be dealt with as frequently. In contrast, a holiday is an event so infrequent for most people that it cannot be an individual's *only* means of restoration. One might interpret this observation as doubt that restoration is a part of tourist motivations at all or, instead, one may speculate that people find just enough restoration day to day to survive, but seek a deep, prolonged restoration when they can afford to (financially and otherwise). Hence, relaxation, specifically the refreshment of body and mind and restoration continue to be listed as key physical motivations to travel (Hall, 2007).

It is not claimed here that all of nature tourism is motivated by restoration. The limits of restoration have not yet been precisely defined and it is possible that the concept may break down if stretched too far. For example, although it should seem reasonable that people seeking peace and quiet in nature are seeking restoration from overstimulation in their everyday environment, it seems less convincing to say that those seeking a challenge in nature (e.g. hikers and climbers) are seeking restoration from a drain on challenges. This pattern of thinking turns *every* interaction with nature into one of compensation for a loss, when there are surely times when we are fully restored and still seek nature; although perhaps this is an issue with needs-based theories of motivation in general – they leave little room for active choice. Assuming that restoration is confirmed – to some greater or lesser degree – as a motivating factor for tourists, how would it fit in with existing theories?

ART and Existing Theories of Tourist Motivation

It is interesting to consider how far ART could be taken as a theory of tourist motivation in itself and also how it could supplement existing theories. To consider the first question, I will use Pearce's (1993) seven criteria for assessing the worth of tourist motivation theories. Pearce claims that a sound theory of tourist motivation would do the following: it would function as a true theory, appeal to different users, be easy to communicate, be methodologically accessible, adopt a dynamic approach, account for both intrinsic and extrinsic motivations and adopt a multimotive approach.

To function as a true theory, ART would have to explain and predict tourist motivations and be empirically verified. In its own domain, ART fulfils these criteria: it is a theoretically consistent explanation of the human preference for nature and it makes predictions that have been validated by a number of studies. As an explanation of at least some tourist behaviour, ART seems *prima facie* reasonable and its methods could easily be applied to tourism-specific studies. ART predicts that environments possessing Kaplan's four properties would be preferred by those tourists seeking restoration and this is possible to verify using existing ART methodology. For these reasons, ART is considered to function provisionally as a true tourist motivation theory.

For ART to appeal to different users, it would have to be applicable to a significant number of tourism researchers. Nature-based tourism is undoubtedly one of the most significant areas of research in tourism studies today (Hall & Boyd, 2005), which could benefit from this fresh perspective and understanding. The third criterion of being easy to communicate seems well met by ART. One might concisely summarise ART's position on tourist motivations as follows: Tourists are drawn to natural environments because those environments possess properties which help restore fatigued psychological faculties and provide relaxation. The specific psychological facility that is restored is directed attention and the specific properties of the environment are 'being away', 'extent', 'fascination' and 'compatibility'.

For ART to be methodologically accessible it would have to provide a set of techniques for measuring its constructs that could be reasonably applied to study tourist motivations. It seems reasonable to expect that the existing techniques for measuring restoration, discussed earlier and in the literature, could be applied to tourists before, during and after their holiday. To adopt a dynamic approach, a theory would have to accommodate new findings and changing tastes. ART is, to some extent, immune to this because it describes human motivations so fundamental that they could be said to be universal and not subject to change. To account for intrinsic and extrinsic motivation is to be able to address those motivations to travel that are desirable in themselves and also those that are a means to an end. Here, the components of 'being away' and 'compatibility' could be seen as intrinsic factors, whereas 'fascination' and 'extent' would serve as extrinsic factors. The challenge would be to assess the range of potential criteria to include in such a list. The final criterion of adopting a multimotive approach would be met if a theory accounted for many different motivations for the same behaviour. By definition, ART explains behaviour in terms of a single motivation – restoration – and therefore does not provide this. It is for this reason that this paper does not assert ART to be a complete description of tourist motivation. However, as shown, it fulfils several other of Pearce's criteria and might be used to refine more comprehensive existing theories as ART offers certain features that they do not. The next section compares ART in relation to a number of popular tourist motivation theories.

Maslow's Hierarchy of Needs

An influential theory of general human motivation and the basis for Pearce's (1988) travel career ladder, comes from Maslow (1943), who defined a hierarchy of five needs that must be met for a healthy and happy life. Individuals must fulfil lower stages of the hierarchy before higher needs can be met, making lower needs more powerful. At the lowest two levels are prerequisites for an individual's bodily survival: *physiological* needs such as thirst, hunger and relaxation, and *safety* needs, such as freedom from threat and danger. Above basic survival, there is a need for *social* relationships that provide love, affection and friendship, and *esteem* that provides self-respect, reputation and a sense of achievement. The highest level of need is that for *self-actualisation* where one fulfils one's highest potential. As it results in relaxation, ART seems to fit most clearly into the physiological level although its actual mechanism is psychological, a distinction not supported by Maslow's basic theory. In the hierarchy of needs, attention restoration would be a basic prerequisite for higher functioning, and studies of extended exposure to the natural environment (Kaplan & Talbot, 1983; Talbot & Kaplan, 1986) have demonstrated the development of higher functioning, in Maslow's terms, as exposure continued. Kaplan and Kaplan (1989) found that participants on an 11-day Outdoor Challenge Programme (similar to the popular Outward Bound system) reported feelings of mastery, self-confidence and inner peace after 11 days. It is tempting to venture that the initial exposure to nature provided restoration that fulfilled lower needs and allowed the higher needs of esteem and self-actualisation to be met.

Push and Pull Factors

Dann (1977) and Crompton (1979) base their theories of tourist motivation around the very general notion of push and pull factors. Push factors, or psychosocial needs, are those aspects of motivation that drive an individual to travel away from home in the first place, whereas pull factors are those properties of destinations that determine which are chosen, given the basic decision to travel. Crompton (1979), in a study of 39 in-depth interviews, identified seven specific push factors and two specific pull factors that motivated tourists. The pull factors were: escape from a mundane environment, exploration and evaluation of self, relaxation, prestige, regression to a childhood state, enhancement of kinship relations and facilitation of social interactions. The two pull factors were those of novelty and education. ART and the theory of restorative environments are accommodated well by the general framework of push-pull factors, with the need for restoration as a push factor towards an environment where restoration can occur and the properties of 'fascination', 'being away', 'extent' and 'compatibility' found in the natural environment 'pulling' individuals to it to meet their need. Regarding Crompton's specific push-pull factors, it is also clear that restoration is most consistent with relaxation, although the restorative property of 'being away' also resonates with 'escape from a mundane environment'.

Social Aspects of ART

An important issue raised by the previous two theories is that of social influences on restoration. Both Maslow and Crompton feature social interactions as important motivations for behaviour, but the social aspects of ART have not yet been made clear. ART currently addresses only the physical, environmental aspects of restoration and it is unclear what role (if any) other people have to play. In the extreme cases, another's presence might be an essential component of, or fatal obstacle to, restoration or instead leave it unaffected. Or, other people might merely enhance or degrade an environment's restorative potential. The only known research to even recognise the absence of knowledge about social aspects of restoration is by Staats and Hartig (2004), who criticise this shortcoming and provide some ideas on how other people might factor into restoration. Their study of 106 participants suggests that the presence of other people does influence restoration in natural environments and may have two positive, enabling effects. The first is to provide an element of *safety*, as it might be hard to relax and mentally recover if one fears injury (or worse) in a natural, uncontrolled environment. Here, 'company enables restoration by providing safety' (Staats & Hartig, 2004: 209). However, it should be noted, 'when safety is not a concern, restoration is enhanced by the absence of company' (Staats & Hartig, 2004: 209). The second effect of company on restoration is to provide someone to help *guide attention* to aspects of the immediate experience: 'independent of safe access, another person might enhance the restorative quality of the environment by providing welcome observations that feed one's curiosity about the environment' (Hartig, 2004: 3). Staats and Hartig's research is a promising start but, as they freely admit, it may not exhaust the social aspects of restoration.

Optimal Arousal Theory

The social aspects of tourist motivation described by Maslow and Crompton are rejected by Iso-Ahola (1982: 257), who claims that 'motivation is purely a psychological concept, not a social one'. Iso-Ahola prefers to consider motivation in terms of *optimal arousal* whereby an individual will seek an environment where they can achieve a personal psychological equilibrium. If an individual is overstimulated, they will seek an environment with less overwhelming stimuli, if they are understimulated, they will choose destinations based on an expectation of excitement. This theory seems most resonant with ART because it highlights an important distinction between restoration and relaxation. Relaxation is not the same as restoration. At one level, the distinction is one of cause and effect: relaxation is a physical feeling, but attention restoration is the renewal of psychological faculties that may lead to relaxation. But there is a more interesting difference here too. The effect of relaxation may also be achieved by closing one's eyes, turning off the world; turning off one's mind and becoming passively 'empty' of stress and worry. For example, wellbeing tourism, specifically the use of spa facilities such as massages, exercises and pampering appears to be oriented towards this approach to relaxation (McNeil, 2005). Restoration, in contrast, is not about passively escaping all perception. Rather, it is to escape a fatiguing mode of interaction with the world and to activate a more primal and natural mode of perception based on effortless fascination, with relaxation as its consequence. Iso-Ahola's theory seems to capture this balance between passivity and activity in different words. ART can extend and refine Iso-Ahola's theory with specific mechanisms of achieving optimal arousal and properties of the environment that facilitate it. Again, dedicated studies will be required to gauge the similarities between ART and optimal arousal or to decide on its applicability.

Implications of Restoration for Tourism Practice

In the field of tourism, much research is dedicated to an under-standing of tourist motivation, vital in the planning, marketing and management of tourist destinations. The questions asked include what initiates the desire to travel and what influences the choice of destination that is selected? Tourist motivation studies seek to explain the patterns of tourism activity, to understand why people leave home and travel, where they go and why they return or move on to different destinations (Page *et al.*, 2001). This knowledge also assists the tourism industry in understanding how customers make travel decisions.

Given that tourists are motivated, to some degree, to visit natural environments by the need for restoration and that Kaplan and Kaplan's four restorative environmental properties are true, what would follow for tourism practice? The form of restoration discussed in this paper requires different facilities than passive relaxation. Restoration is a cause of relaxation and destinations should be sure which they offer. In developing a tourist attraction, for example, a new trail in a nature reserve, the focus can be on ensuring the criteria of 'fascination' and 'extent' are firstly documented and subsequently visibly present, preserved or enhanced through interpretation. Signage and information on different species of wildlife in the nature reserve could serve to exemplify 'extent'.

Within the literature, relaxation is often mentioned as a primary goal by tourists (Pearce, 2005) and thus, the industry sets out to provide relaxation for those individuals planning a holiday months down the line. Consider this scenario: an individual builds up mental fatigue over months, books a holiday three months down the line based on push and pull factors. This does little to address current stress nor does it restore directed attention. Therefore, the theory of restorative environments can be used by the tourism industry to address this gap. A tourist at the end of the day is an individual who has travelled away from home, oftentimes to partake in activities not accessible at home. On the other hand, leisure is accessible, spontaneous and an individual can partake in it as the need arises. So, the tourist industry could set out to promote more short breaks – little and often – as long as the destination offers the four components of ART. The aim would be to provide the sanctuary of a restorative experience as and when you need it. The tourism industry could also set out to change public perception of 'holidays' and leisure breaks, using *restoration* as defined by Kaplan (1995) as its clarion call.

Presented here are arguments to suggest that tourist's preference for nature and relaxation can be explained using the concept of restoration, taken from environmental psychology. It is claimed here that Kaplan and Kaplan's ART and theory of restorative environments can contribute the nature-specific detailed theory, methodological techniques and empirical validation that existing theories of tourism motivation are lacking in this application. Dedicated studies will have to be conducted to definitively settle the issue, but if the claim is found to be true, tourism motivation theory will benefit and implications for tourism practice will follow.

References

Berto, R. (2005) Exposure to restorative environments helps restore attentional capacity. *Journal of Environmental Psychology* 25, 249–259.
Cimprich, B. (1993) Development of an intervention to restore attention in cancer patients. *Cancer Nursing* 16 (2), 83–92.
Cimprich, B. (2003) An environmental intervention to restore attention in women with newly diagnosed breast cancer. *Cancer Nursing* 26, 284–292.
Crompton, J.L. (1979) Motivations for pleasure vacation. *Annals of Tourism Research* 6 (1), 408–424.
Dann, G. (1981) Tourism motivation: An appraisal. *Annals of Tourism Research* 8 (2), 187–219.
Dann, G.M.S. (1977) Anomie, ego-enhancement and tourism. *Annals of Tourism Research* 4 (4), 184–194.
De Botton, A. (2002) *The Art of Travel*. London: Hamish Hamilton.
Eagles, P.F.J. (1999) Nature-based tourism in terrestrial protected areas. In S. Bolton and N. Dudley (eds) *Partnerships for Protection. New Strategies for Planning and Management for Protected Areas* (pp. 144–152). London: Earthscan.
Gifford, R. (2002) *Environmental Psychology* (3rd edn). Canada: Optimal Books.
Gray, J.P. (1970) *International Travel – International Trade*. Lexington Heath: Lexington Books.

Hall, C.M. (2007) *Tourism in Australia. Development, Issues and Change* (5th edn). Australia: Pearson Education.

Hall, C.M. and Boyd, S. (eds) (2005) *Nature-based Tourism in Peripheral Areas: Development or Disaster*. Clevedon: Channel View Publications.

Hartig, T. (2004) Toward understanding the restorative environment as a health resource. Engaging with the environment. Keynote Address. *Open Space. People Space. An International Conference on Inclusive Environments*: Edinburgh. On WWW at http://www.openspace.eca.ac.uk/conference/proceedings/PDF/Hartig.pdf. Accessed 16.06.07.

Hartig, T., Böök, A., Garvill, J., Olsson, T. and Gärling, T. (1996) Environmental influences on psychological restoration. *Scandinavian Journal of Psychology* 37, 378–393.

Hartig, T., Evans, G.W., Jamner, L.J., Davis, D.S. and Gärling, T. (2003) Tracking restoration in natural and urban field settings. *Journal of Environmental Psychology* 23, 109–123.

Hartig, T., Korpela, K., Evans, G.W. and Gärling, T. (1997) A measure of restorative quality in environments. *Scandinavian Housing and Planning Research* 14, 175–194.

Hartig, T., Mang, M. and Evans, G.W. (1991) Restorative effects of natural environment experiences. *Environment and Behaviour* 23 (1), 3–26.

Hartig, T. and Staats, H. (2005) Linking preference for environments with their restorative quality. In B. Tress, G. Tress, G. Fry and P. Opdam (eds) *From Landscape Research to Landscape Planning. Aspects of Integration, Education and Application* (pp. 279–292). Dordrecht: Springer.

Herzog, T.R., Black, A.M., Fountaine, K.A. and Knotts, D.J. (1997) Reflection and attentional recovery as distinctive benefits of restorative environments. *Journal of Environmental Psychology* 17, 165–170.

Herzog, T.R., Chen, H.C. and Primeau, J. (2002) Perception of the restorative potential of natural and other settings. *Journal of Environmental Psychology* 22, 295–306.

Herzog, T.R., Maguire, C.P. and Nebel, M.B. (2003) Assessing the restorative components of environments. *Journal of Environmental Psychology* 23, 159–170.

Holden, A. (2005) *Tourism Studies and the Social Sciences*. London: Routledge.

Iso-Ahola, E.S. (1982) Toward a social psychological theory of tourism motivation: A rejoinder. *Annals of Tourism Research* 6, 257–264.

James, W. (1892) *Psychology. The Briefer Course*. New York: Holt.

Kaplan, R. and Kaplan, S. (1989) *The Experience of Nature. A Psychological Perspective*. Cambridge: Cambridge University Press.

Kaplan, S. (1995) The restorative benefits of nature: Toward an integrative framework. *Journal of Environmental Psychology* 15, 169–182.

Kaplan, S. and Talbot, J.F. (1983) Psychological benefits of a wilderness experience. In I. Altman and J.F. Wohlwill (eds) *Behaviour and the Natural Environment* (Vol. 6, pp. 163–203). London: Plenum Press.

Korpela, K. and Hartig, T. (1996) Restorative qualities of favourite places. *Journal of Environmental Psychology* 16, 221–233.

Laumann, K., Gärling, T. and Stormark, K.M. (2001) Rating scale measures of restorative components of environments. *Journal of Environmental Psychology* 21, 31–44.

Leiper, N. (1995) *Tourism Management*. Victoria: RMIT Press.

Lindberg, K., Wood, M.E. and Engeldrum, D. (1998) *Ecotourism: A Guide for Planners and Managers* (Vol. 2). North Bennington: The Ecotourism Society.

Mace, B., Bell, P. and Loomis, R. (1999) Aesthetic, affective, and cognitive effects of noise on natural landscape assessment. *Society and Natural Resources* 12 (3), 225–242.

Mannell, R.C. and Iso-Ahola, S-E. (1987) Psychological nature of leisure and tourism experience. *Annals of Tourism Research* 14, 314–331.

Maslow, A. (1943) A theory of human motivation. *Psychological Review* 50, 370–396.

McNeil, K.R. (2005) Staying in the spa marketing game: Trends, challenges, strategies and techniques. *Journal of Vacation Marketing* 11 (1), 31–39.

Newsome, D., Moore, S. and Dowling, R. (2001) *Natural Area Tourism: Ecology, Impacts and Management*. Clevedon: Channel View Publications.

Page, S.J., Brunt, P., Busby, G. and Connell, J. (2001) *Tourism: A Modern Synthesis*. Australia: Thomson Learning.

Pearce, P.L. (1988) *The Ulysses Factor: Evaluating Visitors in Tourist Settings*. New York: Springer-Verlag.

Pearce, P.L. (2005) *Tourist Behaviour. Themes and Conceptual Schemes*. Clevedon: Channel View Publications.

Phillip, P.L. (1993) Fundamentals of tourist motivation. In D. Pearce and R. Butler (eds) *Tourism Research; Critiques and Challenges* (pp. 85–105). London: Routledge.

Plog, S. (1973) Why destination areas rise and fall. *Cornell Hotel and Restaurant Administration Quarterly* February, 55–58.

Saegert, S. and Winkel, G.H. (1990) Environmental psychology. *Annual Review of Psychology* 41, 441–477.

Schiffman, B. and Kanuk, W. (1997) *Consumer Behaviour*. Sydney: Prentice Hall Australia.

Staats, H., Kieviet, A. and Hartig, T. (2003) Where to recover from attentional fatigue: An expectancy-value analysis of environmental preference. *Journal of Environmental Psychology* 23, 147–157.

Talbot, J.F. and Kaplan, S. (1986) Perspectives on wilderness: Re-examining the value of extended wilderness experience. *Journal of Environmental Psychology* 6 (3), 177–188.

Tennessen, C.H. and Cimprich, B. (1995) Views to nature: Effects on attention. *Journal of Environmental Psychology* 15, 77–85.

Van den Berg, A.E., Hartig, T. and Staats, H. (2007) Preference for nature in urbanized societies: Stress, restoration, and the pursuit of sustainability. *Journal of Social Issues* 63, 79–96.

Weiler, B. and Davis, D. (1993) An exploratory investigation into the roles of the nature-based tour leader. *Tourism Management* 14 (2), 91–98.

WTO (1998) *Statistical Yearbook of Tourism*. Madrid: World Tourism Organisation.

Chapter 8

Aesthetic Pleasures: Contemplating Spiritual Tourism

SHALINI SINGH and TEJ VIR SINGH

> Travel is nothing if it is not the expansion of the mind – an adventure of the spirit.
>
> Maurice Shadbolt (1976)

If tourism concerns with the pleasures of the material world and spirituality signifies renunciation of the same – could the two shake hands! In simple words: is a synthesis between spirituality and tourism possible or is it just a philosopher's utopia? Thinkers often surmise that the bipolar-unlikes, with their own peculiar attractions, coexist with the opposites – as much as light is often defined alongside darkness, good with bad and beautiful with ugly. If this is the case, then, does spiritual tourism offer a chance for piety and innocuous pleasure to coexist? Again, if this is possible, then can the experiences of and responses to such integration be considered purposeful? and if yes, then, what could be the possible outcomes of such profound encounters? In exploring some possible answers to these complex questions, it would be appropriate to circumscribe the scope of this fusion through brief discourse on spirituality, travel and tourism, wandering journeys and pilgrimages. Such a radical discussion on tourism's good and bad may not be new, but a rethink may be enlightening for further researches.

Spirituality

Somewhat mystic, the concept of spirituality is indeed a philosopher's realm. Despite the fact that specific themes emerge repeatedly in scholarly literature, the term notoriously defies definition (Hasselle-Newcombe, 2005). Ethnohistorical sources have identified spirit(uality) as breath (Latin), wind (Greek) and a cardinal light (Buddhist) (Keegan, 1991). Empirical evidences lend to an acknowledgement of spirituality as a multidimensional phenomenon. Eastern philosophic traditions, namely, Hinduism, Buddhism, Confucianism and Taoism, reverberate themes of consciousness, energy, bliss and dynamic connectedness (Halstead & Mickley, 1997) in explaining spirituality, while Islamic and Judeo-Christian thoughts view truth, surrender and the indivisible supremacy of one God as foundational. These approaches to spirituality may seem almost tangential to one another, but on closer examination of descriptions afforded through human experience and response, both resonate notions of a lived experience, harmonious interconnectedness, belief or affirmation of life/existence and intuitive alignment of sensibilities. Spirituality can be both world affirming and world denying. Hinduism is a classic example of such duality that exalts the man of the world and of retirement (Organ, 1975). Yet another dimension relates to spirituality as a process of dynamic integrative growth that 'leads to ultimate values, meaning and purpose in life' (Halstead & Mickley, 1997). Thus, spirituality adopts a nontheistic approach that permits secular expression in the way people think, behave and act on a daily basis. However, when human response occurs on the basis of some sort of transcendental force, spirituality assumes theistic prowess. It is in this context that religion and/or sanctity finds way in discourses on spirituality.

Religion, like spirituality, is an umbrella term that connotes diverse sets of beliefs, practices and traditions. Hence, the two tend to be used interchangeably, despite religiousness being characterized as 'narrow and institutional' and the latter as 'personal and subjective' (Zinnbauer *et al.*, 1997). It is pertinent to note that while religious theology may enfold spiritual views, it is quite possible for nontheological believers to be deeply involved in spirituality (unchurched). In contemporary times, religion and spirituality are explicitly differentiated, as negative and positive, respectively. The emergence of modern religions, such as New Age and Mystic, claim their foundations in alternative spiritualities (Sutcliffe & Bowman, 2000), thereby reinstating religion in the spiritual domain (Halstead & Mickley, 1997).

Travel and Tourism

Tourists have a ubiquitous presence in both sacred and secular locations. Owing to the dichotomous meanings and uses of sacred and secular spaces by tourists and pilgrims alike, Smith (1992), Cohen (1979) and Collins-Kreiner and Kliot (2000) suggest continua of typology, experiences and perspectives to explain the range. These works seemingly embody the bipolarity of world affirmation (existential) and world denial (renunciation). A typical example of world affirmation may be evidenced in the journeys of 'Goddess pilgrims' – essentially women travelling to ethnic or environmental/historical/heritage destinations with an explicit intention to practice their religious convictions, identity and political consciousness. Their journeys intend to contribute to 'a radical inscription of the female body' (Rountree, 2002: 476) through their exposure to and experience of symbolic activity and ritual at the sites. In allying their female form with that of the sacred, Goddess pilgrims vividly combine religious 'rapture' with hedonic pleasure (rather touristic enjoyment). Another example of world affirmation philosophy is the educational tours of American Jewish students to Israel. Here the Diaspora, motivated by sacred and secular rationalities, visit their homeland as an act of affirmation and allegiance to their 'promised' land (Cohen, 2003). Most modern day spiritualities affirm the existence of spiritual energy in the material world and hence seek experiences through worldliness.

Scholars of tourism, namely MacCannell and Graburn, support a direct relationship of religion and sanctity with modern mass tourism. Studies of tourism in sacred sites/destinations tend to conclude on the indistinguishability of pilgrim behaviour from that of the tourists. Keegan (1991) takes this compatibility one step further by establishing the similarity in the experiences of the tourist with the pilgrim. According to Keegan, the unfamiliarity of other (visited) locations and cultures stimulates the spiritual sensibility by arousing all the senses. It is the 'bombardment' of the numerous and new external stimuli that accelerates 'the mental senses to process and translate new information and experience into meaningful spiritual insights' (Keegan, 1991: 8). A recent study by Sharpley and Sundaram (2005) confirm the relevance of experience as an indispensable factor in the travels of visitors to Auroville (India). Hence, it is not necessary that spiritual outcomes of journeys and visitations are premeditated. Likewise, travels and visits, including route-based travels and pilgrimages, to sacred places may not always yield spiritual experiences. Route-based travel, including pilgrimages, hence cannot ensure spiritual experiences for all.

Wanderings

Travel, for its own sake, can be a spiritual experience – if it obliterates the significance of the destination. Wanderlusters are on a constant itinerary of discoveries of cultural experiences. The journey is oftentimes a pilgrimage. In observing Japanese international tourists, Leiper (1989) notes their peripatetic behaviour that conforms to the wanderlust mode of travel. Constant mobility becomes the only way of ensuring exposure to unfamiliar places, and therefore consistent search for novelty and discovery (Niebuhr in Senn [2002]). This spirit of serendipity, wanderlust, in the traveller, is born out of a yearning to acquaint oneself with the unknown – physically, mentally, emotionally and spiritually. Wanderings of tourists and travellers are rather leisurely though attentive and disciplined in praxis, as they are not undertaken with any special purpose (see Heyd, 2003). These travellers tend to take the longer and arduous routes to and between sites of historical, religious and aesthetic associations.

Spiritual experiences are reported by wanderers, who are differentiated from renouncers, shamans and hermits or adventure-seekers – in that they do not have any serious intent of penance, austerity and agony or the spirited conquests of summits. Wanderers are particularly known for their enjoyment with the journey. Instead, guided by self-propelled ways of travelling, they walk, climb, hike, commune and rest for the sheer joys and pleasures of the activities. Hesse (1972 [1920]) puts this feeling more artistically '. . . in wandering we do not look for a goal, we only look for the happiness of wandering' (Hesse, 1971 [1920]: 24–25). Conventional forms and patterns of travels and tours perhaps offer fairly vivid understandings of spiritual journeying. In ancient Greece, people travelled long distances to witness or participate in a spectacle of wide-ranging significance, such as processions, sacrifices or rituals, artistic performances, athletic competitions and festivals, which afforded the opportunity for 'sacred contemplation' (Rutherford, 2000). Travel was hence interpreted as a 'journey to sanctuary' and watching became synonymous with (sacred) 'sightseeing'. While these travels were premeditated undertakings, unpremeditated journeys are known to engender similar sensibilities. Past routes of wandering men, in some instances have morphed into pilgrimage traditions of route-based travels of innumerable travellers. The poetic wanderings of the Japanese philosopher – Basho, the hike to Santiago, the journey to Lourdes, the walk or cycling to the Camino, and the repetitive visits of nomadic cattle herders in the Nubian Desert in Southern Egypt have all initiated pilgrim movement.

Spiritual Pilgrimages (Journeys)

Spiritual journeys are defined by an indeterminate purpose and momentous experiences. This has held true through civilizations. The purposes of ancient pilgrimages and related phenomenon were as diverse as, and perhaps similar to, present day trends. For instance, the Greeks travelled to sanctuaries to consult oracles, attend festivals, make sacrifices, watch Panhellenic games and seek cures. Reasons for travel can be prescriptive, personal or a combination of both. Travel, in the Islamic faith, is almost a commandment for *Fi-Sabilillah* (the cause of God) – which makes it spiritually purposeful – in that people (especially Muslims) may experience 'the smallness of man and the greatness of God' through the bounties and beauties of His creations (Din, 1989: 552). Hindu pilgrimages are usually subscribed for *darshana* (visit or site) of an auspicious and/or sacred place or shrine, *vrata* (make or fulfill a vow), *snana* (ritual bath), *shraddha* (homage), *daana* (offerings) and *punya* (earning merit) or nirvana (salvations). Pilgrims are thus motivated by a societal, personal or religious interest to visit specific places. When, or whether, the societal intent becomes personal or the interest converts into a need varies with individuals.

Jewish, Christian, Buddhist, Taoist and Confucian pilgrims, on the other hand, undertake journeys with a desire to experience places and paths where holy people had traversed, rested, resided, renunciated, arrived or performed miracles. Sites, such as the burning bush on Mount Sinai (Israel), Gaya in India, Garden of Gethsemane (Jerusalem), Pei-kang in Taiwan, are venues for those with a personal conviction of the sanctity of the place (Hobbs, 1995; Senn, 2002). Such pilgrimages become extraordinarily meaningful, while the experiences of the pilgrims render the locations into places of learning, education and transformation. Though the experiences are heterogenic, they are definitely indicative of the fact that a spiritual journey is as much internally moving as it is physically – in that it is 'not only a matter of the feet, but also a matter of the heart' (Eck, 1981: 340) – or that of the mind as evidenced in the works of many literary compositions. This enlightenment from pilgrimages may be triggered by any incident, engagement or a self-disciplining regimen like abstinence from certain foods or lifestyle, humility, prohibition, interaction/participation, challenge of observances or plain physical movement or sightseeing, or a combination thereof.

In the transformative experience, the fusion of the inner with the outer, the self with the other, the tactile with the intangible, the lesser being with the supreme, the physical with the mental, and the ordinary with the extraordinary is a critical juncture for the traveller. Van Gennep (in Rudwick, 1996) identifies this phase with an initiation rite that occurs in a limen environment. A true pilgrim is thus poised at the threshold of that which separates him/her from the mundane everyday setting while exposing the self to the new and unfamiliar so to experience the spiritual. For the limens to occur, it must involve the spatial, perceptual and intellectual dimensions, simultaneously. Furthermore, the self-amplifying property of the limens affords a spiritual experience and hence a transformation. The threshold calls to question past faith, beliefs, life's purpose and reason for living, and casts a doubt on all that was previously known and accepted. The pilgrim must not only overcome this doubt, but also formulate true meanings and insights and emerge as a new initiate – capable of participating in the all pervading harmony and communion (Senn, 2002).

Experiences of the spirit happen in the sacred and also the secular (e.g. desert, wasteland and wilderness) domains. At established sites, the 'rapture' of the pilgrim invokes, upholds and re-emphasizes the sanctity of the location and the sacred is provoked to reveal itself. Epiphanies of the spirit are thus responsible for the identification and emergence of sacred sites and the lack thereof relegate the locations to enterprises of religion, heritage, power, commerce or profanity. Hierarchical networks of sanctuaries are thus established at local, regional, national and global levels in various forms, such as worship centres, institutes, retreats, ashram(s), healing centres and intentional (spiritual magnet) communities.

The Quest: Odyssey for Personal Fulfilment

In view of the purpose and experiences of pious tourists, spiritual journeys may be described as contemplative travels of seekers in the limens, that can afford transformative learning (true) experiences. At the heart of spirituality is a quest that sets off a need to go forth. Batson and Schoenrade (1991), MacCannell (1973), Senn (2002) and Smith (1992) all allude to 'quest' as the kernel of genuine travel. Senn clearly articulates the questing journey as an arc image for spirituality. Others refer to the seeking as the driving force for spiritual magnetism (Preston, 1992) – of pilgrimage. Again, it is this quest that separates 'religious dwellers' from 'spiritual seekers' (Wuthnow, 1998). The latter are referred to as true or genuine, owing to the fact that all 'goodness' of religion lies within the quest orientation (Hood & Morris, 1985). This dimension, common to spiritual religiosity, and travel/tourism, involves openly facing complex, existential questions and life's uncertainties. In accepting existential finitude – the individual develops true compassion and concern for others and things with which the seeker relates with faith – that in turn leads to creativity and consistent opening to novel experiences (Batson & Ventis, 1982).

Although the spiritual traveller's quest is restricted to physical places and intellectual states that embody valued ideals, it is almost impossible to account for its diversity. For instance, the journey to a sacred centre is a way of finding release for suffering within the Japanese Buddhist tradition; the *Hajj* for the Muslims is an act of submission to the ways of Allah; the *Surot* of the Naciremas (North American ethnic group) is undertaken with the hope of enlightenment (*tsiruot*) and happiness; most Hindu pilgrims travel to Varanasi with the objective of being closer to the sacred, particularly at the time of death (for *nirvana*), while others may wander in the sacrosanct Himalayas for a *darsan* (sacred vision or contemplation) or *moksha* (liberation); most New Age pilgrims seek individual autonomy from religious institutions through the creation of their own space – a process of achieving self-spirituality.

Spiritual Centres

Spiritual seeking invariably takes people away from their hearth and towards outward locations – known and unknown, far away or nearby, manmade and/or natural. The catchment area perhaps determines the power of such locations, sites and landscapes. Griswold (1912) claims that there are only two places or 'creative centres' of the world's great religions, namely; Palestine – Arabia, and India – Persia, which are capable of influencing the largest number of devouts. For the Hebrews, Christians and Muhammadans, the Palestine-Arabian Centre is un-doubtedly a sacred hub, while descendants of the Aryan race, namely Hindus, Zoroastrians and Buddhists, converge to the latter. However, over the centuries, innumerable spiritual magnets have been identified and/or evolved.

The magnetic power of sacred centres is usually perceived as an inherent quality that has a potency to quench the seeker's quest. Nature, in the form of elements, scapes and living and nonliving things, has been (and is) an undeniable source of spiritual quest and quench. Something as simple as light cast upon places orients believers in otherwise undiffe-rentiated spaces (Weightman, 1996). The sacred drama of the movement of wind, sun, water and fire affords the 'initiate' an access to secret sights in the 'mysteries' that may be off limits to the ordinary pilgrim (Goodrich, 1998). Nature has its own ways to connect and communicate its spirit to the human soul. Believers of all faiths, especially Hindus, have contem-plated the divinity of hilltops, mountains, rock outcroppings, headwaters, river confluences, pools and groves of forests, lakes, trees, rocks, stones and other artefacts of nature, both in themselves or as part of the scape. Interestingly, water – a life-giving source – is subjugated to mountains in discourses on spirituality, even though it is the most important element in religiosity.

Of all nature's landscapes, mountains the world over have stirred human consciousness across civilizations and through time. The 'highly photogenic' and vast landscape of Sedona, for example, conveys extraordinary wonderment through its multicoloured sandstones and shales that have been spectacularly sculpted by the elements. Bernbaum (2006) alludes to the aura of mystery and sanctity of mountains through examples from China, Egypt, the USA, Asia, Japan, New Zealand, Australia and Europe. The unending litany on the potency of mountains for the human spirit has led to the belief that mountains could be the meeting-scapes (spaces or places) of the human (earth) with the spiritual (heavens). Gods reveal and express themselves, grant enlightenment and salvation, convey commands, wash sins and heal souls from these lofty abodes. Hindus believe that the high Himalayas are gods' cosmogony; to some they are earthy domiciles of gods.

Many men (holy and common) are known to have traversed the earth in search of spiritual epiphanies and have indeed witnessed the magnetism of iconic nature and culture. Consequently, mortals are known to have been endowed with immortality by later followers who have consecrated those places. MacWilliams' (2000) narration of Japanese Buddhist pilgrimage to the Saikoku and Bando temples (prototype of huts of holy men); Goodrich's (1998) account of pilgrimages to the shrine of T'ien Hsien Sheng Mu Pi Hsia Yuan Chiin (Heavenly immortal Holy Mother Princess of the Crimson Clouds of Dawn) on Miao Feng Shan in China; Sizer's (1999) description of living stories (a type of Protestant pilgrimage) as a journey to the holy land to meet, worship, listen and learn the spirituality and experience of indigenous Christians; Rountree's (2002) exposition on valued ideals enshrined at places such as Mecca, Lourdes, Jerusalem, Benaras – testify to human endeavour to sanctify places. The process of sanctification continues in contemporary times and can be evinced through the movements of holy men like the Dalai Lama (to Dharamsala), Sai Baba (in Puttaparthi) and Aurobindo (in Pondicherry) and the glorification of prominent personalities at secular locations like Lenin's tomb, Mao's Mausoleum, Elvis' shrine at Graceland and Mt. Rushmore, besides war memorials and historic sites. Through the centuries, people – indigenous and migrant settlers – have endowed places, events and people with conceptions of the sacred, perpetuating their beliefs through a consciously cultivated way of life and travels. Cultural meanings bestow places and artefacts with extraordinary power. Perhaps New Age spirituality and pilgrimages serve as exemplars of the process in current times (see Rountree, 2002). As passionate travellers, New Agers manifest their place –specific spirituality (Timothy & Conover, 2006). Furthermore, artefacts of nature and culture evolve into tangible designations of sanctity for pilgrims to reckon with. Thus, abstract spirituality becomes represented in shape and form (made sacred) and made extraordinary (hyped) through rituals and myths. Temples, natural and manmade structures, stones, metals, sand/soil, water, cloth, paintings, bricks, tombs, rocks, twigs, water are just a few dedicated artefacts. Given this context, culture enjoins nature for spiritual fulfilment.

Adventures of the Spirit

The essence of spirituality denies rationalization and/or theorization as the experience is intensely personal and subjective. Even more complex are connections between spirituality and tourism. Perhaps the concern here is the examination of the multifaceted intersection of spiritual experiences with touristic experiences. Through this intersection, both spirituality and tourism lay claim to the common aspects of exposure, leisure and re-creation.

Exposure

Spirituality and tourism have the quality of exposing the seeker to unfamiliar vistas and experiences. The questing traveller observes and absorbs the divinities of places, people, self and others, living and nonliving and actions through the aperture of sacredness. Although such manifestations of the sacred to the seeker are beyond rationalization, Eliade (1987) relates to them as hierophany. The power of hierophany not only brings trees, boulders, forests, landscapes, sites, mountain, elements, artefacts – like incense – to life, but can transform even the inadvertent visitor (Eck, 1981; MacWilliams, 2000; Weightman, 1996). Sacred meanings, connections, interactions and networks are revealed as a consequence of the perceptive realizations, which tend to dispel the disenchantment of the world (Beserke, 2001). In the process, the traveller is affirmed of his/her rootedness in the web of life, the drama of the cosmos and earth's ecology.

Leisure

Spiritual journeys and travels are essentially leisure undertakings, both as means and end, in a variety of ways. Firstly, they afford the seekers with a time to reflect, pause and contemplate (Besecke, 2001; Coleman, 2002; Rutherford, 2000; Snape, 2004). People have a chance to step back or look back and take a pause from the everyday rush and routine in order to be able to contemplate or comprehend themselves and their lives. This serves as a punctuation point in the ongoing drama of life and living. Secondly, the engagement and attunement generates a sense of being that is made evident through self-expression (Ibrahim, 1982; Ivakhiv, 2003; Mazumdar & Mazumdar, 2004; Organ, 1975) and self-actualisation (Abrahams, 1986). Following the possibilities for reflection and contemplation, spiritual engagement enables travellers to be themselves. Their liminoid state encourages a sense of freedom to 'tune' into their surroundings and experience proximity in extraordinary ways. In relating with their external environment, travellers gain a heightened sense of their inner being and capacities for participation and fulfilment. Thirdly, a heightened sense of being and place setting, transports people away from the cares of their everyday life and gives a fresh lease of consciousness to deadened senses and sensibilities. In essence, moments of leisure in new settings stirs the spirit to relish a sense of recovery, healing and wellbeing (Neilson, 2006).

Re-creation

Re-creation of self is a direct benefit to the questing traveller. New and extraordinary experiences, places, cultures, perceptions, feelings and connections have the potency to effect change and energize the spirit. People returning from the spiritual quests are known to perceive and behave with increased sense of consciousness and sensibility towards others as well as settings. According to the *sutras* (Japanese religious text), when people are spiritually exposed, defilements disappear and their bodies and minds become supple and gentle; they experience joy and enthusiasm and they have good thoughts (MacWilliams, 2000).

Effects of Spiritual Journeys

Journeys that engage the tourist/traveller in hierophanic contempla-tions tend to trigger a transformation of some kind in the individual. More often than not, these transformations generate virtues of conduct in people. The combination of contemplation, engagement, actualisation and wellbeing (as previously mentioned) fill people with energy to take actions toward the affirmation of higher goals of humanity, mankind and goodness. Self-transformation occurs in the context of humanity and its social organization (Guo, 2006). In being able to situate themselves in the world, they feel compelled to question, wonder and commit themselves to a harmonizing personal, societal and environmental wellbeing. It is as if the quest was a precursor to an extrinsic commitment (Watson *et al.*, 1988), or a prelude to open-mindedness for existentialism.

In Platonic terms, the individual discovers the true source of being by entering the realm of luminous knowledge, truth and goodness (Weightman, 1996). Hierophantic experiences of spiritual sojourns tend to release the mind, heart and soul of travellers to develop meaningful understanding of life. Personal growth may be in the form of mystic wonderments and/or a personal commitment to negotiate changes in the inner and outer landscape of self and society (Neilson, 2006). For example, Snape's (2004: 149) study, on the Christian Holiday Association (in Lancashire), provides evidence of personal growth through the 'cultivation of character' via comradeship, simplicity and reverence, while Collins and Kakabadse (2006) refer to intuitive contemplation of self, an awareness of their impact on others and a feeling of universal connectedness. It is instructive to acknowledge that commitment to personal growth occurs in the societal context. Tuan (1986) observes that culmination of spiritual journeys, at sacred sites, are characterized by the bonding of similarly inclined strangers, who have liberated themselves from the perils of travel and trials of everyday life.

Similar observations are documented by Eck (1981), whose study of Hindu pilgrimage (*tirtha*) reveals that pilgrim's visitations were socially less restrictive. These pilgrims overcame (crossed) the marginalizing discriminations of caste and gender at the location, as they performed their worship and rituals (e.g. bathing, listening to discourses, singing, giving and walking) – as if pilgrimage levelled all to one status – brought about by the annulment of barriers for the common cause of *bhakti* (devotion). The power of the cause seems to reproduce a transcendental society of equals. Turner explains this enhanced (perhaps equalizing) stature of pilgrims thus: 'Emotionally they gain the feeling of "communitas", socially they gain prominence' (Senn, 2002: 133). Meaningful networks of communes develop offsite and postpilgrimage as well. Ivakhiv's (2003) study of alternative intentional communities, of New Agers, such as the Quaker group, the Scottish Findhorn Community and India's Auroville, explicitly envision neomonastic communitarians. Such locations of spirituality imbue the 'power' to bring about harmony among people, as previously held notions of beliefs and values are replaced by new planetary cultures having their own 'centres of light'. For instance, the shared visions of New Age networks arise from the 'disintegration of industrial society'. This is indeed an interesting phenomenon in view of the fact that modern tourism is a product of industrialization. New Age travel culture, besides charismatic movements, further exemplifies the meltdown of differences and barriers in favour of the all-inclusive *philosophia perennis* (perennial philosophy of one divine truth) (Aupers & Houtman, 2006: 203).

Further, places and landscapes also acquire hierophanic qualities for the questing beholder. Many Eastern cultures (e.g. Indian, Japanese, Chinese), as well as the native groups in the West, have attached religious sentiments to specific locations and landscapes. This aspect of geopiety (pious emotion or sense of reverence) is generally evoked by the wonderment of the earth's bounties, beauties and diversities (Singh, 2004). Landscapes such as those of Stonehenge, Uluru, the Himalaya, Chaco Canyon, Haleakala Crater in Hawaii, Bolivia's Islands of Sun and Moon are named few places of spiritual significance. With time and cultural evolution, sacred landscapes and sites become dedicated to the spirits (Gods) for protection and veneration (Sopher, 1967). For example, the Kannon Temples (in Japan), which originated from 'wonder retreats in the wilderness', have expanded into as many as 66 temples that are founded throughout the Kinai and Kanto regions, all of which now constitute the *Junrei* (pilgrimage circuit) (MacWilliams, 2000). Similar scenic sites and route-based pilgrimages and circuits are found in India (Singh, 2004), China (MacWilliams, 2000), France (Pieper & Van Uden, 1994), Taiwan (Sangren, 1993) and Egypt (El-Aswad, 2006) – to name a few. When the scenery combines with therapeutic qualities, locations gather enhanced prominence and influence (Wilson, 2003).

Aesthetics of Spiritual Journeys

The discussion thus far, affirms that questing journeys and experiential tours/travels are indeed odysseys for personal fulfilment and the context of quest differentiates spiritual travellers and tourists from the rest; thus implying that such journeys fulfill the seeker in ways that are distinguished by the quest in the guest. This assertion leads to an inquiry into the nature of personal fulfilment questing journeys – the understanding of which is possible through a cause-effect approach.

Most scholars of philosophy agree that intellectual rationalization through modern science has wrought disenchantment of this world (Fellows, 2000; Tuan, 1993), making it almost impossible to believe (find meaning) in magical appearances and abstractions. Mathieu *et al.*'s (2006: 303) statement that, '... men ... speak more often to mountains, than mountains to men', aptly illustrates the insipid morbidity of this disenchantment. Besides rationality, pervasive societal strains and tensions have further deepened the disenchantment (Marx & Ellison, 1975). However, philosophical arguments favouring values, perceptions, instinct and consciousness, reinstate enchantment as an inherently aesthetic impulse in humans. A traveller's quest is as much a reflection of the restlessness of disenchanting darkness, as his/her firm belief in the existence of a utopian ideology. The dual needs to escape the darkness and experience mental events (intellectual creativity)ity provides the crucial context for spiritual sojourns, which can be understood via the four aspects of travelling (leisured mobility), exploration, distancing (disengagement) and meaningful engagements.

Travelling

Movements afforded through travel permit suspension from everyday life, and the sojourner enters the realms of the unknown. As an act of leisure, the traveller traverses at a leisurely pace and style. By moving oneself along a path, (s)he is made aware of the value of the journey as it progresses. Wanderers are known to be particularly mindful and appreciative of the leisure afforded by their wanderings. Heyd's (2003) study on the wanderings of Basho (Japanese poet-philosopher), encapsulates the aesthetic pleasure of bodily motion. Pilgrims, who traverse space and scale gradients, engage with their physical and mental efforts to derive a joy from their journey(s). Their movements encapsulate an aesthetic disposition and receptivity towards abandonment that generates a driving passion to move on.

Exploration

In the words of Keegan (1991), the purpose of spiritual journeying is to foster and develop one's spiritual potential. Spiritual seekers tend to be on a soul-searching mission for an enduring purpose for their lifetime. When motivated thus, travelling becomes an agency for exploration, and the people and places visited affords exposures into an array of possibilities. Furthermore, their self-exploration is enriched through the other. In the context of time, past and future ceases to exist – rather they are displaced by the transcendent present. The journeying process brings about maturation and individuation in the seeker.

Distancing

The physical act of distancing (moving away from) alongside the mind's ability to disengage from the everyday, routinised current(s) of life is a precondition for spiritual aesthetics. Tuan (1993) offers an insight through a comparison with mountainscapes that always provide a 'distant' view of all that is below and around. Their panoramic vistas renew the familiar into the unfamiliar and beautiful. Disentanglement from the mundane permits limens where the ordinary becomes extra-ordinary, the extraordinary ordinary, the secular is perceived as sacred, while the sacred becomes secular, and the meaningless is recognized as meaningful and vice-versa. The notion of secular pilgrimages (Eade & Sallnow, 1991; Eliade, 1959) is grounded within this realm of human ability. Psychological distancing affords relief to the mind for synchronized emergences from and immersion of the self in an unusual and vivid way (Porteous in Harrison, 2001). As Harrison indicates, at such 'moments' the perception is aesthetically conditioned to keep the tourist detached from the real world while permitting engagement with the personal experience of being the tourist.

Meaningful engagements

Unlike the consumptive tourist, the pious tourist's quest for enchantment spurs him/herself to engage in intense sensual pleasures that are personally meaningful to themselves. These pleasures are derived from contemplation of the surrounding milieu. The beholder experiences involvement and enwrapment – of being surrounded by divine creations (self, others and landscape). While referring to this state as 'instantiation', Harrison (2001) aligns it with Csikszentmihalyi's concept of 'flow'. Such a peculiar combination of connection with, alongside a disconnection from the world, is possible in a liminoid state – where the attention is fully centred and the ego is dissipated. Meaningful engagements of the kind, especially those pertaining to geo-pious expressions, have been empirically supported (see Singh & Singh, 2004; Hutson, 2007). An emergent sense of reverence in secular settings has led scholars to coin phrases such as secular pilgrimages (Eade & Sallnow, 1991; Eliade, 1959), quasipilgrimages and environmental pilgrims (Singh, 2006).

Consequent upon these aspects of a quest, pilgrims encounter profound experiences that are matched by transcendental awareness and purposive transformations. A Russian astronaut's description encapsulates the experience very simply thus,

I noticed in space a certain shift in perception – you begin to value things ... taken for granted on earth, like fresh air, a mountain stream, sunrise in a forest, a shivering of leaves on trees – all these things we do not pay much attention to down here. Georgei Grechko (in Tuan, 1993: 15)

The quintessence of spiritual experience thus includes an awakening of sensibilities and perceptive acuity for space recovery and community culture. More importantly, it is the integration of space with place, nature with culture, inner with outer being, formless and tangible, finite with the infinite that surfaces in the consciousness. Pilgrims feel energized, transformed and committed to becoming a link in the multitude of interconnections as landscapes and people generate multilevel meanings. Abstractions of truth, beauty and goodness are made comprehensible through the 'synthesia' of senses of the natural and super-natural. One word that somewhat captures the essence of this description is *darsan* – a philosophic term for perceptual viewing – a multifarious 'seeing'. Those whose questing journeys may have come to such fruition will find resonance, of their awakening, in the poetic creations of Wordsworth, Tolstoy, Aurobindo, Basho, Tuan and Tagore – among many other philosophers. Appreciation of the aesthetic reaffirms belief in enchantments of the earth – calling upon travellers to pay homage to its wonders and bounties.

Conclusion

Structures of modern travel and tourism have spurred movements of people in ever-increasing volumes of tourist traffic. How many of these are questing journeys or whether the quest is truly fulfilled, remain uncertain. Although spirituality and tourism are two polarized phenomena, past and current times and events enable a bridge between them. Spiritually meaningful experiences, afforded through a spectrum of alternative tourism, such as solidarity trips, educational travel, dark tourism (Stone, 2006), volunteering vacations (see Zahra, 2006), New Age and/or postmodern travel, besides religious pilgrimages, generate optimism for the future.

While this may augur well for the tourism industry, empirical investigations of religion and tourism document the insensitivity of tourists, and unsustainable irrationalities of modern tourism, at sacred and religious sites (Lee, 2006). Even when places hold sacred meaning to natives and visitors, development agents tend to offend the sense of place through their commercial exploits. Scholars, such as Buck (1978) and D'Amore (1998), are persistent in advocating the engagement of the conscious in the encounters of the visitor, visited and vistas.

Examples of spiritual experiences and related values being upheld over and above tourism development (see Schachenmann, 2006) are few and far between. Primary themes that are characteristic to spiritual tourism are sensibility, sensu'ousity, sustainability, all of which are experienced in *synthesia*. Nonetheless, each of these three dimensions are distinct in their own right – sensibility refers to intellect, perceptiveness and contemplation; sensu'ousity is typified by the aesthetic impulse that triggers wonder, awe and reverence in the initiate; sustainability emerges from our consciousness of, or awakening to, communes – inter and intraconnections of the living and nonliving, the inner and outer and human and divine. This lends to the understanding that spiritual and secular domains are not only interdependent, but also mutually inexclusive.

References

Abrahams, R.D. (1986) Ordinary and extraordinary experience. In V.W. Turner and E.M. Bruner (eds) *The Anthropology of Experience* (pp. 45–71). Urbana, IL: University of Illinois Press.

Aupers, S. and Houtman, D. (2006) Beyond the spiritual supermarket: The social and public significance of new age spirituality. *Journal of Contemporary Religion* 21 (2), 201–222.

Batson, C.D. and Ventis, W.L. (1982) *The Religious Experience: A Social-Psycho-Logical Perspective*. New York: Oxford University Press.

Batson, C.D. and Schoenrade, P.A. (1991) Measuring religion as quest: 2) Reliability concerns. *Journal for the Scientific Study of Religion* 30 (4), 430–447.

Bernbaum, E. (2006) Sacred mountains: Themes and teachings. *Mountain Research and Development* 26 (4), 304–309.

Besecke, K. (2001) Speaking of meaning in modernity: Reflexive spirituality as a cultural resource. *Sociology of Religion* 62 (3), 365–381.

Buck, R.C. (1978) Towards a synthesis in tourism theory. *Annals of Tourism Research* 5 (1), 110–111.

Cohen, E. (1979) A phenomenology of tourist experiences. *Sociology* 13, 179–201.

Cohen, E.H. (2003) Tourism and religion: A case study – visiting students in Israeli Universities. *Journal of Travel Research* 42 (August), 36–47.

Coleman, S. (2002) From the sublime to the meticulous: Art, anthropology and Victorian pilgrimage to Palestine. *History and Anthropology* 13 (4), 275–290.

Collins, P. and Kakabadse, N.K. (2006) Perils of religion: Need for spirituality in the public sphere. *Public Administration and Development* 26, 109–121.

Collins-Kreiner, N. and Kliot, N. (2000) Pilgrimage tourism in the holy land: The behavioural characteristics of Christian pilgrims. *Geo-Journal* 50, 55–67.

D'Amore, L.J. (1998) Spirituality in tourism – A millennium challenge for travel and tourism industry. *Tourism Recreation Research* 23 (1), 87–89.

Din, K.H. (1989) Islam and tourism – patterns, issues, and options. *Annals of Tourism Research* 16, 542–563.

Eade, J. and Sallnow, M. (eds) (1991) *Contesting the Sacred*. London: Routledge.

Eck, D.L. (1981) India's 'Tirthas': 'Crossings' in sacred geography. *History of Religions* 20 (4), 323–344.

El-Aswad, El-Sayed (2006) Spiritual genealogy: Sufism and saintly places in the Nile delta. *International Journal of Middle East Studies* 38, 501–518.

Eliade, M. (1959) *The Sacred and the Profane*. Orlando, FL: Harcourt Inc.

Eliade, M. (1987) *The Sacred and the Profane: The Nature of Religion* (W.R. Trask, trans.). New York: Hawest/Harcourt Brace Jovanovich.

Fellows, R. (2000) Enchantment. In A. O'Hear (ed.) *Philosophy, the Good, the True and the Beautiful* (pp. 91–104). Cambridge: Cambridge University Press.

Goodrich, A.S. (1998) Miao Feng Shan. *Asian Folklore Studies* 57 (1), 87–97.

Griswold, H.D. (1912) Some characteristics of Hinduism as a religion. *The Biblical World* 40 (3), 163–172.

Guo, C. (2006) Tourism and spiritual philosophies of the 'Orient'. In D. Timothy and D.H. Olsen (eds) *Tourism, Religion and Spiritual Journeys* (pp. 121–138). Oxon: Routledge.

Halstead, M.T. and Mickley, J.R. (1997) Attempting to fathom the unfathomable: Descriptive views of spirituality. *Seminars in Oncology Nursing* 113 (4), 225–230.

Harrison, J. (2001) Thinking about tourists. *International Sociology* 16, 159.

Hasselle-Newcombe, S. (2005) Spirituality and 'Mystical Religion' in contemporary society: A case study of British practitioners of the Iyengar method of yoga. *Journal of Contemporary Religion* 20 (3), 305–321.

Hesse, H. 1920. *Wandering; Notes and Sketches* (J. Wright (1972) trans.). New York: Farrar, Straus and Giroux.

Heyd, T. (2003) Basho and the aesthetics of wandering: Recuperating space, recognizing place, and following the ways of the Universe. *Philosophy East and West* 53 (3), 291–307.

Hobbs, J. (1995) *Mount Sinai.* Austin, TX: University of Texas Press.

Hood Jr, R.W. and Morris, R.J. (1985) Conceptualization of quest: A critical rejoinder to Batson. *Review of Religious Research* 26 (4), 391–397.

Hutson, G. (2007) Perceptions of outdoor recreation professionals toward place meanings in natural environments: A Q-method inquiry. Unpublished dissertation, Oklahoma State University.

Ibrahim, H. (1982) Leisure and Islam. *Leisure Studies* 1 (2), 97–210.

Ivakhiv, A. (2003) Nature and self in new age pilgrimage. *Culture and Religion* 4 (1), 93–118.

Keegan, L. (1991) Spiritual journeying. *Journal of Holistic Nursing* 9, 3–14.

Lee, Y-S. (2006) Myth, spirituality and religion in travel: Pre-industrial Korea. *Tourism* 54 (2), 97–106.

Leiper, N. (1989) Tourism and gambling. *GeoJournal* 19 (3), 269–275.

MacCannell, D. (1973) Staged authenticity: Arrangements of social space in tourist settings. *American Journal of Sociology* 79, 589–603.

Macwilliams, M.W. (2000) The holy man's hut as a symbol of stability in Japanese Buddhist pilgrimage. *Numen* 47 (4), 387–416.

Marx, J.H. and Ellison, D.L. (1975) Sensitivity training and communes: Contemporary quests for community. *The Pacific Sociological Review* 18 (4), 442–462.

Mathieu, J., Singh, C. and Hunni, H. (2006) Editorial. *Mountain Research and Development* 26 (4), 303.

Mazumdar, S. and Mazumdar, S. (2004) Religion and place attachment: A study of sacred places. *Journal of Environmental Psychology* 24, 385–397.

Neilson, P. (2006) Christian spirituality: Changes in the inner landscape. *The Expository Times* 117 (7), 277–281.

Organ, T. (1975) Indian aesthetics: Its techniques and assumptions. In Special Issue on Aesthetic Education in Civilization Perspective of *Journal of Aesthetic Education* 9 (1), 11–27.

Pieper, J.T. and Van Uden, M.H.F. (1994) Lourdes: A place of religious transformations? *The International Journal for the Psychology of Religion* 4 (2), 91–104.

Preston, J.J. (1992) Spiritual magnetism: An organizing principle for the study of pilgrimage. In A. Morinis (ed.) *Sacred Journeys: The Anthropology of Pilgrimage.* Westport, CT: Greenwood Press.

Rountree, K. (2002) Goddess pilgrims as tourists: Inscribing the body through sacred travel. *Sociology of Religion* 63 (4), 475–496.

Rudwick, M. (1996) Geological travel and theoretical innovation: The role of 'liminal' experience. *Social Studies of Science* 26 (1), 143–159.

Rutherford, I. (2000) Theoria and darsan: Pilgrimage and vision in Greece and India. *The Classical Quarterly* 50 (1), 133–146.

Sangren, P.S. (1993) Power and transcendence in the Ma Tsu pilgrimages of Taiwan. *American Ethnologist* 20 (3), 564–582.

Schachenmann, P. (2006) Spiritual values in Madagascar: The starting point for endogenous conservation initiatives. *Mountain Research and Development* 26 (4), 323–327.

Senn, C.F. (2002) Journeying as religious education: The shaman, the hero, the pilgrim, and the labyrinth walker. *Religious Education* 97 (2), 124–140.

Sharpley, R. and Sundaram, P. (2005) Tourism: A sacred journey? The case of ashram tourism, India. *International Journal of Tourism Research* 7, 161–171.

Singh, S. (2004) India's domestic tourism: Chaos/crisis/challenge. *Tourism Recreation Research* 29 (2), 35–46.

Singh, S. (2006) Secular pilgrimages and sacred tourism in the Indian Himalayas. *GeoJournal* 64, 215–223.

Singh, S. and Singh, T.V. (2004) Volunteer tourism – new pilgrimages to the Himalayas. In T.V. Singh (ed.) *New Horizons in Tourism: Strange Experiences and Stranger Practices* (pp. 181–194). Wallingford: CABI.

Sizer, S.R. (1999) The ethical challenges of managing pilgrimages to the Holy Land. *International Journal of Contemporary Hospitality Management* 11 (2/3), 85–90.

Smith, V. (1992) Introduction: The quest in guest. *Annals of Tourism Research* 19, 1–17.

Snape, R. (2004) The co-operative holidays association and the cultural formation of countryside leisure practice. *Leisure Studies* 23 (2), 143–158.

Sopher, D.E. (1967) *Geography of Religions.* Englewood Cliffs, NJ: Prentice-Hall.

Stone, P.R. (2006) A dark tourism spectrum: Towards a typology of death and macabre related tourist sites, attractions and exhibitions. *Tourism* 54 (2), 145–160.

Sutcliffe, S.J. and Bowman, M. (eds) (2000) *Beyond New Age: Exploring Alternative Spirituality.* Edinburgh: Edinburgh University Press.

Timothy, D. and Conover, P.J. (2006) Nature religion, self-spirituality and new age tourism. In D. Timothy and D.H. Olsen (eds) *Tourism, Religion and Spiritual Journeys* (pp. 139–155). Oxon: Routledge.

Tuan, Y-F. (1986) Strangers and strangeness. *Geographical Review* 76, 11–19.

Tuan, Y-F. (1993) *Passing Strange and Wonderful: Aesthetics, Nature, and Culture.* Washington, DC: Island Press.

Watson, P.J., Howard R., Hood Jr, R.W. and Morris, R.J. (1988) Age and religious orientation. *Review of Religious Research* 29 (3), 271–280.

Weightman, B.A. (1996) Sacred landscapes and the phenomenon of light. *Geographical Review* 86 (1), 59–71.

Wilson, K. (2003) Therapeutic landscapes and first nations peoples: An exploration of culture, health and place. *Health & Place* 9, 83–93.

Wuthnow, R. (1998) *After Heaven: Spirituality in America Since the 1950s.* Berkeley, CA: University of California Press.

Zahra, A. (2006) The unexpected road to spirituality via volunteer tourism. *Tourism* 54 (2), 173–185.

Zinnbauer, B.J., Pargament, K.I., Cole, B., Rye, M.S., Butter, E.M., Belavich, T.G., Hipp, K.M., Scott, A.B. and Kadar, J.L. (1997) Religion and spirituality: Unfuzzying the fuzzy. *Journal for the Scientific Study of Religion* 36, 549–564.

Chapter 9
Nature, Beauty and Tourism

CAIN SAMUEL TODD

Background

If philosophical discussions of natural beauty have hitherto been limited to the outer margins of Anglo-American 'analytic' aesthetics, the phenomenon of tourism lies well beyond its purview. Although what is sometimes termed 'environmental aesthetics' has quite recently become a burgeoning subfield within aesthetics, there are, as yet, no sustained philosophical treatments of the concept or phenomenon of tourism, with only brief remarks infrequently surfacing within the discussion of 'applied' issues (e.g. Carlson, 2000: 4, 11).[1] Yet the aesthetic appreciation of nature and tourism are closely intertwined (historically and philosophically), and there are important implications for reflecting on the latter that can be drawn out of contemporary accounts of the former.

Doing this is not, however, a straightforward task. In addition to the dearth of philosophical literature, one is immediately confronted by a number of other problematic considerations. For one thing, to say nothing of the scope of 'tourism', the scope of the term 'nature' is vast and immensely varied, encompassing everything from pristine wilderness areas to urban parkland, gardens, environmental art; it embraces individual objects ranging from small pebbles to large elephants, and 'items' ranging from beaches to herds of wildebeest; it ranges through species of fauna and flora, from small to large ecosystems, and it incorporates objects, phenomena and forces that both conform to and elude all of our different senses (Carlson, 2000: xx–xxi; Budd, 2003: 3).

Furthermore, philosophical accounts of the aesthetic appreciation of natural beauty must contend with some of the most difficult conceptual issues in philosophical aesthetics *tout court*. Clear and uncontroversial definitions and demarcations of 'aesthetic' and 'beauty', for instance, have proved continually elusive. Moreover, these fundamental concepts have until recently been considered almost exclusively in relation to the appreciation of art.

Philosophical discussions of natural beauty, common in the 18th century, had all but disappeared by the mid-20th century, during which the field of aesthetics became virtually synonymous with the 'philosophy of art'. Excited in particular by the development of 20th-century *avant garde* art, philosophers turned their attention to features such as: art's expressive capabilities; the role of artistic intention in interpretation; the institutional, historical and social contexts and categories constraining art's production and appreciation; the sophisticated language of criticism. Among other things, many of these features seemed to signal that aesthetic judgements of artworks could be subjected to standards of correctness and objectivity. In this light, it is perhaps unsurprising that some philosophers have even held that aesthetic experience can, properly speaking, only be elicited by works of art, leaving the appreciation of nature either bereft of aesthetic interest and value altogether, or as possessing such only derivatively, from art (e.g. Savile, 1982: ch. 8).

By comparison, nature and its objects came to appear aesthetically uninteresting, its aesthetic value (if allowed such) trivial, and our appreciation of it merely subjective. At best, it was thought that nature could exhibit a limited range of merely 'formal properties' for aesthetic contemplation, such as the arrangements of shapes, colours, patterns and the composition, balance and harmony of these (Carlson, 2000: ch. 1). This was also partly a result of a particular notion of aesthetic appreciation that had been inherited from Kant (1790), whose account of aesthetic appreciation in terms of *disinterested* 'pleasure' provided (and to some extent still provides – e.g. Budd, 2002) the immensely influential paradigm for understanding both aesthetic appreciation and natural beauty.

The idea of 'disinterestedness' demarcates the realm of aesthetic experience, appreciation and judgement from the moral and cognitive realms. It construes aesthetic interest as necessarily detached from everyday practical and personal interests and desires, and hence as comprising an interest or pleasure in an object (and its perceptual properties) 'for its own sake alone' (Budd, 2003: 12–15). Coupled with certain aspects of nature appreciation in the 18th century, particularly a concern with the 'picturesque', and landscapes that conformed to this ideal, the notion of disinterested attention effectively grounded such appreciation in formalist terms.

It is against this background that Ronald Hepburn's groundbreaking paper 'Contemporary Aesthetics and the Neglect of Natural Beauty' (1966) single-handedly rekindled philosophical interest in the aesthetic appreciation of nature and set the agenda for subsequent discussion. Hepburn argued that, unlike art, the appreciation of nature involves 'indeterminacy' because it is not 'framed', not set apart from its environment and is not subject to any intentional constraints. Far from entailing the triviality of nature's aesthetic interest and value, however, Hepburn stressed that, as actors engaged in the multisensory appreciation of our environment, the framelessness of nature requires our aesthetic interest to be creative and imaginative. This, he contended, provides a kind of aesthetic experience fundamentally different to that provided by art, but at least equally rich and rewarding.

Our aesthetic interest in nature, Hepburn argued, is not, and should not, reside merely in the 'uninterpreted' sensory, formal qualities nature offers. Rather, we should seek to understand natural objects *qua* the objects that they are, understanding nature on its own terms, where this involves an element of conceptualisation. For example, at a basic level, this may merely amount to appreciating a tree *as* a tree, or more specifically, appreciating a tree as the type of tree it is. But such conceptualisation need not be so prosaic and can involve the imagination, where our present perception is imbued with imaginative thoughts and feelings; for example, seeing a falling autumn leaf *as* symbolising temporality and vulnerability. Here is a widely quoted example:

> Suppose I am walking over a wide expanse of sand and mud. The quality of the scene is perhaps that of wild, glad emptiness. But suppose I bring to bear upon the scene my knowledge that this is tidal basin, the tide being out. The realization is not aesthetically irrelevant. I see myself now as walking on what is for half the day sea-bed. The wild glad emptiness may be tempered by a disturbing weirdness. (Hepburn, 2004: 50)

Such aesthetic appreciation widens the focus from merely formal properties to what might roughly be called the expressive properties possessed by nature, thereby enriching nature's aesthetic value and interest. More significantly, this enriched notion of the appreciation of nature 'on its own terms' is not arbitrary or merely subjective, but can be appropriate or inappropriate, and it allows Hepburn to contrast what he calls a 'serious' aesthetic interest in nature, with a merely 'trivial' appreciation.

The appreciation of both art and natural objects, Hepburn (1995: 65) contends, can be more or less serious, where the latter means something like being 'hastily and unthinkingly perceived'. Perception can be 'attentive or inattentive, can be discriminating or undiscriminating, lively or lazy ... The reflective component ... can be feeble or stereo-typed, individual, original or exploratory. It can be immature or confused' (Hepburn, 1995: 68). Primarily, 'an aesthetic approach to nature is trivial to the extent that it distorts, ignores, suppresses truth about its objects, feels and thinks about them in ways that falsify how nature really is' (Hepburn, 1995: 69).

The distinction between trivial and serious aesthetic appreciation has had crucial implications for subsequent discussion, and offers some fundamental conceptual tools for assessing the relationship between tourism and the appreciation of nature.

A final issue underpinning Hepburn's nuanced discussion of aesthetic appreciation is an *ethical* concern with the truth, integrity and seriousness of our appreciation of nature. Indeed, part of Hepburn's (1995: 65) argument justifying the trivial/serious distinction is that it 'matters' to us:

> When we see to defend areas of "outstanding natural beauty" against depredations, it matters greatly what account we can give of the appreciation of that beauty: how its value can be set alongside competing and vociferously promoted values involved in industry, commerce and urban expansion. If we wish to attach very high value to the appreciation of natural beauty, we must be able to show that more is involved in such appreciation than the pleasant, unfocused enjoyment of a picnic place, or a fleeting and distanced impression of countryside through a touring-coach window, or obligatory visits to standard viewpoints ...

This concern, coupled with practical policy-oriented environmental considerations, also clearly motivates contemporary accounts of the aesthetic appreciation of nature to attempt to ground the objectivity of such appreciation, and to explore whether there can be a *right* 'model' of interpretation and appreciation.

Thus, there are clearly ethical motivations behind many of the aesthetic theories we shall now examine, and the value of such theories, as well as the notions of aesthetic appreciation they propound, can be readily assessed in terms of their instrumental value in the service of these ethical ends. Further, as there are various ethical implications for nature arising from many types and aspects of modern tourism, the aesthetic attitudes and practices attendant on tourism can be assessed in ethical terms. Given that many of these ethical issues are dealt with more fully in other parts of this book, however, this chapter shall be limited to raising the important, and extremely difficult question of whether, and to what extent, tourism and its relationship to nature can be assessed and evaluated on purely aesthetic grounds. Does the trivial/serious distinction matter to us aesthetically as well as ethically?

Contemporary Models of Nature Appreciation

Natural environmental model

Using Hepburn's discussion as its point of departure, Allen Carlson's 'natural environmental model' represents the most comprehensively developed and influential attempt to delineate a philosophical theory of the aesthetic appreciation of nature. Carlson's primary concern is to defend the idea that there is a right or appropriate way of appreciating nature aesthetically, and this grounds both the seriousness of our appreciation and the objectivity of our aesthetic judgements regarding it.

Carlson notes that, unlike in the appreciation of art, it is unclear both what and how to aesthetically appreciate the natural environment, which lacks frames, artistic intentions, categorical constraints, interpretive conventions and so on. The central aim of his natural environmental model is thus to answer the questions of *what* and *how* to appreciate nature. The model is underpinned by two key claims: (1) 'that, as in our appreciation of works of art, we must appreciate nature as what it in fact is, that is, as natural and as an environment'. This immediately gives rise to (2) 'that we must appreciate nature in light of our knowledge of what it is, that is, in light of knowledge provided by the natural sciences, especially the environmental sciences such as geology, biology, and ecology' (Carlson, 2000: 6).

In order to demonstrate this, Carlson applies the well-known arguments of Kendall Walton (1970), intended to establish the correctness of category-relative aesthetic judgements of works of art, directly to the case of natural objects. Just as art-historical categories guide our knowledge and appreciation of art works, grounding serious and appropriate aesthetic judgements relative to the right category in which the objects are perceived, the categories of natural history and scientific understanding provide the relevant analogous aesthetic guidance for what and how to appreciate in respect of natural objects. The natural sciences and their commonsense predecessors and analogues, claims Carlson, provide knowledge of nature *qua* nature, nature as it actually is, and hence aesthetic appreciation (and the judgements it gives rise to) based on this will be appropriate and objectively valid:

Consider, for example, the aesthetic judgements we take to be true of Shetland ponies (charming, cute) and Clydesdale horses (majestic, lumbering). These judgements are made with respect to the category of horses. Similarly a foal (calf, fawn, etc.) typically strikes us as delicate and nimble when seen in the category of horses (cattle, deer, etc.), but a particularly husky one may strike us as lumbering or perhaps awkward if seen in the category of foals (calves, fawns, etc.). (Carlson, 2000: 60)

Aesthetic appreciation is thus essentially cognitive in nature, for the perception of nature's aesthetic qualities requires conceptualising natural objects relative to the kinds of things they are. Moreover, different types of objects, such as different kinds of landscapes, will call for different ways of perceiving:

we must survey a prairie environment, looking at the subtle contours of the land, feeling the wind blowing across the open space, and smelling the mix of prairie grasses and flowers. But such an act of aspection has little place in a dense forest environment. Here we must examine and scrutinize, inspecting the detail of the forest floor, listening carefully for the sounds of birds … (Carlson, 2000: 50–51)

Carlson thus uses these fundamental components of his model to reject other models of appreciation, which he claims falsify and trivialise nature. Of particular relevance for our purpose is what he labels the 'landscape model', which promulgates the 'scenery cult'. Having its roots in 18th century aesthetic theories, practices and preferences, particularly a concern with the 'picturesque', this model treats nature as if it were a landscape painting (Carlson, 1979). Focussing attention on 'those aesthetic qualities of colour and design which are seen and seen at a distance', the approach to appreciation it advocates is to divide the environment up into 'scenes or blocks of scenery, each of which is to be viewed from a particular point by a viewer who is separated by the appropriate spatial (and emotional?) distance' (Carlson, 1979: 131–132).

This model, according to Carlson, is guilty of misrepresenting nature. By 'flattening' nature into a static two-dimensional pictorial scene, it views nature as what it is not. The 'scenery cult provides a mode of appreciation that is inappropriate to the actual nature of the object of appreciation' (Carlson, 2000: 34). It thereby focuses exclusively on merely formal properties, on objects independently of the sorts of objects they are, and hence fails to accommodate the many other aesthetically salient properties that nature possesses. Indeed, Carlson devotes much effort to arguing against 'environmental formalism', the view that nature's aesthetic value consists primarily in its formal properties, the visual arrangement of shapes, colours and patterns. For this neglects the rich, multisensory, active mode of appreciation that the natural environment both encourages and allows (Carlson, 2000: 34). Instead, nature must be appreciated aesthetically also in terms of nonformal qualities such as expressive qualities:

> in order to appreciate and value the aesthetic quality of the environment, we must appreciate and value qualities such as the gracefulness of an antelope, the delicacy of a flower, the austerity of a desert landscape, the serenity of a quiet meadow, or the ominousness of the sky before a storm. (Carlson, 1977: 158)

There are numerous problems with Carlson's theory. First, Carlson talks of the knowledge necessary for the appropriate or correct aesthetic appreciation of nature as commonsense and/or natural scientific. But the distinction between commonsense and scientific knowledge is not rigidly delineated, and nor is it clear just how much knowledge is relevant or required. As Malcom Budd (2002: 136–137) notes, on the one hand complete knowledge of everything about any natural item seems unnecessary for some instances of aesthetic appreciation. For example, the judgement that a flower is beautiful does not seem to require the ability to describe its sexual functions. While on the other hand, scientific knowledge can, but arguably need not, give rise to or enhance aesthetic appreciation. A complete scientific knowledge of dung does not seem to entail an enhanced aesthetic appreciation of dung, at least not in lieu of an account of which scientific knowledge is relevant/irrelevant to aesthetic appreciation, an account that Carlson does not provide any-where.

Second, any given object will fall under numerous 'correct' categories, more and less general or specific, and hence will possess contrasting, and potentially incompatible sets of aesthetic properties. So, for instance, Hepburn's tidal basin can be equally correctly perceived as both tidal basin and beach, with no obvious reason to prefer, from an aesthetic point of view, one over the other (Budd, 2002: 137–138; Stecker, 1997). There will thus be no one set of right aesthetic properties and judgements about them, but potentially many such sets.

Third, the emphasis on knowledge as a necessary or even important feature of appropriate aesthetic appreciation has been rejected by a number of what have been called 'noncognitive' theories, which possess a common focus on the importance of noncognitive factors, such as emotional, imaginative and sensory engagement, in our appreciation of nature. There is space here only very briefly to mention the most prominent.

The engagement model

Also taking his queue from Hepburn's paper, Arnold Berleant (1995) has developed an 'aesthetics of engagement' model for the aesthetic appreciation of nature. Rejecting the traditional characterisation of aesthetic experience as disinterested contemplation, Berleant stresses the subject's active, multisensory engagement in the environment, and the holistic, perceptual unity of the subject immersed in and continuous with their surroundings.

The arousal model

Noel Carroll (1995) argues that we can have emotional responses to nature that are appropriate, serious and objective, but that are not necessarily dependent upon scientific knowledge of the correct category under which a natural object falls. For example, being exhilarated by the grandeur of a waterfall, or of a blue whale, is an appropriate response irrespective of any detailed knowledge of the nature of waterfalls or whales, the force and magnitude of the water falling or displaced, and so on.

To some extent, this model can be seen as an adjunct to rather than replacement of the natural environmental model, for it does not deny that scientific knowledge might enhance and, in some cases, ground aesthetic appreciation. Moreover, it could be argued that even the basic examples of emotional responses just given require at least some commonsense knowledge of the objects eliciting them, which Carlson's theory seems able to accommodate (Carlson, 2000: 7).

The aloofness or mystery model

A rather more extreme alternative to the kinds of models hitherto discussed is Stan Godlovitch's (2004) notion of an 'acentric natural aesthetic', which advocates the appreciation of nature not as it is 'in itself', but as fundamentally inaccessible and alien, aloof, distant and unknowable. The appropriate experience of nature is one of mystery and incomprehension, and as such nature is, as unknowable, beyond aesthetic appreciation altogether. But although beyond appreciation, nature is not beyond the kind of experience akin to religious worship, and this is the appropriate attitude with which to approach it.

Inevitably, each of these alternative 'noncognitive' models has incurred a number of criticisms (Carlson, 2000: 5–11; Budd, 2002: 129–146), an examination of which would exhaust the scope of the present chapter. However, it should be noted that they do succeed in highlighting the possibility that mere factual knowledge – of whatever degree – may be neither necessary nor sufficient for appropriate aesthetic appreciation of natural objects. Although some thinkers, such as Godlovitch, apparently reject the very idea that our aesthetic appreciation of nature is or should be anything but utterly subjective, others have raised important questions about the relevance of, for instance, myth, religion, poetry and other types of 'fictional', imaginative narrative and associated attitudes as possible groundings for the appropriateness and seriousness of aesthetic appreciation of the natural environment (e.g. Brady, 2003, 2004; Eaton, 2004; Foster, 2004). Indeed, it is important to recognise that Hepburn's own account of serious appreciation preserves the normative dimension of 'appropriateness' without a reliance on scientific knowledge as such.

Scepticism, relativism, freedom

The final 'position' we need to consider here is Malcolm Budd's (2002: 146–148) sceptical view that the very notion of there being an appropriate model for the aesthetic appreciation of nature is a 'chimera'. On the one hand, he holds, if the truth-value of an aesthetic judgement about a natural object is held to be relative – to a particular category, range of properties, perceptual mode etc. – then given, among other things, the changes and transformations to which natural objects are subject, the number of different categories in which any object figures and the many varied ways in which natural objects can be perceived, the range of aesthetic properties is open-ended such that there is no *one* right way of assessing an object's aesthetic properties and no one set that it 'really' possesses (Budd, 2002: 106–109, 127–148).

On the other hand, if aesthetic judgements of nature are not held to be so relative, then, simply, 'there is no such thing as the appropriate aesthetic appreciation of nature' (Budd, 2002: 129). Budd thus concludes that 'the search for a model of the aesthetic appreciation of nature that will indicate what is to be appreciated and how it is to be appreciated – something we have a good grasp of in the case of works of art – is a chimerical quest' (Budd, 2002: 147). First, because we are free to consider any natural item, and any natural context, and second, because:

there are no constraints imposed on manner of appreciation – what actions to perform and mode of perception to engage in – in virtue of the natural category an item belongs to that parallel the constraints imposed by categories of art ... The mistaken search for a model of the correct or appropriate aesthetic appreciation of nature reflects a lack of recognition of the freedom that is integral to the aesthetic appreciation of nature, a freedom which means that much more is up to the aesthetic observer of nature than of art, a freedom which is one aspect of nature's distinctive appeal. (Budd, 2002: 147–148)

It might appear that, were we left with this kind of scepticism, there would be little more to say about aesthetic approaches to nature, including any encompassed specifically by tourism. Instead, we would have to be content merely with listing different types of tourism, their aesthetic interactions with different types of and aspects of nature, and what the various models discussed might say about such interactions; an exercise of little philosophical interest. Fortunately, however, even if Budd is right – both about there being no one model of aesthetic appreciation, and about the integral freedom that gives the aesthetic appreciation of nature its value – his scepticism still leaves open the possibility that there are ways of appreciating nature aesthetically that are more or less appropriate or serious than others. And this has important bearings on how we should understand tourism in relation to the aesthetic appreciation of the natural environment.

Beauty and the Tourist Gaze

Whatever else it might involve, it seems clear that at the very least the aesthetic appreciation of nature must be understood as the appreciation of nature *qua* nature. This need not require the kind of scientific knowledge of nature that Carlson advocates. It requires merely that natural objects be appreciated *as* natural, but it thereby serves to exclude as appropriate any attitudes to nature that distort, falsify or neglect those properties that accrue to them simply as natural. It thus also captures certain intuitions that some types of tourism – and the attitudes, experiences and behaviours associated with them – may be less aesthetically rewarding or rich than others, to say nothing of their relative ethical worth. Just such attitudes have been thought to underpin many common tourist approaches to natural beauty – such as those that fall broadly under the 'landscape model' of appreciation discussed in the last section – which centre on a concern with the picturesque and manifest a 'scenery cult'.

Problems of the picturesque

Carlson (2000: 4) states that 'the picturesque remains the mode of aesthetic appreciation associated with the form of tourism that sees and appreciates the natural world primarily in light of renderings of nature typical of travel brochures, calendar photos, and picture postcards'. It depends on artificially framing landscapes through prescribed viewing points.

Recall that Carlson criticises this model because essentially it 'falsifies' its natural objects. Perhaps even more importantly, the 'cult of scenery' is objectionable because it allows nature only a kind of instrumental value: only insofar as it constitutes pleasing scenes, constructed largely by us from carefully chosen viewpoints, is it valuable. Such a view, it can be argued, does a disservice to nature on its own terms.

Unfortunately, however, this can look like a rather weak, or even misguided objection. After all, if such experiences are held to be aesthetically valuable by the relevant appreciators themselves, the simple falsification of the object of the experience is irrelevant to the aesthetic value of the experience per se, however it is gained.

This issue highlights the difficulty in finding *aesthetic* fault with certain kinds of experiences or attitudes, and suggests why many putative aesthetic criticisms of certain kinds of appreciation are underpinned by consequentialist concerns, often of an ethical nature. For example, from an ethical-environmental perspective, it is easy to see how certain attitudes underpinning modern mass tourism, and the cheap travel that enables it, may lead to a certain lack of awareness and respect, for example, for the fragility or biodiversity of certain 'unscenic' natural environments.

Nonetheless, there are genuine aesthetic reasons that count against certain forms of appreciation, and they appeal both to the state of the appreciator as well as the state of the appreciated, to aesthetic subject and object. For example, in respect of the latter, that mass tourism can come to destroy the very elements that gave rise to it in the first place is manifested not just, say, in physical changes in a place's visual appearance, but in the damage to the aesthetic value of a place, the loss of valuable aesthetic qualities. The imposition of too many constructed viewpoints in an area of scenic beauty, for instance, replete with signs and walkways, and with the building of roads to access them, may result in the loss of the 'wild, glad emptiness' that drew visitors there initially, or perhaps compromise a place's authenticity.

There is additional reason, too, to think that certain aspects of tourism can have negative, impoverishing effects on the nature of the aesthetic experiences one might undergo. For instance, elements of mass tourism, such as the frequent speed and superficiality with which places are visited, may limit the time and physical engagement required fully to understand and aesthetically appreciate them. One may simply miss salient aesthetic properties available for appreciation, such as sounds and smells, which are integral to the surrounding environment. Similarly, attention to conventional scenes and 'beauty spots' can limit our aesthetic experience and awareness of aesthetic properties because it leads to a focus primarily on formal 'scenic' properties at the expense of the many other types of properties and experiences that nature can offer. These might include expressive properties such as the eeriness of a moor, the solitude of a desert or the chaotic exuberance of a swamp.

So, it appears that tourist attitudes limited by conventional notions of the picturesque, and/or governed by the speed and superficiality encouraged by certain elements of modern tourism, can lead to what Hepburn labels 'thin' and 'trivial' experiences of nature, and they may be less rich and rewarding, less imaginative and hence less *intrinsically* valuable than 'thicker', more serious, richer experiences that approach nature on its own terms, rather than on ours.

It is important to realise that, depending on context and whim, the notions of trivial and serious appreciation can be cashed out in any number of different ways. A trivial view of nature might encompass a range of different faults and vices, such as simplification, falsification, sentimentality, lack of authenticity, arbitrariness, romanticisation. One might, under the sway of a Disney upbringing, view all animals anthropomorphically, falsifying their behaviours and needs inappropriately and indulging sentimental attitudes towards them. Or one might have a romanticised view of certain landscapes, desiring to conserve areas that are the way they are because in reality they are full of hardship and poverty (such as many of the pastoral landscapes of Europe).

Sentimentality, simplification, romanticisation and so on may in general be undesirable traits to encourage, but again it is difficult to say precisely what is intrinsically aesthetically wrong with them, as opposed to what is wrong with them in terms of the (ethical) consequences to which they can lead. A sentimental view of animals, for example, may blind one to the need for harsh culling measures to help conserve a particular ecosystem. Yet all of these faults also potentially impose various undesirable limits on our aesthetic experiences of nature. A sentimental conception of animals may hinder one's aesthetic appreciation of their hunting movements, and of the savagery of nature 'raw in tooth and claw'; an overly developed romantic sense of natural beauty may hinder an aesthetic appreciation of parts of nature lacking in grandeur or obvious scenic appeal, such as a beehive or city park.

Insofar as such modes of appreciation hinder or impoverish richer, deeper, more valuable aesthetic experiences of nature, they are to that extent aesthetically undesirable, and hence so too are the types of tourism which encourage them. There is thus good reason to think that there may well be aesthetic advantages to, and hence aesthetic (not just ethical) reasons for preferring some types of tourism (and the attitudes accompanying or manifested by them) in nature over others.

Trivial and serious tourism

Even granted some distinction between trivial and serious appreciation, the difficulty of drawing clear lines of demarcation between them in the hope of providing rule-like generalisations for assessing particular types of tourism and concomitant attitudes towards natural beauty should be evident. There is no one appreciative goal of tourism as such, and even if different general types of tourist attitudes can be roughly distinguished, in practice our attitudes towards nature, tourism and beauty are so varied, mixed, blurred and confused that it would be surprising if we were able to make anything other than rather crude generalisations and relatively cautious claims. Furthermore, these would ideally come packaged with the luxury of fine-grained qualifications that a modest book chapter cannot afford. In light of the previous discussion, however, there are a couple of crucial elements that must be considered in weighing up the aesthetic pros and cons of different types of tourism and tourist attitudes.

First, we must consider what we might call the 'mode of travel'. Given that a serious appreciation of nature is likely to be aided (though in extreme cases may no doubt be hindered) by time spent perceiving and contemplating it, just as the slow food movement urges a deeper, more serious appreciation of food, so slow tourism may encourage and afford the time required for deeper, more serious contemplation of one's surroundings. But this suggests further that it is not merely the speed as such that is important, for slower speeds of travel encourage more direct and deeper physical *engagement* with one's environmental surroundings. Indeed, this should be unsurprising, for in all spheres of aesthetic interest, from wine tasting to artistic contemplation, the rewards of serious attention, interest and value accrue only with the great time and (perceptual and cognitive) effort often necessary to sustain them.

It follows from this that certain forms of tourism and travelling are likely to confer certain aesthetic advantages, namely, any that involves some enhanced and relatively prolonged degree of physical engagement with one's natural surroundings. Concomitantly, it is easy to see that many of the conveniences of modern tourism count against such forms of travel and appreciation, and although they may, of course, bring with them their own new modes of aesthetic appreciation, these are less likely to encompass a rich and serious aesthetic appreciation of nature for its own sake.

A particularly interesting aspect of this concerns the contribution that the quick and convenient nature of modern tourism can make to depleting the sense of wonder that forms one of the primary aesthetic values and motives of travel in the first place. Wonder lies partly in encountering the new and the strange, and in the sheer difficulty and effort often involved in doing so. Once a place becomes a tourist destination, however, this effort may no longer be required to experience the very attributes that drove tourists there initially, and those very attributes themselves are thereby endangered. Instead, more effort may now be spent in trying to maintain serious aesthetic appreciation in the face of all the detritus of modern tourism that has afflicted so many places of natural beauty. In these ways, tourism can be self-defeating and important aesthetic qualities of nature, such as wonder, awe, the sublime, seem particularly threatened by the impositions of certain modes of travel and tourist experience.

Second, insofar as a primary goal of tourism, as such, is to visit and attempt to appreciate a place for its own sake, any tourism that lacks this fundamental attitude will likely lack the resources required to procure the rich and rewarding aesthetic experiences available from it.[2] Moreover, as Alain de Botton (2002) has eloquently pointed out, the escapist pleasures that certain types of tourism are held to provide are easily tarnished and shown to be partly illusory by the constant, inescapable intrusions of banal reality. This problem, de Botton posits, stems fundamentally from the psychological difficulty of changing ourselves to match or reflect a change in place, and hence a preponderance to colour the perception of our surroundings with our everyday cares and troubles. As such, any tourism that aims above all at mere escapism is in danger of harbouring both disappointment and an impoverished appreciation of the surroundings of the natural environment for its own sake.

Inspired by Pascal's thought that 'The sole cause of man's unhappiness is that he does not know how to stay quietly in his room' (de Botton, 2002: 243), de Botton himself advocates a kind of local tourism, which involves taking a heightened aesthetic interest in our everyday, familiar surroundings, perceiving them in greater detail, with greater reflection, and experiencing the aesthetic rewards that any place, not merely the foreign and exotic, can yield up to proper aesthetic effort. In effect, de Botton appears to suggest at least that we should broaden our idea of travel and tourism to incorporate such 'humdrum' aesthetic experiences.

This also offers us a salutary lesson concerning the potential pitfalls of 'serious' tourism where natural beauty is concerned. On the one hand, too much effort to engage with natural beauty, to appreciate nature on its own terms, may actually hinder us from enjoying it; either because of physical discomfort that may interrupt the contemplation necessary to aesthetic appreciation, or because our mere awareness of any (even potential) damage or disturbance to natural beauty may ruin all possible experiences of it for us. Too serious an attitude to tourism and natural beauty, that is to say, may indulge a certain preciousness, in some ways akin to the kind of romantic or sentimental attitudes of which more trivial modes of appreciation stand accused. For the sake of our own aesthetic experiences as tourists, therefore, one ought to be wary not just of appreciating nature trivially, but also of taking serious tourism too seriously.

Notes

1. Alain de Botton's *The Art of Travel* (2002) might appear to be the one exception to this, but his account consists in general, literary-inspired reflections and musings rather than sustained philosophical discussion.
2. Intrinsic and instrumental values are not necessarily mutually exclusive, though an interesting feature of some tourism, for instance, seems to be the value attached to being a tourist and travelling for its own sake, regardless of the objects one is ostensibly aiming to appreciate.

References

Berleant, A. (1995) The aesthetics of art and nature. In S. Kemall and I. Gaskell (eds) *Landscape, Natural Beauty and the Arts* (pp. 228–243). Cambridge: Cambridge University Press.

Brady, E. (2003) *Aesthetics of the Natural Environment*. Edinburgh: Edinburgh University Press.

Brady, E. (2004) Imagination and the aesthetic appreciation of nature. Reprinted in A. Carlson and A. Berleant (eds) *Aesthetics of the Natural Environment* (pp. 156–169). Peterborough, Canada: Broadview Press.

Budd, M. (2002) *The Aesthetic Appreciation of Nature: Essays on the Aesthetics of Nature*. Oxford: Clarendon Press.

Carlson, A. (1977) On the possibility of quantifying scenic beauty. *Landscape Planning* 4, 131–172.

Carlson, A. (1979) Appreciation and the natural environment. *Journal of Aesthetics and Art Criticism* 37, 267–275.

Carlson, A. (2000) *Aesthetics and the Environment: The Appreciation of Nature, Art and Architecture*. London: Routledge.

Carlson, A. (2004) Appreciation and the natural environment. In A. Carlson and A. Berleant (eds) *The Aesthetics of Natural Environments* (pp. 63–75). Ontario: Broadview Press.

Carlson, A. and Berleant, A. (eds) (2004) *The Aesthetics of Natural Environments*. Ontario: Broadview Press.

Carroll, N. (1995) On being moved by nature: Between religion and natural history. In S. Kemal and I. Gaskell (eds) *Landscape, Natural Beauty and the Arts* (pp. 244–266). Cambridge: Cambridge University Press.

de Botton, A. (2002) *The Art of Travel*. London: Penguin.

Eaton, M. (2004) Fact and fiction in the aesthetic appreciation of nature. In A. Carlson and A. Berleant (eds) *The Aesthetics of Natural Environments* (pp. 170–181). Ontario: Broadview Press.

Foster, C. (2004) The narrative and the ambient in environmental aesthetics. In A. Carlson and A. Berleant (eds) *The Aesthetics of Natural Environments* (pp. 197–213). Ontario: Broadview Press.

Godlovitch, S. (2004) Icebreakers: Environmentalism and natural aesthetics. In A. Carlson and A. Berleant (eds) *The Aesthetics of Natural Environments* (pp. 108–126). Ontario: Broadview Press.

Hepburn, R. (1966/2004) Contemporary aesthetics and the neglect of natural beauty. Reprinted in A. Carlson and A. Berleant (eds) *The Aesthetics of Natural Environments* (pp. 43–62). Ontario: Broadview Press.

Hepburn, R. (1995) Trivial and serious in aesthetic appreciation of nature. In S. Kemal and I. Gaskell (eds) *Landscape, Natural Beauty and the Arts* (pp. 65–80). Cambridge: Cambridge University Press.

Kant, I. (1790/1987) *Critique of Judgment* (W. Pluhar trans.). Indianapolis, IN: Hackett.

Kemal, S. and Gaskell, I. (eds) (1995) *Landscape, Natural Beauty and the Arts*. Cambridge: Cambridge University Press.

Matthews, P. (2002) Scientific knowledge and the aesthetic appreciation of nature. *Journal of Aesthetics and Art Criticism* 60, 37–48.

Savile, A. (1982) *The Test of Time*. Oxford: Clarendon Press.

Saito, Y. (1984) Is there a correct aesthetic appreciation of nature?' *Journal of Aesthetic Education* 18, 35–46.

Saito, Y. (1998) The aesthetics of unscenic nature. *Journal of Aesthetics and Art Criticism* 56, 101–111.

Saito, Y. (2004) Appreciating nature on its own terms. In A. Carlson and A. Berleant (eds) *The Aesthetics of Natural Environments* (pp. 141–155). Ontario: Broadview Press.

Sibley, F. (2001) Arts or the aesthetic – which comes first? In F. Sibley (ed.) *Approach to Aesthetics* (pp. 135–141). Oxford: Clarendon Press.

Stecker, R. (1997) The correct and the appropriate in the appreciation of nature. *British Journal of Aesthetics* 37, 393–402.

Walton, K. (1970) Categories of art. *Philosophical Review* 79, 334–367.

Chapter 10
Tourism and the Aesthetics of the Built Environment

ROBERT MAITLAND and ANDREW SMITH

> There is one dimension of place that is easily overlooked – a dimension that may be most critical of all because it concerns experience of the most primary sort – aesthetic. (Berleant, 2003: 42)

Introduction

Philosophers have always wrestled with aesthetics. Indeed, one of the three great questions asked by classical philosophers was 'what do we find attractive?' (Eagleton, 1990: 366). Related discussion cannot help but ask fundamental ontological questions about what it is to be part of this world, as well as more specific questions such as why we find something beautiful, tasteful or pleasurable. Researching aesthetic experiences of built environments can help us to understand more fundamental philosophical issues about how humans respond to, alter and interact with the world around them. This has particular resonance for tourism. Buildings and cities are experienced aesthetically by tourists, and to some extent the desire to impress tourists has always influenced urban design. In this chapter, the relationship between tourism, aesthetics and the built environment is explored through three key dimensions. First, the design of the built environment – and the way in which humans consume it – will naturally affect the tourist experience, and the way visitors understand and navigate cities. Second, 'being a tourist' influences how users of built environments experience them. The experience gained through tourism affects people's aesthetic judgments and demands, and this may influence them when they are back home. Third, the desire of cities to impress tourists shapes the form and appearance of built environments, and affects their aesthetic qualities. In subsequent sections, each of these interrelated elements is analysed.

There are also more specific links between philosophy and urban aesthetics. Alongside issues regarding the aesthetic experience of urbanism, certain philosophical positions are themselves embedded within urban design. Governments and elites dictate the production of the urban environment. So, as Dovey (1999) recognises, we cannot see the relationship between philosophy and urban aesthetics as one that merely concerns humans' experiences of cities. This ignores the 'pronounced effects of social structure and ideology' (Dovey, 1999: 44). A purely phenomenological approach (with its focus on lifeworld) can mean that the ideological dimensions of places 'remain buried and hence powerful' (Dovey, 1999: 44). Therefore, we must also try to unpick the philosophies embedded in urban design. This is particularly important, if, as Short (2006) contends, there exists a notable and growing separation between users of buildings and those who commission them. Accordingly, we need to analyse the production as well as the consumption of the built environment to understand the philosophical basis for urban aesthetics. This should reveal more about: how users of cities interpret urban design philosophies; if tourists consume cities differently than other users; and the extent to which tourism influences urban design. It is important to note that, to provide clarity, this discussion concentrates on developed world cities. For similar reasons, both tourism and aesthetics are discussed in general terms. Tourism is interpreted as visitation outside one's normal environment for leisure purposes (i.e. excluding business and employment-related travel).

Colloquially, 'aesthetics' is the 'beauty' of something, usually its visual appearance. More formally it refers to artistic merit; the value that distinguishes art from ordinary objects. This more restricted definition is difficult to apply to the built environment. As Graham (1997) argues, buildings and cities are usually built for a purpose, whereas a functional dimension is not a priority for art. The influence of place also makes it difficult to understand the built environment aesthetically. Every building, every street, every district, is part of a wider context and cannot be considered independently as artistic work can. Berleant (2003) deals with this by arguing that aesthetics should focus on the experiences we have, as well as the object we call beautiful. This is the approach taken here. Adopting a more inclusive interpretation of aesthetics is not to say that the key characteristic of conventional definitions – the quality of something that has a profound, inspirational (even spiritual) effect on the observer – is inapplicable. Indeed, the great cities and the great buildings are often those that induce effects normally associated with great works of art. This may involve 'an intense sensory presence, directly felt, resonant meaning and expanded awareness' – the very qualities that we praise as aesthetic (Berleant, 2003: 48). And this may be particularly important to tourism, where visitors are often 'disorientated figures' experiencing unfamiliar built environments (Jokinen & Veijola, 1997). Furthermore, if the aesthetic is that which involves the mind passing beyond the facts and glimpsing something of the idea of paradise (Graham, 1997), then it may be particularly relevant to tourism – a practice often understood as a form of escape, pilgrimage or fantasy.

The remaining sections of this chapter address the three-dimensional conceptualisation outlined in the introduction. Initially, we assess how urban aesthetics are produced by city elites and read by city users. This is followed by more specific analyses of the influences of 'being a tourist', and tourism's influence on urban aesthetics.

The Aesthetic Design of the Built Environment and its Consumption

The production of urban aesthetics: Philosophies embedded in urban design

Just as consumption of urbanism takes place at the cultural and individual level, so does the production of the built environment. The built environment may be representative of a certain era, shared identity or regime, or a more narrow expression of personal identity (Vale, 2006). The latter includes the philosophy of the architect or that of the client, or both. These philosophies need to be recognised, as they form the basis for the 'architectural language' or 'dominant reading' of cities. While this may be ignored, contested or distorted by individual users, the material built environment reflects elites' values, tastes and priorities (past and present). Elites utilise specific design philosophies to communicate their values and legitimise their power. The functionality of the built environment noted previously is a key cause of variances in these urban design philosophies and various positions have emerged in architecture to reconcile the use and importance of form within functional structures. These include functionalism (form from function), formalism (function follows form), rationalism (new forms invented to advance new social agendas) and expressivism (buildings express their functions symboli-cally). Architectural convention dictates that form and function should be linked strongly. But one approach to form and function employed in many urban tourist districts is 'façadism' – using ornamental external forms that mask functional interiors. Though derided by purists for its architectural dishonesty, Nasser (2007) argues it satisfies tourists who are more concerned with exterior appearance than the intricacies of cultural heritage. According to Gospodini (2001: 291) impressive façades for cultural institutions may satisfy multiple tourist markets, as functional provision for high culture does not necessarily preclude aesthetic consumption by mass-market tourists – as the external appearance of the building and its relationship to the existing townscape is used as the main pole of visitor's attraction. The emergence of such strategies suggests we need to consider the role of tourism as a key objective of contemporary urban elites – and therefore a key influence on urban aesthetics.

Even when form follows function, structures are imbued with meanings that signify certain values. Therefore, some philosophical analyses extend beyond merely establishing the relationship between form and function, to consider their socioeconomic basis. For Marxists (historical materialists), the form of built environments is connected to the mode of production. Therefore, when we admire the appearance of medieval towns such as Florence, Siena or Bruges 'we are first and foremost respecting a form of production and consciousness – merchant capitalism' (Cuthbert, 2006: 187). Similarly, while Rome and Prague may appear to 'have sprung in some autochthonous manner from their natural sites' (Norberg Scholz cited in Dovey, 1999: 44), their form is the result of political and ideological struggles over centuries.

The experience of urban aesthetics: The users' perspective

Recent analyses have emphasised the pervasiveness of tourism (Urry, 1990; Franklin, 2003). If this is accepted, it makes sense to analyse general ideas about urban aesthetic experiences, as tourist experiences may have commonalities with other city users. Depending on the philosophical position of the researcher, aesthetic experience of built environments is also referred to as 'consumption', 'perception', 'conception' or 'reading'. For many, aesthetically pleasing cities are those that facilitate 'pleasurable' or 'sensory' perception. Therefore, it is unsurprising that the dominant approach is to consider aesthetic experience as a form of environmental perception. According to Cassidy (1997), there are three main conclusions to be drawn from debates within perceptual studies. First, the environment provides information that is both necessary and important in the perceptual process. Second, it shapes our perceptual processes by determining the content of our perceptual memory. Finally, an individual selects, interprets and gives meaning to the information received and constructs a 'phenomic' environment, which then overrides the objective environment. This highlights the importance of understanding the perception of the built environment – and therefore its design – as well as recognising the ultimate consideration, an individual's conception of that environment.

But, it is not enough simply to consider the relationship between individuals and built environments. As well as being material and 'phenomic' entities, cities are also cultural landscapes produced through social and cultural practices. As Pike (1996: 246) states, the city is, 'by any definition, a social image'. Though individuals may feel at the centre of their own experience, they are only able to see within paths and networks of socially constructed meaning (Phillips, 1993). Therefore, some analyses of urban aesthetics (e.g. in iconography) locate them at the shared level, rather than as individually constructed representations. This conforms to Berleant's (2003: 46) approach to urban aesthetics in which we must understand the person and the setting, 'together with the range of historical and cultural influence, knowledge and meaning that imbue that experience'.[1]

Tourism studies have relied heavily on ideas (from behavioural geography and environmental psychology) concerning environmental perception; both for concepts and associated methods. But these ideas have emerged from analyses of peoples' perception of their immediate surroundings. By definition, tourism research is more concerned with perceptions of unfamiliar surroundings. This unfamiliarity helps to justify giving special consideration to *touristic* experiences of urban environments.

Being a Tourist: Tourism and the Development of Aesthetic Preferences and Tastes

Tourism has helped to shape how we perceive the built environment. Urry has famously argued that tourists look at things differently: there is a 'tourist gaze' distinct from 'the non-tourist forms of social experience and consciousness' (Urry, 1990: 2). The tourist gaze is constructed through signs and is 'directed to features of landscape and townscape that separate them off from everyday experience' (Urry, 1990: 3). When people travel, they look at new things and are exposed to a greater variety of aesthetic experiences than if they had simply stayed at home. Of course, tourism is not the only way in which people gaze on new things: in our increasingly multimedia world we are bombarded with images of places and it has been argued that the city is constructed by images and representations as much as by its built environment or investment patterns (Fitzmaurice, 2001). However, the practices of tourism mean that it has a particularly significant effect on how people learn to make aesthetic judgments. Learning takes place not only in formal educational settings, but also through experience – 'experiential learning'. People learn from their experiences, provided these are followed by reflection, analysis and evaluation (Boydell, 1976; Minnaert, 2007). Tourism practices encourage such reflection and analysis. As Urry (1990: 3) says, people 'linger' over the tourist gaze, which is then 'visually objectified or captured' through photographs, videos and their written accounts. This has been reinforced by technical changes that make capturing, sharing, discussing – and reflecting on – images easier and more widespread: digital cameras, mobile phone cameras, blogs, photo-sharing websites for example. But tourism practices are often more explicitly associated with practices of learning. Visitors may be encouraged to reflect on their experiences in a particular way – through consulting guidebooks, visiting interpretation centres or through the way itineraries are assembled by guides. They may plan their own exploration of places and reflect on the aesthetic qualities they have seen (Maitland, 2008).

The practice of tourism then focuses strongly on the aesthetic of places, and encourages the reflection that turns experience into learning. Travel, in particular contexts, has long been linked with learning about taste and aesthetics. In the 18th century 'Grand Tour', members of the upper class toured classical sites and cities of mainland Europe to acquire both aesthetic taste and specific objects to furnish their grand houses. Their taste was cultivated within a world view that emphasised orderliness and restraint in architecture and discouraged what Addison (cited in Styles & Vickery, 2006) termed the mere pursuit of luxury. The idea of decorum reflected a hierarchical view in which the good taste displayed by possession of objects or buildings depended on their appropriateness to one's social station (Styles & Vickery, 2006).

The notion of decorum became less influential after the 18th century with accelerated decline in the later 20th century. This can be associated with the growth of tourism. Travel experiences became accessible to more people as pioneers like Thomas Cook and the Polytechnic Touring Club organised visits in the 19th century. These early ventures were often linked with learning, for example through visits to expositions and World's Fairs, which frequently concerned themselves with the built environment. However, the gradual development of mass tourism can be seen as part of a process of undermining elite taste and exclusivity, and thus both reflecting and reinforcing a decline in decorum. Holidays and resorts were frequently associated with vulgarity, enthusiasm, absence of restraint and the pursuit of luxury. They were separated in time and space from everyday life, and offered distinctly different objects for the tourist gaze, whether on a bank holiday trip to Blackpool in the 19th century or a package holiday to the Costa Brava in the 1960s (Krippendorf, 1987).

The experience of travel has had a growing impact as it shifted from an elite pursuit to a common experience. This might be seen as a refreshing opportunity for city designers to rework the urban aesthetic. Building at the seaside could range from the ostentatious (Blackpool's Pleasure Beach and Tower) to the daring but restrained (the modernist De La Warr Pavilion at Bexhill-on-Sea). However, discussions of tourism and the built environment are inevitably inflected with the derisory tone applied to tourists themselves (MacCannell, 1976). Contemporary commentators frequently see tourism as blight (e.g. Theroux, 1995) and resorts as contrived, banal and without interest – places in which the only effect on aesthetic tastes will be to demean them. But not all tourism is like this (Theroux himself is a serial tourist, after all), and as Judd (2003) says, even in closely regulated tourist environments, visitors can contrive their own experiences through ironic distancing, refusing to conform to the programmed experience of the package tour or escaping from the tourist enclave – especially easy in cities. As Meethan (2001: 112) says, tourists need not be 'passive consumers or even cultural dupes ... easily fooled'. Even in mass tourism resorts, for most visitors, travel offers the opportunity to look with different eyes, and through the practices of tourism reflect on and learn from what they have seen.

Our knowledge about visitors' aesthetic judgement of place is limited, but we can be confident that it develops as a result of travel and will be applied back home. People learn new skills as tourists and this affects their consumption demands (Franklin, 2003) and carries through to their aesthetic judgements in their everyday life. Viewing the 'extraordinary' as a tourist affects the way 'ordinary' places are viewed back home, as users now see them with an 'increasingly informed eye' (Urry, 1999: 74). This is particularly so as touristic experience and behaviours are now less clearly separated in time and space from everyday life (Franklin & Crang, 2001). In cities, residents and visitors enjoy the same activities and consume 'the new urban culture' (Judd, 2003: 32). But what residents want is influenced by their own travel experiences, which affect how they look at and interpret the built environment: 'the rise of the new urban culture devoted to aesthetic pursuits has remade cities into places that provide the consumption opportunities of travel right at home'

(Judd, 2003). Accordingly, the aesthetic of the holiday has been imported into the design of cities – faux Mexican restaurants in shopping malls; the cool and pared-down aesthetic of bars in fashionable areas, borrowed from Barcelona or Manhattan style; in the UK, the new ubiquity of pavement cafes. Travel helps people learn to be more sophisticated consumers of place and as they 'act like tourists in their own city', their aesthetic preferences change, and cities change to accommodate them: 'flourishing districts of urban entertainment concentrate objects, or at least their facsimiles [gathered] from the world over' (Lloyd, cited in Judd, 2003: 32). Tourism's influence on city aesthetics has grown stronger, but has long been important.

Tourism as a Key Influence on Urban Aesthetics

In this section, the influence of tourism on urban aesthetics over the past century is examined. We analyse a series of aesthetic movements chronologically, but recognise that they overlap. The aim is to look at whether cities have changed their appearance to cater for tourists' demands (or what they think tourists demand) and to examine whether we can talk of an emerging tourism imperative, or even a tourism aesthetic, within contemporary urban design.

The role of tourism in city aesthetics during the 'City Beautiful' movement (c. 1890–1930)

The City Beautiful (CB) movement attempted to establish (mainly in US cities) a 'purely visual approach to planning' in the period c. 1893–1932 (Mumford, 1961: 406). CB schemes involved the imposition of monumental architecture with wide road axes, tree-lined boulevards and large civic squares. Commentators expressed their admiration for these aesthetics, particularly the 'beauty and unity of the harmoniously grouped public buildings' (Baldwin Hess, 2006: 515) and some have drawn parallels between the CB movement and today's image conscious 'tourist city' (Smith, 2007). But the aesthetics of the CB movement were not motivated primarily by a desire to impress tourists. Their design ultimately aimed to 'cure' cities of societal ills through a morally uplifting urban environment meant to civilise populations. This explains the introduction of monumental civic buildings, deliberately conceived to 'stir the masses' (Lang, 2003) and around which diverse populations could coalesce (Baldwin Hess, 2006). Yet tourism was a consideration in CB schemes. Civic leaders thought the associated aesthetics could enhance the competitive advantage of a city, including its reputation as a tourist destination (Baldwin Hess, 2006). Indeed, Cocks (2001) suggests that the CB movement was increasingly sustained by the desire to appeal to tourists as well as to improve the urban environment for citizens. This was particularly true in capital cities, such as Washington DC, where 'enhancing the beauty of the ceremonial core took precedent over improving surrounding neighbourhoods because it catered to both patriotism and the tourist industry' (Gournay, 2006: 118). Attracting 'refined tourists' was apparently part of the project to civilise cities, helping them to overcome 'urban parochialism' and inspiring a 'sense of civic belonging' (Cocks, 2001: 172). Several commentators mention the civilising effect that tourists had on late 19th and early 20th century cities. Gruen (2001) suggests that the presence of tourists helped Asian immigrants assimilate in San Francisco. The extent to which the tourists themselves were impressed is hard to gather; some schemes were so big that they were scarcely discernible from ground level. Accordingly, Kolson (2001) dismisses CB schemes as 'meaningless pomp' and 'government ghettos'. Baldwin Hess (2006: 536) is kinder, suggesting that CB projects 'endure as memorable urban places'. Whatever their legacy, during this period tourism had begun to influence urban aesthetics, albeit in an indirect manner.

The role of tourism in the aesthetics of modern cities (c. 1880–1939)

As Gruen (2001: 178) suggests, tourists did not merely wait around for 'broad avenues, stately buildings and gleaming monuments' of the CB movement. They wanted to visit cities to see historic sites and new monumental spaces, but also to see the emerging modernity of cities with more varied aesthetics. Thus, modernity itself became a tourist spectacle (McCannell, 1999). As Gilbert (1999: 281) suggests, during this period tourists visited London 'to see a new world in the making'.

The design of individual structures, and whole urban districts, was influenced by an emerging imperative to impress the lucrative tourist audience. New York, Chicago and other 'New World' cities were able to reinvent themselves as tourist spectacles of modernity, in a way established European cities could not (Gilbert, 1999). Those responsible for urban development began to 'make' cities in a way that impressed visitors. Rodriguez (2000: 69) feels that the construction of new bridges in the San Francisco Bay Area 'stimulated a more general assessment of the city's landscape for its attractiveness to tourists'. The attention to aesthetics and tourism provision in the design of the Golden Gate Bridge certainly implies that tourism was prioritised. Similarly, a desire to facilitate tourists affected later designs for skyscrapers. For example, the building of an observation deck within the Empire State Building in New York suggests it was 'consciously designed with tourism in mind' (Gilbert & Hancock, 2006: 93). So, although tourism cannot claim responsibility for the new vertical dimension of cities, tourism did affect their design, and crucially, their symbolic importance. Ultimately, it was tourism interest that turned buildings like the Empire State Building into modern wonders of the world. Cities knew that being of interest to tourists was a sign of world class status, and they actively invited the tourist gaze. The new skyscrapers also provided ways for tourists to aesthetically consume cities as holistic entities.

Yet, the aesthetics of emerging modern cities in the 1930s were still influenced by established European capitals. Urban authorities and tourists, particularly in the USA, lacked confidence in the attractiveness of new cities, and, accordingly, they used reassuringly conservative architectural styles (e.g. neoclassicism). For Gruen (2001), opinions of whether San Francisco was world class were based on how closely it resembled European 'Grand Tour' cities; the city was promoted as the 'Paris of the West' and early hotels were designed using European styles. When new aesthetics were employed, they were often linked to more established tourism features. Tourist guidebooks compared skyscrapers to medieval cathedrals and to San Gimignano – the medieval Italian city of towers (Gilbert & Hancock, 2006). The established aesthetic of the 'Grand Tour' was still influencing the design of new cities.

The role of tourism in the aesthetics of modernist cities (c. 1945–1970)

City Beautiful schemes and their European equivalents were supplanted by modernist 'rational planning', concentrated on social and housing problems (Baldwin Hess, 2006). According to Doctor (2000) in this new era, beauty was no longer seen as synonymous with the picturesque. Instead, a new engineering aesthetic became prominent – particularly in the immediate post-war period of reconstruction, which involved a conscious rejection of 'grandiose schemes for lining city traffic ways with pompous facades' (Hasegawa, 1992: 6).

Although the buildings, districts and cities built in the 1950s and 1960s were eventually derided for their ugliness, it is too easy to dismiss them as aesthetically misguided or deliberately ugly. Many of the schemes were designed, as with previous ones, to communicate visionary, progressive urbanism. Like CB projects, the idea was often to order and rationalise cities, while incorporating striking statements to communicate a city's status. Beauty, replicating Haussmann's Parisian philosophy, was provided by order, symmetry and vista. So there was continuity between modernist cities and CB antecedents. But, of course, there were also key differences: modernist urbanism continued to use axes and long views, but 'rather than axes that terminate in a single building, modernist urbanism emphasises a complex, balanced symmetry of juxtaposed buildings and framed landscapes' (Vale, 2006: 27). This architecture became closely associated with radical political philosophies and associated regimes, because it communicated the power of government and because of the associated opportunities for surveillance.

It would be a mistake to see tourism as key to the philosophy of modernist cities. The lack of a recognised style and the relentless uniformity in many modernist cities meant that it was 'difficult to sell an image of the town' to tourists (Simson, 2000: 195). But not all modernist cities are considered to be aesthetic failures; some have emerged as tourism destinations. Indeed, the more complete examples of 'high modernism', such as Brasilia, Brazil, now attract tourists because of their aesthetic appearance.[2] Other less coherent examples of modernist schemes, such as Birmingham's city centre, have already been torn apart, denying tourists the chance to view a complete example of 1960s urban design. Birmingham's project, if implemented fully and maintained properly, might have left a city worthy of tourist visitation based on its aesthetic qualities, rather than despite them. Commentators of the period certainly thought so. In 1970, Sutcliffe wrote that the foundations had been laid for 'one of the most visually dynamic and exciting cities in Britain – if not Europe' (cited in Kennedy, 2004: 1). This suggests that there was an expectation that the city would attract tourists because of the innovative new spaces and aesthetics. Ironically, the changes made to cities like Birmingham in the 1960s are now being replaced by structures that have very similar objectives to their maligned precedents: to update the city's image as a progressive city.

Ultimately, the constant regeneration of cities like Birmingham prevents nostalgic aesthetic consumption – something central to the success of most tourist cities. Cities may come to regret hasty demolition, particularly as some modernist urban aesthetics are already being reassessed. According to Doctor (2000: 199), 'the urban districts that came into being in the 1950s and 1960s are appreciated in Rotterdam in the same way other cities cherish their medieval town centre'. But Punter (2005) expresses relief that related sentimentalism did not get in the way of Sydney's urban planning. He dismisses claims that the city has been robbed of its modernist heritage, pointing out that only architectural purists would support preserving modernist spaces 'in a city littered with charmless examples of the genre' (p. 144). This raises the possibility that modernist cities, although not necessarily built with tourism in mind, may be preserved for retrospective consumption by tourists: even if more regular users would prefer them to be consigned to history.

As well as rebuilding towns and cities, the post-war period also involved the construction of new towns designed according to modern principles and priorities (Marr, 2006). Some of them have been very successful from a residential perspective. But their perceived lack of atmosphere and discernible centres severely limits their tourism potential. As Glancey (2006) recognises, city tourists are drawn to a historic centre, grand square or central monument, and the 'jumble and bustle' of cities – none of which is present in these places. Unsurprisingly, there is little evidence that tourism influenced their design. However, at Basildon's inception, the UK's Minister for Town and Country Planning did proclaim that 'Basildon will become a city which people from all over the world will want to visit' (cited in Glancey, 2006). Like Sutcliffe's predictions about Birmingham, this forecast proved optimistic. If it takes 60 to 70 years for an aesthetic style to be regarded nostalgically, these towns may have to wait until c. 2030 before they can compete as tourism destinations.

The role of tourism in the aesthetics of postmodern cities (c. 1970–)

Tourist sites have been redesigned and packaged for mass consumption for over two hundred years (Lasansky & McLaren, 2004). However, as tourist numbers have increased, the process has become more intense and much more widespread. This period of tourism growth broadly coincided with significant changes in attitudes to the aesthetics and design of places. While some modernist' redesign of places proved elegant and successful, more commonly it proved unpopular with users and there was a reaction against 'naïve functionalism, that neglected aesthetics' (Laurence, 2006: 160).

By the 1970s, modernism was under attack on a number of fronts. Architects and planners were criticised as 'evangelistic bureaucrats' (Davies, 1972) – well intentioned but out of touch with what people wanted – and the professions themselves questioned whether they possessed the sophisticated tools of planning and design needed for complex manipulation of places and their aesthetics (McLaughlin, 1994). Left critiques saw modernism's ambitions as futile attempts to resolve capitalism's contradictions (Thomas, 1999), while neoliberals sought to reduce state intervention in city design. The success of neoliberal ideologies meant that power to make aesthetic judgements shifted from professionals and local politicians to developers and users. For example, in the UK, central government instructed local authorities that design was subjective, and they should not use planning control to impose their tastes (DoE, 1980). More broadly, an emerging 'postmodern' architecture rejected the spare modernist aesthetic in favour of eclectic design, borrowing from historic styles, sometimes applied in exaggerated or playful ways and sought to provide a richer, more complex and livelier aesthetic. Venturi, one of its leading practitioners, saw vitality and messiness as interlinked: to Mies van der Rohe's famous modernist epigram 'less is more' he retorted 'less is a bore' (Venturi, 1966). Postmodern design was often intended to be seen in 'knowing' or 'ironic' ways, and explicitly drew lessons from the messy and chaotic, but exuberant and popular cityscapes of resorts like Las Vegas (Venturi *et al.*, 1972). The 'playfulness' associated with tourism and the increasingly eclectic tastes of tourists contributed to the production and consumption of this aesthetic style. It is against this backdrop that we can consider the ways in which tourism has contributed to the aesthetics of places. Three perspectives are outlined: the contribution of tourism to a more consumer-focused aesthetic; its promotion of amenity; and its role in the development of 'iconic' buildings.

First, tourism promoted a more consumer-focused aesthetic as former industrial cities sought to attract visitors when traditional manufacturing and distribution declined (see e.g. Law, 1993; Beioley *et al.*, 1990). For pioneering cities like Baltimore in the 1970s, tourism development was a means of combating both industrial decline and associated images of a decaying and dangerous place. As that very image made it hard to attract visitors, development had to take place in limited areas – 'tourism bubbles' (Judd, 1999) – that not only offered a concentration of attractions to lure visitors, but were both physically and symbolically disconnected from the rest of the city. This meant that visitors could be attracted to an area that felt safe, appealing and provided – in Lynch's terms – a comfortable environment (Pearce & Fagence, 1996). This approach was emulated around the world. Key to it was the reaestheticisation of the built environment (Clark, 2003): tourists had to be persuaded that areas were worth visiting and this required not just new attractions like museums and festival marketplaces, but the revalorisation of heritage and surviving buildings. Disused warehouses, empty textile mills and abandoned docks were given a makeover: no longer ugly, outmoded derelicts, but visually appealing and interesting survivals from an industrial past. While evangelistic bureaucrats could impose an aesthetic they thought city users *should* want, the creators of tourist bubbles had to consider what visitors *would* want – even if that involved contested aesthetic judgments (Silk, 2007).

Second, these lessons about the importance of amenity and aestheticisation were applied as cities sought to make their older central areas attractive to visitors. Retained historic streets and buildings were essential elements (Montgomery, 2003, 2004), but were often little more than façades behind which mixes of new uses could be accommodated (Maitland, 1997): an emphasis on look and appearance that echoes the 'holiday theatre' of resorts (Krippendorf, 1987). The intention was to create a lively atmosphere and street scene, reflecting ideas about the social qualities of space, design and an aesthetic that appeals to users (Lynch, 1960; Jacobs, 1961). There were echoes of the tourist-historic city: historic buildings, heritage, a mix of uses, opportunities to pause and enjoy the street scene or play the role of flaneur in a street cafe. Tourism has a dual role in creating these areas. They are designed by developers to attract visitors – but are intended to appeal to residents too. That means they must appeal to tastes that residents have learnt through being tourists and looking at cities elsewhere. This links tourism to wider discussions of the role of aesthetics in city development. Recent debates focus on the growing importance of amenity in city development, particularly to attract mobile professionals (Florida, 2002; Clark *et al.*, 2001; Clark, 2003). The aesthetic qualities of the built environment are fundamental to the creation of amenity (Silver *et al.*, 2006) so we can see a process of gentrification and reaestheticisation of cities driven by the demands of both visitors and residents, whose tastes increasingly converge (Maitland, 2008; Maitland & Newman, 2008). There are recurring criticisms of the results – standardised appearance, inauthenticity and loss of distinct character (Honigsbaum, 2001; Chrisafis, 2004; Richards & Wilson, 2006). But whatever their imperfections, these areas clearly represent a significantly changed aesthetic, and one in which tourism has played an important but complex role.

Third, the most prominent aesthetic link between tourism and the built environment is through 'iconic' buildings – famously, the Guggenheim, Bilbao – sometimes in association with 'iconic' events – most influentially, the 1992 Barcelona Olympics (Smith, 2005). Destinations have always sought symbols that epitomise their appeal and bring immediate associations with place. They may be natural (Sydney Harbour), achieve iconic status though built for other reasons (Sydney Harbour Bridge) or be deliberately constructed to create a symbolic image (Sydney Opera House). As Smith (2007) says, they can be seen as a contemporary (media-friendly) version of monumentality, used to assert status. In the increasingly intense competition to attract both tourists and mobile professionals, cities see iconic structures – galleries, museums, sports stadia, concert halls – as a means of signalling they are attractive, exciting places offering high levels of amenity. 'Successful' tourism icons prompt emulation by rival cities keen to promote themselves and to offer spectacle for consumers (Richards & Wilson, 2007). Iconic buildings have been part of the process that has transformed the landscape of the modern city as they have been 'promoted without question by countless city boosters from Taiwan and Guadalajara to Edinburgh' (Sudjic, 2005: 23). Tourism, while not the only incentive to build city icons, has had a central role to play in this form of city marketing and the adoption of spectacular environments and 'brandscapes' for an experience economy (Klingmann, 2007).

Conclusion

This chapter has outlined the relationship between tourism, aesthetics and the built environment. Cities are said to be experiencing both increased 'tourismification' and accelerated 'aestheticisation'; and these processes are linked. Tourism is not the only, or even the most important, influence on urban aesthetics and aestheticisation. But it is one that is growing in importance and under acknowledged in the urban literature. Tourists, like other users, are influenced by the aesthetics of built environments, although the most important built environment is the one conceived in individual's own minds. These processes can only be understood via reference to the cultural context in which they take place. This is particularly relevant to tourists because tourism exists not merely as a lived experience through which people learn about aesthetics, but also as a cultural practice, which has established features. 'Being a tourist' may mean the aesthetics of built environment are consumed differently. And the perceived need to provide the aesthetics that tourists demand has influenced the design of built environments. We suggest that a tourism imperative is more influential now that it has ever been. If tourists consume aesthetics differently, and cities are increasingly providing tourism aesthetics, then this constitutes a direct relationship between the consumption and production of urban aesthetics. But an imperative to design cities with tourism in mind does not necessarily mean that city developers are giving tourists what they want. More often, cities are designed for tourism, rather than for tourists. Accordingly, the built environment is increasingly influenced by what city developers think tourists want, both when they are in their own city and when they visit others.

The discussion has also highlighted important philosophical issues. When discussing the built environment, a range of philosophical dimensions needs to be acknowledged. At one end of the spectrum are the specific political philosophies of urban elites, who employ urban design philosophies to achieve their objectives. At the other end of the spectrum are broad philosophical debates about the influence of the resultant designs. The various words used to describe a tourist's aesthetic experience (reading, consuming, perceiving, conceiving) are testament to the wide range of related positions on this matter. The discussion here has highlighted that, while phenomenological perspectives focus on the lived experiences of cities, this may actually allow philosophies embedded in built environments to remain hidden. This leaves us in a quandary about an ideal epistemology that will allow us to gain a comprehensive understanding of urban aesthetics. It is futile to try and resolve these age-old philosophical debates here, but this discussion of the relationship between tourism, aesthetics and the built environment has allowed different positions to be explored.

While acknowledging the dangers of oversimplifying a discussion already based on generalisations, a clear argument emerges from this chapter. Essentially, we have argued that we can only understand the aesthetics of the built environment by looking at tourism. This is not only because a tourism imperative is influencing (and to some extent always has influenced) the design of cities, but also because tourists conceive of built environments differently. And as tourism is becoming more pervasive, we must recognise this to understand more general interpretations of urban aesthetics.

Notes

1. Ontologically, Berleant (2003) is reluctant to separate humans from their environments, and finds it awkward even to talk of interaction between the two, as this presupposes a division. Instead, he prefers to talk of perception, and aesthetic experience, as 'intimate sensing'.
2. The city was included in the UNESCO World Heritage List in 1987 because it is the world's largest complex designed along rigorously functional lines (Batista *et al.*, 2006).

References

Baldwin Hess, D. (2006) Transportation beautiful: Did the city beautiful movement improve urban transportation? *Journal of Urban History* 32 (4), 511–545.

Batista, G., Ficher, S., Leitao, F. and Alves de Franca, D. (2006) Brasilia: A capital in the hinterland. In D. Gordon (ed.) *Planning Twentieth Century Capital Cities* (pp. 164–181). Abingdon: Routledge.

Beioley, S., Maitland, R. and Vaughan, R. (1990) *Tourism and the Inner City.* London: HMSO.

Berleant, A. (2003) The aesthetic in place. In S. Menin (ed.) *Constructing Place: Mind and Matter* (pp. 41–54). London: Routledge.

Boydell, T. (1976) *Experiential Learning.* Manchester: Manchester Monographs.

Burton, A. (1996) Making a spectacle of empire: Indian travellers in Fin de Siecle London. *History Workshop Journal* 42, 127–140.

Cassidy, T. (1997) *Environmental Psychology: Behaviour and Experience in Context.* Hove: Psychology.

Chrisafis, A. (2004) Ibiza on the Liffey: But where are the Irish? *Guardian* (London), 17.

Clark, T.N. (2003) *The City as an Entertainment Machine.* San Diego, CA: Elsevier.

Cocks, C. (2001) *Doing the Town: The Rise of Urban Tourism in the United States.* Berkeley, CA: University of California Press.

Cuthbert, A. (2006) *The Form of Cities; Political Economy and Urban Design.* Oxford: Blackwell.

Davies, J.G. (1972) *The Evangelistic Bureaucrat.* London: Tavistock.

DoE (1980) *Development Control – Policy and Practice.* London: HMSO.

Doctor, R. (2000) Post-war town planning in its mid-life crisis. In T. Deckker (ed.) *The Modern City Revisited* (pp. 197–213). London: Spon Press.

Dovey, K. (1999) *Framing Places: Mediating Power in Built Form.* London: Routledge.

Eagleton, T. (1990) *The Ideology of the Aesthetic.* Oxford: Blackwell.

Fitzmaurice, T. (2001) Film and urban societies in a global context. In M. Shiel and T. Fitzmaurice (eds) *Cinema and the City: Film and Urban Societies in a Global Context* (pp. 19–30). Oxford: Blackwell.

Florida, R. (2002) *The Rise of the Creative Class.* New York: Basic Books.

Franklin, A. (2003) *Tourism. An Introduction.* London: Sage.

Franklin, A. and Crang, M. (2001) The trouble with tourism and travel theory? *Tourist Studies* 1 (1), 5–22.

Gilbert, D. (1999) London in all its glory – or how to enjoy London: Guidebook representations of Imperial London. *Journal of Historical Geography* 25 (3), 279–297.

Gilbert, D. and Hancock, C. (2006) New York City and the transatlantic imagination: French and English tourism and the spectacle of the modern metropolis 1893–1939. *Journal of Urban History* 33 (1), 77–107.

Glancey, J. (2006) Brave New World. *Guardian*, 6 November.

Gospodini, A. (2001) Urban waterfront design in Greek cities. A framework for redesigning space. *Cities* 18 (5), 285–295.

Gournay, I. (2005) Washington: The DC history of unresolved planning conflicts. In D. Gordon (ed.) *Planning Twentieth Century Capital Cities* (pp. 115–129). Abingdon: Routledge.

Graham, G. (1997) *Philosophy of the Arts: An Introduction to Aesthetics*. London: Routledge.

Gruen, J.P. (2000) Everyday attractions: Tourism and the generation of instant heritage in 19th century San Francisco. In N. Al Sayyad (ed.) *Consuming Tradition, Manufacturing Heritage* (pp. 152–190). Abingdon: Routledge.

Hasegawa, J. (1992) *Replanning the Blitzed City Centre*. Buckingham: Oxford University Press.

Hayllar, B. and Griffin, T. (2005) The precinct experience: A phenomenological approach. *Tourism Management* 26, 517–528.

Honigsbaum, M. (2001) McGuggenheim? *Guardian* (London), 27 January, 17.

Jacobs, J. (1961) *The Death and Life of Great American Cities*. New York: Random House.

Jokinen, E. and Veijola, S. (1997) The disorientated tourist. In C. Rojek and J. Urry (eds) *Touring Cultures: Transformations of Travel and Theory* (pp. 23–51). London: Routledge.

Judd, D. (1999) Constructing the tourist bubble. In D. Judd and S. Fainstein (eds) *The Tourist City* (pp. 35–53). New Haven, CT: Yale University Press.

Judd, D. (2003) Visitors and the spatial ecology of the city. In L. Hoffman, S. Fainstein and D. Judd (eds) *Cities and Visitors* (pp. 23–38). Oxford: Blackwell.

Judd, D.R. and Fainstein, S. (eds) (1999) *The Tourist City*. New Haven, CT: Yale University Press.

Kennedy, L. (2004) *Remaking Birmingham. The Visual Culture of Urban Regeneration*. Abingdon: Routledge.

Klingmann, A. (2007) *Brandscapes: Architecture in the Experience Economy*. Boston, MA: MIT Press.

Kolson, K. (2001) *Big Plans: The Allure and Folly of Urban Design*. Baltimore, MD: John Hopkins University Press.

Krippendorf, J. (1987) *The Holiday Makers*. Oxford: Butterworth Heinemann.

Lang, K. (2003) The Hamburg Bismarck as city crown and national monument. In S. Menin (ed.) *Constructing Place: Mind and Matter* (pp. 119–145). London: Routledge.

Lasansky, D.M. and McLaren, B. (eds) (2004) *Architecture and Tourism: Perception, Performance and Place*. Oxford: BERG.

Laurence, P.L. (2006) The death and life of urban design: Jane Jacobs, the Rockefeller Foundation and the New Research in Urbanism 1955–1965. *Journal of Urban Design* 11 (2), 145–172.

Law, C.M. (1993) *Urban Tourism: Attracting Visitors to Large Cities*. New York: Mansell.

Lynch, K. (1960) *The Image of the City*. Cambridge: MIT Press.

MacCannell, D. (1999) *The Tourist: A New Theory of the Leisure Class* (2nd edn). London: Macmillan.

Maitland, R. (1997) Cities, tourism and mixed uses. In A. Coupland (ed.) *Reclaiming the City* (pp. 87–116). London: E&FN Spon.

Maitland, R. (2008) Conviviality and everyday life: The appeal of new areas of London for visitors. *International Journal of Tourism Research* 10 (1), 15–25.

Maitland, R. and Newman, P. (2004) Developing metropolitan tourism on the fringe of Central London. *International Journal of Tourism Research* 6, 339–348.

Marr, A. (2006) *A Modern History of Britain*. Abingdon: Macmillan.

McCabe, S. (2005) Who is a Tourist? A critical review. *Tourist Studies* 5 (1), 85–106.

McLaughlin, B. (1994) Centre or periphery? Town planning and spatial political economy. *Environment and Planning A* 26, 1111–1122.

Meethan, K. (2001) *Tourism in a Global Society*. London: Palgrave.

Minnaert, L. (2007) Social tourism: A potential policy to reduce social exclusion? The effects of visitor-related social tourism for low-income groups on personal and family development. Unpublished PhD thesis, University of Westminster.

Montgomery, J. (2003) Cultural quarters as mechanisms for urban regeneration. Part 1. Conceptualising cultural quarters. *Planning Practice and Research* 18 (4), 293–306.

Montgomery, J. (2004) Cultural quarters as mechanisms for urban regeneration. Part 2 A review of four cultural quarters in the UK, Ireland and Australia. *Planning Practice & Research* 19 (1), 3–31.

Mumford, L. (1961) *The City in History: Its Origins, Its Transformations, and Its Prospects*. London: Secker and Warburg.

Nasser, N. (2007) Planning for urban heritage places: Reconciling conservation, tourism and sustainable development. *Journal of Planning Literature* 17 (4), 467–479.

Parker, D. and Long, P. (2004) 'The mistakes of the past' visual narratives of urban decline and regeneration. *Visual Culture in Britain* 5 (1), 37–58.

Parker, S. (2004) *Urban Theory and the Urban Experience*. Abingdon: Routledge.

Pearce, P.L. and Fagence, M. (1996) The legacy of Kevin Lynch: Research implications. *Annals of Tourism Research* 23 (3), 576–598.

Phillips, R.S. (1993) The language of images in geography. *Progress in Human Geography* 17 (2), 180–194.

Pike, B. (1996) The city as image. In R.T. Legates and F. Stout (eds) *The City Reader* (pp. 242–249). Routledge: London.

Punter, J. (2005) Urban design in central Sydney 1945–2002: Laissez-faire and discretionary traditions in the accidental city. *Progress in Planning* 63 (1), 11–160.

Richards, G. and Wilson, J. (2006) Developing creativity in tourist experiences: A solution to the serial reproduction of culture? *Tourism Management* 27, 1209–1223.

Richards, G. and Wilson, J. (2007) The creative turn in regeneration: Creative spaces, spectacles and tourism. In M. Smith (ed.) *Tourism, Culture and Regeneration*. Wallingford: CABI.

Rodriguez, J. (2000) Planning and urban rivalry in the San Francisco Bay Area in the 1930s. *Journal of Planning Education and Research* 20, 66–76.

Selby, M. (2004) Consuming the city: Conceptualizing and researching urban tourist knowledge. *Tourism Geographies* 6 (2), 186–207.

Short, J. (2006) *Urban Theory: A Critical Assessment*. Basingstoke: Palgrave.

Silk, M.L. (2007) Come downtown & play. *Leisure Studies* 26 (3), 233–257.

Silver, D., Clark, T.N. and Rothfield, L. (2006) *A Theory of Scenes*. Montreal: Urban Affairs Association.

Simson, A.J. (2000) The post-romantic landscape of Telford Town. *Landscape and Urban Planning* 52, 189–187.

Smith, A. (2005) Conceptualizing city image change: The reimaging of Barcelona. *Tourism Geographies* 7 (4), 398–423.

Smith, A. (2007) Monumentality in 'capital' cities and its implications for tourism marketing: The case of Barcelona. *Journal of Travel and Tourism Marketing* 22 (3/4), 79–93.

Smyth, H. (1994) *Marketing the City: The Role of Flagship Developments in Urban Regeneration*. London: E&FN Spon.

Sudjic, D. (2005) Can we still build iconic buildings? *Prospect* (111), 22–26.

Szczgiel, B. (2003) City beautiful revisited: An analysis of 19th century civic improvement efforts. *Journal of Urban History* 29 (2), 107–132.

Theroux, P. (1995) *The Pillars of Hercules: A Grand Tour of the Mediterranean*. New York: GP Putnams and Sons.

Thomas, H. (1999) Social town planning and the planning profession. In C. Greed (ed.) *Social Town Planning* (pp. 15–28). London: Routledge.

Urry, J. (1990) *The Tourist Gaze*. London: Sage.

Urry, J. (1999) Sensing the city. In D. Judd and S.S. Fainstein (eds) *The Tourist City* (pp. 35–53). New Haven, CT: Yale University Press.

Vale, L. (2006) The urban design of twentieth century capitals. In D. Gordon (ed.) *Planning Twentieth Century Capital Cities* (pp. 15–38). Abingdon: Routledge.

Venturi, R.C. (1966) *Complexity and Contradiction in Architecture*. New York: Museum of Modern Art.

Venturi, R.C., Brown, D.S. and Izenour, S. (1972) *Learning from Las Vegas: The Forgotten Symbolism of Architectural Form*. Cambridge, MA: MIT Press.

Chapter 11
Tourism and the Arts

BRIAN WHEELLER

Despite pleas for complete objectivity, as I see it, subjectivity and pragmatism are unavoidably involved, but conveniently ignored, in all research activity. However objective and balanced you might try to be, your inclination dictates what you go searching for. Inevitably there is a (high) degree of subjectivity. Dunn (1998: 136), in the context of travel and tourism, astutely stresses this, 'No process of meaning making exists in isolation. Nothing is totally objective'. Perhaps nowhere is subjectivity more crucial as is its relevance in any exploration of the 'Arts' – where 'beauty' is indeed, in the eye of the beholder: and where, as Landry (2006: 8) succinctly puts it, we are 'in the realm of the subjective'. Attempt to dovetail this complex variable with some of the contentious issues inherent in relevant elements of travel and tourism and ... well, the plot thickens. Inextricably. So, both complex and contentious, it becomes clearly impossible to comprehensively cover every complicated aspect of these relationships in one chapter. Circumstances dictate a degree of inevitable selectivity and subjectivity.

Insightfully, while reviewing Ledbrecht's *Maestros, Masterpieces and Madness*, Mars-Jones (2007: 27) notes 'As for the perverse idea of a critic abstaining from value judgements, it's doomed from the start'. This too is my reading of the situation. What follows is my take on things: a personal, value-laden, anecdotal perspective based on experience. Yet even the ways in which we recollect 'experiences' are personal, open to conjecture. 'There are three sides to every story. Yours, mine and the truth' (Evans, 2004: 1). Observation and examples are drawn mainly from the 'personal' – either directly or indirectly – from what I have read/seen/heard etc ... in turn, therefore, determined primarily by my own subjectivity and preferences. It's a middle-age, white male, Western (English) perspective: working-class background, middle-class trappings, 'onwards and upwards' aspirations (?). Make of it what you will.

I have always believed it difficult, if not impossible, to have precision in the application of definitions. Maybe academically we can ring fence and delineate our field of research: but not practically. There is, then, much wisdom in Humpty Dumpty's 'When I use a word it means just what I choose it to mean – nothing more, nothing less' (Carroll, 1872 [1991]: 135). Given this ambiguity, here we'll settle for vagueness. What then, roughly speaking, constitutes 'the Arts'? A cursory glance at arts reviews in/on so-called quality UK papers, television and radio arts programmes would indicate theatre, opera, ballet, museums, exhibitions, literature, the cinema (art house), architecture, art, photography, classical music ... *The Sun, Mirror* and *Star*, however, would suggest TV soaps, blockbuster films and Richard and Judy's 'ones to read'. {Those that scoff at the latter being regarded as Art will, no doubt, be turning their noses up at the package holiday, be travellers not tourists, and (hypocritically) regard themselves as the vanguard of the pleasure periphery: the Visit Bangladesh before the Tourist Arrive contingent (see Wheeller, 2004). A couple of hours reading Bagginni's (2007) *Welcome to Everytown*, a real Rotherham eye-opener, is in order here. Doctor's order, in fact.}

Here, then, the Arts are seen as a wide, sweeping canvas, painted liberally with a broad brush, under which, deceptively charmingly, 'lie many other coats of paint that colour our lives' (Hamilton, 1999: 4).

Personally, I've never fully understood (and therefore not appreciated?) why a night at the theatre is considered by (high) 'society' to be more edifying than a night, say, in front of the telly. The old maxim 'I don't know much about Art(s) but I know what I like ...' may ring true here. I'm more familiar with the wireless; the seedy, nihilistic aspects of film noir; hard-boiled American detective stories and popular 1960s' music (especially bubblegum) than I am with classical music, opera, the theatre and Shakespeare. More *South Pacific* than *Madame Butterfly*: his sister, not the Bard himself. And The Four Seasons? Think Frankie Valli rather than Vivaldi (see Wheeller, 1996). And this bias undoubtedly restricts my vision. Criticism of such apparent myopia can thus be levelled accordingly. On the other hand, and given ample poetic license, I suppose one could suggest that (by default) I'm therefore in a position to be able to 'focus'. Significantly though, I recognise here that I am in danger of being susceptible to, and falling foul of, culture specificity. *Of being culture specific?* I suppose my retort (re-taught?) would be it is the underlying reasoning and links that are vital to an argument ... the examples being interchangeable embellishments subject, as and when, to reader appropriate appropriation. However, it is recognised here that my cultural/age/gender specific references might make for a difficult read. What is familiar to me might well not be to the reader.

The Arts – like travel and tourism, like society – are driven partly by economics, riven wholly by class. The schism between high and low culture, as manifest in the Arts, is as controversial and divisive as ever. For elucidation, I draw at some length on Carey's (2005) accessible and informative *What Good are the Arts?* 'The arts have traditionally excluded certain kinds of people as well as certain kinds of experience. Writers on the arts have emphasised that their spiritual benefits, though highly desirable, are not available to everyone. The most excellent works of art, the most noble production of genius, Schopenhauer admonishes, "must always remain sealed books to the dull majority of men, inaccessible to them, separated from them by a wide gulf, just as the society of princes is inaccessible to the common people"' (Carey, 2005: x).

And *vice versa*? Well, yes. It seems that the underlying principle applies equally in reverse in that 'low' art is similarly incomprehensible to those (from the 'higher' echelons of society) who don't/can't/won't understand it. Carey astutely observers that 'The most striking deficiency in the case against mass art is the complete lack of interest – illustrated by Adorno, Benjamin, McLuhan and Hartman – in finding out how such art actually affects its recipients' (Carey, 2005: 64). Shalon, reviewing Carey, emphasises this aspect, 'Arguing that there are no absolute values in the arts, that it simply comes down to "a welter of preferences", he (Carey) is unimpressed by the assumption that "high" art puts you in touch with the "sacred" or that it has a "civilising" effect and he is quick to point out *the lack of interest certain critics have shown in finding out how mass art actually affects its recipients*' (Shalan, 2006: 19). This summation applies equally to Carey's lecture given at the 2005 Cheltenham Literary Festival, where he reiterated these arguments.

It is pertinent and (hopefully) worthwhile pursuing this high/low culture theme a little more here. Discussing this schism solely in the context of tourism is provocative enough: but attempting to dovetail said discussion with the Arts is entering dangerous territory. Acute divergence of opinion as to the appropriateness (or otherwise) of staging the 2007 Kylie Monogue exhibition at London's Victoria & Albert museum is testament to this divide. Disagreement rife, statements along the lines of 'Author and academic Lisa Jardine is adamant that she and her fellow trustees of the V&A are delighted to have the show "It is certainly not our job to be elitist"' (Thorpe, 2007: 18), hardly assuaged critics who feared falling standards and a lowering of tone. Not too surprising given that 'Social and cultural divisiveness is inherent in the notion of high art. It can be "high" only by comparison with other art which is "low"' (Carey, 2005: 34). Likewise, in a compelling, yet uneven, article Hamilton

(1999: 4) reasonably contends that 'Popular culture is a dangerous category as it implies the existence of another culture which is either unpopular, or elitist, or both'. How true that is. 'Whereas high art is exclusive, popular art is receptive and accessible, not aimed at an educated minority' (Carey, 2005: 36). Shades of traveller/mass tourist divide?

From the above discussion it is not too hard then to (simplistically and erroneously?) align high art/culture with travel and the traveller and, conversely, low art/culture with tourism and the (mass) tourist. Both unbridgeable, the traveller/tourist divide is as deep and wide as the high culture/low culture chasm. And yet the acceptance of Brian Wilson – the enigmatic, troubled genius of Beach Boys notoriety/fame – is exemplar as to the temporal vicissitudes of attitudes to 'Art'. If ever an artiste suffered for his art ... he's your man. Battered by a drug fuelled 1960s youth and castigated by some, he finally emerged from a 30-year chrysalis of depression, mental breakdown, isolation and exile to be hailed, belatedly in my opinion, as a delicate but sublimely talented artistic butterfly. Having now acquired kudos and status, he has (crucially in this context) gained respectability and acceptance in the eyes of establishment gatekeepers of the arts: to the extent of commissioned performances at the Royal Festival Hall (complete with surfboarding ballerinas on the South Bank) and a 2007 summer exhibition – If Everyone Had an Ocean, at Tate St Ives, Cornwall – dedicated to artwork inspired by Wilson's early music. The gallery's beachfront location at one of the UK's top resorts provided an ideal, evocative, if somewhat overdue, venue for portraying interpretations of his musical vision of youth culture and sun, sand, sea, surf and sex. Accompanying the exhibition, evening showings (on screens erected on the beach itself) of surf movies added to the hedonistic, but simultaneously disturbingly ambiguous, nostalgic atmosphere of misspent youth. Overwhelmingly depressive, in fact – tempered further by being viewed personally from the (disad)vantage of a now misspent middle-age. To add to the gloom, the prospect of that troubled troubadour of dour melancholy, Leonard Cohen, appearing at the (once incongruous) Vienna Opera House (Brown, 2008) serves as another example of the passing of time equating with the acquisition of artistic respectability. Temporally, Carey (2005: 60) believes 'Times, cultures and individuals have differed radically in their artistic preferences'. So too, evidently, within a lifetime.

Graffiti is another case in point, art gaining credibility with age and the passing of time, witness Lord Byron's etching of his name on a column of the Temple of Poseidon, in Attica. Set against this though there is the contemporary, bankable Banksy, the elusive much sought after street artist. They seek him here, they seek him there. But as regards graffiti at its best, what could beat this masterpiece? Painted immaculately on a wall in Amsterdam's Red Light district is a Union Jack, under which an enterprising wag has scrawled the immortal line ... God Shave the Queen. Marvellous.

Hamilton (1999: 4) too, attempts to contextualise culture over time, observing that 'Popular culture is not necessarily meant to last: it captures an age, a period, a generation, a mood of the times'. While a particular type of popular culture might fall into this transitory category (being *in vogue* for only a short time span), the generic concept of popular culture must surely be ongoing – an ever-changing constant. But popular culture as expressed by mass tourism gets short shrift in the arts: tourists usually don't feature too well in literature or film, their depiction often derogatory: impatient and selfish in *Babel*, predatory in *Is Harry on the Boat*, banal in *Leisure* and denigrated in Kerouac's lauded classic where bohemian traveller, not tourist, is King (of the Road?). Tourists often appear fair game, the sop, for the (prejudiced?) 'artiste'. As also, it would appear, is often the case in both the media and tourism academic circles – where (mass) tourism tends not only to be overlooked, but similarly frowned on. These (miss) representations are of considerable import. And a vexed issue.

The media can be regarded as an art form in its own right, especially in its relationship to tourism where 'there are a multitude of tourist practices and an extended range of media. We are, therefore, immediately engaged in a process of multification. There are many connections, overlaps and disjunctures between tourism and the media and equally between the disciplines of tourist and media studies ... (Crouch *et al.*, 2005: 1). And it is taken here, in the context of travel and tourism, that the media and the arts are themselves interlinked. So, even on only one plane, it's not just the inherent 'value' of the Arts per se, or more specifically, individual works of art (however 'defined'), that is significant: in some respects, of more consequence is how they 'reach' (or don't) the audience: of how their 'worth' is represented/presented to the public. And how the audience reaches them. Of how they are 'read' and 'interpreted'. Media coverage and reviews are, therefore, often crucial in instigating and arousing 'awareness', of generating demand for the Arts and subsequent 'Arts Tourism'.

Just as the Arts and Tourism can be seen as 'businesses' so too, lamentably, can Tourism Higher Education in the UK, where the invasion of academia by business mandarins is, it is argued, tightening, squeezing and draining creativity (see Wheeller, 2005). In tourism education provision, there has been some laudable rearguard action against such machinations – an example being the introduction of Arts-related material into tourism teaching. Ask a group of (international) students which books, films and/or music they associate with travel and tourism and the ensuing discussion usually offers scope for the enterprising to embrace a kaleidoscopic range of relevant issues. (The delightful, naïve *Roman Holiday* nearly always features with Chinese students, for example. Never with Westerners.) Specifically, give them (Peter) Carey's short story 'American Dreams' to analyse: maybe show them *The Beach*: or ask them to think about a few paintings ... say Casper David Friedrich's The Traveller or Fischeli's interpretations of beach life: or, perhaps, McGill's exquisite, risque seaside postcards, and then, for good measure, throw in a few of Parr's iconoclastic images depicting England's decaying coastal resorts. With reasonably bright, imaginative students, given full rein, the response is rewarding. And if it is true that the 'doors of imagination' never close then, just as Wallace and Gromit's *A Grand Day Out* exploits in their epic moon shot is an ideal vehicle for teaching tourism impacts (Wheeller, 2005), so their chaotic escapades in their more recent adventure (*The Curse of the Were-Rabbit*) can serve as a way of illustrating the hazards of event management – specifically in the running/ruining of a village's fete/fate. Incidentally, the recent mushrooming of Events Management courses, many under the auspices of Travel and Tourism, is indicative of the trend linking Arts, business, tourism and education. Though, of course, not necessarily arts specific, a proportion of the 'Events' do have an Arts/Cultural content.

In this context of 'education', another ancillary aspect of Art and Tourism is the growing trend in adopting a fetching visual image when promoting forthcoming academic tourism conferences. The use of art in leisure and tourism marketing has long been recognised – early London Underground Art/British Rail posters etc. and a Hockney original for the cover of Bradford's 1992 rather pretentious 'A travel guide' are cases in point. But the practice is no longer restricted to selling the 'tourism product'. Not only is there now an array of conferences covering the wide, eclectic field of 'Tourism/Arts/Culture' but art itself is being employed in the marketing of the overall event. Robinson at Leeds Met is a dab hand at this: so too Burns at the University of Brighton, both past masters, having effectively used artistic/photographic images (Depardon, Muafangejo, Parr etc.) to promote their (consistently high quality) 'product', namely culturally-orientated tourism conferences. As to whether such images employed are always (the most?) appropriate is, of course, debatable (see Wheeller, 1996). But now on conference fliers, juxtaposed alongside the ubiquitous, compulsory university corporate logos, somewhat incongruously yet perfectly understandably, are the works of Seurat, Bosch etc. Art and the commodification of education?

And 'education' in a broader sense? What about the bewildering array of Arts related residential courses on offer - a market segment in itself, a PhD waiting to happen? Would-be lifestyle 'self-enhancer' participants swell the tourist numbers. Writing courses, poetry classes, opera, musical appreciation, learn to paint, gardening. Gardening? Is gardening Art? Carey (2005: 39) suggests so, if only in the sense that 'Landscape gardens for the rich have been art objects since the Renaissance'. (Snared, Carey himself stumbles, inevitably, into the 'culture trap' here, as the Renaissance is probably only a marker to a certain section of [Western] community: to the majority, it'll mean next to nothing.) Again, it is difficult to identify just what Art does, and does not, embrace. Even shopping could, by some, be regarded as an 'art': 'Selfridge, probably the one person who first fully recognised consumption as sensuous entertainment, introduced functional lighting as spectacle so creating the new art of window shopping' (BBC, 2007). And just what is it that constitutes travel as opposed to that which constitutes tourism? 'Staying at a canal side Venetian palazzo isn't a holiday – its art (Greenberg, 1999: 1). In similar vein, a piece in the same Travel section reads 'Ten minutes by car from Benidorm you can escape from the British crowds for a week and visit the village of Villajoyosa for the Moors and Christians festival, otherwise known as the festival of Santa Marta' (Lewis, 1999: 10).

What of religion? Is that too an art form. Possibly not, but the 'trappings' that go with it can be, and are, attributed as such. Magnificent places/palaces of worship and their priceless treasures therein are in themselves revered as 'cultural art'. Yet MacCannell laments 'Throughout the world churches, cathedrals, mosques and temples are being converted from religious to touristic functions' (quoted in Bonami, 2005: 85). But isn't tourism modern pilgrimage, the New Religion? And a secular take on this might see things differently, viewing this 'conversion' of use/purpose as desirable, positive development. Those (of us?) that regard religion as a divisive force from which bitterness, hatred and conflict emanate, but see tourism as (possibly/potential) fun, fun, fun, might well welcome this trend. Subjectivity is All.

Whether they be religious, book, film, music-orientated etc., events/ festivals increasingly feature in the role of tourism generator. And cities vie for status and economic returns that festivals bring (see, for instance,

Manchester takes on Edinburgh in battle of the Festivals [Herbert, 2007: 10]). Besides the larger, familiar venues and excesses of Rio, Notting Hill, Edinburgh, Glyndebourne (memorably miss-pronounced by a Sheffield pub music quiz master as Glyn de Bourne) and Glastonbury etc., multitudes of smaller events are, increasingly, being staged. There are conventions and festivals to meet (almost) all tastes – from the traditional/mundane to the unusual to the downright odd (see '20 great Boutique Festivals' in *the Observer* Escape Guide in which readers are implored to 'Try one of Britain's quirkier events' [Turner, 2007: 8]).

Mainstream or maverick, 'cultural' tours also find their way onto the travel pages of the press. Be it arts/heritage culture/sport – whatever the banner, where there is a market opportunity, the tourism industry, not missing a trick, will be in like Flynn. The Arts, in the context of tourist supply, are ever increasingly being seen as a business opportunity ... an effective weapon in tourism's arsenal of the Big Sell. *Money makes the world go around, the world go around...*

And then there's the marketing jamboree of Liverpool's European Capital of Culture 2008, seen as a great opportunity to 'sell' the city through the arts. Some might consider 'cell' more apposite. This is not a sleight on Liverpool, a city I hold in fond affection from student days spent there. It is, however, a cautionary dampener on the inflated claims of alleviation that cultural tourism can supposedly bring to a city, any city, with serious social deprivation. Some sense of proportion and balance was provided by Ringo Starr's comments in the ominously, but realistically titled, article 'Guns mar Liverpool's culture night' (Townsend & Davies, 2008: 15) in which he sagely observed 'It's a city of ying and yang, both sides of the coin'. Meanwhile, according to Fuchs (2007: 25) 'Valencia's officials have pinned their hopes of boosting the city's cultural profile on the Palau'. Fostering not only the cultural, but also the physical image of a city is considered important. Justifiably acclaimed as an inspirational tour de force, taking 'readers on a tremendous global journey of discovery', *The Art of City Making* opens with 'City making is a complex art' (Landry, 2006: 1): as first lines go not quite Manderley, but still intriguing. With art and aesthetics of architecture at its core, the book emphasises the importance of enhancing the attractiveness of the cityscape, a theme also effectively pursued, though with considerably more brevity, in Glancey's (2007) article 'Light and space: a dozen landmarks of genius'. Of course, much of the architecture 'on show' as, and constituting, the cityscape is either intimately linked with serving the arts ... museums, galleries, theatre, opera, ballet, sculpture ... or with transport/travel (and therefore tourism) supply in the form of railway stations or airports, for example award winning glamour/clamour projects like St Pancras, London or Madrid airport. In the wider arena, there is public art. And image. Gorman's works of art, sculptures that have captured the public's imagination, have (for example) taken on iconoclastic proportions. And not just Gateshead's winged wonder, the *Angel of the North*. His impressive installation *Another Place* on a wind and rain swept Crosby beach has become a tourist attraction in itself.

The actual venue or building can be the main attraction, be it the Gugenheim Bilbao ... 'a building that makes an exhibition of itself' (Glancey, 2007: 34), the Sydney Opera House or, on a rather more modest scale, the Kinema in the Woods at Woodhall Spa, Lincolnshire. But, of course, while (some) galleries and museums are, architecturally, tourist attractions in their own right, the contents on show are usually clearly the major magnates for tourists – drawing, as they do, huge numbers of visitors; witness recent record-breaking Hopper, Monet and Tutankhamen etc. exhibitions in London (and see, Europe's Super Summer of Art [Sharp, 2007]). Obviously a strong case could be made for arguing that much of the art (and artefacts) actually on display are, in one way or another, travel-related, be it in the form of, say, photorealistic landscape, or more tangentially, if only in the sense that any art might trigger abstract thoughts – travel within the mind. There are though, increasingly, examples where travel and tourism play centre stage in that the tourism phenomenon is the key theme of a particular exhibition, play, opera or concert. Recent examples include 'Censored at the Seaside – the Art of Donald McGill' (Brunswick Centre 2004), 'Universal Experience. Art, Life and the Tourist Eye' (Hayworth Gallery 2005), the 'Impressionists by the Sea' (Royal Academy 2007) and 'All-Inclusive: A Tourist World' (Schirn–Kunsthalle, Frankfurt 2008). Assembling work by over 30 international artists, the latter 'presents numerous works depicting and critically questioning various tourist phenomena. Documentation, parodies and defamiliarisations of traditional tourist motifs, and dream images, interlink with subjects like migration, tourist industry, and global communication' ... runs the webpage. Let us hope it is just a touch more comprehensive and comprehensible than the aforementioned, at times baffling – 'You cannot travel on the path before you have become the Path itself' – Universal Experiences extravaganza. But that's art for you.

The Arts are not only attractions in themselves: they are also effectively deployed variously (and nefariously (?)) as advertising vehicles to seduce would-be travellers/tourists. Using culture/art/ music-based puns, references or catch-phrases to 'sell' destinations now appears the norm, examples legion. ... Paradise Found, California

Dreaming, Bohemian Rhapsody well-worn, tired perennials; similarly, 'Hit the road Jack: world's greatest road trips'; 'Beatles Hotel strikes a chord' (Seymour, 2008: 2). The front cover of Escape, *Observer*'s travel supplement, reads 'Poetry in Motion. How a poem remembered from school inspired the trip of a lifetime to Chile' being one of the more prosaic. Mulholland (too young for Johnny Tillotson) cites Padraig de Brun poetry as inspirational. '"Come to paradise says the poem" so I went ... The poem swept me away on a tide of daydreams to a place of promise, sun and light' (Mulholland, 2004: 1): nostalgia, and the journeying back in time, a common feature in travel copy.

Accompanied by glorious vistas adorning the screen, a voice-over cordially drawls 'You've seen the film, now visit the set with Discover America.com' (TV advert 2008). But in the Age of the Cult of Celebrity, not only locations and movie sets, but star's houses, restaurants they've eaten in or had brawls at, hotels the famous have slept in (who the Dickens was 'ere syndrome?). ... whatever, have become fair/fare game for the tourist experience sell. Liverpool's recently opened themed Hard Day's Night Hotel caters for Beatle devotees and features themed rooms full of Lennon and McCartney miscellanea. In his article 'Move over, Marilyn', Crump (2008: 13) observes, 'This is just the latest salvo in a worldwide craze for celebrity hotel suites'.

And the arts and media are instrumental in fuelling demand. Quoted on the inside cover of the *The Atlas of Literature* (Bradbury, 1996) is Melville's typically perceptive 'Nearly all literature, in one sense, is made up of guide-books'. Some perhaps more honest than others? To me, the pernicious deception prevalent in the likes of Mann's *Death in Venice* and Benchley's *Jaws*, both depicting local authority connivance with the tourist industry, say more about travel and tourism and are nearer the mark than the conventional guidebook or the effusive picture painted by novels of say the Mills and Boonesque holiday romance read (Wheeller, 2004). Greene's subversive novels and there oft deceptively exotic locations are usually good value in the 'travel' stakes; none more so than his aptly titled *Travels with my Aunt*. Besides the endearing eccentricities of the eponymous relative, it is another family member, Uncle Jo that catches the eye here. Prevented by a stroke from embarking on a planned world tour, he settles instead by looking for 'a house of three hundred and sixty-five rooms so that he could live a day and night in each' (Greene, 1999: 59). There follows a couple of pages of fine prose in which the itinerant eventually moves into a 52-roomed mansion, 'A room for every week of the year' and then proceeds to move from one to another, treating each week as a new location/vacation. The book is a classic. Not so Fischer's *Voyage to the End of the Room*, a title that flatters to deceive but still, in the context of mind travels, worth a read. (For an excellent review of Greene's work on film see Falk's informative *Travels in Greeneland*.)

Much of 'travel' writing is of escape: of escape from claustrophobic situations as in Saint-Expuery's magical *Little Prince* and its wistful theme of travel, loss and unfulfilled dreams, Bowles' *Sheltering Sky* and Fitzgerald's splendid *Tender is the Night*, where protagonists flee suffocating (America) in search of new environs (North Africa and continental Europe) in vain attempts to add spice by peppering up doomed relationships ... only to discover it is the relationship, not location, that is the constant claustrophobic variable. So, despite William Least Heat-Moon's overwhelming desire to escape the rigours of doomed 'domestic bliss' (he loses his job and his wife leaves him ... on the same day) produced his – some might say – classic *Blue Highways* (most memorable line? 'A man who couldn't make things go right could at least go' Least Heat-Moon, 1999: 2), running away can often be futile and I'm more inclined to go along with the sublime songsmith Harry Chapin (1974) who (as always) was spot on with

Sometimes I get this crazy dream
I just take off in my car
But you can travel on 10,000 miles
And still stay where you are

There is a flip-side to music and tourism. Going back features frequently in song ... considerably more so than it appears to in tourist literature on these matters. While the emphasis of much (travel) writing and commentary on music appears to be on illuminating aspects of escape from the humdrum to locales exotic, there is possibly an equal amount of (overlooked) laments, threnodies almost, about the longing, the desire, for whatever reason, to return, to get back home (again) to the familiar. Check out 'Detroit City', 'My Own Back Yard', 'Little Old Wine Drinker Me', with Dino's melancholic crooning 'And the music takes me back to Tennessee', '(Goin' Back to) Houston', 'Sloop John B's 'This is the worst trip I've ever been on' etc. A long way from the heady early day/ daze of Jan and Dean's 'Surf City' and the Beach Boys early homage to the Californian idyll. Though I'm not sure where the Tradewinds' New York's a Lonely Town [When You're the only Surfer Boy around], or the more familiar Mammas and Pappa's 'California Dreaming' fit into this line of reasoning, as they too feature characters longing to get back home. In both case, though, it is California that's calling. In fact, 'California Girls', the

Beach Boys' evocative anthem eulogising the Golden State falls into this category too: 'But I can't wait to get back to the States, back to the cutest girls in the world' (Wilson, 1965).

Out of the sun: into the shadows – from one extreme, to the other. The maverick Houellebecq's (2004) tourist-related works *Lanzarote* (the only novel/novella I am aware of with photographs) and, particularly, his disturbing, gross – but grossly – under-rated novel *Platform* (Houelle-becq, 1999) leach tourism's darker, seamier undercurrents. When adapted to theatre and presented at the Edinburgh Festival, *Platform* caused a kafuffle and prompted caustic reviews (Brennan, 2006). But, then again, in academic circles, so does its contentious subject matter ... greed, religion and sex tourism. According to exploratory work by Botterill (2008), a similar hostile reception befell Adam's controversial opera *The Death of Klinghoffer*, which provoked protest when first performed at the Brooklyn Academy of Music. Inspired by events of the 1985 Palestinian hijacking of the cruise ship the Achille Lauro and the murder of a wheelchair-bound Jewish terrorist, this presentation also raises delicate issues ... including the dark spectre of arts censorship in democracies.

> Pretty much anything worthwhile in the way of books, paintings and music has usually had a rough ride from self-appointed guardians of decency. (Decharne, 2003: 13)

Censorship can take many forms ... political pressure/influence being a relatively common phenomenon. In a previous article, 'Travel, Tourism and Popular Music', I drew attention to the hypocrisy of censorship when the Brazilian authorities attempted to prevent Michael Jackson from filming his video in the favelas of Rio de Janeiro for fear it would present the wrong image of Rio to the world, thereby hitting their tourist trade. 'The video, for his single They Don't Care About Us is meant to highlight the plight of children in poverty-stricken areas of cities ... Rio's authorities took legal action to ban him from filming in the filthy alleys of the Dona Marta slum, home to 4000 people ... Marcelo Alenear, the governor of Rio, said the video would reflect a "negative and damaging image of the city, especially when it is trying to promote its flamboyant carnival which starts on Saturday".... Dona Marta favela, or shantytown, is a stark reminder of the vast gap that exists between rich and poor in the seaside city. ... The fact that the authorities had, for the previous 30 years been more than happy with the positive (though to many very) misleading images of the city as created and portrayed by Gilberto's Girl from Ipanema is typically hypocritical' (Wheeller, 1996).

Nothing new here then. Business ethics, tourism and art? What better example than with the Lake poet Wordsworth and his 'daffodils'. To his chagrin, Wordsworth was aware that his lyrical contributions were, in themselves, partly responsible for luring hordes of would-be visitors to 'his' beloved Lake District and was acutely conscious of the desecration that he feared would inevitably accompany them. Objecting to this, he resented, and resisted strongly, the incursion of the railway as its tentacles spread North. But then, recognising that 'progress' was inevitable, and the battle lost, he turned full circle, and 'sold-out', or rather 'bought-in' ... shares, that is: in the railway. Wordsworth's relationship with tourists and the inherent threats of tourism development via the railways makes for a good story. Unfortunately, it's (probably?) only apocryphal. But, then again, so what? Where is the truth in tourism? How 'true', for example, is travel writing? Many claim to write from the heart, few from the groin ... notable exceptions being O'Brien's *All the Girls* and Williams' *No Particular Place to Go*. Yet, in its many guises, isn't sex (and the prospect thereof) one of the motivators for travel? And as for 'from the heart'? As if. Hand on heart? – well, only true when wearing jackets and their wallets are in their left, inside coat pocket. *Money makes the world go around, the world go around.*

Ralph Fiennes, interviewed on the subject of 'movies of conscience', is quoted as saying 'Films are a kind of weapon. They are a tool for good or evil' (Maher, 2006: 18). The Dream/Nightmare Factory? Parallels with tourism? Perhaps travel writers, and come to think of it, tourism and tourists should have consciences too? But do they? And what of tourism officials who have honed their powers of selectivity of media coverage and tourism to the proverbial fine art?

A measure of the significance that the media has to tourism can be gleaned from the Tourism Society's recognition of this in the awarding of their 2007 annual award for 'contribution to tourism' to the impressive television series *Coast*. The concomitant, lavishly illustrated BBC books that accompanied the series *Coast: A Celebration of British Coastal History*; *Coast: The Journey Continues*; *Coast from the Air* and *Coast* Series 1 and 2 DVD boxsets, while somewhat excessive, further help 'sell' the coast to potential customers. And boosting tourist demand and expanding markets are, understandably, high on the Tourism Society agenda. They would, I'm sure, also be pleased with Dimbleby's beautifully crafted, sumptuous *A Picture of Britain*. In similar vein, featuring, amongst others, Elgar, Vaughan Williams and Holst, The BBC Philharmonic's ''An English Journey' in which 'Orchestral descriptions of the English countryside abound ... ' was accompanied by a programme depicting England's bucolic green and pleasant land: 'manor' from heaven for the tourism establishment? Whereas *Crap Towns* (Jordison, 2003), *Boring Postcards* (Parr, 2002) and the Viz Tourist Map of the British Isles were, perhaps, received rather less enthusiastically; the latter prompting Morison's 2001 article 'Viz's vision of Britain riles the big nobs of tourism'.

There is little doubt, then, as to the power of the media influencing tourist demand. 'We call it the Palin Effect. The Himalayas have been doing well [in the wake of Palin's television series] and *Pole to Pole* did a lot for Peru and that continent. Documentaries that captivate, that are about travel, have a positive effect on our bookings' (Roseveare, 2005). So, too, 'positive' literature in general – Japanese Invasion sparked by Peter Rabbit (Paul, 2007: 45) and the sentiments of Pickles' (2007: 24) travel article The Quiet Poetry of the Lakes, 'you can do the arty sights (the houses and views associated with Wordsworth and Ruskin) or revert to childhood with Beatrix Potter'. The association between character (real or fictional) and place is well documented. Some personal favourites include Pryce's peculiar detective stories very much set in a surreal Aberystwyth, the town's name featuring in each of the titles of the four book series, Robert B. Parker's Spencer novels with Boston (Massachusetts, not Lincolnshire) as backdrop, Chandler's California ('the most of everything and the best of nothing'); Harvey's curmudgeonly anti-hero Resnik roaming Nottingham's mean streets. And the more mainstream Dexter equals Morse equals Oxford.

Headlines along the lines Wizard! Harry saves tourist industry (O'Connor, 2003) and Universal grasps Potter's magic (Ellis, 2007) are common place. Rowling's phenomenon has created a tourist magnate – be it to the film locations or to Harry's Florida theme park, opening shortly. But leaving aside this and other now familiar well/overdocumented 'success' stories lauded by tourist boards ... of the *Four Weddings, Notting Hill, Lord of the Rings, Da Vinci Code* ilk. ... I'd like to give some attention to instances where literature and film, with darker connotations, may have a more ambiguous, even negative, impact on tourism.

This downside of tourism and the arts has always intrigued me. While Billy Hayes tortured plight in Midnight Express did little for Turkish tourism, was the impact short-lived? 'Cinema has always been about transport, taking the viewer out of a darkened room and into the world' (Sutcliffe, 2007: 5). It's about being somewhere else. 'Around the world in 16 days as 182 movies hit London' (Solomons, 2007: 9). And it is in this context of virtual mobility that Hillaby, in Journey through Britain (1979), introduced his 'skull cinema', the dream factory of the mind and its ability to escape from present circumstances. The emphasis is on cerebral travel. But travel to where? A review of the film *Paradise Lost* reads 'Originally entitled Turistas, this off-the-peg post Hostel schlocker follows backpackers on holiday to Brazil where they find themselves on the wrong end of an organ transplant programme ... despite the thematic echoes of *The Beach*, which hint at wider social subtext, it all boils down to boring body parts ... leery gore' (Kermode, 2007: 8). Hardly one for the Brazilian Tourist Board's portfolio then. And the rather violent Antipodean *Wolf Creek*, was reviewed thus – 'An impressive debut, though one imagines the Australian tourist board wouldn't agree' (Sturges, 2007: 66). Perceptive questioning at the 'Things that Move' Leeds conference pursued this line of reasoning. In response to a generally upbeat presentation on film tourism, it was pointed out that films such as *This is England*, highlighting skinhead culture, *Last Resort* concerning the lives of asylum seekers in a grim Margate and *Twin Town* with drug culture in Swansea are 'films that Visit Britain are unlikely to be featuring soon' (Long, 2007).

Hard to establish what (negative) impact the unsavoury aspects of Greene's *Brighton Rock* or the writings of Patrick Hamilton had on the South coast town's (then) thriving tourist trade. Or elsewhere, contemporarily, Lewis' *Swansea Terminal* which, reviewing, Wilson (2007: 18) describes the city surroundings as 'dark, bleak, sordid, and sinister' while a review of *Night Fisher* reads 'Just in case the Hawaiian tourism board's sun swept propaganda has been too effective lately, here comes a depiction of the seamier side of tropical paradise ... dark, claustrophobic and foreboding, even the palm trees look threatening' (Taylor, 2006: 19). And then there are Carl Hiaasen's Floridian novels (*Native Tongue*, *Tourist Season* etc.), devastating indictments of tourism development in the Sunshine State. But, then again, it's difficult to see a downturn in tourist numbers resulting from his caustic commentary. Given the perversities of human nature, maybe all publicity is, indeed, good publicity with the voracity of the old maxim underpinning the spectacular growth of Dark Tourism. Dracula films would lend obvious support here, while the remakes of the *Poseidon Adventure* or, even, *Titanic* don't appear to have negatively affected demand for cruises. Quite the reverse, apparently.

But, conversely, publicity through the 'arts' does not always guarantee a favourable touristic outcome. There is, of course, the not insignificant matter of the 'product' in question. While New York, New York (I left my heart in) San Francisco and April in Paris may have a certain nuance, songs and/or music extolling the virtues of a destination do not necessarily mean success in the tourism stakes. Despite featuring the longest brick-built viaduct in the world, the nation's hat museum, Strawberry Studios and the Fred Perry Way (commemorating one of, if not the only, town's famous sons) the release of Wimple Winch's much sought after 'Rumble on Mersey Square South' and Frankie Vaughn's subsequent epic, the eponymous 'Stockport', the town has failed to prosper as a tourist Mecca. Even the release of Pete Farrow's 'Who says there's no beach in Stockport' had failed to do the trick. Not too surprisingly, a pleasing musical signature alone is not always a sufficient incentive; sometimes more of a deterrent?

I asked a colleague (twice) for advice on this particular matter of association. His response? 'I've had another think about works of art that might put people off locations, but as before I've run up against a brick wall. The obvious suggestions are *Deliverance* and the American wilderness; Pittsburgh and the films of George A Romro; New York and the films of Abel Ferrara, or small town America and *Blue Velvet*. After that it all comes down to personal taste. So, for example, I immediately want to leave any place where music by Queen, Phil Collins or Dire Straits is playing' (Boland, 2007). Couldn't agree more.

If there have been themes to the chapter then one would be the (symbiotic?) selective appropriation and commodification of the arts by tourism. Another the edgy, dark notion that art can (and does) portray place, travel and tourism in a less than flattering light – and the allusion made to vested tourist interests media manipulation to minimise any resulting adverse impact of this seamier presentation. Of paramount import throughout, though, is the over-riding recognition as to the crucial significance of the subjective in any interpretation of the arts and tourism.

So, it seems appropriate to conclude on a personal note by drawing attention to two of my favourite artistes. No writing of mine on the Arts and Tourism could be complete without reference to John Cooper-Clarke's paean to the package holiday, the classic 'Majorca'.

> I got drunk with another fellah,
> Who'd just brought up a previous paella
> Wanted a fight but said they were yella
> in Majorca. . . . (Cooper-Clarke, 1983: 98)

Somewhat removed from poet laureate material this gem just fails, unfortunately, to feature in *The Oxford Book of Travel Verse*. Nevertheless – indeed, for that very reason – a listen to a live version (replete with laconic style and staccato delivery) is surely a must for any would-be aficionados of the Arts and Tourism. How the other half lives?

And similarly, also a 'must', are Harland Miller's bleak, yet richly evocative, quirky works of Northern seaside resorts and his ironic take on their (re)branding – 'Bridlington: 93 million miles from the Sun': 'Blackpool: Its All Fun and Games until Someone Loses an Eye' – are understated masterpieces in the nostalgic melancholy of faded glory. And an antidote to the contemporary gloss of the 'Experience Economy'.

So there you have it, some subjective personal thoughts. Rather than an objective, dispassionate, coherent, cogent analysis on the Arts and Tourism I've opted instead for a seemingly irreverent eclectic, erratic random ramble around the subject – a personal journey reflected in the thoughts aired and examples proffered by way of illustration.

And to finish with a final flourish? All together now one more time, a rousing karaoke Cabaret chorus. ... *Money makes the world go around, the world go around* ...

References

Baggini, J. (2007) *Welcome to Everytown*. London: Granta.
Boland, R. (2007) In conversation. NHTV, Breda, the Netherlands.
Bonami, F. (2004) *Universal Experience*. Chicago, IL: Museum of Contemporary Art Press.
Botterill, D. (2008) Comic and tragic representation of tourism in twentieth century opera. Paper presented at the Association for Tourism in Higher Education Annual Conference, Canterbury UK.
BBC (2007) *Shopping, Seduction and Mr Selfridge*. BBC Radio 4 22.10. 07.
Bradbury, M. (2006) *The Atlas of Literature*. London: De Agostinti.
Brennan, C. (2006) Northern Exposure. *Observer*, 3 September, 17.
Brown, J. (2008) Still Miserable after all these Years. *Independent* 12 March, 7.
Carey, J. (2005) *What Good are the Arts?* London: Faber.
Carroll, L. (1872/1991) *Through the Looking Glass*. Manchester: World International Publishing.
Chapin, H. (1974) W.O.L.D. *Electra Records*. Los Angeles, CA: British Lion Music.
Cooper-Clarke, J. (1983) *Ten Years in an Open-necked Shirt*. London: Arena.
Crump, V. (2008) Move Over, Marilyn. *Sunday Times*, 27 January, 13.
Decharne, M. (2003) *Hardboiled Hollywood*. Harpenden: No Exit Press.
Dunn, D. (1998) Home truths from abroad. PhD thesis, University of Birmingham.
Ellis, J. (2007) Universal Grasps Potter's Magic. *Bangkok Post*, 5 April, B5.
Evans, R. (2004) *The Kid Stays in the Picture*. New York: New Millennium.
Fuchs, D. (2007) Mud Slung at Valencia's Opera House. *Guardian*, 27 October, 25.
Glancey, J. (2007) Light and Space. *Guardian*, 6 October, 34.
Greenberg, S. (1999) Life Inside a Canaletto. *Independent on Sunday* Travel, 27 March, 1.
Greene, G. (1999) *Travels with my Aunt*. London: Vintage.

Hamilton, A. (1999) From C.B. Fry to Fried Fish. *The Times Weekend*, 25 October, 4.
Herbert, I. (2007) Manchester takes on Edinburgh in Battle of the Festivals. *Independent*, 21 March, 7.
Houellebecq, M. (1999) *Platform*. London: Heinemann.
Houellebecq, M. (2004) *Lanzarote*. London: Vintage.
Jordison, S. (2003) *Crap Towns*. London: Boxtree.
Kermode, M. (2007) Paradise Lost. *Observer Review*, 7 October, 8.
Landry, C. (2006) *The Art of City Making*. London: Earthscan.
Least Heat-Moon, W. (1999) *Blue Highways*. London: Little Brown & Co.
Lewis, M. (1999) What's on Worldwide. *Independent on Sunday Travel*, 27 March, 10.
Long, P. (2007) Email correspondence. Leeds Metropolitan University.
Maher, K. (2006) Sitting in the Dock of the Bay. *Times Screen*, 9 March.
Mars-Jones, A. (2007) What a Bum Note, Norman. *Observer Review*, 15 April, 27.
Mulholland, J. (2004) Poetry in Motion. *Observer Escape*, 25 June, 1.
O'Brien, M. (1983) *All the Girls*. London:Macmillan.
Parr, M. (1999) *Boring Postcards*. London: Phaidon.
Paul, D. (2007) Japanese Invasion Sparked by Peter Rabbit. *Sunday Express*, 21 January, 45.
Pickles, H. (2007) The Quiet Poetry of the Lakes. *Telegraph*, 10 October, 24.
Price, S. (2007) Best Literary Museums. *Independent*, 15 December, 15.
Seymour, T. (2008) Beatles Hotel Strikes a Chord. *Sunday Tasmanian*, 17 February, 2.
Shalan, A. (2006) Review of What Good are the Arts. *Guardian*, 17 June, 19.
Sharp, R. (2007) Europe's Super Summer of Art. *Independent*, 9 June, 10.
Solomons, J. (2007) Around the World in 16 days. *Observer Review*, 14 October, 9.
Sturges, F. (2007) Review of Wolf Creek. *Independent*, 15 December, 66.
Taylor, C. (2006) Review of Night Fisher, Kikuo Johnson. *Guardian*, 11 March, 2.
Townsend, M. and Davies, C. (2008) Guns Mar Liverpool's Culture Night. *Observer*, 13 January, 15.
Thorpe, V. (2007) V&A Under Fire over Kylie Show. *Observer*, 4 February, 18.
Turner, S. (2007) 20 Great Boutique Festivals. *Observer*, 15 April, 8.
Wheeller, B. (1996) No particular place to go: Travel, tourism and music, a mid-life crisis perspective. In M. Robinson, N. Evans and P. Callaghan (eds) *Tourism and Culture Change* (pp. 323–340). Sunderland: Business Education Publishers Ltd.
Wheeller, B. (2004) The truth? The hole truth. Everything but the truth. Tourism and knowledge: A sceptic septic's perspective. *Current Issues in Tourism* 7 (6), 467–477.
Wheeller, B. (2005) Wallace and Gromit's Grand Day Out: Imagery, Metaphor and Postgraduate Tourism Teaching. *Conference Proceedings*, Buckingham Chilterns, pp. 17–21.
Williams, H. (1981) *No Particular Place to Go*. London: Jonathon Cape.
Wilson, B. (1965) *California Girls*. Los Angeles, CA: Rondor Music.
Wilson, L. (2007) Review of Swansea Terminal (Lewis). *Guardian*, 10 November, 18.

Part 4

Virtue: Ethics, Values and The Good Life

Chapter 12

Ethics and Tourism

DAVID FENNELL

Introduction

The focus of this chapter is on giving readers a basis from which to understand the more formal side of ethics, including key philosophical traditions that have emerged in ethics along the path of 2500 years of discourse. This includes a discussion on deontology, or seeking the means; teleology, or seeking the best ends or consequences from our actions; and existentialism, which is the pursuit of individual authenticity and responsibility. Behaviour, both from the individual and organisational standpoints, is a function of what we value, so a brief discussion of values is included as an important aspect of the chapter, especially in regards to how values link with ethics. It is indeed surprising that the willingness of researchers to explore ethics in tourism has been marginal, especially given that tourism, by its nature, emphasises the value of one over the value of others. This axiom is supported by the fact that tourism creates innumerable negative costs (impacts) that stem from the pursuit of primarily hedonistic ends (Fennell, 2008; see also Przeclawski, 1996). Positioning tourism research from an ethical standpoint, especially in light of a better understanding of human nature, might open up new possibilities for better grounding the many new forms of alternative or responsible tourism that continue to agitate against the mass tourism model. Ethical theory, therefore, provides the most appropriate means by which to build a platform for expressing a shared responsibility in tourism.

Ethical by Nature

Ethics should be an expression of what it means to be a human; the deepest truths of human nature as described by Somerville (2006). This is no coincidence because we are ethical beings by nature. So, ethics is not something we choose to have or not (although it is a quality that we can use and exercise or one that we can suppress and let atrophy), because millions of years of evolution have allowed humans to cross an evolutionary threshold, paving the road towards intelligence, anticipation, abstraction and self-awareness. In this vein, Ayala (1987) writes that humans are ethical because we can: (1) anticipate the consequences of our actions, (2) make value judgments and (3) choose between alternative courses of action (see also Ehrlich, 2000). Mayr (1988) contends that the evolution of larger brains in association with larger social groups provided the foundation for morality, leading to selection rewards (in the biological sense) for the demonstration of unselfish traits benefiting the group, as well as the evolution of ethical behaviour by choice and freewill (see Mayr [1988] and Fennell [2006a] for a discussion of how reciprocal altruism evolved as the basis for morality).

This knowledge provides the basis from which to conclude that morality is a human universal. But even so, we must be careful when we apply this reasoning because although we have evolved with the capacity to be moral, the various normative approaches to ethics in existence around the world are variable from culture to culture (see Williams [1993a] for a good discussion on the biological and cultural coevolution that have endowed us with the capacity to be ethical). So, the moral standards and ethical principles that we follow

> constitute a structure of interlocking behavioural guidelines that have been growing organically since our ancestors first became human, if not earlier. We worked them out through a long and arduous evolutionary process marked by many wrong turns and much social discord. Indeed, the structure is still imperfect and we continue trying to make improvements. We are building a sense of humanity-as-a-whole as the ultimate in-group, which exists over and above our sense of national consciousness and whatever residual loyalties we retain from the earlier, culture-based periods. The need is increasingly urgent, for galloping technological change is forcing new global problems on us that demand global solutions. (Coon, 2005: 43–44)

Ethics is often confused with the closely related concept of morality. It is this latter concept, however, which is seen to be the more general and that which informs our various ethical maxims. Morality, therefore, refers to the rational and natural inclinations of humanity to do good and avoid evil (e.g. preserving life, forming an ordered society, pursuing the truth, etc.). By contrast, ethics, stemming from the Greek word *ethos* (meaning a habitual mode of conduct), is concerned with answering the question: What should one do in order to be good? Defined, ethics is the *rules, standards, and principles that dictate right, good, and authentic conduct among members of a society or profession* (Fennell & Malloy, 2007). We see these standards, rules and principles in many different walks of life, including medicine, engineering, law, marketing, sport, business and environment. In tourism, ethics usually surfaces in the form of codes of ethics – prescriptions and proscriptions – which are designed to help individuals and groups act with the best interests of a range of sociocultural, economic and ecological considerations in mind.

Not unlike the fields of endeavour noted above, tourism involves making decisions on a personal level, e.g. where to go as a tourist and perhaps how; or group decisions, e.g. which stakeholder groups to include in tourism policy and planning, and what level of involvement to include them at. Because these decisions are often politically, economically, socially and ecologically charged, they become difficult in the presence of so many competing demands. This means that if we as decision-makers are to honour the commitment that we have to balance such demands in an ethical way, there are some basic steps that might be employed in doing so. Following Somerville (2006), these include:

(1) Problem recognition. We make mistakes as tourism decision-makers because we often don't know that we have a problem in the first place, which might also mean, therefore, that we may be ignorant of the consequences of our actions.
(2) Problem analysis. Once the problem has been identified, those with ethical training might help decision-makers further by identifying as much as possible the problem(s) at hand, including all facts and any uncertainties.
(3) Ethical issues. An ethical approach helps to identify the ethical issues that surface as well as the different values that inform decisions.
(4) Values analysis. The ethicist examines whether any of the relevant values conflict; if not then there is no ethical dilemma.
(5) Prioritisation. Finally, if the values are in conflict, the ethicist can help prioritise these based on three different ethical traditions. Because ethicists don't always agree on one best way to solve a problem, it is important to examine these traditions in understanding which is best under different circumstances.

Before we look at these traditions more closely, the reader may pause in reflecting on the aforementioned steps. The employment of individuals with ethical training in tourism seems almost counterintuitive. I say this because not unlike commerce in general, the *modus operandi* of tourism is to make money. If we employ someone to help us make ethical decisions in our businesses, we potentially detract from our ability to maximise profits. I say this because there is a broad movement in business that assumes the position that, 'Business must fight as if it were a war. And, like a good war, it should be fought gallantly, daringly, and, above all, *not* morally' (Levitt, 1979: 141).

Values

Behaviour is a function of what we value, both in individual and organisational contexts. Our values push us – they motivate us to do something. If they don't inspire action, then they are not values we actually hold. Using the example of a code of ethics in tourism, the primary purpose is to inspire ethical behaviour and the primary criticism is that they are platitudes (Vinton, 1990; Wheeller, 1994). In other words, the individual and the group must value the code if it is to serve its overall purpose. Value has been defined by Hodgkinson (1983: 36) as 'a concept of the desirable with a motivating force'. This definition implies the following:

(1)   A value is an abstraction (i.e. a concept). It is imposed by humans on something that may have no inherent value (e.g. diamonds).
(2)   A value is something that is socially acceptable (i.e. desirable) as opposed to individually desired. For example, sadism may be desired by some but not desirable by most.
(3)   A value pushes us into action (i.e. motivating force). Another way to see this is that our behaviour is a manifestation of what we value.

This is a rather powerful definition that renders much of what we say rather impotent if it does not translate into action. If I say that I value the environment, yet freely pollute it by driving a large vehicle to and from work (when I could reasonably walk to my destination), then this value is rhetoric.

Beyond definition, Hodgkinson (1996) felt that values could be arranged according to a hierarchy based on four disparate levels. The example of a tourism code of ethics can be used to characterise these four levels. At the base level, we value something because we simply like it. Little cognitive thought is present in this almost instinctual level of *preference*. So, I might value the code because it makes me feel content/ secure just knowing its there to guide and protect me (Adams *et al.*, 2001). The next level incorporates the preferences of the collective or *consensus*. I make my choice to value something based upon the activity of others – a democracy of value so to speak. I value the code because everyone else does – I am socialised or pressured to conform by the organisation. The third level is much more robust in its cognitive activity. Here, one values based upon the *consequence* of valuing. In other words, if through a rational/logical assessment of the outcome of valuing 'X', I determine that it has a positive benefit for society or the environment, then I will value it – otherwise I will not. I value the code, therefore, because I actually see the positive outcome of it in terms of heightened awareness and ethical behaviour. At the highest level of valuing, I base my behaviour not upon what I like or what others like or what science tells me, but upon a transrational and authentic *principle*. I may well consider these levels of valuing; however, my deepest sense of valuation comes from this sense of personal will, genuineness and faith. I value the code because it coalesces with my personal values and those I authentically believe everyone should follow. Of all that we do value, the vast minority will be based upon the highest level of principle (Table 12.1).

Table 12.1 The value paradigm

Value type	Grounds of value	Psychological orientation	Philosophical orientation
4	Preference	Affect	Hedonism
		Emotion	Behaviourism
		Feeling	Positivism
3	Consensus	Cognition	Democracy
		Reason	Liberalism
		Thinking	
2	Consequence	Cognition	Pragmatism
		Reason	Utilitarianism
		Thinking	
1	Principle	The will	Existentialism
		Conation	Religion/faith
			Kantianism

Source: Hodgkinson (1983)

Ethical Traditions

Table 12.1 provides the basis from which to understand values from a hierarchical perspective. Written into this hierarchy is the psychological orientation associated with each level as well as a philosophical orientation. It is the latter orientation that is the focus of this section in relation to seeking the end, the means, as well as authenticity.

Teleology: Seeking the end

There are two dominant approaches to seeking the moral end. The first has its roots in Aristotelian philosophy in which the end we ought to seek is the Greek term *eudaimonia*. The most accurate translation of this term is 'to flourish' as opposed to seeking simple happiness. The target then is to flourish and therefore any decision we make that does not lead instrumentally to our flourishing is a bad decision. Good or virtuous decisions aim us in the direction of *eudaimonia*. Virtuous decisions, Aristotle believes, are the result of selecting the mean between excess and deficit. In other words, 'all things in moderation' or the 'golden mean' would be the watchword for Aristotelians. For example, the mean between being a coward and being rash is the virtue of courage; the mean between underdevelopment of a natural resource and scorched-earth policy would be the virtue of sustainable development. Our ability to reason allows us to choose and (the potential) to choose well. If not for reason we could not be decision-makers in the first place. If all we had were instinct and emotion, then it would be nature choosing not us! Reason then gives us the ability to think through options and to determine the quality of happiness we seek (this phrase will come back to haunt us below).

This approach is also known as virtue ethics and is perceived to be universal in its application. Where simple forms of happiness can be relative and subjective according to the particular tastes of individuals and cultures, the target of *eudaimonia* is a universal and objective good (see Tribe, 2002). Hultsman (1995) used the concept of 'just' tourism (see below) as a metaphor to suggest that ethical tourism is that which is virtuous, e.g. fair and honourable. Other virtues like truthfulness, honesty and sympathy have been identified by Smith and Duffy (2003) as being important in the development of codes of ethics for groups, such as tour operators, in making these groups more responsive to tourists and the environment. Conversely, Butcher (2003) argues that hedonism, once a virtue of tourism, has now become a sin because of the new moral authority (Wheeller, 1994; Munt, 1994) in tourism – an activity that used to be more about fun and adventure. Instead, these aspects have been removed from tourism because of the new ethical imperative where pleasure seeking has been regulated in the face of social and environmental concerns.

A second approach to seeking the moral end is based upon the pursuit of happiness in a way that is substantially different from Aristotle's view. This theory can be subdivided into two themes, one seeking individual pleasure and the other seeking the pleasure of the group. Seeking pleasure and avoiding pain, as the end we should seek, is the moral view of the hedonists (see 'preference' in Table 12.1). While this approach doesn't hold a great deal of moral stock among philosophers, it is certainly an apparent basis for much of human behaviour – particularly with regard to the realm of tourism. Pleasure is the end to be sought; however, the kind of pleasure we ought to seek varies considerably among hedonists. Hedonism in general is the basis for what we today may better understand as relativism. This view posits that what an individual or a culture perceives as pleasure is relative to that individual or particular culture and no external judgement of morality ought to be made. This subjectivist view is in obvious conflict with the objective and universal beliefs of Aristotle.

Group hedonism is the democratic expansion of individual hedonism. Seeking the greatest pleasure or happiness for the greatest number is the end that is coveted. Also known as utilitarianism (see 'consequence' in Table 12.1), this moral school of thought has a number of variations. The earliest treatise, written by Jeremy Bentham, led the individual to believe that quality of pleasure was not an issue, but only quantity. In other words, if sex tourism resulted in more pleasure than ecotourism, for example, then the former was the more obvious choice among decision-makers. These choices were made by way of the hedonistic calculus that is not unlike our contemporary rational decision-making process in which alternatives are weighed against a particular criterion (i.e. pleasure). The alternative that maximises the intended goal (i.e. greatest good for the greatest number) is the 'best' choice. J.S. Mill followed Bentham's lead, however, he responded to the criticism of utilitarianism by distinguishing between qualities of pleasure. He argued, not unlike the misunderstood hedonists, that not all pleasures were of the same value. The goal of the maximisation of happiness remained for Mill; however, higher order pleasures are preferred over lower order pleasures. Distinguishing between the two requires the wisdom of expert judges who have experienced both and will naturally choose the higher over the lower (i.e. ecotourism over sex tourism).

Criticism of the implicit denial of rights (see 'Justice and Rights' below) to the individual in favour of those of the group lead contemporary utilitarians to devise a somewhat hybrid version that incorporate rules to the calculus of ethical behaviour. Rule-utilitarianism suggests that an act is moral if it follows the *rule* that ultimately leads to the greatest goodness rather than placing emphasis upon the *act* that will bring about the greatest good. For example, let's look at the environmental impact of the periodic practice of oil tankers dumping their refuse into the ocean. In order to put an end to this practice, local officials board the next tanker that enters their waters (not knowing if they have polluted or not) and publicly execute the crew in an effort to establish a very powerful message and deterrent for other ships. While this extreme utilitarian act may result in the greatest good for the greatest number (i.e. pollution will come to an end), it also involves the denial of rights of the potentially innocent crew. Cultural relativism aside, the basic human right to live is generally regarded as a 'rule' that results in the maximisation of goodness. Therefore, establishing laws that maintain this basic assumption would result in the utilitarian end mediated through a rule. Returning to our polluters, lopping off the heads of the crew may put an end to the problem of polluting waters, however it may, in turn, cause a greater degree of collective pain if the public then becomes uneasy about the status of their basic rights (e.g. I can lose my head if it serves the public good despite my innocence).

Utilitarianism in general (act or rule) can be criticised on the basis of the vagueness of the ends sought. What exactly is the greatest good and who make up the greatest number? Is this goal set for our immediate goodness or that of the next generation? Do animals count? Does the environment count? While there have been attempts to rein in the notion of whose happiness is maximised (e.g. the culture, the society, the group, the organisation), it remains a contentious aspect of this approach to moral decision making. Karwacki and Boyd (1995) observed that ecotourism is unethical because those who stand to gain the most from it (political figures and service providers), do so at the expense of the poverty-stricken citizenry (the majority or greatest number). Under utilitarian scrutiny, ecotourism fails because its economic benefits (to a few) do not come close to its externalities (e.g. pollution, loss of culture and local resources).

Utilitarianism is pervasive in our Western society, as almost implicitly we seek to act or at least are encouraged to act for the greatest good for the greatest number. Hedonism, while in full bloom in many aspects of our life, is not the epitome of the moral life that most would proclaim. In many respects, utilitarianism was an offspring of the age of science in which calculations of moral virtue seemed possible. As well, it was a rebellion against the firm grasp that the Church had upon the decision-making ability of the masses. Utilitarianism took the process of moral choice out of the hands of the priest and into the control of the individual who was then able to consider the weight of various options in a secular manner. The Church's perspective of moral decision making was and is based upon the followers' obligation to do their duty to God and to the Church. It is this sense of duty to follow rules that is our next focus.

Deontology: Seeking the means

Moral theories that are based upon duty are formally termed deontology (see 'principle' in Table 12.1 for all three forms of deontology). From this perspective, what is moral is that which abides by the rule or principle and not what results in a particular outcome. That I do my duty is enough. The obvious question is, 'what is the basis of my duty?' Some deontologists will argue that the principles based upon a religious source are the foundation of moral behaviour. For example, the Koran and the Bible provide devotees with the information required to live moral lives. Doing one's duty to abide by these rules can be perceived as a form of prayer or yoga (i.e. practice).

A second source of deontological behaviour is understood as social contract ethics. This secular perspective sees ethical behaviour as that which adheres to the rules, principles and norms that we as a civil society agree to uphold. The American Constitution, the Canadian Charter of Rights and Freedoms, the Australian Bill of Rights are all examples of social contracts to guide moral behaviour. From a micro view, codes of ethics in organisations and professional associations are rules and principles that have been formulated by stakeholders to guide and monitor ethical conduct – deontological tools for the organisation. In one of the earlier papers on hospitality and ethics, Whitney found that the value of a company's code of ethics, and whether profit should be the sole factor in influencing business decision, was based on traditional values rather than those that violate traditions. These latter situations create ethical dissonance (ethical conflict) between stronger ideological aspects (that which they believe in) versus operational ones (that which they practice) (Whitney, 1990). Hultsman's (1995) concept of 'just' tourism has a deontological link to it in how it is premised on the work of Aldo Leopold's land ethic, which is essentially a limitation on the notion of freedom in the interests of appropriate social conduct – do nothing that will harm the natural world. Like the medical equivalent of 'do no harm', his work stands as a first principle from which to plan and develop tourism in view of sustainability and the precautionary principle (see also Holden, 2003).

A third source of deontology is intuitive. This is not the intuition of a hunch to buy a lottery ticket when I 'feel' lucky. This is based upon the capacity of reason that only humans share. Immanuel Kant is the dominant proponent of this ethical perspective. He argues that because humans, regardless of their individualism based upon gender, ethnicity, age, etc., have the capacity to think, they can reach similar ethical conclusions. His intuitive rule is that ethical conduct must be universalisable (or, based on our definition, it must also be moral). He termed this global rule 'the categorical imperative' and described it as follows: 'act only according to that maxim by which you can at the same time will that it should become a universal law' (Kant, 1968: 45). This rule implies then that for a decision to be morally worthy, it must be suitable for all, not just for me in this particular instance. For example, promise keeping could be perceived as a universally desired law – we should all keep our promises and expect others to do so. If we do not, then when we make a so-called promise, we could never be sure that it will be kept. The outcome would be the impossibility of making any sort of formal or informal agreements or contract between individuals, organisations and nations. Theoretically, this seems reasonable – intuitively right in fact. However, when real life enters into the picture the ideal breaks down. For example, I am driving my car to the airport to meet my wife for a trip – an occasion we promised each other to keep. On the way, I notice an elderly woman sitting in a park being accosted by some young tuffs. I have a decision to make, do I assist the woman or do I continue on in order to keep my promise with my wife? The strict Kantian would argue in favour of keeping the original promise, however, such a decision strikes most of us as, on face value, the wrong action to take – we should help the elderly woman.

A second universal law, termed the *practical imperative*, is in some respect easier to handle. It states that you should never treat someone simply as a means to an end, but rather as an end in themselves. This does not mean that you cannot use someone at all, as we all must 'use' the skills and attributes of others to survive in any form of community. What is meant here is that while we do use others, we must also at the same time respect these others and accept them as individuals with dignity. For example, we use a tour guide to prevent us from being lost on a trek and at the same time, he or she uses us as a means for livelihood. As long as we treat the guide with respect and take a reasonable interest in his or her life (or life projects) and if he or she does the same with us, then all is well according to Kant. If, however, the guide perceives us only as a source of revenue and if we see the guide only as a means to our personal survival, then we both have failed to exercise Kant's practical imperative.

Deontology has been criticised on a number of different levels. The principle concern is related to where specific duties originate. A code of ethics, for example, is not very useful if the guidelines themselves are developed by organisations that have their own best interests in mind. The same can be said about organisational policies that serve the interests of some at a cost to others. As such, do some people have special rules and guidelines over others? If so, why?

Justice and rights

Two terms introduced above which have direct relevance to tourism at a number of levels, include justice and rights. Justice does not fit neatly into any one of the main theoretical perspectives above, but rather has been discussed in the context of many different themes, including utilitarianism, human rights and virtue ethics (see Smith & Duffy, 2003). Rawls (1971) writes that the sufficient condition for equal justice among people is a moral personality; there is no race or recognised cohort within society that lacks this attribute. Moral persons are thus distinguishable by two main features. First, they are found to have a conception of the good, and second they have a sense of justice through the desire to use and act upon principles of justice. Philosophers often refer to six principles of distributive justice in trying to understand what is fair in society. These include: (1) to each person an equal share, (2) to each person according to individual need, (3) to each person according to that person's rights, (4) to each person according to individual effort, (5) to each person according to societal contribution and (6) to each person according to merit (Beauchamp & Bowie, 1983: 41–42). In this way, justice provides an avenue by which to further explore the link between theory, as stressed above, and the applied side of ethics (applied issues are those that are controversial enough to spawn support from more than one side, and which have moral relevance at a broad scale).

D'Sa (1999) argues that tourism is very much a justice issue in consideration of disparities, racism and corporate power. Tourism that may be considered 'unjust' perpetuates the problems that have been created around disparities, racism and such, in the name of profit and priority. By contrast, tourism that is considered 'just' is that which is fair and honourable and which seeks to do no harm as a first principle (Hultsman, 1995). Perhaps the most frequently cited issue that has relevance to justice, at least to the six principles listed above, is with regards to people's rights. The example of the Paduang human zoo serves to illustrate how the actions of a few have such dire repercussions on the lives of so many. Drummond (1988) reported on the fate of 33 people – an entire tribe from Burma – who were kidnapped by a Thai businessman (Thana Nakluang) and put on display for international tourists. As one of the world's rarest indigenous tribes, the 'giraffe women' of this tribe wear several rings around their necks, which elongate the muscles. The group was lured from their home in the South of Burma through the promise of being reunited with their relatives over the border in Thailand. Instead, they were taken to a jungle area and presented to the authorities under the guise of helping the group develop a model tourist village. Soon thereafter, tourist agencies found out about the village and began promoting it in Bangkok and Chiang Mai. The villagers were paid in rice and oil and the equivalent of 42 pounds per month, depending on their behaviour. Those who attempted to escape were beaten by guards patrolling the perimeter of the village. Having learned about the village through a report in the London *Times*, Prime Minister Chuan Leekpai ordered the closure of the camp and had formal charges laid against Nakluang. With no rights to speak of, this group's future is said by Drummond to hang in the balance. If they are deported back to Burma, they face a similar fate, or a risk of being treated as rebels by a brutal military regime.

Not unlike situations where local people are restricted from the use of resources, or where invasive chemicals have endangered local people's lives, tourism often fails to consider the rights of the many who must bear the costs of the few who stand to gain so much. When we recognise that people cannot be treated as a means to an end, but rather as an end in and of themselves (using Kant's practical imperative above), we acknowledge their right to fair and equal treatment. As such, rights in tourism need to be discussed in the context of a duty owed to an agent (the right-holder) in supporting the agent's important interests. Rights, therefore, are often supported by social contracts, where there is a duty or burden that *should* be assumed by a duty-bearer (e.g. government). While it is encouraging to see the involvement of government in the case of the Paduang human zoo, rights can often be ignored or rejected on utilitarian bases, depending on the desired consequences of institutional action.

Existentialism: Seeking authenticity

The subjectivist realm of existentialism is centred on the experience of what it is like to exist as a human being (Collinson, 1987) in the pursuit of personal authenticity – acts that are self-determined, based on freedom of choice and where one assumes responsibility for action (see Guignon, 1986). Existentialists, therefore, reject pre-existing normative ethical theories (i.e. deontology and teleology) and moral authorities, and instead make ethical decisions on the basis of their own subjective value set (see 'principle' in Table 12.1). While it is noticeably the most individualistic of moral perspectives it is also cosmopolitan in nature, for when the existentialist chooses for one's self, the choice is made for all – in the global sense.

Existentialists as a group are suspect about the influence that society has over their pursuit to be true to themselves. Kierkegaard (1859/1939) referred to this as 'state morality' or 'the crowd', whereby actions are deemed worthy only in the context of what government or organisations deem to be appropriate. So, dumping bilge water at sea becomes ethical if this is an accepted practice by industry, but this doesn't mean, however, that this behaviour is ethical by other standards. What becomes even more confounding is when individuals are asked to subscribe to mixed ethical systems (Jacobs, 1994). Guardian (e.g. government) and commercial (e.g. industry) moral systems may be opposed to one another and, as such, we get mixed messages and either fail to understand what is indeed the best course of action, or we elect to subscribe to one over the other if it corresponds to our own value set (as noted above).

Not surprisingly, the worlds of business and government have tended to steer clear of existentialism for fear that it may breed chaos and excessive individualism in an environment in which solidarity, efficiency, effectiveness and productivity are the watchwords (Hodgkinson, 1996). Included here, of course, is the acceptance of organisational imperatives (e.g. Scott & Hart, 1980) that dictate that the survival and growth of the organisation supersedes the survival and *eudaimonia* of the individual. This organisational imperative strips away any chance of being an individual, as we tend to rely on and favour that which is imposed on us from the group standpoint. When we do this we remove our own cloak of personal responsibility because decision-making – and the consequences of our actions – somehow becomes someone else's responsibility. However, despite the apparent contradictory nature between systems and existentialism, the existentialist can operate as a profoundly 'moral' individual within society – furthermore, the existentialist's overt behaviour may be remarkably similar to those individuals promoting other moral orientations – what differentiates is intention. So, rules, systems and obligations can be accepted, followed – even created by existentialists – the key is that they are carried out in good faith. Good faith implies that choices are made and action taken as a function of the individual's own will. From a Kierkegaardian perspective, exercising our will as individuals to perform selfless acts for the other helps us on our way to building capacity for responsible citizenship – the move towards responsible tourism (Fennell, 2008). This means that if we continue to place ourselves as tourists and service providers as the only locus of concern in tourism interactions, then we can do little to actualise an ethic of responsibility in tourism for the larger whole.

Conclusion

Only recently has ethics been a topic of interest to tourism scholars. This is indeed unfortunate because the act of travel, and the inherent freedom tied to it, is perhaps the most self-oriented expression of the individual. The reasons for the dearth are open to debate. Perhaps other disciplines like law, medicine and business have longer and more rigorous histories, allowing them to arrive at ethics as a matter of progression. Perhaps still, the ethical transgressions in tourism do not have the same social implications as medicine or law. It may also be that tourism research has not embraced knowledge from other fields to the extent that it might (Fennell, 2006b). Tourism by nature is said to be interdisciplinary – whether it is truly interdisciplinary is subject to debate. A strong case can be made for too much insularity in tourism research (e.g. our focus on impacts) as opposed to a receptiveness that would welcome the theory on ethics from other fields in attempts to strengthen our field. At any rate, a stronger understanding of values and how values link to ethics and ethical traditions should better prepare us in considering what we ought to do in order to be responsible or ethical in tourism. If we simply cannot take this leap from the aesthetic state of being to the ethical, as individuals and organisations, there is very little chance of reaching the lofty goals set out in sustainable, alternative or responsible tourism forms (see Fennell, 2008).

References

Adams, J.S., Tashchian, A. and Shore, T.H. (2001) Codes of ethics as signals for ethical behavior. *Journal of Business Ethics* 29, 199–211.
Ayala, F.J. (1987) The biological roots of morality. *Biology and Philosophy* 2, 235–252.

Beauchamp, T.L. and Bowie, N.E. (1983) *Ethical Theory and Business* (2nd edn). Englewood Cliffs, NJ: Prentice-Hall, Inc.

Butcher, J. (2003) *The Moralisation of Tourism: Sun, Sand . . . and Saving the World?* London: Routledge.

Collinson, D. (1987) *Fifty Major Philosophers: A Reference Guide*. London: Croom Helm.

Coon, C. (2005) The architecture of ethics. *Humanist* 65 (1), 43–45.

Drummond, A. (1998) The Padaung 'human zoo'. *In Focus* 29, 8–9.

D'Sa, E. (1999) Wanted: Tourists with a social conscious. *International Journal of Contemporary Hospitality Management* 11 (2/3), 64–68.

Ehrlich, P.R. (2000) *Human Natures: Genes, Cultures, and the Human Prospect*. New York: Penguin.

Fennell, D.A. (2006a) Evolution in tourism: The theory of reciprocal altruism and tourist-host interactions. *Current Issues in Tourism* 9 (2), 105–124.

Fennell, D.A. (2006b) *Tourism Ethics*. Clevedon: Channel View Publications.

Fennell, D.A. (2008) Responsible tourism: A Kierkegaardian interpretation. *Tourism Recreation Research* 33 (1), 3–12.

Fennell, D.A. and Malloy, D.C. (2007) *Codes of Ethics in Tourism: Practice, Theory, Synthesis*. Clevedon: Channel View Publications.

Guignon, C. (1986) Existential ethics. In J. Demarco and R. Fox (eds) *New Directions in Ethics: The Challenge of Applied Ethics* (pp. 73–91). New York: Routledge & Kegan Paul.

Hodgkinson, C. (1983) *The Philosophy of Leadership*. Oxford: Basil Blackwell.

Hodgkinson, C. (1996) *Administrative Philosophy*. New York: Pergamon Press.

Holden, A. (2003) In need of a new environmental ethics for tourism? *Annals of Tourism Research* 30 (1), 95–108.

Hultsman, J. (1995) Just tourism: An ethical framework. *Annals of Tourism Research* 22 (3), 553–567.

Jacobs, J. (1992) *Systems of Survival: A Dialogue on the Moral Foundations of Commerce and Politics*. Toronto: Vintage.

Karwacki, J. and Boyd, C. (1995) Ethics and ecotourism. *A European Review* 4, 225–232.

Kierkegaard, S. (1959/1939) *The Point of View for my Work as an Author* (W. Lowrie, trans.). London: Oxford University Press.

Levitt, T. (1979) The dangers of social responsibility. In T.L. Beauchamp and N.E. Bowie (eds) *Ethical Theory and Business* (pp. 138–141). Englewood Cliffs, NJ: Prentice-Hall.

Mayr, E. (1988) *Toward a New Philosophy of Biology: Observations of an Evolutionist*. Cambridge, MA: The Belknap Press.

Munt, I. (1994) The 'other' post-modern tourism: Culture, travel and the new middle classes. *Theory, Culture and Society* 11, 101–123.

Przeclawski, K. (1996) Deontology of tourism. *Progress in Tourism and Hospitality Research* 2, 239–245.

Rawls, J. (1971) *A Theory of Justice*. Cambridge, MA: The Belknap Press.

Scott, W.G. and Hart, D.K. (1979) *Organizational America*. Boston, MA: Houghton Mifflin.

Smith, M. and Duffy, R. (2003) *The Ethics of Tourism Development*. London: Routledge.

Sommerville, M. (2006) *The Ethical Imagination: Journeys of the Human Spirit.* Toronto: Anansi Press.

Tribe, J. (2002) Education for ethical tourism action. *Journal of Sustainable Tourism* 10 (4), 309–324.

Vinton, G. (1990) Business ethics: Busybody or corporate conscience? *Leadership & Organizational Development Journal* 11 (3), 4–11.

Wheeller, B. (1994) Egotourism, sustainable tourism and the environment – a symbiotic, symbolic or shambolic relationship. In A.V. Seaton (ed.) *Tourism: The State of the Art* (pp. 647–654). Chichester: John Wiley and Sons.

Whitney, D.L. (1990) Ethics in the hospitality industry: With a focus on hotel managers. *International Journal of Hospitality Management* 9 (1), 59–68.

Williams, P.A. (1993) Can beings whose ethics evolved be ethical beings? In M.H. Nitecki and D.V. Nitecki (eds) *Evolutionary Ethics* (pp. 233–239). Albany, NY: State University of New York.

Chapter 13

Good Actions in Tourism

TAZIM JAMAL and CHRISTOPHER MENZEL

Introduction

This chapter explores the notion of good actions in tourism. Such an inquiry could perhaps successfully rely upon a simple, unanalyzed, common sense notion of 'good', but we are a bit sceptical of our common sense intuitions. Hence, we will draw upon several major analyses of the notion that can be found in the history of philosophy. Note that our purpose here is *not* to provide airtight philosophical accounts of these analyses. Nor is it our intent to try to apply these theories to touristic actions with a high degree of rigor and precision. As with all philosophical theories, controversies and disagreements abound, and discussion can easily devolve into nit-picking over fine points of detail. Our goal is simply to isolate the (very different) underlying intuitions that drive them and draw upon those intuitions in each case to develop a useful idea of what it is that constitutes a good action. We then try to apply these notions specifically to actions in tourism.

Three Ethical Paradigms

Three major ethical paradigms are particularly relevant to tourism:

(1) The utilitarian ethic of the greatest good.
(2) A Kantian ethic of respect for persons.
(3) An Aristotelian virtue ethics.

In this section, we will provide a brief overview of each paradigm, and identify corresponding notions of good action in tourism. We must stress 'overview', as this section is not intended to be an exhaustive scholarly review of these paradigms. Rather, its purpose is primarily to tap the strong (occasionally conflicting) moral intuitions that drive each of the paradigms in order to develop a general notion of good action in tourism. On the basis of this notion, examples of good action, actions that are not good and actions that are questionable (either ambiguous or requiring further analysis) are presented in subsequent sections.

Utilitarianism

Utilitarianism is an ethical theory most associated with the British philosophers Jeremy Bentham and John Stuart Mill. Utilitarianism can tell us what a good action is but, it is more fundamentally concerned with (morally) *right* actions. The fundamental intuition behind utilitarianism is that actions are judged as right or not for an agent in accordance with the *consequences* of performing them, in particular, with the amount of good and bad that result. For our purposes good and bad can be understood simply to mean *pleasure* and *pain*, respectively. Importantly, however, pleasure should not be understood crassly to mean simply pleasant physical sensation. Rather, it should be understood to encompass all aspects of pleasure, from simple physical pleasures to social and aesthetic pleasures of, e.g. good company or fine entertainment. Moreover, it should not be understood so as to exclude such pleasures as the satisfaction one might gain from a job well done or from helping others. Parallel remarks apply to pain, which should be understood to encompass not only physical pain, but also less tangible experiences as sorrow over loss of one's property, community or cultural traditions.

To clarify the idea of a right action in the utilitarian sense, note first that, intuitively, good and bad (in the senses above) offset one another: when good and bad come in intuitively equal quantities, the *overall* goodness can be said to be zero, nothing. Intuitively, then, we can say that the *overall goodness* of an act (i.e. the performance of an action) is the 'sum' of the good and bad of its consequences. To emphasize: 'sum' is meant informally here; we do not assume that it is genuinely possible to quantify precisely the good and bad that result from an action. Rather, we rely here simply on the intuition that good and bad (in the senses above) come in degrees and that we are capable of making intuitive judgments about how good the consequences of one action are compared to another. Given this, let us say that, of two actions A1 and A2 available to an agent, A1 is *better than* A2 for that agent if his or her performing A1 would bring about more overall good (i.e. would result, on balance, in more good than bad) than would his or her performing A2. An action is *right* for an agent, then, if it is better than any other action that is available to the agent. An action can then be said simply to be *good* for an agent if the overall good that would result from performing it were to outweigh the overall good that would result from its nonperformance.

Utilitarianism captures a very important ethical intuition, viz., that, other things being equal, at least, the goodness of an action is judged in terms of its consequences. However, it is clear that, as it stands, it will not do as a general ethical principle. Simple counterexamples are easy to construct. For instance, suppose that a new tourist development in an economically underdeveloped tropical setting would bring in huge amounts of money to its investors and an infusion of cash to the surrounding towns. Suppose, however, that building the development would destroy habitat that is essential to the survival of several small, indigenous communities. Quite likely, good would significantly outweigh bad in this scenario; many people would profit and only indigenous communities would suffer. Utilitarianism would therefore dictate that the development is well warranted. Intuitively, however, to move ahead despite the fact that it would destroy the indigenous communities seems morally dubious, to say the least. The utilitarian, however, has no basis on which to defend that community. There must therefore be more to the ethical story than utilitarianism. Our next ethical perspective addresses this sort of case.

Kantianism and respect for persons

The moral philosophy of Immanuel Kant is best known for the idea that every moral action is guided by a *categorical imperative*. Unlike *hypothetical imperatives*, which dictate what one ought to do if one wishes to achieve a particular end – e.g. *If you want a good red wine, you ought to buy one from Bordeaux* – categorical imperatives are absolute; one is obligated to obey them regardless of one's desired ends. A central question, then, is: Whence these imperatives? Kant famously answers that individual categorical imperatives are grounded in a principle of reason, which he named the Categorical Imperative (CI). The connection between CI and particular imperatives that guide our actions in particular circumstances is straightforward: CI provides a general principle from which particular categorical imperatives can be inferred by applying the principle to a given context in which moral action is required.

CI itself takes a number of forms in Kant's ethical writings. The most famous of these reflected the influence of Newton on the 18th century mindset by appealing to the notion of universal laws: 'Act only in accordance with that maxim through which you can at the same time will that it become a universal law' (Kant, 1998 (4:421)[1], as cited in Johnson 2008). The idea is that an action is morally permissible only if one can rationally envision a world in which everyone acted in accordance with the principle underlying the action. A well-known example concerns lying to achieve a goal. Suppose that Sam is a developer who is wondering whether, to increase the likelihood of a successful bid, it would be permissible for him to add to his bid the false claim that he is a LEED-certified[2] 'green' builder. In doing so, he would be acting upon the general maxim: *I will tell lies whenever it suits my ends*. Being a good Kantian, Sam tries to envision a world in which everyone acted in accordance with that principle. Clearly, he cannot. For lying is possible only in a world in which communication is built upon a foundation of trust that permits people justifiably to assume that others tend to be truthful about what they claim. In a world in which everyone abided by the maxim in question, everyone would suspect everyone else of lying to achieve their ends and, hence, the foundations of trust that make lying possible would not exist. Sam, therefore, rightly infers that it is not permissible for him to make the false claim in question.

The 'Universal Law' formulation of CI captures an important aspect of our moral thinking – in a nutshell, the intuition that is tapped when we ask of someone pondering a dubious action: 'What if everyone did that?' However, the version that is most germane to our purposes here is often known as the humanity formulation: 'Act in such a way that you treat humanity, whether in your own person or in the person of another, always at the same time as an end and never simply as a means' (Kant, 1998 (4:432), as cited in Johnson 2008).[3] By saying that we should treat humanity – one's own or another's – as an end and never simply as a means, Kant is highlighting the commonality that we share with all others, the characteristics that make us all human. In this way, Kant points us beyond the particularities of any given individual to the enduring basis for the ethical treatment of all individuals, to the foundation that requires the equal treatment of others, regardless of their personal features or their particular situation in life. For all of us possess humanity in equal measure. In particular, humanity requires a certain kind of respect – not the respect that is earned or deserved in virtue of one's actions, intelligence or social standing, but rather, a respect that is simply recognized in virtue of who the person is (Darwall, 1985). For example, most US citizens believe that a certain respect is owed the US President simply in virtue of his being president, irrespective of the respect, or lack thereof, he may be owed in virtue of the way he has executed the duties of the office. Thus, as Johnson (2008) puts it: 'We are to respect human beings simply because they are persons and this requires a certain sort of regard. We are not called on to respect them insofar as they have met some standard of evaluation appropriate to persons'.

What is it, exactly, to treat another person as an end and not solely as a means to an end? The clearest sort of answer for Kant is what we might call *passive*: person A treats another person B as an end by *refraining* from actions that exploit or otherwise harm B in the service of achieving A's own ends. Thus, for example, suppose our developer Sam has a brother who is a powerful Texas state politician. Sam could be seen to be treating his brother as an end if he refrains from exploiting that connection to win state contracts for his business. Again, Sam might show proper respect for the members of an indigenous community who depend on their surrounding ecosystem by choosing to build a resort according to 'green' principles that leave the ecosystem intact.

Additionally, there is also clearly a more *active* sense in which one treats another as an end: one acts in such a way as to further that person's well-being. And this, of course, seems highly germane to issues of the good in tourism. However, it is rather difficult to flesh the notion of well-being in an intuitively satisfying way in Kant's framework. Intuitively, for most people, well-being suggests living a full, well-rounded life. For Kant, however, humanity's highest good is to have a 'good will', that is, roughly, to develop one's character in such a way that all of one's ethically significant actions are motivated entirely by the moral considerations dictated by reason. This seems to have several unintuitive consequences. First, if having a good will is the highest human good, it would seem to follow that, in acting so as to promote the well-being of others, one should always seek to further another's ability to develop a good will. It is, at the least, not obvious that this is always consistent with acting so as to enable one to live a fuller, more well-rounded life. Perhaps, for example, some people might be able to develop the intellectual discipline necessary for having a Kantian good will only by living a difficult and ascetic existence. In such cases, Kant's ethics might actually require that one act in a way that deprives such people of many of life's joys and pleasures. Second, somewhat paradoxically, for Kant, one cannot take one's *own* well-being into consideration in one's moral deliberations when deciding to act in a way that furthers the well-being of others without sullying the moral worth of the act. For insofar as we are motivated by personal benefit of any kind, we are not motivated by moral considerations only, and thus any actions so motivated lose their moral value.

Kant's ethics therefore seem to be missing an aspect of treating others with respect that seems important to formulating a fully robust notion of a good action. The humanity formulation of Kant's CI clearly captures a critical intuition about the overriding value of humanity in our moral thinking, but seems only to deliver a notion of a *bad* action in a given set of circumstances – it is an action that, in those circumstances involves treating another person solely as a means, not an end. But a more active sense is needed to be able to say what a *good* action is. Our third ethical framework – Aristotle's ethics of virtue – seems to address these intuitive shortcomings in Kant's account.

Aristotle and living well

For Aristotle, *eudaimonia* – happiness, or 'living well' – is the highest good. All particular goods that one chooses to pursue – health, friends, community, even the austere Kantian *summum bonum* of a good will – are pursued for the sake of the general, highest good of living well. Aristotle thus explicitly recognized the moral significance of well-being in our thinking, and thereby provides us with the ingredient that seems to be missing from the Kantian notion of respect for persons. For we show respect for others not only passively, by refraining from treating them merely as means in the service of achieving our ends, but also actively, by acting in such a way that promotes their happiness, their ability to live well. This, in turn, provides us with an Aristotelian notion of good action: other things being equal, we should treat others so as to facilitate and enhance their ability to live a 'good' life, in a word, to *flourish*, to live a life that is full and well-rounded.

For our purposes, however, it is important to explore Aristotle's notion of character and its relation to good action more deeply. For out of this notion emerges a particularly cogent concept of good action that is relevant to all of tourism's stakeholders, particularly those in positions of power.

Living well, it must be emphasized, is most definitely not to be confused with 'living large', i.e. with the mere possession and enjoyment of wealth and worldly goods. To the contrary, for Aristotle, living well involves the development of a certain *character*, which, in turn, involves the acquisition of certain *virtues*. The most central of these for Aristotle is *phronesis*, or *practical wisdom*. For Aristotle, the mere pursuit of perceived goods in and of itself does not really distinguish human beings from other animals. What sets humans apart is their ability to use *reason* to guide them in their pursuit of happiness, in particular their use of reason to make decisions, set goals and establish plans to achieve them. Obviously, some decisions/goals/plans are better than others. Practical wisdom, for Aristotle, is the ability to make wise decisions, set appropriate goals and to develop effective plans for achieving them.

Thus, living well involves (among other things) the development and exercise of *phronesis* to set, pursue and achieve the goals that lead to a full life.

How does one develop *phronesis*, practical wisdom? *Phronesis* is not an inert quality; it cannot be attained simply by, e.g. thinking noble thoughts. Rather, one cultivates it through the *practice and repetition* of good actions until the performance of such actions becomes a consistent aspect of one's character – one has not truly acquired *phronesis* if one is wise one day and not wise the next. To illustrate the idea, let us suppose that Sarah was initially disinclined to participate in a new neighbourhood recycling program. However, convinced intellectually that recycling is a good thing for both her community and her own character, Sarah made the decision to do her recycling consistently, her disinclination notwithstanding. Eventually, her disinclination faded and the once burdensome task became an easy part of her routine that flowed naturally from her character. In making her initial decision, Sarah exercised good judgment and thereby cultivated her capacity for practical wisdom. And the transformation of her attitude toward recycling from burdensome task to natural routine was a concomitant manifestation of the development of her character and thus, more generally, moved her closer to the ideal of living well.

As hinted at above, the development and exercise of practical wisdom is not all there is to living well. Practical wisdom is but one of several component 'virtues' that constitute the sort of character that is exhibited by a person who is living well. Virtues are traits of character (dispositions) that are manifested in daily action, the possession of which are what make for a good person (Rachels, 1999). Aristotle conceived of virtues as midpoints, or *means*, between extremes of deficiency and excess. Thus, for example, courage is the mean between cowardice and rashness; honesty the mean between prevarication and indiscretion.

It is perhaps questionable whether all virtues can be so conceived, but the strong intuition that Aristotle is tapping in his doctrine of the mean is that the virtuous life is marked by *moderation*, by the consistent exercise of wise and measured judgment followed by appropriate action. Good habits that cultivate moral and intellectual virtues help to build good character and enable good conduct in daily life. Consider Sarah and the recycling example above – moral virtues can come about by regular practice – we become just by repeatedly doing just acts (just acts are based on virtue). Similarly, intellectual virtues can be cultivated by engaging in good habits regularly at home and during travel – the virtue of learning, for instance, may be cultivated by seeking new knowledge about the destination and its people, history, culture and its biophysical environments (e.g. by reading, participating in dialogue with locals, educational tours, etc.).

For Aristotle, then, good action is virtuous action. It is not enough to do the right thing – *good action must spring from a virtuous character*. A person with excellent knowledge of sustainability principles and practices who does not act in accordance with it may be lacking in the necessary moral virtues, such as the virtue of caring for future generations who may suffer the consequences of resource depletion. Or he or she may act justly or courageously but does so out of fear of punishment or desire for praise. These would not be good actions to Aristotle because they do not spring from a virtuous character. The goal of the good person, therefore, should be the continued development of the sort of virtuous character that consistently produces good actions.

It is important to note briefly that Aristotle situates the good life of the individual within a larger sociopolitical context (the Greek *polis*). Part of good action involves social and political praxis – being active in the day-to-day affairs of the city-state (the *polis*) and exercising good judgment in decision making. Attending to social well-being is important to ensure individual flourishing. This drives home the fact that a truly ethical life must to some extent, at least, be *other-regarding*. For one cannot expect oneself to be able to flourish in a decaying natural environment or social infrastructure. This, of course, has immediate and dramatic implications for tourism, where situations are generally embedded in a complex mix of environmental, social, cultural, economic and political factors. We address this briefly in the next section.

Discussion

We commenced our discussion earlier in the chapter by stating that the starting point for ethical deliberation in regard to good actions in tourism is utilitarian: *other things being equal*, significant actions ought to maximize utility – understood broadly to include such goods as pleasure, wealth, security and general happiness. The qualification 'other things being equal' is critical, as certain goods may arrive to the larger population within a society at a significant cost to a smaller group of individuals within it. Ethical action then has to consider the well-being of the smaller group, which the Kantian notion of respect of persons in the humanity formulation of CI helps to address. Aristotle's concept of *eudaimonia* – living well – and the concomitant notion of a virtuous character, supplements the more passive, or negative, character of the

Kantian notion by providing a more active, positive goal for ethical action, viz., the obligation to further the ability of others to flourish and live well.

As healthy ecosystems are essential for human health and flourishing, good tourism includes good actions towards the biophysical world. *Phronesis* is required in assessing impacts and making ethical choices between several development options for an environmentally or culturally sensitive tourism destination. Active participation in tourism development and management by those who stand to be most impacted by decisions is key to developing *phronesis* and good actions. Aristotelian notions of virtue and character play an important role here, for a virtuous person accords respect to others, exercises *phronesis* to ensure that resource use and the commodification of culture and nature are done in a responsible manner (tempering utilitarian motives with the other two ethical perspectives described above). Among developers, character in particular tempers the desire to maximize profits with concern for the effects of design and management decisions on local communities and on tourist visitors. Among tourists, character tempers the desire for personal pleasure with concern also for the well-being of local communities and service workers. And among service workers, character tempers the inclination to view tourists not only as sources of income, but as individuals towards whom hospitality is extended in the truest sense of the term. The ethical concepts described above are further illustrated by three types of examples provided below.

Practicing good tourism similarly involves becoming engaged in the social and environmental well-being of the destination place and space, and being able to exercise good judgment and virtue in the conduct and practice of tourism. Note that the premise here is that there is a *telos* or purpose (end) for tourism. Good tourism is tourism that meets its end or fulfils its purpose (Jamal, 2005). To be more specific, good tourism is the manifestation of those virtues that achieve the *telos* (purpose) of tourism in the places, spaces and stakeholders of the tourism system.

Applying the theory

In this section, we apply our 'synthesis' of the three ethical paradigms to several examples to illustrate good, bad and questionable touristic actions.

Example 1: Good actions in tourism: Building and business practices

The BC Visitor Centre (BCVC) in Golden, British Columbia, is a state-of-the-art facility located just off Trans-Canada Highway that runs alongside the town of Golden. The town's strategic location near the border between the provinces of Alberta and British Columbia makes it an ideal gateway community to several national parks that surround it. The Centre is a good example of cooperation and contribution to the good of visitors and to the character and culture of the area. Financing and building of the Centre was a collaborative project between the public and private sector. Leadership was provided in the main by the following regional and local stakeholders: Tourism BC, the BC Ministry of Transportation, the Ministry of Agriculture, Golden Area Initiatives and the Kicking Horse Mountain Resort. Additional support was provided by the Government of Canada, the Government of BC, the Columbia Shushwap Regional District, the Town of Golden, the Kicking Horse Mountain Resort, the Canadian Imperial Bank of Commerce and Canada BC Infrastructure Project. The BCVC is the first provincial visitor center to obtain LEED Silver Certification. Requirements for materials, etc., were met, and the building's design and form represents a strong commitment to sustainability and to local cultural heritage – the timber frame design, local materials blend with modern architectural aesthetics to represent the community's traditional economy (forestry) and a new technologically informed tourism. As described on the plaque within the Centre (on 19 June 2006):

> The project attempts to manifest the place that is Golden, an industrial and industrious community derived from the railroad and forestry industry of the Columbia River Valley. The project looks to the simple forms, honest material strategy and indigenous building techniques, while attempting to create a contemporary and progressive architectural language. It utilizes several local wood product materials . . .

Like the BC Visitor Centre, good actions in constructing tourism-related facilities are also demonstrated by the efforts of developers to build 'green' hotels, resorts and conference centers. The landmark David L. Lawrence Convention Center is a symbol of a new Pittsburgh and regional destination place. Certified with a Gold LEED rating by the US Green Building Council, it is the first 'green' convention center and is stated to be the largest 'green' building in the world (http://www.pittsburghcc.com/html/index.htm. Accessed 31.3.08). As stated on its web site, natural daylight and natural ventilation are used to light and heat the building, a water reclamation system reduces potable water use and recycling is a well-established aspect of this facility. Enviro-friendly actions are also being implemented in areas such as downhill skiing whose cumulative impacts tend to type it as a traditionally unsustainable activity. In Vail, Colorado, plans have been announced to build North America's largest green resort, Ever Vail, with 'enviro-friendlier' condos, shops, restaurants and a gondola. In New England (USA), the mountain resort Jiminy Peak (http://www.jiminypeak.com. Accessed 31.3.08) has installed a 1.5 megawatt wind turbine that is expected to meet one third of the resort's electrical demands; the resort claims to be the first in North America to install a wind turbine for power (Beehner, 2007). In the popular year-round mountain destination of Jackson Hole, the new Hotel Terra Jackson Hole (http://www.hotelterrajacksonhole.com. Accessed 31.3.08) is a 72-room eco-boutique hotel with energy-efficient windows, custom mattresses made from organic cotton, environmentally friendly cleaning products and a goal to offset 100% of energy usage with wind, biomass and other renewable energy forms. Beehner's article ends rhetorically with the comment: 'Who said green and luxury don't mix?' (Beehner, 2007: 13).

Laying aside (for now) the ethical questions surrounding the provision of luxury, one might respond by saying that good actions in tourism aim not only for resource conservation and good experience for guests, but also fair distribution of related costs and benefits, responsible treatment of employees (including fair living wage) and attention to local cultural heritage. Ecolodge development and ecotourism are generally aimed at minimizing adverse resource impacts, aiding conservation and social-cultural sustainability. Part of this is ensured through thoughtful building and facility design, and involving residents in the planning, development and management process. As Example 2 demonstrates, public and private sector actions have to consider those who stand to be most impacted by a (proposed) development. In other words, utilitarian arguments for the greater good (e.g. providing mountain experiences for visitors, facilitating local and area-based economic benefit, contributing to a successful tourism industry) must be tempered by respect for persons (e.g. local residents in the resort destination and the mountain-cultural aspects that are important to their well-being).

Example 2: Actions lacking goodness in tourism: Disrespecting environment and culture

Dracula Park is an example of a failed top-down planning attempt to provide local and regional economic development. The utilitarian aim of the Romanian government combined with profit-making business interests resulted in a theme park proposal that was seen by many to be disrespectful of local residents and religious sensibilities, as well as detrimental to local ecosystems. Hoping to stimulate international tourism and take advantage of a lucrative myth (Dracula-based films, novels, clubs, etc.), the Romanian Ministry of Tourism initiated Dracula Park, a large theme park to be located on Breite Plateau near the historic town of Sighisoara (Transylvania), three hundred kilometers North-west of Bucharest. The location was selected in 2001, with project completion slated for 2004. Sighisoara is seen to be the birthplace of Vlad Tepes, a 15th-century prince whose reputation for cruelty towards his prisoners (he was known as Vlad the Impaler) apparently helped to inspire Bram Stoker to create his fictional character Dracula (Jamal & Tanase, 2005). Accommodation and facilities at the proposed theme park were to include a 700-room hotel (there were around six hotels in Sighisoara at that time), pension lodgings, apartments, camping, restaurants (fast foods, snack bar, medieval restaurant and theme bar), sports grounds and a theatre hall. The on-site International Institute of Vampirology would house a resource center with books, movies and historical information. A replica of Dracula's Castle, catacombs, an artificial lake and a labyrinth garden were also proposed. In addition to various adverse environmental impacts (including the potential destruction of 400-year-old oaks on Breite Plateau) that concerned NGOs, the projected economic, social and cultural costs appeared to far outweigh potential benefits. Local residents and religious leaders expressed vocal opposition, and strong conflict resulted. Early in 2003, the Romanian government announced a new Park location at Snagov, twenty-five miles Northwest of Bucharest. Snagov Lake contains an island with a monastery said to house the remains of Vlad Tepes. This attempt to relocate the park to a different site also met with continued resistance and eventual failure (Jamal & Tanase, 2005).

The Dracula Park project was aborted by the Ministry of Tourism and its public-private partners (local and international). The policy-making power of government, and the financing/development expertise of various corporate groups afford power and control over the flow of benefits and costs. Good actions and lack of good actions result; low income, minority populations and the poor are especially vulnerable to resource appropriation and degradation of biophysical goods on which their livelihoods and survival depend. In other words, activities that do not comport with good actions in tourism include those that result in inequitable distribution of costs and benefits (Lee & Jamal, 2008). For example, research by Stonich (1998) found unequal distribution of clean water between incoming tourists (primarily international visitors) and local residents in the Honduras. Visitors had more access to environmental resources while residents received a disproportionate share of the resulting environmental problems and costs. High water usage by hotels (especially noticeable in showering use) translated into increasing water scarcity for residents. While clean water was available to tourists, lack of sanitation and water filtration facilities created health problems for the Bay Islanders. The poor also received the least benefits from tourism as measured by income and patterns of consumption (Stonich, 1998). Many residents felt that those who controlled tourism opportunities, namely the government, international interests and local elites, benefited vastly and to the exclusion of the poorer residents.

In both the examples above, it can be argued that respect for the local resident is lacking. Vocal resistance by local residents combined with the protests of local and area-based NGOs was needed to avert a poorly thought-out (lacking in practical wisdom among other things) project with high risk to local residents, local ecosystems and to local-global cultural heritage (Sighisoara). In the Honduras example, little attention was being paid to the plight of Bay Islander residents affected by increased development-related costs and lack of access to a precious commodity (water). Lack of respect, and lack of moral character (resulting in lack of concern) by more powerful stakeholders is part of the ethical scenario here. Neither are the tourists blameless for their lack of knowledge or lack of concern – education, learning and prudential actions is part of ecotourist ethics, but virtue ethics shows that these should be part of good actions by all tourists regardless of activity type. Developing intellectual and moral virtues (good character) helps tourists to exercise practical wisdom in their behavior and in their use of a destination's resources. They can be assisted by good corporate actions that include 'green' practices (Example 1) and visitor education about the destination's environment, people, and economic and cultural dimensions. Corporate social responsibility (CSR) is facilitated by developing virtues such as fairness, honesty, plus developing practical wisdom, for instance, by actively and habitually involving those who stand to be most impacted (e.g. local residents in the destination) in the planning, development and management of tourist attractions, facilities and services. Such organizations and individuals demonstrate good character and the ability to conduct good actions in tourism.

Example 3: Questionable actions in tourism: Marketing a post-disaster site

The examples above support the following view, which draws upon the three philosophical perspectives outlined earlier. Good actions in tourism provide for individual and collective flourishing, prudent use of environmental and cultural resources (conserving as needed) and ensuring that actions for the greater (economic) good are taken with regard to the well-being of individual and smaller groups. The utilitarian view generally adopted by government policymakers and planners, therefore, has to be tempered by the Kantian notion of respect for persons powered, in turn, by the Aristotelian conception of good character. Yet, despite the guidance provided by these three perspectives, it is not always easy to identify whether an action is good or not good (existential questions are especially problematic). In some situations, identifying who benefits and who loses may be a helpful start to discussing good (or not good) actions in tourism.

Prior to the devastation of New Orleans by Hurricane Katrina in August 2005, New Orleans was a popular tourist destination known for its diverse cultural offerings, including a vibrant culinary and musical heritage, and a deviant touristic space for sexual 'play'. The Mardi Gras carnival was one moment for this, but year-round activities had been re-created by reproducing the city's short history of legalized prostitution (Storyville) in the space of Bourbon Street. As little remained physically to show of Storyville, bars, strip clubs and sex shops helped create a 'nostalgia' excuse for tourists to experience those times of vice through exhibitions of sexual nudity, obscenity and excess (Vessey & Dimanche, 2003). Vessey and Dimanche noted that excessive behavior such as genital display during Mardi Gras and on Bourbon Street had led to public criticism that pressured city officials to enact obscenity laws; some tourists ended up in jail for violating these laws – they were under the impression that 'Bourbon Street is a place to really let go ...' (Vessey & Dimanche, 2003: 64). Post-Katrina New Orleans raises even more troubling questions on the actions of destination marketers (which include not only the destination marketing organization, but also the other intermediaries whose advertising and promotional actions contribute to destination image construction). Would the continued re-presentation of New Orleans as a play destination constitute good action in tourism?

Good Actions in Tourism: What Ought We to Do?

Climate change and global warming are no longer a matter of dispute; for us in travel and tourism the challenge revolves around prioritizing issues and engaging in good actions to tackle existing problems and minimize future harm to living and nonliving systems affected by global warming and rising global population. A globalized and technologically interconnected world offers opportunities and challenges to facilitating good actions in tourism. While jet engines contribute significantly to global warming, efforts are being made to develop alternative fuels and other means of limiting carbon dioxide and other harmful emission. The argument is utilitarian (sustainability for the greater good), where 'good' translates to current and future generations (intra and intergenerational equity). As international travel continues to democratize, aided by increasing per capita wealth and technological innovations (consider the rapidity with which events and place translate around the globe today) in the 'Western' world, luxury travel and medical tourism are only two of many new forms of tourism that are emerging. Yet, even in luxury-oriented resorts, boutique hotels and tours catering to the wealthy, evidence of good actions to build character and enable respect and care for other persons can be seen.

The popularization of philanthropic activities by celebrities like Angelina Jolie who brought attention to the plight of refugees from Darfur and Afghanistan, and Bono's sustained actions to address poverty in the developing world, has influenced charitable actions by luxury travellers. Nonprofit organizations and tour operators have facilitated this partnership between two extremes (the very wealthy and the underserved poor) by organizing tours where charitable actions are built in or are an optional part of the travel experience. Artisans of Leisure, based in New York, organized a trip to Paris and Morocco for a mother and daughter that included direct interaction with children at orphanages to which they also delivered supplies they had purchased (Alsever, 2007). Guests of Exquisite Safaris will tour Kenya, Tanzania and Uganda, visiting farmers and other small business enterprises that have been funded by donations from similar luxury travellers; travellers with the luxury tour operator Abercrombie and Kent recently gave $100,000 over two years to the Living with Elephants Educational Outreach Program (Alsever, 2007). Direct face-to-face interaction and experience at the destination enables learning and development of moral virtue, as well as practical wisdom (*phronesis*) in performing charitable acts. Respect for persons is facilitated, too, when one encounters the Other, who then is no longer nameless or part of a larger abstract concept (poverty). Encountering the vulnerability and humanity of the Other while experiencing the destination's environmental and cultural rich-ness, is an important factor in the success of such philanthropic luxury tours. Meanwhile, other forms of tourism have arisen that also aspire to provide for good actions in tourism, e.g. pro-poor tourism, volunteer tourism (see the rising popularity of 'volun-tourism' in newspaper travel sections, e.g. Conlin, 2007).

The three historical perspectives presented in this chapter offer an avenue for investigating the ethics of tourism, specifically, good tourism and what constitutes good actions in tourism. Further research and analysis will be required to construct a well-supported ethical claim about what tourism ought to provide and how to facilitate good actions in tourism. Here, our approach leads to a proposition for future discussion: Tourist development should be focussed on the design, creation and management of tourist sites that naturally encourage equitable distribution of costs and benefits among its local-global stakeholders, respect for others (including nonhuman others) and the development of character in site developers, service providers, NGOs, tourists and residents.

Notes

1. We are following Johnson, 2008 in using a standard citation scheme for Kant's *Groundwork* here.
2. LEED = Leadership in Energy and Environmental Design. See the US Green Building Council web site for information on the LEED green building rating system. On the World Wide Web at http://www.usgbc.org/DisplayPage. aspx?CMSPage ID=222. Accessed 3/31/08.
3. The qualification 'simply' in the principle is important. For it would be impossible to make one's way around in the world without treating others as means to an end – anyone performing a service for pay, for example, is being so treated by the beneficiary of the service. What Kant's principle proscribes is treatment of another *solely* as a means to an end.

References

Alsever, J. (2007) When a luxury vacation cultivates philanthropy. *New York Times,* 9 December, B6.

Aristotle (1980) *Nichomachean Ethics* (D. Ross, trans.). Oxford: Oxford University Press.

Beehner, L. (2007) Going green, luxuriously. *New York Times,* 2 December, C6, C13.

Conlin, J. (2007) Trips to help shape the world. *New York Times,* 9 December, Travel Section, TR6.

Darwall, S. (1985) Kantian practical reason defended. *Ethics* 96, 89–99.

Jamal, T. (2005) Virtue ethics and sustainable tourism pedagogy: Phronesis, principles and practice. *Journal of Sustainable Tourism* 12 (6), 530–545.

Jamal, T. and Tanase, A. (2005) Conflict over the proposed Dracula Park location near Sighisoara, Romania: The role of sustainable tourism principles. *Journal of Sustainable Tourism* 13 (5), 440–455.

Johnson, R. (2008) Kant's moral philosophy. *The Stanford Encyclopedia of Philosophy (Fall 2008 Edition),* Edward N. Zalta (ed.), URL=< http://plato. stanford.edu/ archives/fall2008/entries/kant-moral/ > .

Kant, I. (1998) *The Groundwork of the Metaphysics of Morals* (M. Gregor ed.). Cambridge: Cambridge University Press.

Lee, S. and Jamal, T. (2008) Environmental justice and environmental equity in tourism: Missing links to sustainability. *Journal of Ecotourism* 7 (1), 44–67.

Stonich, S.C. (1998) Political ecology of tourism. *Annals of Tourism Research* 25 (1), 25–54.

Vessey, C. and Dimanche, F. (2003) From Storyville to Bourbon Street: Vice, nostalgia and tourism. *Journal of Tourism and Cultural Change* 1 (1), 54–70.

Chapter 14
Against 'Ethical Tourism'

JIM BUTCHER

Who could be against ethical tourism? To argue against it is to court the charge of being unethical, which at a time when ethical living is such a prominent issue would seem bizarre.

However, I will argue that ethical tourism, as constituted through the many debates and discussions in universities and beyond, is a thoroughly bad idea. Not only does its advocacy amount to a slight on the holidaymaker in search of fun and relaxation, it is also premised upon assumptions that, far from being ethical, are profoundly reactionary when viewed from a humanist standpoint.

In this spirit, it is worth considering what could be regarded as the social construction of ethical tourism – why is it that the extension of leisure travel, generally seen in the past as a part of economic and social progress, is now (for some at least) characterised by ethical dilemmas? Why is ethical tourism more often than not associated with small-scale initiatives that make a virtue of changing little, even in places wracked by poverty?

A Pervasive Agenda

Calls for ethical tourism have a relatively recent vintage. In the 1980s, Krippendorf's *The Holiday Makers* (1987) painted a grim picture of modern tourism, and at times reads as a manifesto for a new, 'ethical' tourist. More recent titles such as *Preserve or Destroy: Tourism and the Environment* (Croall, 1995) and *The Paving of Paradise and What You Can Do To Stop It* (MacLaren, 1998) exemplify a pervasive negative view of the development of mass leisure travel. Along with GM food and supermarkets, the growth of holiday making – something we may have expected to be worthy of celebration – is viewed through a dark lens and seen as exemplary of damaging globalisation. Ethical tourism, for its advocates, is a counter to this.

More recently, authors such as Fennell (2006) and Smith and Duffy (2003) have sought to develop a more substantial understanding of ethical tourism, the former elaborating an impressive survey of philoso-phical thought on ethics as a means to confront contemporary ethical dilemmas, the latter's focus being tourism development.

NGOs concerned with the deleterious effects of mass tourism have been vocal. In Germany, *Studienkreis für Tourismus und Entwicklung* (Students for Tourism and Responsibility) operate their prestigious *To Do!* awards. The winners are almost invariably small-scale, locally oriented and green. This organisation, typical of others throughout Europe, state in their aims and objectives that they 'support forms of tourism which contribute to intercultural encounter, which allow for joint learning processes, mutual respect as well as respect for cultural diversity and the sustainable use of natural resources' (STE, nd).

Industry groups such as The International Ecotourism Society are influential in marketing and promoting the ethical credentials of green holidays. Their role is not just to network with like-minded tourists with a love of the natural world, but also to advocate the superiority of eco holidays for both parties concerned, tourists and hosts. The society claim that: 'Ecotravel offers an alternative to many of the negative effects of mass tourism by helping conserve fragile ecosystems, support endan-gered species and habitats, preserve indigenous cultures and develop sustainable local economies' (TIES, nd). They encourage prospective tourists to, 'travel with a purpose – a personal purpose and a global one' (TIES, nd).

Calls for ethical tourism feature ever more prominently in the media, too. British social commentator Libby Purves argues that: 'Tourists should not travel light on morals', and paints a bleak picture of the effects of the industry (Purves, 2001). The UK *Guardian* newspaper environment editor, in an article entitled 'Tourism is bad for our health', asserts that mass tourism, 'wreak(s) havoc on the environment' and that despite attempts to clean up the industry, 'tourism is essentially and inescapably, environmentally destructive' (Griffiths, 2001).

Advocacy of ethical tourism is also evident in the commercial sector. A host of companies, spurning the four Ss (sun, sea, sand and sex) in favour of the three Ts (travelling, trekking and trucking) have set out to appeal to the ethical sensibility. Their advocacy of ethical tourism is often met with scepticism by the NGOs and campaigns, who question whether their concern to be ethical is genuine or merely a marketing ploy. Nonetheless, many such companies echo the criticisms of package tourism made by the NGOs and express a similar commitment to the environment and the host's culture. They also display a similar disdain for package tourists. *Explore*, a trekking holiday company, have advertised their holidays as being for 'people who want more out of their holiday than buckets of cheap wine and a suntan' (cited in Butcher, 2003: 14). *Dragoman* view their trucking holidays as visiting places that have been 'shunned by the masses who prefer resorts and beaches' (Butcher, 2003). Other brochures set out the important role expected of their clientele in relation to supporting the culture and environment of their hosts in the Third World. *Encounter Overland* regard their customers as 'today's custodians of the ancient relationship between traveller and the native which throughout the world has been the historic basis for peaceful contact' (Butcher, 2003).

Romantic Disdain?

If the ethical lobby were simply indulging in romantic disdain for the growth of leisure travel then this would be nothing new. The eminent Victorian gentleman Sir Lesley Stephen argued that the only saving grace of resorts was that they confined 'the swarm of intrusive insects to one place' (cited in Feifer, 1986: 179), and Thomas Cook was frequently criticised for developing travel opportunities for those deemed incapable of benefiting from them (Brendon, 1991).

Today's critique less often carries the overt snobbery and sense of superiority that was good coin in Victorian England (although it is certainly still there). Rather, today's package tourists are deemed thoughtless and unaware – thoughtless with regard to their environmental footprint and unaware of the damaging impact on the culture of their hosts. In the view of a vocal ethical tourism lobby, there is a need to reign in their pleasure seeking for the sake of the planet and the cultures that inhabit it.

George Monbiot sums up this gloomy view when he asserts: 'Tourism is, by and large, an unethical activity, which allows us to have fun at everyone else's expense' (Monbiot, 1999). *Guardian* ethical-living correspondent Leo Hickman (2002) concurs in his apocalyptically titled book *The Last Call: In Search of the True Cost of Our Holidays*. He describes tourism as 'a self-centred act', before proceeding to draw a comparison between drunken men on stag weekends in Tallinn and invading Nazi armies in World War II. Hickman's glum journalism is not untypical of assertions in mainstream academic literature, which not infrequently refer to tourism as a form of colonialism or imperialism (a comparison that succeeds in simultaneously grossly exaggerating any damaging effects of tourism and, more importantly, trivialising colonialism and imperialism).

Given the extent of the advice industry at home, covering what to eat, how to bring up children, how often to exercise and much else, one might have expected holidays to remain immune from this trend, as an antidote to angst and personal insecurity. Yet simply 'leaving your cares behind' is presented as part of the problem, and yet more advice is offered as the solution. For example, codes of conduct on how to 'travel well', such as those now included in *Rough Guides* series, are widely advocated in the academic literature (Butcher, 2003). The emphasis on formal codes for negotiating other cultures on holiday presupposes that host and tourists inhabit different cultural worlds, and that cross-cultural encounters are fraught (Butcher, 2003).

Culture or Cultures?

The academic literature offers some depth to the popular cultural criticisms of tourism. Anthropological concepts such as 'acculturation', 'the demonstration effect' and 'staged authenticity' are commonly invoked in the context of examining intercultural encounters, and have certainly sensitised researchers to cultural differences. However, as Kay Milton (1996) argues in *Environmentalism and Cultural Theory*, anthropology's influence in rural development thinking from the 1970s brought with it cultural relativism. This is certainly true for the discussion on tourism, where hosts and tourist are defined by their differences, and common aspirations for development are rarely alluded to. Hence, these concepts are often invoked in the context of a desire to protect communities from the excesses of modernity in the form of tourism and tourists. A one-sided sympathy for victims of a cultural imposition, rather than empathy with the aspirations of our hosts (including the desire to travel itself) is the result. This is very much in line with what Raymond Williams identified as a distinctive anthropological conception of culture, one that sees culture first and foremost in its plural, as *cultures* (Williams, cited in Young, 1995: 44).

There is a sense in which the advocacy of ethical tourism, or 'New Moral Tourism' as I describe it in *The Moralisation of Tourism* (Butcher, 2003), is a little like amateur anthropology. Just as the anthropological study of tourism emerged with concerns over cultural contact between hosts and guests (Nash & Smith, 1991), New Moral Tourism has reflected growing misgivings with Mass Tourism (Poon, 1993). Both anthropologists and New Moral Tourists are interested in learning about the culture of the host. Both may also seek to minimise their own impact on the hosts' society – anthropologists seek to blend in order to avoid eliciting behaviour different from the norm, and New Moral Tourists may be wary of their own capacity to damage the local culture. Also, neither is satisfied with staged aspects of the hosts' culture, in which traditional festivals and rituals are presented as spectacles for tourists (MacCannell, 1976; Goffman, 1959). Both seek to go beyond that, potentially into the authentic 'backstage' world of their host.

Many ethical New Moral Tourism companies and development initiatives utilising nature-based tourism appeal to this desire to go 'backstage'. Tanzania's NGO-funded cultural tourism programme offers tourism 'the People to People way' (Fisher, nd). The literature says that the tours 'offer visitors insights into the life – traditional and modern – of Tanzanians at home and at work, at play and at rest' (Fisher, nd). The brochure is filled with pictures of cultural life – predominantly villagers working on the land and taking produce to be sold, as well as one of a mother feeding her baby. The photographs would fit well alongside an anthropological account of village life in poor, rural Tanzania.

David Lodge's novel *Paradise News* is insightful with regard to this cultural debate (Lodge, 1991). The book follows the fortunes of a group of tourists to Hawaii. Anthropologist Rupert Sheldrake spends his time studying the behaviour of the other tourists and warning them of the futility and destructive nature of their leisure. Sheldrake comments: 'I'm doing to tourism what Marx did to capitalism, what Freud did to family life. Deconstructing it' (Lodge, 1991: 64). Sheldrake's theory is that the sheer repetition of the word Paradise in brochures, in hotels and in the resorts brainwashes the tourists into thinking that they really are in Paradise.

Sheldrake is a fictional character, but definitely a man of our times. He voices grave concerns about tourism's ill effects, which chime with those of many of tourism's critics. His unease at what tourists do and how they behave is echoed in the wary pronouncements of academics and the steady stream of ethical advice given out to tourists today.

Yet, an oversensitivity to cultural difference can easily be a self-fulfilling prophecy. If we look for difference we will no doubt find it, but if we don't assume it we are more likely to find our hosts share much with us, be it in perhaps very different circumstances. This latter view is perhaps a sound outlook for researchers, Sheldrake included, and holidaymakers alike.

Sheldrake travels alone – his fiancée ended their engagement: 'She said I spoiled her holidays, analysing them all the time' (Lodge, 1991).

In Defence of the Masses

Is mass tourism really as bad as it is painted by champions of ethical holidays? One place I have never heard associated with ethical tourism is the Spanish resort of Torremolinos, immortalised by Monty Python's *Watney's Red Barrel* sketch as the resort of choice for drunken Brits abroad. The *Cadogan's Guide* description of it as a 'ghastly, hyperactive, unsightly holiday inferno' (Facaros & Paul, 1999: 603) is different in tone only from some references to the Spanish Costas in academic literature. Yet 50 years ago, Torremolinos was a poor fishing community, with high rates of infant mortality and low levels of literacy. In part due to the development of mass package tourism, it now enjoys levels of wealth and education that enable many Spanish people to join the (still exclusive) club of leisure travelers. Indeed, in late season, the Costas are frequented by Spanish people from the cities, who come to enjoy the cool breezes and conviviality – hardly an alien invasion, more of a cause for optimism surely.

Moreover, the impact of tourism revenues from the 1960s played an important part in Spain's economic modernisation, and some even argue in breaking down social conservatism. For all its faults, the balance sheet in Spain, Torremolinos included, is surely very positive. Julio Aramberri, former Professor of Sociology turned tourism development expert in the Spanish government in the 1980s, is rightly proud of the role of the development of tourism in bringing greater affluence to his country, and remains frustrated at the indifference to the benefits of the industry, warts and all, of many social scientists (Aramberri, 2007).

A further example is Malta, a small island, population around 450,000, with approaching one third of its land mass urbanised, in receipt of well over a million tourists annually. But are the Maltese up in arms over the colonisation of their island? Far from it, opinion polls have consistently shown a favourable view from the large majority. This is in some contrast to the view of many academic commentators, who are often quick to disparage the resort, preferring to laud the 'sustainable' benefits of the ecolodge.

In the advocacy of ethical tourism, the adjectives 'small', 'local' and 'participatory' are treated as articles of faith, and most often associated with sustainability. 'Mass' and 'big' (especially when followed by 'business') less often feature. This serves to accentuate the limiting philosophy of 'small is beautiful' and deny the many benefits of large-scale development.

Ethical Consumerism and Life Politics

Of course ethical tourism is just one aspect of a wider development – that of ethical consumerism. Ethical consumerism takes people's role as consumers as an important arena for social change. Such an outlook seems almost commonsense today – it has become a central feature of contemporary politics – but only really developed in the 1980s (Harrison *et al.*, 2005). Indeed, it represents a fundamental shift in politics, from the politics of production to those of consumption (Baumann, 2000). The former involved a contestation of how production, and society, was organised, and is essentially the politics of Left and Right. The protagonists in this political configuration bought in to the idea of progress – politics was characterised by competing claims to be able to modernise societies through economic development (Baumann, 2000). However, the ascendancy of the politics of consumption elevates people's role as consumers in shaping identities and in social change. It often eschews 'progress' and modernity in favour of green thinking (Heartfield, 2002).

Advocates of ethical consumerism argue that consumers can force a more ethical agenda onto companies through exercising choice in favour of products that are deemed more sustainable. Such a view was personified by Bodyshop founder, the late Anita Roddick: 'Don't just grin and bear it. As consumers we have real power to affect change … we can use our ultimate power, voting with our feet and wallets – in buying a product somewhere else, or not buying it at all' (cited in Pepper, 1996: 85). A radical version of this view – one that chimes with some of the advocacy of ethical tourism – is Noreena Hertz's (2001) *Silent Takeover*, which postulates ethical demand as the driver for radical social change.

Tourism can have an edge in discussions of ethical consumerism – it is distinctive for a number of reasons:

Firstly, the tourist travels to a destination, at which the 'service' is produced – in a sense production and consumption are simultaneous, and involve both an economic and a cultural encounter. Hence, existential dilemmas (a feature of Giddens's 'Life Politics' (1991), of which ethical consumerism is a part) are central to ethical tourism. For some, the weakness of the old political identities was precisely their lack of recognition of such existential dilemmas, and the efficacy of the new politics of consumption and lifestyle is precisely that it is a politics based around lived experience (Giddens, 1991).

Second, some argue that tourism involves the visual 'consumption' of other cultures through the 'tourist gaze' (Urry, 1995, 2002). This refers to important aspects of the host's culture being moulded through commercial tourism encounters, and altered in ways that may have a deleterious effect on the community and environment.

Third, ethical tourism has been argued to have two elements key to ethical 'alternative' consumption: solidarity and caring for the environment (Meletis & Campbell, 2007). For example, ecotourism's claims to be ethical are based upon its capacity to integrate conservation (caring for the environment) and development (solidarity with people through supporting local culture) in what some term a 'symbiotic', or mutually reinforcing relationship. Some even argue that alternative tourism can be a radical counter to the domination of global business over the lives of communities (Pleumaron, 1994; Wearing, 2001).

Moreover, the solidarity shown overcomes a potential problem identified recently by some cultural geographers; that of *caring at a distance* (see Meletis & Campbell, 2007). Ethical tourism involves caring up close and personal, and is often accompanied by a sense of mission, something that would not have been associated with holidays in the past.

Ethical consumerism is in line with the growth of the wider category of Life Politics (Giddens, 1991). Giddens identified a shift from the traditional politics of emancipation, embodied in collective ideas such as trade unionism, and grand narratives of Left and Right, towards Life Politics. Life Politics refers to individuals' attempts to reposition themselves culturally in the context of their own lives and through this to try to make a difference to their immediate environment and also more broadly in the political realm. Hence, Giddens argues that Life Politics is a reconfiguration of the relationship of the individual to their society – personal identity becomes a site of political change (Giddens, 1991).

The growth of Life Politics reflects important shifts in the way people relate to society more broadly – the issues they prioritise and the ways in which they may seek to have an impact upon these issues. How we consume has grown in prominence relative to the workplace as the terrain on which identities are formed and social issues are debated. Sociologist Zygmunt Baumann puts it thus:

> ... in present day society, consumer conduct (consumer freedom geared to the consumer market) moves steadily into the position of, simultaneously, the cognitive and moral focus of life, the integrative bond of the society ... In other words, it moves into the self same position which in the past – during the 'modern' phase of capitalist society – was occupied by work. (Bauman, 1992: 49)

Bauman makes the widely accepted point that in previous periods, the realm of production, or work, was more central to identity, but that today it is more as consumers that we develop a sense of ourselves in the world. The growth of the importance of consumption is often viewed in positive terms (Giddens, 1991; Featherstone, 1991). The world of consumption and identities, personal and political, takes the appearance of a world of choice and freedom – one can break free of traditional collective identities connected to class, race or gender and develop one's own identity and experiment in ways not evident in the past. In political terms, too, it has been argued that consumers can generate pressure for change in a way traditional, discredited political institutions are unable to (Hertz, 2001).

However, Life Politics is a very limited arena for our moral and ethical aspirations. The backdrop to Life Politics is the collapse of perceived alternatives to capitalism. The collapse of communism seemed to confirm that alternatives to the market do not work. This is reinforced by the adoption, or at the very least acceptance of market forces as positive or ineffaceable even by capitalism's erstwhile critics on the Left. This has contributed to a lack of questioning of the market, which has taken on the appearance of an eternal reality in political and social debates. Francis Fukuyama's *End of History* (1992) thesis, following soon after the end of the Cold War, presenting a contemporary world in which all the big ideological issues have been settled, is perhaps emblematic of a sense of closure of grand politics.

Margaret Thatcher, the former Conservative Prime Minister of the UK asserted in the 1980s the 'TINA doctrine', that 'There Is No Alternative' to the market. Once this becomes the backdrop for politics, change *through* the market, through our role as consumers, becomes the only channel through which to act upon the world. We have agency as consumers, but little prospect of influencing the way in which production is organised. As individuals, we may be 'empowered', but collectively we are impotent. It is only in such times that how and where we holiday can become a focus for acting upon the world.

The advocacy of ethical tourism makes a virtue of this closure of political options and debate, and substitutes 'ethics' for politics. Hence, ethical tourism is tourism for our times. It focuses people's aspirations to 'make a difference' onto individualised, and often egotistical acts of charity. It, in a sense, cashes in on the anti-political mood of our times, through which collective solutions of any kind appear redundant and old fashioned (Furedi, 2005; Heartfield, 2002). As an expression of anti-politics, the scope for ethical tourism to tackle social and political problems is incredibly limited.

Welfare, Economic Growth and 'Responsibility'

The debate about ethical tourism is not solely focused on the consumer. Calls for corporate social responsibility in the tourism industry, as elsewhere, have become more of an issue (Kalisch, 2002). As is the case with ethical business generally, it is on the face of it hard to take issue with calls for greater 'responsibility' in tourism development.

Yet ethical, 'responsible' tourism has come to be associated with localism, smallness of scale and environmental conservation. It is commonplace for a casual association to be made between ecotourism and ethical tourism. It is nigh on unknown for mass tourism to be championed as ethical, in spite of the latter's contribution to economic wellbeing. In fact, there is a real sense in the debate that small-scale, green ethical tourism is ethical precisely in relation to the unethical record of mass tourism in the past (Butcher, 2003).

One perverse outcome of this is *that human welfare has become detached from economic growth* in the discussion. Ethical tourism projects claim to aid welfare for 'local' people. Welfare benefits are often discussed in terms of support of the local way of life, or providing economic incentives for environmentally friendly practices. Yet this is seen in contradistinction to large scale, national economic development, seen by the advocates of a new ethical tourism as damaging.

Take for example Scheyvens' (2002) *Tourism for Development: Empowering Communities*. Scheyvens makes explicit that the locality is the most appropriate unit for development in terms of human wellbeing. She says of her book: 'It is not a book about how governments can extract the greatest economic benefits from encouraging foreign investment in tourism. [...] Rather, the interests of local communities in tourism development are placed at the forefront' (Scheyvens, 2002: 8). In her estimation, it is governments that benefit from a more traditional approach to development, whilst ecotourism and other 'ethical' niches can be oriented towards local people in their communities, and are hence deemed to be what prominent advocate of neopopulist development Robert Chambers refers to as 'good change' (Chambers, 1983). This is typical of the neopopulist outlook on development – it presents large-scale development as beneficial to distant governments, with local community level development as holding out greater potential for 'people', the latter mode of development hence acquiring ethical status.

This assumption is widely made and rarely questioned in the ethical tourism debate.

Yet national economic growth is, in general, a prerequisite for significant improvements in health, education and literacy – this is evident in the experience of any developed country. It is notable that China, the world's fastest growing economy, is also the society that has gone the furthest in meeting the UN Millennium development goals. Yet, grand development projects that can contribute to significant economic growth are eschewed in the advocacy of ethical tourism. Instead, small-scale projects make a virtue of changing little, and often of providing meagre benefits based upon charity. In fact, rarely are 'ethical' tourism projects lauded for their contribution to national economic growth – rather 'welfare' on a local level is stressed, and the provision of basic needs (a laudable goal that, in some circumstances, ecotourism can contribute too) is liberally conflated with 'sustainable' development (Butcher, 2007).

Ecotourism: An 'Ethical' Alternative?

At the forefront of attempts to make tourism 'ethical' – and archetypical of the trend to detach welfare from economic growth (ecotourism eschews growth and economic transformation but is constantly rationalised in terms of its welfare benefits) – is ecotourism. In 1989, Karen Ziffer, ecotourism pioneer and co-founder of The International Ecotourism Society, set the tone in her book *Ecotourism: Potentials and Pitfalls*, arguing that ecotourism can be more than a type of holiday – it can also be philosophy and a model of development. Her view was prescient – in the last two decades ecotourism has undergone a transition from green niche market to favoured ethical type of leisure travel and innovative rural development option.

As a model of development, ecotourism's claims to be 'sustainable' and 'ethical' reside in its ability to link conservation and development. As such, it is part of the growth of integrated conservation and development projects (ICDPs) that attempt to bring together these two apparently competing aims within biodiversity rich areas. The argument is carried by its own circular logic – revenue through ecotourism means that conservation is incentivised, and conservation ensures that the ecotourist revenue will keep on coming. This has been characterised as a 'win-win' situation, in which both conservation and development benefit. This view is rehearsed in numerous studies and books, the majority of which constitute a critical advocacy of ecotourism, often by favourable comparison to mass tourism.

Yet, this formulation assumes a static view of human aspiration. Ecotourism can certainly offer the prospect of limited development, but simultaneously relies on capping development at a level that maintains a localised 'harmony' between people and nature. Such a notion, at a stroke, rules out development on any transformative scale, as experienced by the economically developed countries. It is paradoxical that such limited horizons are consistently associated with 'sustainable tourism development' and occupy the moral high ground in debates on tourism development in much academic literature.

Mark Ewen, in an insightful paper at the Royal Geographical Society Annual Conference of 2006, looked at reactions in Nepal to a new road being built near to the Annapurna Conservation Area, a popular area for trekkers and ecotourists (Ewen, 2006). The road links the ascendant economies of China and India and follows a key trekking route alongside the Kali Gandaki river. Trekkers and ecolodge owners, and even a World Bank consultative report, objected to the road on the grounds of environmental damage and the knock-on effect of this on tourism. Local people, however, were found to be positive, favouring transport by road vehicle to mule and porters, and citing the beneficial impact of improved road links on trade, food prices and access to hospitals. Here, the interests of the ecotourism industry, both private and NGO-funded, not to mention the sensibilities of their clientele, were to cap development in the interests of maintaining the environment and way of life. For many locals this was akin to maintaining poverty.

Ecotourism's philosophy is distinctly anti-modern, and likely to take sides against any desire for substantial development, even in economically poor societies. Take the *Quebec Declaration* arising from the United Nations International Year of Ecotourism of 2002 (UNEP/WTO, 2002). This influential document lauds ecotourism as being able to 'strengthen, nurture and encourage the community's ability to maintain and use traditional skill, particularly home based arts and crafts, agricultural produce, traditional housing and landscaping, in a sustainable manner' (UNEP/WTO, 2002: 7). This begs the question as to whether the community would freely – outside of the staged participation exercises conducted by conservation NGOs where funding is invariably tied to predetermined priorities – choose 'traditional skill' over modern technology, 'traditional agriculture' over high yielding genetically modified seeds and 'traditional housing' over modern methods better able to stand up to the ravages of nature.

Tourism for Our Times

The rise of ethical tourism perhaps says more about the times we live in than anything intrinsic to different types of holiday. These are holidays for our post-political times.

The failure of mainstream politics and collective political identities to engage people's aspirations has tended to promote the individualised politics of consumption and lifestyle as channels through which to 'make a difference'. Ethical travel companies, keen to appeal to this sentiment, point out that travel can be all about a personal mission to do just that.

The mission, typically, is to help a local community by encouraging them to preserve their way of life and the environment on which they depend. Any notion of transforming the way poor societies relate to the natural world through economic development plays second fiddle to adapting to localised environmental limits. These limits are presented as closely linked to local tradition, and hence culture is tied in to the project. Some environmental NGOs even refer to the need to preserve 'bio-cultural diversity' in this vein (Maffi & Oviedo, 2000). Given that the richest biodiversity and greatest impoverishment are often congruent, this outlook comes close to being a rationalisation of poverty. Yet, it is championed as 'ethical tourism'.

Ethical tourism tends to divert our attention from the big picture, and focus it back onto what we can do, as individuals, on our travels. The narrow confines of this realm of moral behaviour need to be questioned. The hard truth is that as ethical tourists we can change little. Buy the coral necklace and you contribute to the destruction of the coral, refuse to buy it, and the hawker's family are poorer. Hardly a 'win–win' scenario.

The criticisms of mass tourism, considered earlier, are also telling with regard to the social climate. In the past, negative conceptions of the masses would have been contested by political movements that stood for their interests, and tempered by a belief that growing affluence for the majority was a sign of progress. For example, Thomas Cook championed tourism for 'the millions' who could 'o'er leap the bounds of their own narrow circle, rub off rust and prejudice by contact with others, and expand their sails and invigorate their bodies by an exploration of some of nature's finest scenes' (Withey, 1997: 145).

Today, in the absence of a sense that more opportunities for people to travel is part of human progress, 'the millions' can be presented as the object, not the subject, of society, duped by voracious advertising and in need of ethical direction. According to one popular analysis, package tourism is 'consumed en masse in a similar, robot like and routine manner, with a lack of consideration for the norms, culture and environment of the host country visited' (Poon, 2003). Such statements betray a contemptuous view of ordinary tourists.

Ethical Tourism Under Fire

It is perhaps no surprise that the critique of mass tourism has turned in on itself, and now the ethical alternatives themselves are under fire. If one starts from the premise that environments and the communities that inhabit them are innately fragile, then while mass tourism is the obvious target, inevitably ecotourism also becomes a fraught activity. Adventurers going somewhere off the beaten track, traveling independently, may, it is argued, be blazing a trail for the masses to follow, spreading the net of tourism to ever more remote and fragile parts of the planet.

Some, following this logic, cynically suggest that maybe Blackpool and Benidorm are the best examples of sustainable tourism, as they keep the masses in one place, thus preserving the bulk of the planet from their deleterious impact. Such a view regards people as problem, and more people as more of a problem – a sort of holiday Malthusianism.

Of course, in recent years leisure travel has become the focus of debates on global warming, in particular the carbon footprint associated with flying (a relevant statistic in the Stern Report is that world aviation accounts for less than 2% of global greenhouse gas emissions, possibly rising to 5% by 2050). Certainly, reigning in leisure travel would have an impact on manmade carbon emissions.

But it will also have an impact on economies in which tourism plays an important role. In the developing world, more often than not the focus for ethical tourism, nature's vagaries have often disrupted lives and devastated harvests and homes, irrespective of the recent findings in relation to human contribution to global warming. Economic development, perhaps partly based on foreign exchange generated through tourism, creates the prospect of being able to adapt to climatic changes and shield against natural disasters. Yet, ethical tourism, in the form either of the advocacy of ecotourism or staying close to home, eschews development as damaging, and offers little prospect of liberation from poverty.

Humanism and Travel

A critique of attempts at green ethical living lays itself open to the charge of being entirely negative, defeatist or alternatively as being caricatured as an advocacy of big business with all the negative connotations associated with this in the minds of liberal people.

However, whilst I think an attempt to deproblematise leisure mobility as a human activity is entirely positive in and of itself, I would also advocate a rather different approach to leisure travel than that featured in many discussions of ethical tourism. In response to the green focus of ethical tourism, it is important to champion mobility as part of a humanist philosophy that is optimistic about the capacity of people to adapt and overcome the limits that nature bequeaths. It is an outlook that, in contrast to the preoccupation with the 'host–tourist relationship', and the cultural relativism characteristic of so much discussion around ethical tourism, sees the opportunity to travel – for business or for pleasure – as a part of a common human progress. Such a philosophy simply proposes that we should aspire to the opportunities – pleasurable, educational and commercial – that many in the wealthy countries of the world benefit from being made available for all. That would be a truly ethical vision. It is unlikely to be one that finds favour with those who have lost sight of equality and development, caught up in moralising about our holidays.

References

Arramberri, J. (2007) Personal communication.

Bauman, Z. (1992) *Intimations of Postmodernity*. London: Routledge.

Bauman, Z. (2000) *Liquid Modernity*. Oxford: Polity

Brendon, P. (1991) *150 Years of Popular Tourism*. London: Secker and Warburg.

Butcher, J. (2003) *The Moralisation of Tourism*. London: Routledge.

Butcher, J. (2007) *Ecotourism, NGOs and Development: A Critical Analysis*. London: Routledge.

Chambers, R. (1983) *Rural Development: Putting the Last First*. London: Longman.

Facaros, D. and Paul, M. (1999) *Cadogan's Spain*. London: Cadogan.

Croall, J. (1995) *Preserve or Destroy? Tourism and the Environment*. London: Calouste Gulbenkian Foundation.

Ewan, M. (2006) Conflicts between policy and practice: Sustainable development through tourism in the Annapurna region, Nepal. Unpublished paper.

Fennell, D.A. (2006) *Tourism Ethics*. Clevedon: Channel View Publications.

Feifer, M. (1985) *Going Places*. London: Macmillan.

Fisher, S.H. (ed.) (nd) *Tanzanian Cultural Tourism Programme Brochure*. Written, designed and edited by Stephen H. Fisher.

Fukuyama, F. (1992) *The End of History and the Last Man*. London: Penguin.

Furedi, F. (2005) *Beyond Left and Right: The Politics of Fear*. London: Continuum.

Giddens, A. (1991) *Modernity and Self Identity: Self and Society in the Late Modern Age*. Cambridge: Polity.

Giddens, A. (1994) *Beyond Left and Right: The Future of Radical Politics*. London: Polity Press.

Giddens, A. (1998) *The Third Way: The Renewal of Social Democracy.* Cambridge: Polity.

Goffman, I. (1959) *The Presentation of Self in Every Day Life.* Harmondsworth: Penguin.

Harrison, R., Newholm, T. and Shaw, D. (2005) *The Ethical Consumer.* London: Sage.

Heartfield, J. (2002) *The 'Death of the Subject' Explained.* Sheffield: Sheffield Hallam University Press.

Hertz, N. (2001) *The Silent Takeover: Global Capitalism and the Death of Democracy.* London: Heinemann.

Hickman, L. (2007) *The Last Call: In Search of the True Cost of Our Holidays.* London: Guardian Books.

Kalisch, A. (2002) *Corporate Futures: Social Responsibility in the Tourism Industry.* London: Tourism Concern.

Krippendorf, J. (1987) *The Holiday Makers: Understanding the Impact of Leisure Travel.* Oxford: Heinemann.

Lodge, D. (1991) *Paradise News.* London: Penguin.

MacCannell, D. (1996) *The Tourist: A New Theory of the Leisure Class.* London: MacMillan.

MacLaren, D. (1998) *Rethinking Tourism and Ecotravel: The Paving of Paradise and What You Can Do to Stop It.* Bloomfield, CT: Kumarian Press.

Maffi, L. and Oviedo, G. (2000) *Indigenous and Traditional Peoples of the World and Eco-region Based Conservation: An Integrated Approach to Conserving the World's Biological and Cultural Diversity.* WWF-International (People and Conservation Unit)/Terralingua.

Mann, M./Tourism Concern (2000) *The Community Tourism Guide.* London: Earthscan.

Meletis, Z.A. and Campbell, L.M. (2007) Call it consumption! Reconceptualising ecotourism as consumption and consumptive. *Geography Compass* 1 (4), 850–870.

Milton, K. (1996) *Environmentalism and Cultural Theory.* London: Routledge.

Monbiot, G. (1999) An unfair exchange. *The Guardian*, 15 May.

Nash, D. and Smith, V. (1991) Anthropology and tourism. *Annals of Tourism Research* 18, 12–25.

Pepper, D. (1996) *Modern Environmentalism.* London: Routledge.

Pleumaron, A. (1994) The political economy of tourism. *The Ecologist* 24 (4), 142–148.

Poon, A. (1993) *Tourism, Technology and Competitive Strategy.* Wallingford: CABI.

Purves, L. (2001) Tourists Should Not Travel Light on Morals. *The Times*, 10 July.

Scheyvens, R. (2002) *Tourism for Development: Empowering Communities.* Harlow: Prentice Hall.

Smith, M. and Duffy, R. (2003) *Ethics of Tourism Development.* London: Routledge.

Studienkreis für Tourismus und Entwicklung (Students for Tourism with Responsibility) (nd) Aims and Objectives. On WWW at http://www.studien kreis.org/engl/wer/ziele.html. Accessed 17.02.08.

The International Ecotourism Society (nd) 'Ecotourism Explorer' advice initiative. On WWW at http://www.ecotourism.org/travelchoice/investigate.html. Accessed 16.05.02.

UNEP/WTO (2002) *The World Ecotourism Summit Final Report*. Paris: UNEP and WTO.

Urry, J. (1995) *Consuming Places*. London: Routledge.

Urry, J. (2002) *The Tourist Gaze*. London: Sage.

Wearing, S. (2001) *Volunteer Tourism: Experiences that Make a Difference*. Wallingford: CABI.

Withey, L. (1997) *Grand Tours and Cooks Tours: A History of Leisure Travel 1750–1915*. London: Aurum.

Young, R.C. (1995) *Colonial Desire: Hybribity in Theory, Culture and Race*. London: Routledge.

Ziffer, K. (1989) *Ecotourism: The Uneasy Alliance*. Washington, DC: Conservation International.

Chapter 15

Development and its Discontents: Ego-tripping Without Ethics or Idea(l)s?

MICK SMITH

> It is impossible to escape the impression that people commonly use false standards of measurement – that they seek power, success and wealth for themselves and admire them in others, and yet that they underestimate what is of true value in life. (Freud, 1972 [1929]: 1)

There are several ways of interpreting this passage with which Freud begins his 1930 essay 'Civilization and its Discontents'. Some are less critical than others, taking what is said at face value, others might seek to look behind appearances, to think through this statement's implications and question its assumptions. Does everyone really seek power, success or wealth? What kind of person admires these 'achievements'? If most people do seek and admire these qualities then why does Freud suggest that their standards of measurement might be false? What, then, is of *true* value in life? Is there an alternative standard by which to measure this value? These already sound very much like ethical questions.

It is not accidental that such questions should be raised in the context of an essay, the main theme of which is, in its editor's words 'the irredeemable antagonism between the demands of instinct and the restrictions of civilization [or society]' (Strachey in Freud, 1972: x). Not accidental, because the restrictions Freud is discussing in this essay are primarily *moral* restrictions. This being so, should we simply assume then that the desire for power, success and wealth are expressions of instinctual (and amoral) presocial demands? This is certainly a fairly common view but, if this is so, does this mean that when Freud speaks of the 'true value of life' he is merely moralising, that is, preaching the higher value of civilization's ideals over and against 'selfish' instinctual desires? This hardly seems likely, as a key aspect of Freud's argument is that such social restrictions are potentially psychologically damaging precisely because they involve the *repression* of certain natural instincts. There is then an ambiguity here about how Freud views the role of civilization, about whether, all told, it is a force for good or ill, an ambiguity that Freud does not resolve, but leaves open for the reader to make their own assessment: 'it is' he says 'very far from my intention to express an opinion upon the value of human civilization' (Freud, 1972: 81).

As one might expect with Freud, there is obviously more going on here than surface appearances suggest. The antagonism between individual instincts and social restriction is not something, Freud thinks, which can be simply decided in favour of one or the other. It is indeed 'irredeemable', a fundamental and lasting tension present (although certainly not always consciously recognised) in every human life; a tension within which the individual's psyche is composed and yet which constantly threatens that composure, even in some cases resulting in neuroses. We can already see then that Freud offers a much more sophisticated picture of the human individual than one simply domi-nated by irrepressible selfish urges (let's call this the cartoon caveman model) or, on the other hand, by the total subjugation of the individual to externally imposed social norms (as, for example, in caricatures of mind-washing political cults where everyone follows a formulaic party-line).

Nevertheless, Freud's framework still relies on these characterisations of instinct and social restriction as the poles between which that which is truly valuable in life might emerge and against which ethics is under-stood. And so, although his essay raises fundamental ethical questions, including questions about the very nature of ethics itself, these too tend to be answered within this extremely limiting framework. For example, he argues, the 'commandment "Love thy neighbour as thyself" [a social restriction] is the strongest defence against human aggression' [which is, broadly speaking, instinctual], but because the demands made on individuals by such an ethics are excessive they are 'impossible to fulfil'. And so 'anyone who follows such a precept in present-day civilization only puts himself at a disadvantage *vis-à-vis* the person who disregards it'. Such ethics has nothing to offer the individual 'except the narcissistic satisfaction of being able to think oneself better than others'. The conclusion to be drawn from this, Freud argues, is, that 'so long as virtue is not rewarded here on earth ethics will ... preach in vain'. To think otherwise is to rely on an 'idealistic misconception of human nature' (Freud, 1972: 80)

Now we might qualify such conclusions, just as Freud immediately qualified his opening passage, by saying that in any 'general judgement of this sort, we are in danger of forgetting how variegated the human world and its mental life are' (1). Generalisations about human nature are fraught with difficulties and dangers and are, themselves, almost always closely associated with defining certain (politically contestable) normative expectations. Freud's comment about 'idealistic misconceptions of human nature' was, for example, quite explicitly, targeted at ethical forms of 'socialism' (80), which he claims, like Jesus Christ, expect the impossible from people and so are bound to fail. Perhaps, however, a critical examination of the limits of Freud's own model of human nature might view human possibilities in a rather different light. Thinking *through* the assumptions underlying Freud's essay, that is, thinking with Freud against Freud, might reveal important insights into ethics, despite the fact that this was not his work's primary intention. This 'detour', via psychoanalysis and philosophy, is worth taking because how we think about the relations between tourism and ethics will clearly depend on how we understand ethics in the first place.

Indeed, this attempt to interpret Freud's essay has already begun to throw into relief several important, and unfortunately influential, misunderstandings of ethics that stand in the way of our re-cognition (our being aware of and rethinking) the problems and possibilities that emerge with our fleeting encounters with other beings, environments and ways of life. All too often, debates about tourism ethics fall back, albeit in more or less sophisticated ways, into the kind of opposition that structured Freud's essay. In their crudest forms, they tend to simply reiterate the predominant neoliberal (almost Hobbesian) model of *Homo economicus*, that totally self-interested, atomistic, hedonistic, although supposedly 'rational' individualism characterised by complete scepticism about the very possibility of anyone actually being motivated by genuine ethical concerns for others. From this perspective, ethics is just a repressive social conjuring trick played on the gullible.

This, of course, is *not* Freud's view, as one of his main interests is to explain the psychosocial origins and operations of a (guilty) conscience understood as an *integral* (albeit troubling) part of the individual self's formation. However, even more sophisticated discussions (to some extent including Freud's) continue to emphasise a struggle between (largely internal) biologically generated self-centred desires (egoism) and (largely external) impositions of social solidarity where any expression of concern for others is implicitly or explicitly associated with the cultural repression of the necessary satisfaction of more primal 'natural' (instinctual) needs, that is, of whatever is deemed to be our 'human nature'. Such strategies allow ethical critiques of current practices to be labelled simultaneously unrealistic (fighting against an irrepressible human nature), irrational and moralistic (preaching the acceptance of rules, codes of conduct, sanctions etc.) to *guilt-trip* people into fulfilling their social obligations against their 'naturally' self-interested inclinations. In this way ethics is, quite wrongly, regarded primarily as a means of placing restrictions on individual freedoms, especially the kind of freedoms supposedly enjoyed by entrepreneurs and consumers in 'free markets', and supposedly facilitated by tourism developments.

The Moralisation of Tourism?

Jim Butcher's (2003) recent book *The Moralisation of Tourism* seems to be a forthright version of this thesis, one that will certainly appeal to those hard-line neoliberals who believe ethics has absolutely no place in business, or to those who just want an excuse for not caring (or even recognising) the 'downside' of tourism developments. Butcher portrays those advocating the recognition of ethical concerns in tourism as developmental malcontents, profoundly unhappy with the current directions taken by the tourism industry and hypercritical of the mixed 'blessings' its unrestricted growth brings to resident human and ecological communities. The problem with this view is not the accuracy of its portrayal (many people are indeed deeply unhappy about tourism's more destructive effects), but the implications drawn from it in terms of how ethics is understood and how it is articulated within actual debates about tourism. Butcher (2003: 1) complains about critics of tourism who 'try to make us feel slightly guilty about our fortnight of fun through their advocacy of "ethical" alternatives' who strive to impose a 'moralistic agenda of dubious merit' over and against the 'wants and needs' of both visitors and their 'hosts' and the 'freedom to please oneself'. Unknowingly echoing Freud's remarks, he derides the narcissistic 'sense of moral superiority' (Butcher, 2003: 2) that seems to be the only benefit to be derived from promoting ethical tourism. What is worse, these 'self-appointed campaigners' and 'angst-ridden academics' (Butcher, 2003: 2) are never satisfied with the results of their moralising, continually subjecting even 'celebrated alternatives' to mass tourism, like ecotourism, 'to their own critique' (Butcher, 2003: 2). It seems, like ethical socialists and Jesus Christ, these critics just expect too much from 'real' people; they have instigated a new 'moral crusade' (Butcher, 2003: 93) that tries to impose impossible ethical standards on those just looking for 'innocent fun' (Butcher, 2003: 30).

If we ignore, for the moment, Butcher's polemical excesses, and concentrate instead on his portrayal of ethics, reading this through Freud's essay allows several interesting features to emerge. First, that ethics is, indeed, understood by Butcher primarily in terms of placing socially imposed constraints on the satisfaction of more primal wants and needs, on individuals' self-interested, (but, because supposedly entirely natural) *innocent* pleasures. Butcher implies that only those who are already guilt and 'angst-ridden', those socially repressed individuals who we might (in Freud's terms) regard as being subject to neurotic tendencies, those who have become incapable of feeling or appreciating *innocent* pleasure, would still gain some kind of warped pleasure from guilt-tripping others and thereby enabling themselves to feel morally superior. That is to say, on his model, even those who claim to be ethically concerned are ultimately motivated by their own vicarious and narcissistic pleasures.

What Butcher cannot and will not recognise then is any kind of ethics that really is an expression of a genuine concern for other people's plight, a desire to conserve diverse languages, cultures or traditions, a felt need to offer an *ethical* critique of injustice, racism, poverty or exploitation, or that someone might be pained (for other than selfish reasons) by the extinction of other species or the bulldozing of ecological communities.

His failure to appreciate this possibility is bolstered by the bizarre belief that (mass) tourism developments (and the modern Western developmental model) are actually always in the best interests of everyone, or at least everyone that matters. It is perhaps on this last point that he differs most from Freud, as this would seem to suggest that modernity (in the form of corporate capitalism) is a unique form of 'civilization' that resolves what Freud mistakenly took to be the 'irredeemable' tensions between instinct and restriction, precisely because, as the best of all possible worlds, modernity apparently has no need whatsoever of ethics or moralising restrictions. We can all be left to get on with our innocent fun and 'guilt-free enjoyment' (Butcher, 2003: 141) even if that new luxury golf-course development happens to mean our eviction from the lands that traditionally fed our family.

It is worth delving a little further into Butcher's thesis lest this characterisation be thought interpretively inaccurate and/or (which would be doubly ironic) ethically unfair. Butcher frequently claims that ethical concerns are getting in the way of alleviating poverty or restricting people's personal 'freedom' to enjoy themselves. However, it is not at all clear why he would even be so concerned if he didn't have an ethical (and a moral) agenda of his own. His position then is not *necessarily* unethical. Might it be then that it is the *form* taken by the 'moralisation of tourism' that he objects to, its supposedly vicarious and narcissistic elements, its purported lack of political efficacy, and so on, rather than ethics per se. If so, one would have hoped that his book would clearly state this up-front. Unfortunately, though, it doesn't, and Butcher proceeds to a blanket condemnation of the 'new tourism'. But, quite frankly, it beggars belief that every single form of ethical, eco, or community, tourism, no matter how varied its motivations, how different its organisation, how much local community input or control it entails, could be accurately described as moralising, as both repressive and yet (simultaneously) ineffectual, while somehow Butcher's own, unspoken 'ethical' concerns (if that is what they are) remain pure in intent and, so it seems, if enacted, would be universally effective, progressive and liberating.

As Butcher only ever describes his own (not necessarily unethical) views negatively, that is, in terms of what they are not and all other positions are – moralising, banal, patronising, proscriptive (Butcher, 2003: 74) and so on – it is difficult to judge whether this apparently miraculous perspicacity has any grounding in reality. It would certainly help if, rather than just criticising everyone involved in tourism that professes ethical concern for others or tries to act on this basis, Butcher would say plainly whether or not *he* himself is actually ethically concerned about any of the repercussions of mass tourism. If he is then we need to know what distinguishes his ethical concerns from those he condemns. If he isn't then one can't help but think that his entire critique is disingenuous.

What, for example, about the numerous instances cited in (and beyond) the tourism literature where local communities, cultures and individuals in the global South have resisted the imposition of what *they* regard as inappropriate and insensitive tourism developments. How does Butcher respond to such situations? Well, he never seems to mention them. He simply continues to promote the Western developmental model, business as usual, with absolutely no attempt whatsoever to discriminate between 'good' or 'bad' or even 'better' or 'worse' ways of following this model. The only criteria seem to be the size of the development – the bigger the better – and the more 'fun' that results for tourists, the better. He does this on the basis that he (certainly no less a 'self-appointed' academic expert than those he criticises) knows what kind of 'civilization' is in the best interests of the poor. And what if local people (and not just hyper-sensitive, angst-ridden, do-gooders) complain about disparities in wealth? Butcher's advice: 'Get rid of the all-inclusive resorts, the conspicuous displays of wealth and privilege, and poor people are, if anything worse off' (Butcher, 2005: 8).

This seems such a bizarre position that many will have difficulty understanding where it originates. Interestingly, he explains the moral turn in tourism (and in ethical consumerism in general) as being brought about by the 'closure of grand politics' (Butcher, 2003: 105) following the purported collapse of all ideological alternatives to the market (a thesis-based in Fukuyama's [1992] controversial quasi-Hegelian claims about *The End of History*). This 'lack' leaves the individual feeling a need to re-establish an alternative sphere of political action and, given our current socioeconomic situation, this most frequently takes the form of a moralisation of consumer choice. This form of 'individualised' politics, Butcher thinks, degrades *real* politics (although what *that* involves is not explained anywhere) and is 'deceitful' (Butcher, 2003: 109) as it can 'make no difference to the broader inequality that exists between nations and peoples' (Butcher, 2003: 110).[1] Of course, by describing any and all calls for individual tourists/hosts to be concerned and try to make a difference as 'deceitful' (Butcher, 2003: 109) we might at least presume that Butcher finds deceit ethically reprehensible. Again, though, we might ask why Butcher is otherwise so coy about expressing his own ethical ideals.

Indeed, there are so many problems here that it is difficult to know where to start. For example, it seems any and *all* attempts to ameliorate social disparities or environmental damage caused by tourism by working within, parallel to or even in explicit opposition to, a system of consumer capitalism merely exemplifies an ineffectual moralising.[2] Yet, as we have 'apparently' reached the end of history, there is no longer any 'outside' of the system, no other viable alternative, so all forms of resistance are, apparently, equally ineffectual. In other words, it's difficult to read Butcher as saying anything other than stop worrying and whining, because it won't make any difference anyway unless we can change everything, which is impossible, as 'the collapse of communism seems to confirm that all alternatives to the market system do not work' (Butcher, 2003: 104). So, while espousing the individual's liberation from 'moral repression' and the hedonistic benefits of consumer choice for holidaymakers, he is actually saying that anything an individual may chose to do (other than push for more tourism development) is absolutely immaterial? There is no alternative to, or way to even influence, the current socioeconomic system. How liberating!

It is important to notice that Butcher's account of moralisation, of lifestyle politics, actually depends upon the fact that (even after the demise of socially repressive nonmarket-oriented regimes) individuals still desire an avenue for *political* participation. There is, then, much more at stake here than simply (and rightly) pointing out the inadequacies of (ethical) consumerism when it comes to fulfilling this broader task.[3] But, of course, this then leads back to asking questions about the individual's motivations for desiring the development of an alternative political sphere (e.g. might some of these motivations be best described as ethical?) and what a wider alternative politics might involve, both questions his book studiously avoids. Indeed, Butcher selectively quotes social theorist Zygmunt Bauman's work in support of his views about 'individualisation', but entirely fails to mention Bauman's (1993) advocacy of forms of ethics and politics that take cognisance of our current *postmodern* condition without in any sense making them mere matters of consumer choice.

It is revealing to quote Bauman on tourism and compare (or rather contrast) this with Butcher because Bauman, like Freud, recognises the impossibility of 'indulging in a daydream about a balance sheet that has only a credit side' (Bauman, 1997: 4) and of elevating the pleasure principle to the role of 'presiding judge' (Bauman, 1997: 2). The book *Postmodernity and its Discontents*, from which these quotations are taken, is, of course, explicitly referring to the tensions Freud revealed in his essay, but which the tourist, according to Butcher, can and should be able to avoid. 'Tourism need only be about enjoyment' (Butcher, 2003: 142). And for Bauman, this (Butcher's) figure of the perfect pleasure-seeking tourist, epitomises the postmodern idea of an ironic 'hero', whose 'freedom' and 'autonomy' depend upon keeping their emotional distance from the people and places visited, on constantly shifting (in)attention to what happens around them, and a refusal of other-directed social involvement. But, this celebration of ego-tripping is problematic for a number of reasons. First, as Bauman points out, this kind of self-understanding is only possible to the extent that the tourist 'haves' can blot out or excise their metaphorical 'alter egos' the 'have nots', which he refers to figuratively as 'vagabonds' (Bauman, 1997: 93), those *forced* by *social pressures* (including the pressures created by tourism developments) *rather than by choice*, to be mobile and detached from ethical relations with others. In other words, this requires the tourist's suppression of all ethical (other-oriented) inclinations or sentiments, the denial of their existence and/or relevance, and the abdication of any sense of *personal responsibility* that, for Bauman, is the starting point for all ethics and politics (Bauman, 1993: 34).

This leads to a second point. The 'choice' celebrated in the image of the perfect 'guilt-free' tourist, is, as Bauman indicates, not actually as free from social restrictions as it might seem. Indeed this image itself, while actually lived by so few, plays an important role in comprising 'an effective system of social control' (Smith, 1999: 153) in various ways. Reading Butcher, you might get the impression that only NGOs, environmentalists and moralising academics pose a threat to individuals' freedom and pleasures, while the corporate capitalism that motivates mass tourist developments simply responds to already free individuals' choices. This modern 'civilization' apparently has no limiting effect whatsoever on the kind of individual we are, the possibilities open to us, or the kind of social system we must inhabit, despite the fact that its spread is global (and according to Butcher inescapable) and it shapes almost every aspect of our lives, including the framing of our self-understandings, our possibilities for work and leisure, our wants and desires. This isn't plausible, and it certainly isn't Bauman's point, which is that the privatisation of 'moral' responsibility comes hand in glove with the social conditions in which 'life-politics', including the moralisation of consumerism, is presented as the only (a)political alternative. In other words, *the situation which Butcher objects to so strongly, is precisely the product of the kind of developmental model he advocates following.*

For Bauman this postmodern situation is inherently ambiguous, it *'is the moral person's bane and chance at the same time' and 'which of the two faces of the postmodern condition will turn out to be its lasting likeness, is itself a moral question'* (Bauman, 1995: 8, emphasis in original) Why both bane and chance? Why is this itself a moral question? Well, precisely because Bauman views ethics and (ethically motivated) politics as ultimately based in feelings of individual responsibility. The social structures of modernity, for example, massive centralised bureaucracies, often took that responsibility from individuals even as they relied upon and redistributed it to apportion obligations and blame. That we are now called upon from all kinds of quarters to behave in terms of a privatised, individualised, responsibility (even if this 'calling' is sometimes only a deceitful way of those promoting the developmental model of global capitalism avoiding the blame for its downside, its systemic destructive repercussions) actually offers individuals a real chance to recognise the limits and possibilities of responsibility (ethics) as such. In other words, it might provide a chance to think about why ethical responsibility can be such an important part of our self-identities – about the place of exercising ethical judgements and the importance of an ethically motivated politics in what Hannah Arendt (1958) termed, the 'human condition' (see also Smith, 2005).

This 'human condition' is not simply Arendt's term for human nature. The conditions in which we find ourselves are historically and socially variable, not biologically or metaphysically fixed, but, nevertheless, Arendt argues, the test of one's 'humanity', in the sense of revealing who one is as a person, emerges from how we respond to our being caught up in these particular circumstances. Do we respond by allowing social circumstances to provide an excuse for suppressing any ethical and political agency we might have or, alternatively, by exercising our individual capacity to make ethical and political 'choices', whether or not we think our actions will make much difference. Arendt discusses this emergence of one's individual character, in terms of those who, on the one hand, claimed they could do nothing to stop the supposedly inexorable rise to power of the Nazis and, on the other hand, those individuals who felt that their responsibility was to speak out and/or act despite the apparent hopelessness of their circumstances. Fortunately, most people in today's global North don't face anything like those kinds of tough, life-threatening decisions (precisely because some other people made them in the past). That, however, should not stop us thinking about Arendt's point more generally, in terms of whether or not, for example, we would visit Myanmar (Burma) knowing what we do about the military junta in power there, its abuse of child labour, its repression of political dissent, and so on. In making these kinds of decisions, and in presenting arguments for them, we can still exercise our individuality demonstrating something of *who* we are in however limited a fashion and when we debate such issues we are, in Arendt's terms, engaged in politics.

Ethics are, then, in Arendt's and Bauman's (and in a more limited way, Freud's) view, not just socially imposed norms, they are also ways of composing who we are. To reject ethics as simply a form of social repression is like refusing to speak or think on the basis that language too is just a social imposition, a form of constraining indoctrination. And just as we can learn to use language to question the way things are, to challenge as well as accept the norms of our particular 'civilization', thereby expressing our individuality and experiencing a degree of liberty that is otherwise impossible, so too ethics (concern for others) provides a basis for questioning the way things are, informs how we might relate to others, and is a mode of being in which we exercise our *individual* responsibilities in concert, though not necessarily agreement, with others. Ethics as such can also be an expression of our discontent with civilization.

Thus, as Bauman argues, 're-personalising morality means returning moral responsibility from the finishing line (where it was exiled) to the starting point (where it is at home) of the ethical process. We realise now – with a mixture of apprehension and hope – that unless moral responsibility was "from the start", somehow rooted in the very way humans are – it would never be conjured up at a later stage . . .'. In other words, and this is Bauman's point, you can't guilt-trip anyone if they don't already have a *capacity* to exercise *their own* conscience, and these 'human' possibilities – to be able to care about others, be it loved ones, distant strangers, or even other nonhuman beings, other species and environments – are part of being a human individual *from the beginning*.[4] Some might go so far as to say, (*re* Freud's opening remark) that it is only through experiencing these kinds of relationships, not just the (also socially constrained) search for power, success and wealth for oneself, or in envying them in others, that one is able to come to any kind of estimation of what might be 'of true value in life'.

Wish You Were Here? Or Why Ethics Matter

> I speak of responsibility as the essential, primary, and fundamental structure of subjectivity. For I describe subjectivity in ethical terms. Ethics here, does not supplement a preceding existential base; the very node of the subjective is knotted in ethics understood as responsibility. (Levinas, 1985: 95)

So, where does this discussion leave us? First, it is vital to understand that ethics *as such* is not a later add-on to the individual, a social imposition on an already formed individual's self-interested instincts. This capacity is actually an integral part of the way the individual is composed as an individual, in and through the delicate inter-relations between their biological capacities *and* their social relations with other people. Because of this, *and only because of this*, it certainly becomes possible to try to socially manipulate this ethical capacity just as it is possible (indeed often much easier) to manipulate people's selfish tendencies. But that doesn't mean we can, or more importantly should, take every call to behave responsibly as simply a form of social manipulation. The degree to which it is, or is not, a form of manipulation is itself, as Bauman suggests, an *ethical* question, and one that most people are capable of judging on that basis for and amongst themselves. Making such judgements, about what one thinks is right and wrong, and about the extent of one's responsibilities, about the motives of other people, is a vital (living and changing) aspect of what ethics, and being an individual, is all about. And, as Alphonso Lingis' (2004) philosophical travelogues suggest, this is something we are capable of even in the company of complete strangers in lands that seem entirely foreign to us.

This difficult balancing act in terms of how, when and even *if* we exercise our individual ethical responsibilities has no easy solution. There are no strict rules one can follow, no infallible codes of conduct, no mathematical formulae for working out what is right, no language that can fully encompass and perfectly express how to feel about innumerable different circumstances, let alone define exactly how our actions might affect others. That is one reason why civilizations have developed so many different kinds of ethical language, in terms of rights, virtues, care, duties and so on (Smith & Duffy, 2003). Each way of expressing ethics provides a different kind of approximation to certain ethical intuitions in different social/historical circumstances. Those that are more theoretical and less like lists of rules offer more flexibility when it comes to critical reflection, more scope for exercising individual responsibility.

This is also why Emmanuel Levinas (1985) describes ethics as a relation of 'infinity' not 'totality'. That is to say, the question of what is good is *always* (infinitely) an open question, never something definitively settled. Ethics as such is not at all a matter of mindlessly following socially imposed rules. Being ethical involves keeping on asking, is that really good enough? are there alternative possibilities? what if? and so on. This is precisely why ethically motivated criticisms of tourism keep on asking whether ecotourism, for example, is always the best solution to a particular set of circumstances, whether it can be more sensitive to local needs, less ecologically damaging, more democratically organised and so on.

The critical possibilities of ethics, the way it can, potentially, place everything in question, especially our own self-centredness, is very like certain idea(l)s of rationality. But ethics can't be reduced to simply a matter of rational choice either, as it requires passionate involvement, it is based in a sense of responsibility, a concern for others. What is more, as Freud was perhaps the first to recognise, we don't have full conscious control over every aspect of our individual being, not everything that happens within and between us is, or can be made, transparent to our consciousness, made subservient to a rational ordering. Some of our 'gut-reactions' to circumstances may depend upon our past dispositions and long-dormant experiences as well as on our instincts, desires and social history, all of which together with our self-critical reflections combine to compose a more, or less, stable and troubled ethical 'character', an integral aspect of who we are. Of course, some of our past actions may haunt us in the form of a guilty conscience, but this too, unless overwhelming, is not always a bad thing, as it may allow us to reflect on circumstances and make different kinds of decisions in the future, ones we are happier being party too. Ethics is messy, complicated, and difficult precisely because we are not cartoon cave men. Its unsettling, questioning, presence is also what distinguishes an individual from the other extreme, the caricature cult follower, that person seeking *absolution* from all troubling aspects of their individuality and their conscience, an absolution only possible to the extent that they cease to evaluate their own actions in anything but the framework approved by this narrow scion of 'society'.

Nothing then is as innocent as it might appear, and this is surely part of Freud's point too. Only someone entirely lacking ethical capacities can be entirely *innocent* (amoral), which explains why we don't generally blame animals for the pain they inflict on their prey, and why we tend to regard a person who knowingly inflicts avoidable harm on others as immoral not amoral. Innocence is a mythic (and also, ironically, an ethical) ideal of a kind of unattainable presocial purity (amorality) that stands as a point of contrast to a supposedly 'corrupted' world, the real world in which our responsibilities are often unclear and our identities, if we are at all reflexive, are constantly troubled.[5] It is a necessary ideal with great political power (one frequently extolled but constantly compromised by contemporary civilization) but for this reason, its deployment, even in the form of defending 'innocent holiday fun', is never itself entirely politically innocent.

Even if we would sometimes like to bury our heads, ostrich-like, in those sandy holiday beaches, being an individual means leaving open the task of composing *who* we are in terms of our decisions, involvements and concerns with other beings. This is an infinite task bounded only by our mortality just as, analogously, (and contra Fukayama) no civilization ever actually reaches the end of its history so long as those composing it believe they can still make a difference. As already argued, when, how and even if we feel responsible is all part of working out who we are. Certainly, holding ourselves under constant moral supervision or subjecting ourselves to continual ethical questioning is not, as Freud recognised, good for our mental health. Being ethical all the time, as Freud noted in terms of Christ's exhortations, is an impossible ideal, (just like pure innocence),[6] but then no ideal is ever fully realisable and all, when taken to extremes, have downsides, the 'free-market' or 'revolutionary communism' for example. Why should this seem strange? After all, despite what the brochures promise, no holiday is ever perfect either, but this doesn't stop us assessing whether some were better than others for all kinds of complex reasons. This is similarly true with ethics; the aim is not unachievable perfection, but to employ our ideas and ideals to judge what might, after all, be better or worse. And so we need to recognise the difference between 'choosing' to take a 'moral holiday', in the sense of a break from all the infinite claims *our* conscience might make on us, and the kind of claim Butcher makes, that all holidays are situations where ethics should have *no* place, where it is always irrelevant, where we should always be entirely absolved of all our responsibilities for others. This latter view has nothing to do with liberating people from social oppression and everything to do with shielding one aspect of what currently passes for civilization from critique.

Regarding individual responsibility as the starting place of ethics means rejecting the claim that ethics is all about weighing people down with guilt. It also means rejecting the naïve idea that ethics is somehow opposed to pleasure, that it straightforwardly represses the satisfaction of our more fundamental desires, or is equivalent to saying that there is something morally wrong with having 'fun'. To argue this would indeed be indicative of a neurosis. There really is something liberating and immensely enjoyable about temporarily shedding normal everyday responsibilities, about a change of scene, about encountering other, diverse, ways of living in the world, about taking a rest from those everyday, socially imposed, restrictions that enjoin us to sit at that desk or work-station from 9–5. (Indeed our tourist experiences might actually allow some to realise just how restricting and unenjoyable their work-world is.) But there is no such thing as an ethics-free zone. After all, even the capitalist system, as Weber (2001 [1930]) long ago recognised, is deeply indebted to a work *ethic*.

Being a tourist is clearly about enjoyment, (who actually denies this?) but it is never '*only* about enjoyment' (Butcher, 2003: 142, my emphasis). The escapism of the relatively wealthy is evidently, and ironically, dependent upon the global extension of the same socioeconomic system they seek respite from, and, like all industries, tourism has a downside. That some people recognise this and might choose to holiday in ways they think minimise the effects of this downside, that might reduce, however fractionally, the extent to which others have to become, in Bauman's terms, 'vagabonds', *forcibly* ejected from the social and environmental settings within which they had previously composed their identities, is not ineffectual moralising. It is an example of someone taking just a little ethical and individual responsibility for their decisions and expressing something of who they are (and if this eases their conscience a little, or even provides pleasure, then that too can be a good thing, not something they should be blamed for). Only forms of moral absolutism could argue that only that which doesn't give any pleasure is ethical, or that we should do nothing because the little we can do is not enough by itself to set the entire world to rights.

What we need to remember is that everyone is, as Freud and Bauman agree, always potentially one of civilization's discontents, but that's why we struggle within, for, *and against* social and economic restrictions for ethical, and not just egoistic, reasons. That's why some of us want a more, rather than less, ethical tourism.

Notes

1. The tactic of deliberately provoking controversy by attacking any and all those who show any critical ethical or political concerns about the socially dominant (and dominating) aspects of Western capitalism is more than a little reminiscent of the now defunct 'journal' *Living Marxism* (later LM), the house journal of the Revolutionary Communist Party (RCP). LM morphed, after losing a libel case concerning its accusation that ITN journalists had distorted the truth about film they shot of severely malnourished prisoners of war in Serbian concentration camps (Vulliamy, 2000), into several rather more innocuously named organisations, most notably the 'Institute of Ideas', launched in 2000 by previous editor of LM Claire Fox (aka Clare Foster) (lobbywatch, 2007) and a web-site called spiked-online.com. Those contributing to these sites continue the LM tradition of contrarian politics, attacking environmentalism, supporting GM foods, denying global warming and decrying anything that might constrain or oppose corporate capitalism (Monbiot, 2003). Butcher's book explicitly acknowledges the Institute of Ideas as inspirational and at least two of his previous papers appear on the spiked website. His latest book attacking environmental NGOs is fulsomely praised by Ceri Dingle of WORLDwrite (Canterbury Christ Church, 2007), another organisation linked to the Institute of Ideas, whose far from witty and compassionate 'campaigning slogan is "Ferraris for All"' (Dingle, 2007).
2. See, e.g. Butcher's (2006) attack on Wearing, McDonald and Ponting's (2005) 'Building a Decommodified Research Program in Tourism', and Wearing and Ponting's (2006) reply.
3. Though, of course, the argument that consumer choice is an *inadequate* vehicle for political discourse and change doesn't mean that it is *entirely* ineffectual, as the development of ethical tourism itself suggests. An important part of the point in raising questions of ethics in tourism is also to initiate wider political debates about the possibility of making developments more ethical and what that might mean, but then the continual questioning of how ethical the new tourism actually is, is precisely what Butcher objects to (Butcher, 2003: 2).

4. I would qualify Bauman's statement somewhat. First, because it assumes that this is *only* a human possibility and not something that at least some other animals might be capable of feeling. Second, because there are also dangers (already noted above) about how easily such claims might be turned into a generalised definition of human nature. People are diverse, even in their capacities. It is likely that not all humans develop this capacity to the same degrees. It is even more certain that many people who have it succeed in their attempts to entirely suppress it in different areas of their life to avoid being troubled by it. That they manage to do this is obviously not a mark of their heroic status, or of individual freedom.

5. The loss of an original innocence is a recurrent mythological theme in everything from biblical narratives of the fall to Enlightenment narratives of the presocial 'state of nature'.

6. Though I'm reminded of a scene in Woody Allen's film Manhattan. When his duplicitous friend excuses his behaviour by exclaiming 'You are so self-righteous you know, I mean we're just people. You think you're God'. Allen replies 'Well I gotta model myself after someone'.

References

Arendt, H. (1958) *The Human Condition*. Chicago, IL: University of Chicago Press.

Bauman, Z. (1993) *Postmodern Ethics*. Oxford: Blackwell.

Bauman, Z. (1995) *Life in Fragments*. Blackwell: Oxford.

Bauman, Z. (1997) *Postmodernity and its Discontents*. Cambridge: Polity.

Butcher, J. (2003) *The Moralisation of Tourism: Sun, Sand … and Saving the World?* London: Routledge.

Butcher, J. (2006) A response to 'building a decommodified research program in tourism: The contribution of NGOs' by Stephen Wearing, Mathew McDonald and Jess Ponting. *Journal of Sustainable Tourism* 14 (3), 307–310.

Canterbury (2007) New book on negative impact of ecotourism. Canterbury Christ Church University. On WWW at http://Canterbury.ac.uk/News/newRelease. Accessed 27.11.07.

Dingle, C. (2007) Ceri Dingle. On WWW at http:www/battleofideas.org.uk. Accessed 27.11.07.

Freud, S. (1972) *Civilization and its Discontents* revised and edited by James Strachey, London: Hogarth Press.

Levinas, E. (1985) *Ethics and Infinity.* Pittsburgh, PA: Duquesne University Press.

Lingis, A. (2004) *Trust*. Minneapolis, MN: University of Minnesota Press.

lobbywatch (2007) On WWW at http://www.lobbywatch.org. Accessed 23.11.07.

Monbiot, G. (2003) Invasion of the entryists. On WWW at http://monbiot.com. Accessed 23.11.07.

Smith, D. (1999) *Zygmunt Bauman: Prophet of Postmodernity.* Oxford: Polity.

Smith, M. (2005) Ecological citizenship and ethical responsibility: Arendt, Benjamin and political activism. *Environments* 33 (3), 51–63.

Smith, M. and Duffy, R. (2003) *The Ethics of Tourism Development*. London: Routledge.

Spiked-online (2007) On WWW at http://www.spiked-on-line.com. Accessed 23.11.07.

Vulliamy, E. (2000) Poison in the Well of History. *Guardian* (15 March). On WWW at http://www.guardian.co.uk. Accessed 23.11.07.

Wearing, S., McDonald, M. and Ponting, J. (2005) Building a decommodified research paradigm in tourism: The contribution of NGOs. *Journal of Sustainable Tourism* 13 (5), 424–455.

Wearing, S. and Ponting, J. (2006) Reply to Jim Butcher's response. *Journal of Sustainable Tourism* 14 (5), 512–515.

Weber, M. (2001) *The Protestant Ethic and the Spirit of Capitalism*. London: Routledge.

Chapter 16

Transmodernity: Remaking Our (Tourism) World?

IRENA ATELJEVIC

Prologue

This chapter is a product of my life's interesting serendipity that deserves to be traced and revealed here for two main reasons. Firstly, to acknowledge people and events who have inspired me and led to the birth of the ideas that will be discussed in this chapter. The process of creativity is fascinating in itself, as I do not believe in the concept of purely original ideas. This project in particular has convinced me of the 'synchronicity phenomenon' (Jarowski, 1996), whereby people on a similar frequency are all engaged in the parallel intellectual universes around the globe who articulate related ideas, but often express them in different wor(l)ds and terminologies. Secondly and perhaps more importantly, I have claimed elsewhere about the need for tourism scholars to be more transparent about their own positioning and to reveal the geo-body-political location of the subject that speaks (see Ateljevic *et al.*, 2005). In times when we ought to get a more coherent picture of the ever-growing but seriously dispersed tourism studies field (Airey, 2007), positionality remains one of the least travelled roads of tourism scholars. So, here I present the background story of this chapter that, at the end of this philosophical book, sets its sights on the possible desirable ends of tourism, by invoking a new paradigm of transmodernity.

I heard about the term transmodernity for the first time in 2006 when I was invited to provide a keynote at the Annual Nordic Tourism Studies Conference in Finland (Ateljevic, 2006a). In its call the conference organizers stated:

> The title of this year's conference "Visions of Transmodern Tourism" directs the focus of the venue at the future of tourism. At this point of the postmodern era, a debate has started on transmodernism, the return of values and critical analysis after a period of

technology-driven developments. Information society has not delivered the quality of life many expected to see. The advancing climate change paints a rather bleak picture of future. In the center of the 'silent revolution' is the human experience; consumption and growth through learning and self-discovery rather than meritocratic performance, long-term solutions instead of the insecurity of quartal life. (http://www.tourismuninet.org)

When I read these lines, I became truly excited. It had echoed similar ideas of the project I have been working for the last few years in collaboration with my dear colleagues Nigel Morgan, Annette Pritchard and Candice Harris. The ideas that we have encapsulated under the critical turn in tourism studies have communicated similar issues by questioning the neoliberal discourses of our personal, academic and tourism lives (Ateljevic *et al.*, 2007). By reading the conference call, I was delighted to learn that our vision of tourism scholarship's potential to create an academy of hope that nurtures open minds and open hearts and is founded on principles of humanity, respect and equity, coincided with a much bigger paradigm shift of values. This so-called 'coincidence' just proves that there is a subconscious collective knowledge that is emerging within our joint, universal consciousness, so we can finally dare to think and speak what we deeply feel and intuitively know.

Another keynote speaker present at the conference was Marc Luyckx Ghisi who was introduced to me as an expert on transmodernity, as explained by the conference organizer Petri Hottola on my subsequent inquiry: 'Marc certainly appears to be one of the key figures here, especially with his Internet presence and his way of bringing different ideas together' (Email communication, 11/01/2008). Marc's speech (Ghisi, 2006) was revealing as he spoke from the capacity of a theologian, philosopher and researcher on global cultural transformation and had worked in the Forward Studies Unit of the European Commission for 10 years, advising presidents Delors and Santer on EU visions, ethics and culture shifts. His 'good news' talk based on his book (Ghisi, 2001) entitled: *Au Delà de la Modernité, du Patriarcat et du Capitalisme: la Société Réenchantée?*[11] was intriguing, and encouraged me to investigate the notion of transmodernity further. The journey of exploration has been purely fascinating and has not stopped since. As I had engaged with broader literature in arts, humanities, social science and popular culture, I had begun to connect the pieces of the puzzle and became even more excited. Reading major works of renowned social historians, political scientists and sociologists, I am now convinced that the new global consciousness is awakening and fundamental changes are to occur. I also realized that my preceding engagement with love ethics, inspired by women writers such as bell hooks (Ateljevic, 2005, 2006b), was leading me in a similar direction, which made even more sense as the holistic picture was forming right in front of me.

Introduction

> Dreams require optimism, a sense that one's hopes can be fulfilled. (Rifkin, 2005: 384)

This chapter sets its sights on the possible positive ends of tourism in the context of the so-called 'post-9/11' world, which has climaxed with the global crisis of wars, 'terrorism', climate change, overconsumerism, increasing gaps between the rich and poor, social alienation, and individual feelings of pressure, anxieties, chaos and powerlessness worldwide. These processes have raised a whole range of futurist scenarios from the 'softer' questions of environmental sustainability to the radical argument that humanity is in danger of a collective death (e.g. Brown, 2006; Rooney *et al.*, 2005). The questions of (the earth's) sustainability that have penetrated public discourse only recently are speeding ahead faster than we can comprehend. The problem is that we still frame it within the existing economic and political framework that continues to use rationality, money and technology as the most dominant measurements of progress and human development. Reflectively, social scientists, economists, political activists, writers, spiritual leaders and many successful entrepreneurs argue that humanity needs (and is actually going through) a major global mind change and a paradigm shift.

In this chapter, I will review various standpoints and research that suggests a major global change in consciousness and I will offer the concept of transmodernity as an umbrella term that connotes the emerging sociocultural, economic, political and philosophical shift. I will begin with the elaboration of the concept as given by Ghisi (2001, 2006, 2008) followed by reference to other writings in the fields of critical economics, social anthropology and psychology, cultural studies, political science and social activism literature. Given that many of the tenets provided by Ghisi's notion of transmodernity relate to other writings that do not necessarily use the same term, but communicate a similar idea of the emerging paradigm shift as the next cultural and material development in the human (although dominantly Western) history, I have opted to use the concept as a medium to convey what appears to be a single message: '[h]umanity finds itself, once again, at a crossroad between a dying old order and the rise of a new age' (Rifkin, 2005: 181).

However, in the obvious recognition that most of the reviewed writings here are written by Europeans/Americans, I have also looked at the opinions of postcolonial and subaltern writers who similarly offer a positive view of the transmodern world potentialities. Actually, once I ventured into this complex field of literature I found that the transmodern ideas lead primarily to publications in Spanish by its leading advocate, Enrique Dussel, which may explain 'transmodernism's "newness" in the North' (Cole, 2005: 90). So, I do need to acknowledge that Dussel's views (and of his followers) deal more with philosophical issues of the postcolonial, epistemological and political liberation, which go beyond the scope of this chapter and would require a separate paper in itself. The logic behind this choice lies in the recognition that the newness of transmodernity (not only in tourism studies but also across all social science) requires one general overview of the main trends and arguments, before we get into debates of its various aspects. In order to avoid the trap of the postmodern deconstruction process that Rifkin (2005: 5) claims brought us to 'modernity reduced to intellectual rubble and an anarchic world where everyone's story is equally compelling and worthy of recognition', I am tracing the commonalities of what transmodernity offers in this fresh and promising move in the new era of humanity.

Once the main philosophical tenets and levels of change are explained, I will proceed to discuss our tourism academy of hope (Ateljevic et al., 2007) as one of responses to calls for inclusivity, partnership and love ethics, which appear to drive the transmodern voices. In anticipation of criticism by political economy pessimists that my discussion on love ethics is rather naïve, I want to clarify my position. Being originally educated as a neo-Marxist geographer I cannot deny the dominant and overwhelming evidence of structural inequalities around the globe, out of which tourism appears to be one of their most visible manifestations (Bianchi, 2002). However, in the process of my career, I have learned to agree with the later works of Gloria Steinem and bell hooks, who claim that marking oppressed difference creates the mindset of victimization that seriously affects personal and collective confidence about oneself, hence subtly reproducing further marginalization. I have claimed elsewhere how (early anthropological and sociological) critical voices of pessimistic views on tourism have paradoxically reproduced the notion of the passive and victimized 'Other' (e.g. Ateljevic & Doorne, 2003, 2005). So, in my hope that we can truly remake the world, I opt to focus on signs that signal the potential move in the collective consciousness.

In the plethora of pessimistic views and bad news I leave that (admittedly important) job to others and commit myself to trace and discover what is positive and possible in our human development potential.

The tourist as a metaphor of the social world (Dann, 2002) has been staring us in the face for quite some time – from the early claims of MaCannell's (1976) theory of international tourism being the quest of modernity to a whole array of postmodern forms of travel, such as the boom in backpacking and so-called New Age and spiritual tourism. In recognition of the interpretations of either inward-looking and market-oriented special interest tourisms (Ateljevic & Hannam, 2008) or critical views of dominant tourisms of fear and despair (Franklin 2003, 2007), I will rather offer possibilities of *hope* for tourism (studies) to be remade and to remake the world.

Transmodernity: The Dialectic Triad

In speaking about the emerging paradigm shift of transmodernity, Ghisi (1999, 2006, 2008) primarily refers to the changing underlying values in which humans make their judgments and decisions in all areas of their activities – economy, politics and everyday life. He begins his thesis with an overview of five levels of change that he describes through the 'iceberg metaphor' of the human global (un)consciousness and its (un)awareness and (in)visibility, whereby the first two levels are the least visible in terms of the awareness of their 'slow death'. The first level is at the darkest and coldest bottom, where our global civilization finds itself today at the edge of unsustainability and what he describes as the collective suicide of humanity. The second level relates to the death of 'command, control and conquest' patriarchal values, which have turned the world into a competitive and territorial battleground. Level three refers to the death of modernity as a dominant paradigm through which we see the world as an objective reality rooted in impartial truth. Level four refers to the death of the industrial type of businesses and decline of the material economy, while level five concerns the overall crisis of overtly bureaucratic and pyramidal institutions.

While these can be seen as typical postmodern claims, Ghisi continues to explain, a transmodern way of thinking is now emerging, as our hope for a desperately needed and newly reconstructed vision, after the endless postmodern (albeit necessary) deconstructions of modernity in which intellectuals engaged for the last few decades. The postmodern rubble in which we have found ourselves is quite neatly captured by Rifkin (2005: 5):

> If post-modernist razed the ideological walls of modernity and freed the prisoners, they left them with no particular place to go. We became existential nomads, wandering through a boundaryless world full of inchoate longings in a desperate search for something to be attached to and believe in. While the human spirit was freed up from old categories of thought, we are each forced to find our own paths in a chaotic and fragmented world that is even more dangerous than the all-encompassing one we left behind.

According to Ghisi, the very concept of transmodern implies that the best of modernity is kept while at the same time we go beyond it. As such, it is not a linear projection that takes us from (pre)modernity via postmodernity to transmodernity, but rather transcends modernity in that it takes us trans, i.e. through, modernity into another state of being, 'from the edge of chaos into a new order of society' (Sardar, 2004: 2). This argument reflects the original meaning of the term itself that was actually coined by the Spanish philosopher and feminist Rosa Maria Rodriguez Magda (albeit not acknowledged by Ghisi) in her essay *La Sonrisa de Saturno: Hacia una teoria transmoderna* (1989),[2] in which she uses Hegelian logic whereby modernity, postmodernity and transmodernity form the dialectic triad that completes a process of thesis, antithesis and synthesis. As expressed in her own words: 'the third tends to preserve the defining impetus of the first yet is devoid of its underlying base: by integrating its negation the third moment reaches a type of specular closure' (Magda, 1989: 13). In other words, transmodernism is critical of modernism and postmodernism while at the same time drawing elements from each. In a way it is a return to some form of absolute 'logic' that goes beyond the Western ideology and tries to connect the human race to a new shared story, which can be called *a* global consciousness (Rifkin, 2005).

So, what exactly does this complex philosophical premise mean in terms of its translation into the social, economic and political arrangements of the world and our human existence? To explain this, the discussion will be divided into three sections – first the main theoretical tenets of the concept, second the social factors of change and finally economic and political changes. Yet, as my view is that people form and are formed by structures, it is important to note that this division is only provided for the sake of the reader's comprehension and not to artificially divorce powers of structure and agency.

The main transmodernity tenets

Ghisi describes transmodernity as the planetary vision in which humans are beginning to realize that we are all (including plants and animals) connected into one system, which makes us all interdependent, vulnerable and responsible for the Earth as an indivisible living community. In that sense, this paradigm is actively tolerant and genuinely democratic by definition, as the awareness of mutual inter-dependency grows and the hierarchies between different cultures dismantle. It is also essentially post-patriarchal in a sense that women's visions and intuitions are to be recognized as indispensable in order to invent innovative urgent solutions. This is radically different from the (preceding and indeed necessary) (post)modern feminist movements that have primarily fought for women's rights only. In contrast, it is about a joint effort of both men and women to fight for tomorrow's better world by rejecting values of control and domination. It is also essentially postsecular in a sense that it redefines a new relation between religions and politics in a way that re-enchants the world towards a new openness to spiritual guidance as a basis for 'private' behavior and 'public' policy, while rejecting religious divisions and dogmas. It is open to the transcendental, while resisting any authoritarian imposition of religious certainty. In doing so, it aims to rediscover the sacred as a dimension of life and of our societies.

Transmodernity opposes the endless economic progress and obsession with material wealth and instead promotes the concept of the quality of life as a measure of progress. This is expressed in the form of the knowledge economy, which moves emphasis from material capital to intangible assets and the nourishment of human capital. It challenges the rationalized notions of work in its artificial divorce from life. It combines rationalism with intuitive brainwork. It shifts away from vertical authority towards 'flatter', more 'horizontal' organizations; away from 'recommendations-up-orders-down' management and toward more consensual decision making. It redefines the relation between science, ethics and society to reach for real transdisciplinarity. It downsizes the concept of clergy, technocrats and experts in order to raise self-awareness, self-knowledge and individual accountability of all. It promotes Earth citizenship and draws from the highest potentials of humanity. Within the global vision of connected humanity, it claims that each community or region needs to be free to develop in ways that are uniquely suited to its culture, ecology, climate and other characteristics. It wants us to see that the danger of today is less between cultures and religions, than the conflict between different paradigms. It transcends modernity clashes 'to jump over' into the transmodern world and as such it offers a powerful path to peace and a new platform of dialogue between world cultures. Overall, it is generally characterized by optimism to provide hope for the human race.

Sociocultural change: The silent revolution of cultural creatives

Ghisi substantiates his claims with reference to the phenomenon of the 'silent revolution' led by the growing numbers of so-called 'Cultural Creatives' (Ray, 1998; Ray & Anderson, 2000), 'who create new values and who, without knowing it, are activating the 21st century paradigm' (Ghisi, 2008: 158). The concept of the silent revolution of cultural creatives comes from the historian Arnold Toynbee who analyzed the rise and fall of 23 civilizations in world history and who claims that when a culture shift occurs, usually 5% of 'creative marginals' are preparing the shift in silence. This concept has been borrowed by sociologist Paul H. Ray and psychologist Sherry Ruth Anderson, who have applied it to their market cluster research of politics in America. Drawing upon 13 years of survey research studies on over 100,000 Americans, plus over 100 focus groups and dozens of in-depth interviews, they have discovered that around 24% of Americans are departing from traditional or modern cultures to weave new ways of life. They describe this new subculture as the cultural creatives, who care about ecology and saving the planet, about relationships, peace, social justice, self-actualization, spirituality and self-expression. They are both inner-directed and socially concerned. They are activists, volunteers and contributors to good causes – more so than other Americans. Among many interesting behavoural indicators, they are those who read and listen to the radio the most, and watch television the least. They reflect on themselves, actively travel and are looking for a spiritual dimension in life that goes beyond religious dogmas. In everyday life they search for the harmony of the body, mind and spirit; hence their travels often consist of spiritual and educational trips (e.g. retreats and events focused on spirituality and inner search, wellbeing, alternative medicine, etc.). Interestingly, 66% in this group are women.

The evidence goes beyond the North American continent however. The Statistics Office of the European Commission (Eurostat) used a similar method to the American study and confirmed a similar trend of approximately 20% of the European population who exhibit a similar set of values (Tchernia, 1997). In his latest work, Ghisi (2008) also gives numerous anecdotal evidence showing that this trend is quietly spreading throughout Eastern Europe, Asia and the Middle East. Ray and Anderson (2000) claim however, that the visibility of cultural creatives and their power to produce serious change are overshadowed by the fact they are often disregarded as the esoteric New Agers, who simply opt for an alternative lifestyle. Subsequently and typically for tourism scholars, this significant sociocultural shift has been promptly recognized to feed the market of 'New Age tourists' (Pernecky & Johnston, 2006) who consume spa, wellness and spirituality tourism (Smith & Kelly, 2006; Mansfeld & McIntosh, 2006).

In parallel, another scholar Duane Elgin (1997) similarly provides social indicators that suggest the new emerging world-view that he calls a reflective/living-systems paradigm. He derives his claims from the comprehensive overview of cultural transformation literature as well as the empirical evidence of world statistics on main behavioral trends, emerging social values and sustainable ways of living. Many of Elgin's claims have also been based on the well-known World Values Survey, run by Ronald Inglehart, who also spoke about the silent revolution (Inglehart, 1977), although more in terms of a general intergenerational shift in the values of the people living in advanced industrial societies. More recently, he examined the relationship between the sacred and the secular, based on new evidence of the World Values Survey in 80 societies, which found that a growing proportion of the population in both rich and poor countries spends time thinking about the meaning and purpose of life (Inglehart & Norris, 2004).

Economic and political changes

For the sceptics who often too easily disregard these claims as being rather an elitist, upper/middle class luxury, I would like to cite two renowned social and political scientists – Riane Eisler (1987, 1996, 2002, 2007), a macrohistorian,[3] and Jeremy Rifkin (1995, 2005), a social critic and advisor to government leaders and heads of state (in Europe and the USA). Although these two authors do not use the term transmodernity as such, I intentionally use their work because they speak, in a similar vein, about the new technological, economic and political arrangements that are creating and manifesting the change.

Based on her work as a cultural historian and evolutionary theorist over the last 20 years, Riane Eisler introduced the *partnership* and the *domination* system as two underlying possibilities for structuring our beliefs, institutions and relations. It is her particularly brilliant historical analysis (1987) over 30,000 years that provides us with a refreshing view of our past and 'givens' in all areas of our personal, communal, economic and political life. With reference to recent archaeological discoveries, she shows that ancient times (before 3500BC) were based on matrifocal values, which did not mean the opposition to patriarchy (i.e. the domination of women over men), but rather the societal organization focused on the values of giving life, fertility, the pleasure to exist, artistic creations and sexual pleasure. In the 'new' world, of which we are the last heirs, 'power' is no longer viewed as the ability to give life, but is construed as the power to bring death, destroy life, dominate others and be obeyed at all cost. In deconstructing the long history of domination however, she now gives us a beacon for our tired world of an ongoing mistrust, blood, misery and injustice. By transcending the trap of polarized thinking, she offers a way forward by pointing to the partnership model in which social structure is more generally egalitarian, with difference (be it gender, race, religion, sexual preference or belief system) not automatically associated with superior or inferior social and/or economic status. In providing us with an impressive range of worldwide evidence of personal, communal and economic initiatives, organizations and policies she claims that we are finally witnessing the worldwide movement towards this new model (Eisler, 1996, 2002).

In her latest groundbreaking work (Eisler, 2007) *The Real Wealth of Nations*, she deconstructs Adam Smith's theory of the 'invisible hand of the market' to unpack its deep-seated culture of domination and exploitation that has devalued all activities that fall outside of the market's parameters of buying and selling. Instead, she proposes a new concept of 'caring economics' that takes into account the full spectrum of economic activities of the household, to the life-enriching activities of caregivers and communities, to the life-supporting processes of nature. Her claims of critical and caring businesses is further supported by evidence that many mainstream businesses have been requestioning the main purpose of their 'bottom-line' existence (i.e. going for profit only), which has led to the concept of spiritual economy and spiritual entrepreneurs conscious of her/his mission towards the common good of humanity (see Allee, 2003; Harman, 1998; www.worldbusiness.org).

Whilst Riane Eisler provides us with a new economic model for the future, Jeremy Rifkin (2005: 7–8) claims that it is the 'European dream of the United Europe' (in all its potentiality) that is already a political manifestation of the new coming era that is quietly eclipsing the American dream:

The new European dream is powerful because it dares to suggest new history, with an attention to quality of life, sustainability, and peace and harmony ... The new dream is focused not on amassing wealth but rather, on elevating the human spirit ... It takes humanity out of the materialist prison in which it has been bound since the early days of the eighteenth-century Enlightenment and into the light of a new future motivated by idealism.

To substantiate his claims which could be easily interpreted as overtly idealistic in light of many EU controversies, hypocrisies and problems, he stresses two main points. First, he clearly states that dreams reflect hopes, not achievements, hence the notion of the *potentiality* in many of the tenets provided by the ideal of European dream. Second, to contextualize the possibilities more strongly, he provides us with a painstaking overview of the historical making of the Enlightenment/modern age, which created the earth-shattering changes for the medieval era.

In elaborating his thesis, he gives an overview of how the fundamental pillars of the modern era: individualism; the market-exchange economy, the ideology of property; and territory-bound-nationstate governance (forged with capitalistic markets) were once created and how they are now also slowly being replaced with the new spatial, economic, social and political arrangements of the global (or what I would call transmodern) era. By giving us as an overview of its political architec-ture, and the historical making of the united Europe, its unique features of extra-territorial governance, constitution, internal workings and various policies, he gives us the realistic picture of its many hypocrisies and contradictions yet many of its many achievements and potentialities. He presents a neat insight into the workings of the knowledge economy concept based on the cooperative commerce of reciprocity and trust; the three-sector politics that include civil society organizations; environ-mental sustainability policies, etc.

Being acutely aware of the word limits of this chapter and for the sake of not diluting the argument on transmodernity, I cannot summarize here all his convincing evidence of the new history in making. Yet, one of his key underlying arguments needs to be stressed, as it neatly supports the main contention I am trying to display here. Namely, he also speaks about the shift to a new relational consciousness in which humans are increasingly becoming aware of shared risk and vulnerability, economic, social and environmental interdependencies that together make up the Earth's indivisible living community. In other words, he moves us from the current geopolitics (and its assumption that the environment is a giant battleground where we all fight for our own individual survival) to a truly innovative concept of *biosphere* politics (the premise of the Earth as a living organism made up of interdependent relationships in which we are all connected as one).

The subaltern view of transmodernity

When speaking of geopolitics, finally the postcolonial and subaltern literature needs to be consulted, as (after all) transmodernity is a term that originated in Spanish-speaking circles and is particularly associated with its leading advocate, Enrique Dussel and his neo-Marxist philosophy of liberation (Dussel, 1995). However, as I previously stressed in the introduction, it goes beyond this chapter to engage seriously with the epistemological and political aspects of Dussel's way to unsettle the Eurocentric coloniality. Yet, a few commonalities with the preceding discussion can be identified. First, Dussel's acknowledgement that postmodernity has been critical of various modern Eurocentricisms but in his opinion not enough, as it still represents the Eurocentric critique of the included negation which has paradoxically reinforced the process of 'Othering' by the further demarcation of difference and identity politics.

Second and in consequence, Dussel sees the potentiality in transmodernity to move us beyond traditional dichotomies; to articulate a critical cosmopolitanism beyond nationalism and colonialism; to produce knowledges beyond third world and Eurocentric fundamentalisms; to produce radical postcapitalist politics beyond identity politics; to overcome the traditional dichotomy between the political economy and cultural studies and to move beyond economic reductionism and culturalism (Grosfoguel *et al.*, 2007). In a similar vein, Ziauddin Sardar (2004) sees the positive potentiality of the transmodern world to bridge what appears currently the impassable gap between Islam and the West due to the concept of 'tradition' as an idée fixe of Western society. He shows how transmodern tenets of consensual politics and modalities for adjusting to change are at the very heart of Islam. Yet he warns us that in developing a transmodern framework to open discussions it is important to think of the Muslim world beyond the strait jackets of either ultramodernist or ultratraditionalist governments (neither of whom have any understanding of transmodernism) and involve ordinary people instead – activists, scholars, writers, journalists, etc. In doing so, Sardar (2004) argues we will discover that most people have critical but positive attitudes towards the West; and women will be as willing, if not more so, to participate in such discussions and the transformations they may initiate, as men. He is of the opinion that if the West shift towards transmodernism, the involvement of the public will open up massive new possibilities for positive change and fruitful synthesis, which would replace homogenizing globalization with a more harmonious and enriching experience of living together.

Love Ethics and (Our Tourism) Academy of Hope

The preceding discussion has clearly shown that the transmodern paradigm shift on the whole points to the intuitive aspirations for inclusivity, diversity, partnership, sacredness and quality of life, deep play, sustainability, universal human rights, the rights of nature and peace on Earth. The synchronicity phenomenon of the universal seemingly unconnected 'coincidences' (Jarowski, 1996) are further illustrated by the fact that I primarily learned about many of those ideas through the feminist writings focused on love ethics (bell hooks) and what Gloria Steinem described as the *circularity paradigm* (1993, 2004), which we cited in our book on the critical turn in tourism studies (Ateljevic *et al.*, 2007). Her words (Steinem, 1993: 189–190) very much resonate with the ideas elaborated above:

> If we think of ourselves as circles, our goal is completion – not defeating others. Progress lies in the direction we haven't been … Progress is appreciation. If we think of work structures as circles, excellence and cooperation are the goal – not competition. Progress becomes mutual support and connectedness. If we think of nature as a circle, then we are part of its reciprocity. Progress means interdependence. If we respect nature and each living thing as a microcosm of nature – then we respect the unique miracle of ourselves. And so we have come full circle.

The realization that human powers come from within has been translated into the political arena, producing a sociopolitical movement of so-called 'sacred activism', which reaffirms an individual growth, spirituality and actions that counter contemporary global discourses of fear, alienation and disempowerment (e.g. Fonda, 2004; Fox, 2000; Maathai, 2005; Tacey, 2004; Steinem, 2004).

In many ways, some of those ideas can be traced in my latest work where I put forward the poststructural concept of embodiment (Ateljevic & Swain, 2006; Ateljevic & Hall, 2007; Wilson & Ateljevic, 2008). I have argued that the poststructural perspective gives us the opportunity to engage with subtle norms and values shaping our lives in the process of which both the normalized discourse of dehumanized structures and the resisting power of agency can be revealed in parallel. Yet, in my deconstructions I want(ed) to remain positive and hopeful, as I have begun to be inspired by the feminist work on the importance of embracing love ethics and the tracing of positive structures, changes and potentialities that give us hope and models of acting and behaving in our personal and professional lives (Ateljevic, 2005, 2006b; Ateljevic *et al.*, 2007). As Steinem (1993: 129) aptly asks:

> And where is the routine study of social forms other than hierarchy, patriarchy, and competition – or even an understanding that they exist? Where are the campuses as pioneers of the powers of self-esteem and human possibilities?

bell hooks (2000, 2002, 2003) has particularly engaged with those ideas in her work of conceptualizing love that goes beyond only exceptional-individual phenomenon. To promote the overall cultural embrace of a global vision wherein we see our lives and our fate as intimately connected to those of everyone else on the planet, she urges both men and women to challenge the patriarchal culture of lovelessness, sexist stereotypes and dehumanization and to engage in the art of loving for themselves and their universal humanity. She has translated those ideas particularly into the most obvious academic area of influence for potential social change – our teaching, and in doing so has produced the concept of so-called 'democratic educators' and a pedagogy of hope (hooks, 2003). In presenting her ideas and looking at what works, she urges us teachers to resist oppressive structures by exposing their dehumanization and to embrace the values that motivate progressive social change – spirit, struggle, service, love, the ideals of shared knowledge and shared learning.

It is in this context of (what I now recognize as) transmodern calls to 'shift to a new level of consciousness, to reach a higher moral ground . . . to shed our fear and give hope to each other' (Wangari Maathai 2004 Nobel Peace Prize lecture) that our tourism academy of hope and so-called critical turn in tourism studies has been created (see Ateljevic *et al.*, 2007). The objectives of this endeavor have been twofold: firstly, to move the dominant business treatment of tourism to obtain a richer under-standing of the tourism phenomenon in the broader context of material, discursive and social practices (see, e.g. Pritchard *et al.*, 2007); secondly, to create a community of resistance in which we seek to transgress the oppressing teaching and research structures. Indeed, we have been contesting the dehumanizing academic ideologies and practices that stifle our creativity in research (see Tribe [2003] for its impact on tourism enquiry), promote a collective fear of radical change and entrenches a culture of domination that ensures our obedience.

In our endeavors to produce true transformational knowledge, we have been searching for strategies and practices to legitimize our professional, emotional and spiritual responsibilities to those with whom and for whom we co-create tourism knowledge, to our students and also to ourselves. In doing so, we are not seeing this as some self-centered self-indulgence, but rather as a necessary deconstruction of the geo-body politics of academic knowledge and its deeply embedded destructive dichotomies and hierarchies of rational/emotional; feminine/masculine; subject/object; internal/external; mind/body/spirit; winner/loser; dominant/passive; man/nature; and agency/structure/resistance. We are seeking to examine not just the world as it is, but to reflect on the world as we in Tourism Management/Tourism Studies make it, as Keith Hollinshead pointed out at our second critical tourism studies conference in Split (2007). With his concept of tourism world-makings he reveals the manner in which those who deal with tourism (scholars, students, planners, entrepreneurs, etc.) do not just represent or open up the world to others, but how they actually routinely redefine, reconstitute and refabricate that very universe, hence the urge to scrutinize our 'actual or potential role in conjuring up visions of the world, in providing access to the world, and in revealing realities about the world for the golden hordes whose journeying' we enable and may be also empowering (Hollinshead, 2002: 1–2, 2007). At the same conference, John Tribe also critically examined our role in tourism education in order to identify if there are lost aspects of universities that we wish to reclaim, and asked us a vital question: 'What are our hopes for students of tourism, the micro-academies that we construct and inhabit within our Universities and indeed ourselves as academics?' (Tribe, 2007: 14).

Transmodern Tourism

In sketching out what the embrace of the circularity paradigm of partnership/love ethics, or in other words – transmodernity philosophy – has already brought to (one corner of) tourism studies, I will end with outlining a few other possible ends of what this new frame of thinking can potentially bring. Its dialectic potentialities and implications are indeed manifold.

Firstly, whilst it is not new that tourism serves as an apt metaphor through which modernity (MacCannel) or postmodernity (Urry) has been criticized and displayed, it is unique to transmodernity that it finally gives us the opportunity of the true epistemological liberation from the inherent nature of tourism (studies) as the 'Otherness machine' (Aitchison, 2001). Indeed, even when we are critical in our writings and political agendas, it is in the language itself (e.g. pro-poverty tourism) or identity (geo-body) politics (e.g. the subaltern or feminist studies) that the connotations of inferiority associated around marking of difference are further reproduced. In contrast, transmodernity gives us the necessary political and epistemological position to transcend all (post)es-sentialist contradictions and treatments of race, gender, tradition, culture, economy, etc., and to provide us with a theoretization that can give us a 'ground zero' of *biosphere politics* with no inherent domination and superiority of one over another. Once the grounds of the shared risk, vulnerability and interconnectedness of all humans occupying our Earth are acknowledged, the true dialogue with no patronising can be open. Or what Margaret Swain (2007) invokes in her hopes of critical cosmopo-litanism for critical tourism studies that she ties into an idea of 'panhumanity' – combining a universalistic conception of human rights with cosmopolitan awareness of difference.

Secondly, I would argue that tourism is actually one of the key indicators that manifest the global shift in human consciousness. It is enough to look at the profile of cultural creatives to establish the case in point. Actually, all our 'special interest tourisms' clearly reveal the changing mindset of the ever-growing (international and domestic) tourism populations. Actually, this is one of the most critical points that can significantly move forward the historical frustration of tourism scholars in their efforts to create a 'serious field of study' (Airey, 2004, 2007; Nash, 2007). If the contemporary tourism phenomenon indicates the new step in development of human global consciousness, one can easily see the enormous political power of such shift in the public discourse of tourism.

Thirdly (and consequently), tourism has genuine powers to help the world in reaching the higher level of consciousness, as Margaret Silf (2006: 178) states in her elaborations to find possible ways to wisdom:

To travel is to discover that human beings in other lands and cultures are also people with whom we can share our laughter and our tears, and that what we have in common is a great deal more than the sum of all our differences.

Therefore, if governments, civil society, tourism producers and consumers begin to recognize such deeper meanings of tourism potentialities, tourism can become a leader 'industry' in the emerging concept of caring/spiritual global economy. In consequence, this realization gives us an enormous political weight to point to the agency and authority of tourism to possibly change the world for the better and assist it in its longings for interconnectedness and communion. Invoking the power of Hollinshead's concept of worldmakings, we can finally penetrate public discourses and change their dominant interpretations of tourism as being nothing more than a frivolous leisure activity or yet another form of economic development. Actually, it is often people outside of our field who give us a way of how to lift tourism discourse to another level.

For example, Theodore Zeldin is an Oxford-based historian and public intellectual (e.g. an advisor to the current French (Sarkozy) government and a regular BBC speaker) who is interested in human development potential, and in doing so challenges the traditional ideas of work and human conversations. In his motivation to genuinely connect the human community, he has initiated numerous projects by creating the Oxford Muse Foundation. One of those Muse projects relates to his interest of raising the potentiality of tourism to help more open human dialogue at the global scale (Telephone communication, 14/01/2008). To that end, for example, he initiated the concept of so-called Muse hotels in order to redesign the very idea of a hotel, and create a model for how any business can rethink from scratch what it is doing. Zeldin argues that hotels (like corporations) have not changed their basic goals since the late 19th century, when César Ritz said that the purpose of his hotel was to 'teach you how to live'. For him, that meant to be able to enjoy luxury and to live like royalty, with servants ministering to your every whim. But where can they go next, after they have fitted every kind of gold tap, electronic gadget and leisure facility? Zeldin asks and immediately replies that: 'they could become important cultural institutions, playing a significant part in the dialogue of civilizations, giving tourists a chance to do what conventional ambassadors cannot'. Apparently, a number of hotels in Britain, France, Spain and the USA have expressed an interest in using some of the ideas of the Muse to enrich the experience of their guests and to make their hotels into a new sort of cultural centers (http://www.oxfordmuse.com/projects/projects.htm).

Zeldin's intiative can be read as what Hollinshead describes as the necessary *creativity* in tourism interpretations and doings, in which he invites both tourism scholars and tourism industry to recognize 'how tourism is indeed potentially connected to all of our industries, to all of our civilities, and to all of our other aspirations' (Hollinshead, 2002: 11). To sum, in my commitment to trace the positive transformational potentiality of tourism, I am joining Franklin's (2007: 145) claim that the initial grounds of our critical views of tourism studies were founded by social disciplines that were predisposed to look for negative impacts (while admitting there have been many), which should make us 'wonder whether because of our fears and anxieties we have ever properly looked at the positive benefits of tourism'. When saying positive however, I do not mean the positivist affirmations of satisfying narrow tourism industry agendas (and in doing so reproducing unjust capitalistic relations), but rather of the systematic pursuit of identifying the global transformational capacities for human interconnectedness that tourism can and does offer.

Final Reflections

In this paper I have engaged with a broad range of literature that provides us with many signals and evidence of an emerging and significant paradigm shift in our human evolution. To suggest so, different authors use many terms to capture the main forces behind the potentiality of creating the brave new transmodern world – the reflective/living-systems paradigm (Elgin); the partnership model of caring economics (Eisler); the relational global consciousness of bio-sphere politics (Rifkin); love ethics (hooks); the circularity paradigm of interdependence (Steinem); the transmodern philosophy of political liberation (Dussel). The plethora of these terms echoes the argument of Riane Eisler (2002) that the reason why we do not hear much about this movement is because it is not centralized and coordinated under a single unifying name.

In conveying 'good news' however, I do not deny the harsh reality of structural inequalities around the world and my own privileged position in it – to speak, to write and to live comfortably. Yet, it wasn't always like that. As a person who experienced the Balkan war in the 1990s and subsequent displacement with its all challenges during which I encountered both beautiful human support and random discrimination, I attest to the powers of positive mindset and human compassion that helps one to empower and to be empowered. In the light of my own experience, I want to promote values of wisdom and compassion and individual powers to make a difference and in doing so to point to the possibilities of creating unity by celebrating diversity, which I believe represents the only way to the sustainable future of humanity. And it is in this context that I am stressing the transformational powers of tourism to which potential I have witnessed in many corners of the world that I visited in my capacity as a researcher and a traveler– from the peripheral regions of New Zealand, the Pacific and China to the islands of the Adriatic sea (to name a few). Of this potential I was made aware early in my life when every summer tourists flooded my little island in Croatia where I grew up in the 1970s and 1980s (see Ateljevic & Hall, 2007), when and where the benefits of tourism's international nature planted many seeds of hope and continues to do so.

Notes

1. In translation: *Beyond Modernity, Patriarchy and Capitalism: Re-enchanted Society?*, although not published in English as such. However, its extended version under a different title (2008) has been translated into the English.
2. Rosa Maria Rodriguez Magda is a Spanish philosopher and feminist whose work is mainly published in Spanish, which explains why her work is not so well-known in the English-speaking world of the West. I managed to find on the Internet only one of her essays in English in which she explains in general terms the main philosophical tenets of her concept.
3. Riane Eisler is the author of the international bestseller *The Chalice and the Blade: Our History, Our Future*, which has been published in 23 foreign editions, making Riane the only woman who has been selected among 20 great thinkers (including people like Hegel, Marx and Toynbee) for inclusion in *Macrohistory* and *Macrohistorians*.

References

Airey, D. (2007) Tourism education: Life begins at 40! A keynote presented at the ATHE Annual Conference: *Shaping the Future of Tourism Education*, St. Anne's College, Oxford, 5–7 December.
Aitchison, C. (2001) Theorizing other discourses of tourism, gender and culture: Can the subaltern speak (in tourism)? *Tourist Studies* 1, 133–147.
Allee, V. (2003) *The Future of Knowledge: Increasing Prosperity Through Value Networks*. Burlington, MA: Elsevier.
Ateljevic, I. (2005) The art of loving and de-humanization of the world: The concept of embodiment in tourism studies education and research. ATHE Annual Conference: *The Future of Tourism in Higher Education*, Liverpool, UK, 30 November – 2 December.
Ateljevic, I. (2006a) Promoting an academy of hope: A way of knowing and way of being. A keynote presented at the 15th Nordic Symposium in Tourism and Hospitality Research: *Visions of Modern Transmodern Tourism*, Savonlinna, Finland, 19–22 October.
Ateljevic, I. (2006b) The process of (un)learning and becoming: Being a student and teacher of *what*? ATHE Annual Conference: *Knowledge, Communication,*

Networking: Locating Tourism Knowledge, Cambridge University, UK, 6–8 December.

Ateljevic, I. and Doorne, S. (2003) Unpacking the local: A cultural analysis of tourism entrepreneurship in Murter, Croatia. *Tourism Geographies* 5 (2), 123–150.

Ateljevic, I. and Doorne, S. (2005) Dialectics of authentification: Performing 'exotic otherness' in a backpacker enclave of Dali, China. *Tourism and Cultural Change* 3 (1), 1–27.

Ateljevic, I. and Hall, D. (2007) Tourism embodiment of the macho gaze in the South Eastern Europe: Performing masculinity and femininity in Albania and Croatia. In A. Pritchard, N. Morgan, I. Ateljevic and C. Harris (eds) *Tourism and Gender: Essays on Embodiment, Sensuality and Experience* (pp. 138–157). London: CAB International.

Ateljevic, I. and Hannam, K. (2008) Conclusion: Towards a critical agenda for backpacker tourism. In K. Hannam and I. Ateljevic (eds) *Backpacker Tourism: Concepts and Profiles* (pp. 247–256). Clevedon: Channel View Publications.

Ateljevic, I., Harris, C., Wilson, E. and Collins, F. (2005) Getting 'entangled': Reflexivity and the 'critical turn' in tourism studies. *Tourism Recreation Research: Theme – Tourism and Research* 30 (2), 9–21.

Ateljevic, I., Pritchard, A. and Morgan, N. (eds) (2007) *The Critical Turn in Tourism Studies: Innovative Research Methodologies*. Oxford: Elsevier.

Ateljevic, I. and Swain, M. (2006) Embodying tourism research: Gender performance among Sani and Bai women in Yunnan's ethnic tourism. Paper presented at the CAUTHE International Tourism Conference, Victoria University, Melbourne, Australia, 6–9 February.

Bianchi, R.V. (2002) Towards a new political economy of global tourism. In R. Sharpley and D. Telfer (eds) *Tourism & Development: Concepts and Issues* (pp. 265–299). Clevedon: Channel View Publications.

Brown, L. (2006) *Plan B 2.0*. London: Norton NY.

Cole, M. (2005) Transmodernism, Marxism and social change: Some implications for teacher education. *Policy Futures in Education* 3 (1), 90–105.

Dann, G. (ed.) (2002) *The Tourist as a Metaphor of the Social World*. Wallingford: CABI.

Dussel, E. (1995) *The Invention of the Americas: Eclipse of 'Other' and the Myth of Modernity*. New York: Continuum.

Eisler, R. (1987) *The Chalice and the Blade: Our History and Our Future*. San Francisco, CA: Harper and Row.

Eisler, R. (1996) *Sacred Pleasure: Sex, Myth and the Politics of the Body*. New York: HarperSanFrancisco.

Eisler, R. (2002) *The Power of Partnership: Seven Relationships that will Change Your Life*. Novato: New World Library.

Eisler, R. (2007) *The Real Wealth of Nations*. San Francisco, CA: Berret-Koehler.

Elgin, D. (1997) *Global Consciousness Change: Indicators of an Emerging Paradigm*. San Anselmo, CA: Millennium Project.

Fonda, J. (2004) The new feminism. A keynote speech. *Proceedings of the Women and Power Omega Institute 4th and V-Day Annual Conference*, New York, September 9–11.

Fox, M. (2000) *One River, Many Wells*. Dublin: Gateway.

Franklin, A. (2003) The tourist syndrome: An interview with Zygmunt Bauman. *Tourist Studies* 3, 205–217.

Franklin, A. (2007) The problem with tourism theory. In I. Ateljevic, A. Pritchard and N. Morgan (eds) *The Critical Turn in Tourism Studies: Innovative Research Methodologies* (pp. 131–148). Oxford: Elsevier.

Fromm, E. (2006) *The Art of Loving* (50th Anniversary edition). New York: Harper Perennial; Modern classics.

Ghisi, L.M. (2001) *Au Delà de la Modernité, du Patriarcat et du Capitalisme: la Société Réenchantée.* L'Harmattan, Paris. On WWW at http://von2020.canalblog.com. Accessed 20.01.07.

Ghisi, L.M. (2006) Transmodernity and transmodern tourism. A keynote presented at the 15th Nordic Symposium in Tourism and Hospitality Research: *Visions of Modern Transmodern Tourism*, Savonlinna, Finland, 19–22 October.

Ghisi, L.M. (2008) *The Knowledge Society: A Breakthrough Towards Genuine Sustainability.* India: Stone Hill Foundation.

Grosfoguel, R., Saldivar, J.D. and Torres, N.M. (eds) (2007) *Unsettling Postcoloniality: Colonilaity, Transmodernity and Border Thinking.* Durham, NC: Duke University Press.

Harman, W. (1998) *Global Mind Change: The Promise of the XXIst century* (2nd edn). San Francisco, CA: Berret and Koelher.

Hollinshead, K. (2002) Tourism and the making of the world: The dynamics of our contemporary tribal lives. In J. Kneski (ed.) *Honors Excellence Occasional Paper Series* (Vol. I: 2, pp. 1–27). Miami, FL: The Honors College at Florida International University.

Hollinshead, K. (2007) The 'world-making' drive of tourism: A broadening of Meethan's analysis of culture and place production. A keynote presented at the Second International Critical Tourism Studies Conference, Split, 20–23 June. Abstract in C. Harris and M. van Hal (eds) *Conference Proceedings: The Critical Turn in Tourism Studies: Promoting an Academy of Hope.* Zagreb: Institute for Tourism.

hooks, b. (1994) *Teaching to Transgress: Education as the practice of Freedom.* New York: Routledge.

hooks, b. (2000) *All About Love: New Visions.* New York: Harper Perennial.

hooks, b. (2002) *The Communion: The Female Search for Love.* New York: Harperscollins.

hooks, b. (2003) *Teaching Community: A Pedagogy of Hope.* New York: Routledge.

Inglehart, R. (1977) *The Silent Revolution: Changing Values and Political Styles among Western Publics.* Princeton, NJ: Princeton University Press.

Inglehart, R. and Norris, P. (2004) *Sacred and Secular: Religion and Politics Worldwide.* New York: Cambridge University Press.

Jarowski, J. (1996) *Synchronicity: The Inner Path of Leadership.* San Francisco, CA: Berret & Koelher.

Maathai, W. (2005) A keynote speech. *Proceedings of the Women and Power Omega Institute and V-Day 4th Annual Conference.* New York, September 10–13.

MacCannell, D. (1976) *The Tourist: A New Theory of Leisure Class.* New York: Schocken Books.

Magda, R.M.R. (1989) *Transmodernity.* Online essay. On WWW at http://es.geocities.com/circulocero/magda.html. Accessed 22.01.07.

McIntosh, A. and Mansfeld, Y. (2006) Spiritual hosting: An exploration of the interplay between spiritual identities and tourism. *Tourism: An Interdisciplinary Journal* 54 (2), 1–24.

Nash, D. (ed.) (2007) *The Study of Tourism: Anthropological and Sociological Beginnings.* Tourism Social Science Series. Amsterdam: Elsevier.

Pernecky, T. and Johnston, C. (2006) Voyage through numinous space: Applying the specialization concept to New Age Tourism. *Tourism Recreation Research* 31 (1), 37–46.

Pritchard, A., Morgan, N., Ateljevic, I. and Harris, C. (2007) *Tourism and Gender: Essays on Embodiment, Sensuality and Experience.* London: CAB International.

Ray, H.P. (1998) What might be the next step in cultural evolution? In D. Loye (ed.) *The Evolutionary Ryder* (pp. 87–102). Twickenham: Adamantine Press.

Ray, H.P. and Anderson, S.R. (2000) *The Cultural Creatives: How 50 Million People are Changing the World.* New York: Harmony Books.

Rifkin, J. (1995) *The End of Work.* New York: Penguin Group.

Rifkin, J. (2005) *The European Dream: How Europe's Vision of the Future is Quietly Eclipsing the American Dream.* New York: Penguin Group.

Rooney, D., Hearn, G. and Ninan, A. (2005) *Handbook on the Knowledge Economy.* Cheltenham: Edvard Elgar.

Sardar, Z. (2004) Islam and the West in a Transmodern World. Article on Contemporary Issues 18/08/2004. On WWW at http://www.islamonline.net/english/Contemporary/2002/05/article20.shtml. Accessed 15.04.07.

Silf, M. (2006) *The Way of Wisdom.* Oxford: Lion Hudson.

Smith, M. and Kelly, C. Wellness tourism, Editorial. *Tourism Recreation Research* 31(1), 1–4.

Steinem, G. (1993) *Revolution From Within.* Boston, MA: Little, Brown and Company.

Steinem, G. (2004) New leaps of consciousness. A keynote speech. *Proceedings of the Women and Power Omega Institute 4th and V-Day Annual Conference*, New York, September 9–11.

Stewart, T. (2002) *The Wealth of Knowledge: Intellectual Capital and the XXIst Century Organization.* London: N Brealey.

Swain, M. (2007) The cosmopolitan hope of tourism: 'If it's tourist season why can't we shoot them?' bumper sticker, Northern California. A paper presented at the Second International Critical Tourism Studies Conference. Split, 20–23 June. Abstract in C. Harris and M. van Hal (eds) *Conference Proceedings: The Critical Turn in Tourism Studies: Promoting an Academy of Hope.* Zagreb: Institute for Tourism.

Tchernia, J.F. (1997) *Les styles de valeurs des Européens.* Paris: Tchernia Etudes Conseil (Research International).

Tacey, D. (2004) *The Spirituality Revolution.* New York: Brunner-Routledge.

Tribe, J. (2003) The RAE-ification of tourism research in the UK. *International Journal of Tourism Research* 5, 225–234.

Tribe, J. (2007) Promoting an academy of hope. A keynote presented at the Second International Critical Tourism Studies Conference, Split, 20–23 June. Abstract in C. Harris and M. van Hal (eds) *Conference Proceedings: The Critical Turn in Tourism Studies: Promoting an Academy of Hope.* Zagreb: Institute for Tourism.

Wilson, E. and Ateljevic, I. (2008) Challenging the 'tourist-other' dualism: Gender, backpackers and the embodiment of tourism research. In K. Hannam and I. Ateljevic (eds) *Backpacker Tourism: Concepts and Profiles* (pp. 95–110). Clevedon: Channel View Publications.

Index